2014
SUPPLEMENT TO
MANUAL FOR
COURTS-MARTIAL

UNITED STATES
MILITARY RULES OF EVIDENCE
(2012 EDITION)

The Supplement to the 2012 Edition of the Manual for Courts-Martial (MCM) is a complete revision of the Military Rules of Evidence (Mil. R. Evid.). On May 15, 2013, the President signed Executive (Exec.) Order 13643 implementing the 2013 Amendments to the MCM. This Exec. Order completely replaces Part III (Mil. R. Evid.) of the MCM. The Mil. R. Evid. were amended to conform to Federal Rules of Evidence.

PREFACE

The Supplement to the 2012 MCM is a complete revision of Part III (Mil. R. Evid.) of the MCM and incorporates changes made by Exec. Order 13643, dated May 15, 2013.

Summary of Changes to Mil. R. Evid. in Part III of the MCM:

• All Military Rules of Evidence were amended for stylistic reasons and to align them with the Federal Rules of Evidence.

• Mil. R. Evid. 101(a) is amended to delete the words "including summary courts-martial" because Mil. R. Evid. 1101 already addresses the applicability of this rule to summary courts-martial.

• Mil. R. Evid. 101(b) is amended to change the word "shall" to "will."

• Mil. R. Evid. 101 is amended to add a discussion section.

• Mil. R. Evid. 105 is amended to change the title to "Limiting evidence that is not admissible against other parties for other purposes."

• Mil. R. Evid. 201(d) is subsumed into subsection (c). The remaining subsections are renumbered accordingly.

• Mil. R. Evid. 201A is renumbered so that it now appears as Rule 202. The phrase "in accordance with Mil. R. Evid. 104" was added to subsection (b) to clarify that Rule 104 controls the military judge's relevancy determination.

• Mil. R. Evid. 201(b) is amended to move subsection (b)(2) to a discussion section.

• Mil. R. Evid. 301(c) is amended to remove the phrase "concerning the issue of guilt or innocence."

• Mil. R. Evid. 301(d) and (f)(2) are combined for ease of use. The remaining subsections are renumbered accordingly.

• Mil. R. Evid. 304(c) is moved so that it immediately follows subsection (a) and is highly visible to the practioner.

• Mil. R. Evid. 304(h)(3) is moved to subsection (a)(2) so that it is included near the beginning of the rule to highlight the importance of an accused's right to remain silent. The remaining subsections were renumbered.

• Mil. R. Evid. 304(b) is amended to add the term "allegedly."

• Mil. R. Evid. 304(c)(5), (d), (f)(3)(A), and (f)(7) are amended to replace the word "shall" with "will" or "must."

• Mil. R. Evid. 305 is amended to revise the definition of "person subject to the code" to clarify that it includes a person acting as a knowing agent only in subsection (c).

• Mil. R. Evid. 305 is amended to move the definition of "custodial interrogation" from subsection (b) to subsection (d) in order to co-locate the definition.

• Mil. R. Evid. 305(c)(2) and (c)(3) are amended to change the titles to "Fifth Amendment right to counsel" and "Sixth Amendment right to counsel" respectively because practioners are more familiar with those terms.

• Mil. R. Evid. 305(c)(2) is amended to add the words "after such request" to clarify that any statements made prior to a request for counsel are admissible, assuming, of course, that Article 31(b) rights were given.

• Mil. R. Evid. 305(a)(d), and (f) are amended to change the word "shall" to "will."

• Mil. R. Evid. 305(f)(2) is amended to replace the word "abroad" with "outside of a state, district, commonwealth, territory, or possession of the United States."

• Mil. R. Evid. 311 is amended to move the definition of "unlawful" from subsection (c) to subsection (b) so that it immediately precedes the subsection in which the term is first used in the rule.

• Mil. R. Evid. 312(b)(2) is moved to a discussion paragraph because it addresses the conduct of the examiner rather than the admissibility of evidence.

• Mil. R. Evid. 312(c)(2)(a) is amended to replace the words "clear indication" with "probable cause."

• Mil. R. Evid. 312(d) is amended to replace the term "involuntary" with "nonconsensual."

• Mil. R. Evid. 312(e) is amended to add a discussion paragraph to address a situation in which a person is compelled to ingest a substance in order to locate property within the person's body.

• Mil. R. Evid. 312(f) is amended to add a line at the end of the subsection to conform with the rule from CAAF's holding in *United States v. Stevenson*, 66 M.J. 15 (C.A.A.F. 2008).

• Mil. R. Evid. 313(c) is amended to add the definition of "inventory" to further distinguish inventories from inspections.

• Mil. R. Evid. 314(a) is amended to add language to clarify that the rules as written afford at least the minimal amount of protection required under the Constitution as applied to servicemembers.

• Mil. R. Evid. 314(c) is amended to limit the ability of a commander to search persons or property upon entry or exits from the installation alone, rather than anywhere on the installation, despite the indication of some courts in dicta that security personnel can search a personally owned vehicle anywhere on a military installation based on no suspicion at all.

• Mil. R. Evid. 314(c) is further amended to add a discussion section below the rule.

• Mil. R. Evid. 314(f)(2) is amended to change the phrase "reasonably believed" to "reasonably suspected."

• Mil. R. Evid. 314(f)(3) is amended to change the phrase "reasonably believed" to "reasonably suspected."

• Mil. R. Evid. 315 is amended to move former subsection (h) so that it immediately follows subsection (a).

• Mil. R. Evid. 315(b) is amended to change the term "authorization to seach" to "search authorization."

• Mil. R. Evid. 315 is amended to move the second sentence from subsection (d)(2) to subsection (d) to clarify that its content applies to both commanders under subsection (d)(1) and military judges under subsection (d)(2).

• Mil. R. Evid. 315(f)(2) is amended to change the word "shall" to "will."

• Mil. R. Evid. 315(g) is amended to include a definition of exigency rather than to provide examples that may not encompass the wide range of situations where exigency might apply.

• Mil. R. Evid. 316(a) is amended to add the word "reasonable."

• Mil. R. Evid. 317 is amended to move former subsections (b) and (c)(3) to a discussion paragraph.

• Mil. R. Evid. 401 is amended to change the title to "Test for relevant evidence."

• Mil. R. Evid. 402 is amended to change the title to "General admissibility of relevant evidence."

• Mil. R. Evid. 404 is amended to change the title to "Character evidence: crime or other acts."

• Mil. R. Evid. 408 is amended to change the title to "Compromise offers and negotiations."

• Mil. R. Evid. 409 is amended to change the title to "Offers to pay medical and similar expenses."

• Mil. R. Evid. 410 is amended to change the title to "Pleas, plea discussion, and related statements."

• Mil. R. Evid. 413 is amended to change the title to "Similar crimes in sexual offense cases."

• Mil. R. Evid. 414 is amended to change the title to "Similar crimes in child-molestation cases."

• Mil. R. Evid. 501 is amended to change the title to "Privilege in general."

• Mil. R. Evid. 504 is amended to add subsection (c)(2)(D).

• Mil. R. Evid. 505 is amended to significantly restructure the rule to bring greater clarity and regularity to military practice. The changes focus primarily on expanding the military judge's explicit authority to conduct ex parte pretrial conferences in connection with classified information.

• Mil. R. Evid. 506 is amended to significantly revise the rule to bring greater clarity and also to align it with changes made to Mil. R. Evid. 505.

• Mil. R. Evid. 507 is amended to add subsection (b) to define terms that are used throughout the rule and add subsection (e)(1) to permit the military judge to hold an in camera review upon request by the prosecution.

• Mil. R. Evid. 509 is amended to add the language "courts-martial, military judge" in light of CAAF's holding in *United States v. Matthews*, 68 M.J. 29 (C.A.A.F. 2009).

• Mil. R. Evid. 511 is amended to add titles to subsections of the rule for clarity and ease of use.

• Mil. R. Evid. 513 is amended to delete the words "spouse abuse" and "the person of the other spouse or" from subsection (d)(2), thus expanding the overall scope of the privilege.

• Mil. R. Evid. 513(e)(3) is amended to change the language to further expand the military judge's authority and discretion to conduct in camera reviews.

• Mil. R. Evid. 601 is amended to change the title to "Competency to testify in general."

• Mil. R. Evid. 602 is amended to change the title to "Need for personal knowledge."

• Mil. R. Evid. 603 is amended to change the title to "Oath or affirmation to testify truthfully."

• Mil. R. Evid. 605 is amended to change the title to "Military judge's competency as a witness."

• Mil. R. Evid. 606 is amended to change the title to "Member's competency as a witness."

• Mil. R. Evid. 607 is amended to change the title to "Who may impeach a witness."

• Mil. R. Evid. 608 is amended to change the title to "A witness's character for truthfulness or untruthfulness."

• Mil. R. Evid. 609 is amended to change the title to "Impeachment by evidence of a criminal conviction."

• Mil. R. Evid. 609 is amended to conform subsections (a), (b)(2), and (c)(1) to conform with the Federal Rules of Evidence.

• Mil. R. Evid. 611 is amended to change the title to "Mode and order of examining witnesses and presenting evidence."

• Mil. R. Evid. 611(d)(3) is amended to conform with the United States Supreme Court's holding in *Maryland v. Craig*, 497 U.S. 836 (1990) and the Court of Appeals for the Armed Forces' holding in *United States v. Pack*, 65 M.J. 381 (C.A.A.F. 2007).

• Mil. R. Evid. 612 is amended to change the title to "Writing used to refresh a witness's memory."

• Mil. R. Evid. 613 is amended to change the title to "Witness's prior statement."

• Mil. R. Evid. 614 is amended to change the title to "Court-martial's calling or examining a witness."

• Mil. R. Evid. 614(a) is amended to substitute the word "relevant" for "appropriate."

• Mil. R. Evid. 615 is amended to change the title to "Excluding witnesses."

• Mil. R. Evid. 702 is amended to change the title to "Testimony by expert witnesses."

• Mil. R. Evid. 703 is amended to change the title to "Basis of an expert's opinion of testimony."

• Mil. R. Evid. 705 is amended to change the title to "Disclosing the facts or data underlying an expert's opinion."

• Mil. R. Evid. 706 is amended to change the title to "Court-appointed expert witnesses."

• Mil. R. Evid. 801 is amended to change the title to "Definitions that apply to this section; exclusions from hearsay."

• Mil. R. Evid. 801(2) is amended to change the title of the subsection from "Admission by party-opponent" to "An opposing party's statement" to conform to the Federal Rules of Evidence.

• Mil. R. Evid. 802 is amended to change the title to "The rule against hearsay."

• Mil. R. Evid. 803 is amended to change the title to "Exceptions to the rule against hearsay – regardless of whether the declarant is available as a witness."

• Mil. R. Evid. 803(24) is removed as it is unnecessary.

• Mil. R. Evid. 804 is amended to change the title to "Exceptions to the rule against hearsay."

• Mil. R. Evid. 806 is amended to change the title to "Attacking and supporting the declarant's credibility."

• Mil. R. Evid. 901 is amended to change the title to "Authenticating or identifying evidence."

• Mil. R. Evid. 902 is amended to change the title to "Evidence that is self-authenticating."

• Mil. R. Evid. 902(11) is amended to add language permitting the military judge to admit non-noticed documents even after the trial has commenced if the offering party shows good cause to do so.

• Mil. R. Evid. 903 is amended to change the title to "Subscribing witness's testimony."

• Mil. R. Evid. 1001 is amended to change the title to "Definitions that apply to this section."

• Mil. R. Evid. 1005 is amended to change the title to "Copies of public records to prove content."

• Mil. R. Evid. 1006 is amended to change the title to "Summaries to prove content."

• Mil. R. Evid. 1007 is amended to change the title to "Testimony or statement of a party to provide content."

JOINT SERVICE COMMITTEE
ON MILITARY JUSTICE

CONTENTS

PART III   MILITARY RULES OF EVIDENCE

PART III
MILITARY RULES OF EVIDENCE

SECTION I
GENERAL PROVISIONS

Rule 101. Scope

(a) *Scope.* These rules apply to courts-martial proceedings to the extent and with the exceptions stated in Mil. R. Evid. 1101.

(b) *Sources of Law.* In the absence of guidance in this Manual or these rules, courts-martial will apply:

(1) First, the Federal Rules of Evidence and the case law interpreting them; and

(2) Second, when not inconsistent with subdivision (b)(1), the rules of evidence at common law.

(c) *Rule of Construction.* Except as otherwise provided in these rules, the term "military judge" includes the president of a special court-martial without a military judge and a summary court-martial officer.

Discussion

Discussion was added to these Rules in 2013. The Discussion itself does not have the force of law, even though it may describe legal requirements derived from other sources. It is in the nature of treatise, and may be used as secondary authority. If a matter is included in a rule, it is intended that the matter be binding, unless it is clearly expressed as precatory. The Discussion will be revised from time to time as warranted by changes in applicable law. *See* Composition of the Manual for Courts-Martial in Appendix 21.

Practitioners should also refer to the Analysis of the Military Rules of Evidence contained in Appendix 22 of this Manual. The Analysis is similar to Committee Notes accompanying the Federal Rules of Evidence and is intended to address the basis of the rule, deviation from the Federal Rules of Evidence, relevant precedent, and drafters' intent.

Rule 102. Purpose

These rules should be construed so as to administer every proceeding fairly, eliminate unjustifiable expense and delay, and promote the development of evidence law, to the end of ascertaining the truth and securing a just determination.

Rule 103. Rulings on evidence

(a) *Preserving a Claim of Error.* A party may claim error in a ruling to admit or exclude evidence only if the error materially prejudices a substantial right of the party and:

(1) if the ruling admits evidence, a party, on the record:

(A) timely objects or moves to strike; and

(B) states the specific ground, unless it was apparent from the context; or

(2) if the ruling excludes evidence, a party informs the military judge of its substance by an offer of proof, unless the substance was apparent from the context.

(b) *Not Needing to Renew an Objection or Offer of Proof.* Once the military judge rules definitively on the record admitting or excluding evidence, either before or at trial, a party need not renew an objection or offer of proof to preserve a claim of error for appeal.

(c) *Review of Constitutional Error.* The standard provided in subdivision (a)(2) does not apply to errors implicating the United States Constitution as it applies to members of the Armed Forces, unless the error arises under these rules and subdivision (a)(2) provides a standard that is more advantageous to the accused than the constitutional standard.

(d) *Military Judge's Statement about the Ruling; Directing an Offer of Proof.* The military judge may make any statement about the character or form of the evidence, the objection made, and the ruling. The military judge may direct that an offer of proof be made in question-and-answer form.

(e) *Preventing the Members from Hearing Inadmissible Evidence.* In a court-martial composed of a military judge and members, to the extent practicable, the military judge must conduct a trial so that inadmissible evidence is not suggested to the members by any means.

(f) *Taking Notice of Plain Error.* A military judge may take notice of a plain error that materially prejudices a substantial right, even if the claim of error was not properly preserved.

Rule 104. Preliminary questions

(a) *In General.* The military judge must decide any

preliminary question about whether a witness is available or qualified, a privilege exists, a continuance should be granted, or evidence is admissible. In so deciding, the military judge is not bound by evidence rules, except those on privilege.

(b) *Relevance that Depends on a Fact.* When the relevance of evidence depends on whether a fact exists, proof must be introduced sufficient to support a finding that the fact does exist. The military judge may admit the proposed evidence on the condition that the proof be introduced later. A ruling on the sufficiency of evidence to support a finding of fulfillment of a condition of fact is the sole responsibility of the military judge, except where these rules or this Manual provide expressly to the contrary.

(c) *Conducting a Hearing so that the Members Cannot Hear It.* Except in cases tried before a special court-martial without a military judge, the military judge must conduct any hearing on a preliminary question so that the members cannot hear it if:

(1) the hearing involves the admissibility of a statement of the accused under Mil. R. Evid. 301-306;

(2) the accused is a witness and so requests; or

(3) justice so requires.

(d) *Cross-Examining the Accused.* By testifying on a preliminary question, the accused does not become subject to cross-examination on other issues in the case.

(e) *Evidence Relevant to Weight and Credibility.* This rule does not limit a party's right to introduce before the members evidence that is relevant to the weight or credibility of other evidence.

Rule 105. Limiting evidence that is not admissible against other parties or for other purposes

If the military judge admits evidence that is admissible against a party or for a purpose – but not against another party or for another purpose – the military judge, on timely request, must restrict the evidence to its proper scope and instruct the members accordingly.

Rule 106. Remainder of or related writings or recorded statements

If a party introduces all or part of a writing or recorded statement, an adverse party may require the introduction, at that time, of any other part – or any other writing or recorded statement – that in fairness ought to be considered at the same time.

SECTION II
JUDICIAL NOTICE

Rule 201. Judicial notice of adjudicative facts

(a) *Scope.* This rule governs judicial notice of an adjudicative fact only, not a legislative fact.

(b) *Kinds of Facts that May Be Judicially Noticed.* The military judge may judicially notice a fact that is not subject to reasonable dispute because it:

(1) is generally known universally, locally, or in the area pertinent to the event; or

(2) can be accurately and readily determined from sources whose accuracy cannot reasonably be questioned.

(c) *Taking Notice.* The military judge:

(1) may take judicial notice whether requested or not; or

(2) must take judicial notice if a party requests it and the military judge is supplied with the necessary information.

The military judge must inform the parties in open court when, without being requested, he or she takes judicial notice of an adjudicative fact essential to establishing an element of the case.

(d) *Timing.* The military judge may take judicial notice at any stage of the proceeding.

(e) *Opportunity to Be Heard.* On timely request, a party is entitled to be heard on the propriety of taking judicial notice and the nature of the fact to be noticed. If the military judge takes judicial notice before notifying a party, the party, on request, is still entitled to be heard.

(f) *Instructing the Members.* The military judge must instruct the members that they may or may not accept the noticed fact as conclusive.

Rule 202. Judicial notice of law

(a) *Domestic Law.* The military judge may take judicial notice of domestic law. If a domestic law is a fact that is of consequence to the determination of the action, the procedural requirements of Mil. R. Evid. 201 – except Rule 201(f) – apply.

(b) *Foreign Law.* A party who intends to raise an

issue concerning the law of a foreign country must give reasonable written notice. The military judge, in determining foreign law, may consider any relevant material or source, in accordance with Mil. R. Evid. 104. Such a determination is a ruling on a question of law.

SECTION III
EXCLUSIONARY RULES AND RELATED MATTERS CONCERNING SELF-INCRIMINATION, SEARCH AND SEIZURE, AND EYEWITNESS IDENTIFICATION

Rule 301. Privilege concerning compulsory self-incrimination

(a) *General Rule.* An individual may claim the most favorable privilege provided by the Fifth Amendment to the United States Constitution, Article 31, or these rules. The privileges against self-incrimination are applicable only to evidence of a testimonial or communicative nature.

(b) *Standing.* The privilege of a witness to refuse to respond to a question that may tend to incriminate the witness is a personal one that the witness may exercise or waive at his or her discretion.

(c) *Limited Waiver.* An accused who chooses to testify as a witness waives the privilege against self-incrimination only with respect to the matters about which he or she testifies. If the accused is on trial for two or more offenses and on direct examination testifies about only one or some of the offenses, the accused may not be cross-examined as to guilt or innocence with respect to the other offenses unless the cross-examination is relevant to an offense concerning which the accused has testified. This waiver is subject to Mil. R. Evid. 608(b).

Discussion

A military judge is not required to provide Article 31 warnings. If a witness who seems uninformed of the privileges under this rule appears likely to incriminate himself or herself, the military judge may advise the witness of the right to decline to make any answer that might tend to incriminate the witness and that any self-incriminating answer the witness might make can later be used as evidence against the witness. Counsel for any party or for the witness may ask the military judge to so advise a witness if such a request is made out of the hearing of the witness and the members, if present. Failure to so advise a witness does not make the testimony of the witness inadmissible.

(d) *Exercise of the Privilege.* If a witness states that the answer to a question may tend to incriminate him or her, the witness cannot be required to answer unless the military judge finds that the facts and circumstances are such that no answer the witness might make to the question would tend to incriminate the witness or that the witness has, with respect to the question, waived the privilege against self-incrimination. A witness may not assert the privilege if he or she is not subject to criminal penalty as a result of an answer by reason of immunity, running of the statute of limitations, or similar reason.

(1) *Immunity Requirements.* The minimum grant of immunity adequate to overcome the privilege is that which under either R.C.M. 704 or other proper authority provides that neither the testimony of the witness nor any evidence obtained from that testimony may be used against the witness at any subsequent trial other than in a prosecution for perjury, false swearing, the making of a false official statement, or failure to comply with an order to testify after the military judge has ruled that the privilege may not be asserted by reason of immunity.

(2) *Notification of Immunity or Leniency.* When a prosecution witness before a court-martial has been granted immunity or leniency in exchange for testimony, the grant must be reduced to writing and must be served on the accused prior to arraignment or within a reasonable time before the witness testifies. If notification is not made as required by this rule, the military judge may grant a continuance until notification is made, prohibit or strike the testimony of the witness, or enter such other order as may be required.

(e) *Waiver of the Privilege.* A witness who answers a self-incriminating question without having asserted the privilege against self-incrimination may be required to answer questions relevant to the disclosure, unless the questions are likely to elicit additional self-incriminating information.

(1) If a witness asserts the privilege against self-incrimination on cross-examination, the military judge, upon motion, may strike the direct testimony of the witness in whole or in part, unless the matters to which the witness refuses to testify are purely collateral.

(2) Any limited waiver of the privilege under subdivision (e) applies only at the trial in which the answer is given, does not extend to a rehearing or

new or other trial, and is subject to Mil. R. Evid. 608(b).

(f) *Effect of Claiming the Privilege.*

(1) *No Inference to Be Drawn.* The fact that a witness has asserted the privilege against self-incrimination cannot be considered as raising any inference unfavorable to either the accused or the government.

(2) *Pretrial Invocation Not Admissible.* The fact that the accused during official questioning and in exercise of rights under the Fifth Amendment to the United States Constitution or Article 31 remained silent, refused to answer a certain question, requested counsel, or requested that the questioning be terminated, is not admissible against the accused.

(3) *Instructions Regarding the Privilege.* When the accused does not testify at trial, defense counsel may request that the members of the court be instructed to disregard that fact and not to draw any adverse inference from it. Defense counsel may request that the members not be so instructed. Defense counsel's election will be binding upon the military judge except that the military judge may give the instruction when the instruction is necessary in the interests of justice.

Rule 302. Privilege concerning mental examination of an accused

(a) *General rule.* The accused has a privilege to prevent any statement made by the accused at a mental examination ordered under R.C.M. 706 and any derivative evidence obtained through use of such a statement from being received into evidence against the accused on the issue of guilt or innocence or during sentencing proceedings. This privilege may be claimed by the accused notwithstanding the fact that the accused may have been warned of the rights provided by Mil. R. Evid. 305 at the examination.

(b) *Exceptions.*

(1) There is no privilege under this rule when the accused first introduces into evidence such statements or derivative evidence.

(2) If the court-martial has allowed the defense to present expert testimony as to the mental condition of the accused, an expert witness for the prosecution may testify as to the reasons for his or her conclusions, but such testimony may not extend to state-

ments of the accused except as provided in subdivision (b)(1).

(c) *Release of Evidence from an R.C.M. 706 Examination.* If the defense offers expert testimony concerning the mental condition of the accused, the military judge, upon motion, must order the release to the prosecution of the full contents, other than any statements made by the accused, of any report prepared pursuant to R.C.M. 706. If the defense offers statements made by the accused at such examination, the military judge, upon motion, may order the disclosure of such statements made by the accused and contained in the report as may be necessary in the interests of justice.

(d) *Noncompliance by the Accused.* The military judge may prohibit an accused who refuses to cooperate in a mental examination authorized under R.C.M. 706 from presenting any expert medical testimony as to any issue that would have been the subject of the mental examination.

(e) *Procedure.* The privilege in this rule may be claimed by the accused only under the procedure set forth in Mil. R. Evid. 304 for an objection or a motion to suppress.

Rule 303. Degrading questions

Statements and evidence are inadmissible if they are not material to the issue and may tend to degrade the person testifying.

Rule 304. Confessions and admissions

(a) *General rule.* If the accused makes a timely motion or objection under this rule, an involuntary statement from the accused, or any evidence derived therefrom, is inadmissible at trial except as provided in subdivision (e).

(1) *Definitions.* As used in this rule:

(A) "Involuntary statement" means a statement obtained in violation of the self-incrimination privilege or Due Process Clause of the Fifth Amendment to the United States Constitution, Article 31, or through the use of coercion, unlawful influence, or unlawful inducement.

(B) "Confession" means an acknowledgment of guilt.

(C) "Admission" means a self-incriminating statement falling short of an acknowledgment of guilt, even if it was intended by its maker to be exculpatory.

(2) Failure to deny an accusation of wrongdoing is not an admission of the truth of the accusation if at the time of the alleged failure the person was under investigation or was in confinement, arrest, or custody for the alleged wrongdoing.

(b) *Evidence Derived from a Statement of the Accused.* When the defense has made an appropriate and timely motion or objection under this rule, evidence allegedly derived from a statement of the accused may not be admitted unless the military judge finds by a preponderance of the evidence that:

(1) the statement was made voluntarily,

(2) the evidence was not obtained by use of the accused's statement, or

(3) the evidence would have been obtained even if the statement had not been made.

(c) *Corroboration of a Confession or Admission.*

(1) An admission or a confession of the accused may be considered as evidence against the accused on the question of guilt or innocence only if independent evidence, either direct or circumstantial, has been admitted into evidence that corroborates the essential facts admitted to justify sufficiently an inference of their truth.

(2) Other uncorroborated confessions or admissions of the accused that would themselves require corroboration may not be used to supply this independent evidence. If the independent evidence raises an inference of the truth of some but not all of the essential facts admitted, then the confession or admission may be considered as evidence against the accused only with respect to those essential facts stated in the confession or admission that are corroborated by the independent evidence.

(3) Corroboration is not required for a statement made by the accused before the court by which the accused is being tried, for statements made prior to or contemporaneously with the act, or for statements offered under a rule of evidence other than that pertaining to the admissibility of admissions or confessions.

(4) *Quantum of Evidence Needed.* The independent evidence necessary to establish corroboration need not be sufficient of itself to establish beyond a reasonable doubt the truth of facts stated in the admission or confession. The independent evidence need raise only an inference of the truth of the essential facts admitted. The amount and type of evidence introduced as corroboration is a factor to be considered by the trier of fact in determining the weight, if any, to be given to the admission or confession.

(5) *Procedure.* The military judge alone is to determine when adequate evidence of corroboration has been received. Corroborating evidence must be introduced before the admission or confession is introduced unless the military judge allows submission of such evidence subject to later corroboration.

(d) *Disclosure of Statements by the Accused and Derivative Evidence.* Before arraignment, the prosecution must disclose to the defense the contents of all statements, oral or written, made by the accused that are relevant to the case, known to the trial counsel, and within the control of the Armed Forces, and all evidence derived from such statements, that the prosecution intends to offer against the accused.

(e) *Limited Use of an Involuntary Statement.* A statement obtained in violation of Article 31 or Mil. R. Evid. 305(b)-(c) may be used only:

(1) to impeach by contradiction the in-court testimony of the accused; or

(2) in a later prosecution against the accused for perjury, false swearing, or the making of a false official statement.

(f) *Motions and Objections.*

(1) Motions to suppress or objections under this rule, or Mil. R. Evid. 302 or 305, to any statement or derivative evidence that has been disclosed must be made by the defense prior to submission of a plea. In the absence of such motion or objection, the defense may not raise the issue at a later time except as permitted by the military judge for good cause shown. Failure to so move or object constitutes a waiver of the objection.

(2) If the prosecution seeks to offer a statement made by the accused or derivative evidence that was not disclosed before arraignment, the prosecution must provide timely notice to the military judge and defense counsel. The defense may object at that time, and the military judge may make such orders as are required in the interests of justice.

(3) The defense may present evidence relevant to the admissibility of evidence as to which there has been an objection or motion to suppress under this rule. An accused may testify for the limited purpose

of denying that the accused made the statement or that the statement was made voluntarily.

(A) Prior to the introduction of such testimony by the accused, the defense must inform the military judge that the testimony is offered under subdivision (f)(3).

(B) When the accused testifies under subdivision (f)(3), the accused may be cross-examined only as to the matter on which he or she testifies. Nothing said by the accused on either direct or cross-examination may be used against the accused for any purpose other than in a prosecution for perjury, false swearing, or the making of a false official statement.

(4) *Specificity.* The military judge may require the defense to specify the grounds upon which the defense moves to suppress or object to evidence. If defense counsel, despite the exercise of due diligence, has been unable to interview adequately those persons involved in the taking of a statement, the military judge may make any order required in the interests of justice, including authorization for the defense to make a general motion to suppress or general objection.

(5) *Rulings.* The military judge must rule, prior to plea, upon any motion to suppress or objection to evidence made prior to plea unless, for good cause, the military judge orders that the ruling be deferred for determination at trial or after findings. The military judge may not defer ruling if doing so adversely affects a party's right to appeal the ruling. The military judge must state essential findings of fact on the record when the ruling involves factual issues.

(6) *Burden of Proof.* When the defense has made an appropriate motion or objection under this rule, the prosecution has the burden of establishing the admissibility of the evidence. When the military judge has required a specific motion or objection under subdivision (f)(4), the burden on the prosecution extends only to the grounds upon which the defense moved to suppress or object to the evidence.

(7) *Standard of Proof.* The military judge must find by a preponderance of the evidence that a statement by the accused was made voluntarily before it may be received into evidence. When trial is by a special court-martial without a military judge, a determination by the president of the court that a statement was made voluntarily is subject to objection by any member of the court. When such objection is

made, it will be resolved pursuant to R.C.M. 801(e)(3)(C).

(8) *Effect of Guilty Plea.* Except as otherwise expressly provided in R.C.M. 910(a)(2), a plea of guilty to an offense that results in a finding of guilty waives all privileges against self-incrimination and all motions and objections under this rule with respect to that offense regardless of whether raised prior to plea.

(g) *Weight of the Evidence.* If a statement is admitted into evidence, the military judge must permit the defense to present relevant evidence with respect to the voluntariness of the statement and must instruct the members to give such weight to the statement as it deserves under all the circumstances.

(h) *Completeness.* If only part of an alleged admission or confession is introduced against the accused, the defense, by cross-examination or otherwise, may introduce the remaining portions of the statement.

(i) *Evidence of an Oral Statement.* A voluntary oral confession or admission of the accused may be proved by the testimony of anyone who heard the accused make it, even if it was reduced to writing and the writing is not accounted for.

(j) *Refusal to Obey an Order to Submit a Body Substance.* If an accused refuses a lawful order to submit for chemical analysis a sample of his or her blood, breath, urine or other body substance, evidence of such refusal may be admitted into evidence on:

(1) A charge of violating an order to submit such a sample; or

(2) Any other charge on which the results of the chemical analysis would have been admissible.

Rule 305. Warnings about rights

(a) *General rule.* A statement obtained in violation of this rule is involuntary and will be treated under Mil. R. Evid. 304.

(b) *Definitions.* As used in this rule:

(1) "Person subject to the code" means a person subject to the Uniform Code of Military Justice as contained in Chapter 47 of Title 10, United States Code. This term includes, for purposes of subdivision (c) of this rule, a knowing agent of any such person or of a military unit.

(2) "Interrogation" means any formal or informal questioning in which an incriminating response ei-

ther is sought or is a reasonable consequence of such questioning.

(3) "Custodial interrogation" means questioning that takes place while the accused or suspect is in custody, could reasonably believe himself or herself to be in custody, or is otherwise deprived of his or her freedom of action in any significant way.

(c) *Warnings Concerning the Accusation, Right to Remain Silent, and Use of Statements.*

(1) *Article 31 Rights Warnings.* A statement obtained from the accused in violation of the accused's rights under Article 31 is involuntary and therefore inadmissible against the accused except as provided in subdivision (d). Pursuant to Article 31, a person subject to the code may not interrogate or request any statement from an accused or a person suspected of an offense without first:

(A) informing the accused or suspect of the nature of the accusation;

(B) advising the accused or suspect that the accused or suspect has the right to remain silent; and

(C) advising the accused or suspect that any statement made may be used as evidence against the accused or suspect in a trial by court-martial.

(2) *Fifth Amendment Right to Counsel.* If a person suspected of an offense and subjected to custodial interrogation requests counsel, any statement made in the interrogation after such request, or evidence derived from the interrogation after such request, is inadmissible against the accused unless counsel was present for the interrogation.

(3) *Sixth Amendment Right to Counsel.* If an accused against whom charges have been preferred is interrogated on matters concerning the preferred charges by anyone acting in a law enforcement capacity, or the agent of such a person, and the accused requests counsel, or if the accused has appointed or retained counsel, any statement made in the interrogation, or evidence derived from the interrogation, is inadmissible unless counsel was present for the interrogation.

(4) *Exercise of Rights.* If a person chooses to exercise the privilege against self-incrimination, questioning must cease immediately. If a person who is subjected to interrogation under the circumstances described in subdivisions (c)(2) or (c)(3) of this rule chooses to exercise the right to counsel, questioning must cease until counsel is present.

(d) *Presence of Counsel.* When a person entitled to counsel under this rule requests counsel, a judge advocate or an individual certified in accordance with Article 27(b) will be provided by the United States at no expense to the person and without regard to the person's indigency and must be present before the interrogation may proceed. In addition to counsel supplied by the United States, the person may retain civilian counsel at no expense to the United States. Unless otherwise provided by regulations of the Secretary concerned, an accused or suspect does not have a right under this rule to have military counsel of his or her own selection.

(e) *Waiver.*

(1) *Waiver of the Privilege Against Self-Incrimination.* After receiving applicable warnings under this rule, a person may waive the rights described therein and in Mil. R. Evid. 301 and make a statement. The waiver must be made freely, knowingly, and intelligently. A written waiver is not required. The accused or suspect must affirmatively acknowledge that he or she understands the rights involved, affirmatively decline the right to counsel, and affirmatively consent to making a statement.

(2) *Waiver of the Right to Counsel.* If the right to counsel is applicable under this rule and the accused or suspect does not affirmatively decline the right to counsel, the prosecution must demonstrate by a preponderance of the evidence that the individual waived the right to counsel.

(3) *Waiver After Initially Invoking the Right to Counsel.*

(A) *Fifth Amendment Right to Counsel.* If an accused or suspect subjected to custodial interrogation requests counsel, any subsequent waiver of the right to counsel obtained during a custodial interrogation concerning the same or different offenses is invalid unless the prosecution can demonstrate by a preponderance of the evidence that:

(i) the accused or suspect initiated the communication leading to the waiver; or

(ii) the accused or suspect has not continuously had his or her freedom restricted by confinement, or other means, during the period between the request for counsel and the subsequent waiver.

(B) *Sixth Amendment Right to Counsel.* If an accused or suspect interrogated after preferral of charges as described in subdivision (c)(1) requests counsel, any subsequent waiver of the right to counsel obtained during an interrogation concerning the same offenses is invalid unless the prosecution can demonstrate by a preponderance of the evidence that the accused or suspect initiated the communication leading to the waiver.

(f) *Standards for Nonmilitary Interrogations.*

(1) *United States Civilian Interrogations.* When a person subject to the code is interrogated by an official or agent of the United States, of the District of Columbia, or of a State, Commonwealth, or possession of the United States, or any political subdivision of such a State, Commonwealth, or possession, the person's entitlement to rights warnings and the validity of any waiver of applicable rights will be determined by the principles of law generally recognized in the trial of criminal cases in the United States district courts involving similar interrogations.

(2) *Foreign Interrogations.* Warnings under Article 31 and the Fifth and Sixth Amendments to the United States Constitution are not required during an interrogation conducted outside of a State, district, Commonwealth, territory, or possession of the United States by officials of a foreign government or their agents unless such interrogation is conducted, instigated, or participated in by military personnel or their agents or by those officials or agents listed in subdivision (f)(1). A statement obtained from a foreign interrogation is admissible unless the statement is obtained through the use of coercion, unlawful influence, or unlawful inducement. An interrogation is not "participated in" by military personnel or their agents or by the officials or agents listed in subdivision (f)(1) merely because such a person was present at an interrogation conducted in a foreign nation by officials of a foreign government or their agents, or because such a person acted as an interpreter or took steps to mitigate damage to property or physical harm during the foreign interrogation.

Rule 306. Statements by one of several accused

When two or more accused are tried at the same trial, evidence of a statement made by one of them which is admissible only against him or her or only against some but not all of the accused may not be received in evidence unless all references inculpating an accused against whom the statement is inadmissible are deleted effectively or the maker of the statement is subject to cross-examination.

Rule 311. Evidence obtained from unlawful searches and seizures

(a) *General rule.* Evidence obtained as a result of an unlawful search or seizure made by a person acting in a governmental capacity is inadmissible against the accused if:

(1) the accused makes a timely motion to suppress or an objection to the evidence under this rule; and

(2) the accused had a reasonable expectation of privacy in the person, place or property searched; the accused had a legitimate interest in the property or evidence seized when challenging a seizure; or the accused would otherwise have grounds to object to the search or seizure under the Constitution of the United States as applied to members of the Armed Forces.

(b) *Definition.* As used in this rule, a search or seizure is "unlawful" if it was conducted, instigated, or participated in by:

(1) military personnel or their agents and was in violation of the Constitution of the United States as applied to members of the Armed Forces, a federal statute applicable to trials by court-martial that requires exclusion of evidence obtained in violation thereof, or Mil. R. Evid. 312-317;

(2) other officials or agents of the United States, of the District of Columbia, or of a State, Commonwealth, or possession of the United States or any political subdivision of such a State, Commonwealth, or possession, and was in violation of the Constitution of the United States, or is unlawful under the principles of law generally applied in the trial of criminal cases in the United States district courts involving a similar search or seizure; or

(3) officials of a foreign government or their agents, where evidence was obtained as a result of a foreign search or seizure that subjected the accused to gross and brutal maltreatment. A search or seizure is not "participated in" by a United States military or civilian official merely because that person is present at a search or seizure conducted in a foreign nation by officials of a foreign government or their agents, or because that person acted as an interpreter or took steps to mitigate damage to property or physical harm during the foreign search or seizure.

(c) *Exceptions.*

(1) *Impeachment.* Evidence that was obtained as a result of an unlawful search or seizure may be

used to impeach by contradiction the in-court testimony of the accused.

(2) *Inevitable Discovery.* Evidence that was obtained as a result of an unlawful search or seizure may be used when the evidence would have been obtained even if such unlawful search or seizure had not been made.

(3) *Good Faith Execution of a Warrant or Search Authorization.* Evidence that was obtained as a result of an unlawful search or seizure may be used if:

(A) the search or seizure resulted from an authorization to search, seize or apprehend issued by an individual competent to issue the authorization under Mil. R. Evid. 315(d) or from a search warrant or arrest warrant issued by competent civilian authority;

(B) the individual issuing the authorization or warrant had a substantial basis for determining the existence of probable cause; and

(C) the officials seeking and executing the authorization or warrant reasonably and with good faith relied on the issuance of the authorization or warrant. Good faith is to be determined using an objective standard.

(d) *Motions to Suppress and Objections.*

(1) *Disclosure.* Prior to arraignment, the prosecution must disclose to the defense all evidence seized from the person or property of the accused, or believed to be owned by the accused, or evidence derived therefrom, that it intends to offer into evidence against the accused at trial.

(2) *Time Requirements.*

(A) When evidence has been disclosed prior to arraignment under subdivision (d)(1), the defense must make any motion to suppress or objection under this rule prior to submission of a plea. In the absence of such motion or objection, the defense may not raise the issue at a later time except as permitted by the military judge for good cause shown. Failure to so move or object constitutes a waiver of the motion or objection.

(B) If the prosecution intends to offer evidence described in subdivision (d)(1) that was not disclosed prior to arraignment, the prosecution must provide timely notice to the military judge and to counsel for the accused. The defense may enter an objection at that time and the military judge may

make such orders as are required in the interest of justice.

(3) *Specificity.* The military judge may require the defense to specify the grounds upon which the defense moves to suppress or object to evidence described in subdivision (d)(1). If defense counsel, despite the exercise of due diligence, has been unable to interview adequately those persons involved in the search or seizure, the military judge may enter any order required by the interests of justice, including authorization for the defense to make a general motion to suppress or a general objection.

(4) *Challenging Probable Cause.*

(A) *Relevant Evidence.* If the defense challenges evidence seized pursuant to a search warrant or search authorization on the ground that the warrant or authorization was not based upon probable cause, the evidence relevant to the motion is limited to evidence concerning the information actually presented to or otherwise known by the authorizing officer, except as provided in subdivision (d)(4)(B).

(B) *False Statements.* If the defense makes a substantial preliminary showing that a government agent included a false statement knowingly and intentionally or with reckless disregard for the truth in the information presented to the authorizing officer, and if the allegedly false statement is necessary to the finding of probable cause, the defense, upon request, is entitled to a hearing. At the hearing, the defense has the burden of establishing by a preponderance of the evidence the allegation of knowing and intentional falsity or reckless disregard for the truth. If the defense meets its burden, the prosecution has the burden of proving by a preponderance of the evidence, with the false information set aside, that the remaining information presented to the authorizing officer is sufficient to establish probable cause. If the prosecution does not meet its burden, the objection or motion must be granted unless the search is otherwise lawful under these rules.

(5) *Burden and Standard of Proof.*

(A) *In general.* When the defense makes an appropriate motion or objection under subdivision (d), the prosecution has the burden of proving by a preponderance of the evidence that the evidence was not obtained as a result of an unlawful search or seizure, that the evidence would have been obtained even if the unlawful search or seizure had not been made, or that the evidence was obtained by officials who reasonably and with good faith relied on the issuance of an authorization to search, seize, or apprehend or a search warrant or an arrest warrant.

(B) *Statement Following Apprehension.* In addition to subdivision (d)(5)(A), a statement obtained from a person apprehended in a dwelling in violation R.C.M. 302(d)(2) and (e), is admissible if the prosecution shows by a preponderance of the evidence that the apprehension was based on probable cause, the statement was made at a location outside the dwelling subsequent to the apprehension, and the statement was otherwise in compliance with these rules.

(C) *Specific Grounds of Motion or Objection.* When the military judge has required the defense to make a specific motion or objection under subdivision (d)(3), the burden on the prosecution extends only to the grounds upon which the defense moved to suppress or objected to the evidence.

(6) *Defense Evidence.* The defense may present evidence relevant to the admissibility of evidence as to which there has been an appropriate motion or objection under this rule. An accused may testify for the limited purpose of contesting the legality of the search or seizure giving rise to the challenged evidence. Prior to the introduction of such testimony by the accused, the defense must inform the military judge that the testimony is offered under subdivision (d). When the accused testifies under subdivision (d), the accused may be cross-examined only as to the matter on which he or she testifies. Nothing said by the accused on either direct or cross-examination may be used against the accused for any purpose other than in a prosecution for perjury, false swearing, or the making of a false official statement.

(7) *Rulings.* The military judge must rule, prior to plea, upon any motion to suppress or objection to evidence made prior to plea unless, for good cause, the military judge orders that the ruling be deferred for determination at trial or after findings. The military judge may not defer ruling if doing so adversely affects a party's right to appeal the ruling. The military judge must state essential findings of fact on the record when the ruling involves factual issues.

(8) *Informing the Members.* If a defense motion or objection under this rule is sustained in whole or in part, the court-martial members may not be informed of that fact except when the military judge must instruct the members to disregard evidence.

(e) *Effect of Guilty Plea.* Except as otherwise expressly provided in R.C.M. 910(a)(2), a plea of guilty to an offense that results in a finding of guilty waives all issues under the Fourth Amendment to the Constitution of the United States and Mil. R. Evid. 311-317 with respect to the offense, whether or not raised prior to plea.

Rule 312. Body views and intrusions

(a) *General rule.* Evidence obtained from body views and intrusions conducted in accordance with this rule is admissible at trial when relevant and not otherwise inadmissible under these rules.

(b) *Visual examination of the body.*

(1) *Consensual Examination.* Evidence obtained from a visual examination of the unclothed body is admissible if the person consented to the inspection in accordance with Mil. R. Evid. 314(e).

(2) *Involuntary Examination.* Evidence obtained from an involuntary display of the unclothed body, including a visual examination of body cavities, is admissible only if the inspection was conducted in a reasonable fashion and authorized under the following provisions of the Military Rules of Evidence:

(A) inspections and inventories under Mil. R. Evid. 313;

(B) searches under Mil. R. Evid. 314(b) and 314(c) if there is a reasonable suspicion that weapons, contraband, or evidence of crime is concealed on the body of the person to be searched;

(C) searches incident to lawful apprehension under Mil. R. Evid. 314(g);

(D) searches within a jail, confinement facility, or similar facility under Mil. R. Evid. 314(h) if reasonably necessary to maintain the security of the institution or its personnel;

(E) emergency searches under Mil. R. Evid. 314(i); and

(F) probable cause searches under Mil. R. Evid. 315.

Discussion

An examination of the unclothed body under this rule should be conducted whenever practicable by a person of the same sex as that of the person being examined; however, failure to comply with this requirement does not make an examination an unlawful search within the meaning of Mil. R. Evid. 311.

(c) *Intrusion into Body Cavities.*

(1) *Mouth, Nose, and Ears.* Evidence obtained from a reasonable nonconsensual physical intrusion into the mouth, nose, and ears is admissible under the same standards that apply to a visual examination of the body under subdivision (b).

(2) *Other Body Cavities.* Evidence obtained from nonconsensual intrusions into other body cavities is admissible only if made in a reasonable fashion by a person with appropriate medical qualifications and if:

(A) at the time of the intrusion there was probable cause to believe that a weapon, contraband, or other evidence of crime was present;

(B) conducted to remove weapons, contraband, or evidence of crime discovered under subdivisions (b) or (c)(2)(A) of this rule;

(C) conducted pursuant to Mil. R. Evid. 316(c)(5)(C);

(D) conducted pursuant to a search warrant or search authorization under Mil. R. Evid. 315; or

(E) conducted pursuant to Mil. R. Evid. 314(h) based on a reasonable suspicion that the individual is concealing a weapon, contraband, or evidence of crime.

(d) *Extraction of Body Fluids.* Evidence obtained from nonconsensual extraction of body fluids is admissible if seized pursuant to a search warrant or a search authorization under Mil. R. Evid. 315. Evidence obtained from nonconsensual extraction of body fluids made without such a warrant or authorization is admissible, notwithstanding Mil. R. Evid. 315(g), only when probable cause existed at the time of extraction to believe that evidence of crime would be found and that the delay necessary to obtain a search warrant or search authorization could have resulted in the destruction of the evidence. Evidence obtained from nonconsensual extraction of body fluids is admissible only when executed in a reasonable fashion by a person with appropriate medical qualifications.

(e) *Other Intrusive Searches.* Evidence obtained from a nonconsensual intrusive search of the body, other than searches described in subdivisions (c) or (d), conducted to locate or obtain weapons, contraband, or evidence of crime is admissible only if obtained pursuant to a search warrant or search authorization under Mil. R. Evid. 315 and conducted in a reasonable fashion by a person with appropriate

medical qualifications in such a manner so as not to endanger the health of the person to be searched.

Discussion

Compelling a person to ingest substances for the purposes of locating the property described above or to compel the bodily elimination of such property is a search within the meaning of this section.

(f) *Intrusions for Valid Medical Purposes.* Evidence or contraband obtained in the course of a medical examination or an intrusion conducted for a valid medical purpose is admissible. Such an examination or intrusion may not, for the purpose of obtaining evidence or contraband, exceed what is necessary for the medical purpose.

Discussion

Nothing in this rule will be deemed to interfere with the lawful authority of the Armed Forces to take whatever action may be necessary to preserve the health of a service member.

(g) *Medical Qualifications.* The Secretary concerned may prescribe appropriate medical qualifications for persons who conduct searches and seizures under this rule.

Rule 313. Inspections and inventories in the Armed Forces

(a) *General Rule.* Evidence obtained from lawful inspections and inventories in the Armed Forces is admissible at trial when relevant and not otherwise inadmissible under these rules. An unlawful weapon, contraband, or other evidence of a crime discovered during a lawful inspection or inventory may be seized and is admissible in accordance with this rule.

(b) *Lawful Inspections.* An "inspection" is an examination of the whole or part of a unit, organization, installation, vessel, aircraft, or vehicle, including an examination conducted at entrance and exit points, conducted as an incident of command the primary purpose of which is to determine and to ensure the security, military fitness, or good order and discipline of the unit, organization, installation, vessel, aircraft, or vehicle. Inspections must be conducted in a reasonable fashion and, if applicable, must comply with Mil. R. Evid. 312. Inspections may utilize any reasonable natural or technological aid and may be conducted with or without notice to those inspected.

(1) *Purpose of Inspections.* An inspection may include, but is not limited to, an examination to determine and to ensure that any or all of the following requirements are met: that the command is properly equipped, functioning properly, maintaining proper standards of readiness, sea or airworthiness, sanitation and cleanliness; and that personnel are present, fit, and ready for duty. An order to produce body fluids, such as urine, is permissible in accordance with this rule.

(2) *Searches for Evidence.* An examination made for the primary purpose of obtaining evidence for use in a trial by court-martial or in other disciplinary proceedings is not an inspection within the meaning of this rule.

(3) *Examinations to Locate and Confiscate Weapons or Contraband.*

    (A) An inspection may include an examination to locate and confiscate unlawful weapons and other contraband provided that the criteria set forth in subdivision (b)(3)(B) are not implicated.

    (B) The prosecution must prove by clear and convincing evidence that the examination was an inspection within the meaning of this rule if a purpose of an examination is to locate weapons or contraband, and if:

        (i) the examination was directed immediately following a report of a specific offense in the unit, organization, installation, vessel, aircraft, or vehicle and was not previously scheduled;

        (ii) specific individuals are selected for examination; or

        (iii) persons examined are subjected to substantially different intrusions during the same examination.

(c) *Lawful Inventories.* An "inventory" is a reasonable examination, accounting, or other control measure used to account for or control property, assets, or other resources. It is administrative and not prosecutorial in nature, and if applicable, the inventory must comply with Mil. R. Evid. 312. An examination made for the primary purpose of obtaining evidence for use in a trial by court-martial or in other disciplinary proceedings is not an inventory within the meaning of this rule.

Rule 314. Searches not requiring probable cause

(a) *General Rule.* Evidence obtained from reasonable searches not requiring probable cause is admissible at trial when relevant and not otherwise inadmissible under these rules or the Constitution of the United States as applied to members of the Armed Forces.

(b) *Border Searches.* Evidence from a border search for customs or immigration purposes authorized by a federal statute is admissible.

(c) *Searches Upon Entry to or Exit from United States Installations, Aircraft, and Vessels Abroad.* In addition to inspections under Mil. R. Evid. 313(b), evidence is admissible when a commander of a United States military installation, enclave, or aircraft on foreign soil, or in foreign or international airspace, or a United States vessel in foreign or international waters, has authorized appropriate personnel to search persons or the property of such persons upon entry to or exit from the installation, enclave, aircraft, or vessel to ensure the security, military fitness, or good order and discipline of the command. A search made for the primary purpose of obtaining evidence for use in a trial by court-martial or other disciplinary proceeding is not authorized by subdivision (c).

Discussion

Searches under subdivision (c) may not be conducted at a time or in a manner contrary to an express provision of a treaty or agreement to which the United States is a party; however, failure to comply with a treaty or agreement does not render a search unlawful within the meaning of Mil. R. Evid. 311.

(d) *Searches of Government Property.* Evidence resulting from a search of government property without probable cause is admissible under this rule unless the person to whom the property is issued or assigned has a reasonable expectation of privacy therein at the time of the search. Normally a person does not have a reasonable expectation of privacy in government property that is not issued for personal use. Wall or floor lockers in living quarters issued for the purpose of storing personal possessions normally are issued for personal use, but the determination as to whether a person has a reasonable expectation of privacy in government property issued for personal use depends on the facts and circumstances at the time of the search.

(e) *Consent Searches.*

(1) *General Rule.* Evidence of a search conducted without probable cause is admissible if conducted with lawful consent.

(2) *Who May Consent.* A person may consent to a search of his or her person or property, or both, unless control over such property has been given to another. A person may grant consent to search property when the person exercises control over that property.

Discussion

Where a co-occupant of property is physically present at the time of the requested search and expressly states his refusal to consent to the search, a warrantless search is unreasonable as to that co-occupant and evidence from the search is inadmissible as to that co-occupant. *Georgia v. Randolph*, 547 U.S. 103 (2006).

---

(3) *Scope of Consent.* Consent may be limited in any way by the person granting consent, including limitations in terms of time, place, or property, and may be withdrawn at any time.

(4) *Voluntariness.* To be valid, consent must be given voluntarily. Voluntariness is a question to be determined from all the circumstances. Although a person's knowledge of the right to refuse to give consent is a factor to be considered in determining voluntariness, the prosecution is not required to demonstrate such knowledge as a prerequisite to establishing a voluntary consent. Mere submission to the color of authority of personnel performing law enforcement duties or acquiescence in an announced or indicated purpose to search is not a voluntary consent.

(5) *Burden and Standard of Proof.* The prosecution must prove consent by clear and convincing evidence. The fact that a person was in custody while granting consent is a factor to be considered in determining the voluntariness of consent, but it does not affect the standard of proof.

(f) *Searches Incident to a Lawful Stop.*

(1) *Lawfulness.* A stop is lawful when conducted by a person authorized to apprehend under R.C.M. 302(b) or others performing law enforcement duties and when the person making the stop has information or observes unusual conduct that leads him or her reasonably to conclude in light of his or her experience that criminal activity may be afoot. The stop must be temporary and investigatory in nature.

(2) *Stop and Frisk.* Evidence is admissible if seized from a person who was lawfully stopped and who was frisked for weapons because he or she was reasonably suspected to be armed and dangerous. Contraband or evidence that is located in the process of a lawful frisk may be seized.

Discussion

Subdivision (f)(2) requires that the official making the stop have a reasonable suspicion based on specific and articulable facts that the person being frisked is armed and dangerous. Officer safety is a factor, and the officer need not be absolutely certain that the individual detained is armed for the purposes of frisking or patting down that person's outer clothing for weapons. The test is whether a reasonably prudent person in similar circumstances would be warranted in a belief that his or her safety was in danger. The purpose of a frisk is to search for weapons or other dangerous items, including but not limited to: firearms, knives, needles, or razor blades. A limited search of outer clothing for weapons serves to protect both the officer and the public; therefore, a frisk is reasonable under the Fourth Amendment.

---

(3) *Vehicles.* Evidence is admissible if seized in the course of a search for weapons in the areas of the passenger compartment of a vehicle in which a weapon may be placed or hidden, so long as the person lawfully stopped is the driver or a passenger and the official who made the stop has a reasonable suspicion that the person stopped is dangerous and may gain immediate control of a weapon.

Discussion

The scope of the search is similar to the 'stop and frisk' defined in subdivision (f)(2) of this rule. During the search for weapons, the official may seize any item that is immediately apparent as contraband or as evidence related to the offense serving as the basis for the stop. As a matter of safety, the official may, after conducting a lawful stop of a vehicle, order the driver and any passengers out of the car without any additional suspicion or justification.

(g) *Searches Incident to Apprehension.*

(1) *General Rule.* Evidence is admissible if seized in a search of a person who has been lawfully apprehended or if seized as a result of a reasonable protective sweep.

(2) *Search for Weapons and Destructible Evidence.* A lawful search incident to apprehension may include a search for weapons or destructible evidence in the area within the immediate control of a person who has been apprehended. 'Immediate control' means that area in which the individual search-

ing could reasonably believe that the person apprehended could reach with a sudden movement to obtain such property.

(3) *Protective Sweep for Other Persons.*

(A) *Area of Potential Immediate Attack.* Apprehending officials may, incident to apprehension, as a precautionary matter and without probable cause or reasonable suspicion, look in closets and other spaces immediately adjoining the place of apprehension from which an attack could be immediately launched.

(B) *Wider Protective Sweep.* When an apprehension takes place at a location in which another person might be present who might endanger the apprehending officials or others in the area of the apprehension, a search incident to arrest may lawfully include a reasonable examination of those spaces where a person might be found. Such a reasonable examination is lawful under subdivision (g) if the apprehending official has a reasonable suspicion based on specific and articulable facts that the area to be examined harbors an individual posing a danger to those in the area of the apprehension.

(h) *Searches within Jails, Confinement Facilities, or Similar Facilities.* Evidence obtained from a search within a jail, confinement facility, or similar facility is admissible even if conducted without probable cause provided that it was authorized by persons with authority over the institution.

(i) *Emergency Searches to Save Life or for Related Purposes.* Evidence obtained from emergency searches of persons or property conducted to save life, or for a related purpose, is admissible provided that the search was conducted in a good faith effort to render immediate medical aid, to obtain information that will assist in the rendering of such aid, or to prevent immediate or ongoing personal injury.

(j) *Searches of Open Fields or Woodlands.* Evidence obtained from a search of an open field or woodland is admissible provided that the search was not unlawful within the meaning of Mil. R. Evid. 311.

Rule 315. Probable cause searches

(a) *General rule.* Evidence obtained from reasonable searches conducted pursuant to a search warrant or search authorization, or under the exigent circumstances described in this rule, is admissible at trial when relevant and not otherwise inadmissible under

these rules or the Constitution of the United States as applied to members of the Armed Forces.

Discussion

Although military personnel should adhere to procedural guidance regarding the conduct of searches, violation of such procedural guidance does not render evidence inadmissible unless the search is unlawful under these rules or the Constitution of the United States as applied to members of the Armed Forces. For example, if the person whose property is to be searched is present during a search conducted pursuant to a search authorization granted under this rule, the person conducting the search should notify him or her of the fact of authorization and the general substance of the authorization. Such notice may be made prior to or contemporaneously with the search. Property seized should be inventoried at the time of a seizure or as soon thereafter as practicable. A copy of the inventory should be given to a person from whose possession or premises the property was taken. Failure to provide notice, make an inventory, furnish a copy thereof, or otherwise comply with this guidance does not render a search or seizure unlawful within the meaning of Mil. R. Evid. 311.

(b) *Definitions.* As used in these rules:

(1) "Search authorization" means express permission, written or oral, issued by competent military authority to search a person or an area for specified property or evidence or for a specific person and to seize such property, evidence, or person. It may contain an order directing subordinate personnel to conduct a search in a specified manner.

(2) "Search warrant" means express permission to search and seize issued by competent civilian authority.

(c) *Scope of Search Authorization.* A search authorization may be valid under this rule for a search of:

(1) the physical person of anyone subject to military law or the law of war wherever found;

(2) military property of the United States or of nonappropriated fund activities of an Armed force of the United States wherever located;

(3) persons or property situated on or in a military installation, encampment, vessel, aircraft, vehicle, or any other location under military control, wherever located; or

(4) nonmilitary property within a foreign country.

Discussion

If nonmilitary property within a foreign country is owned, used, occupied by, or in the possession of an agency of the United States other than the Department of Defense, a search should be conducted in coordination with an appropriate representative of the agency concerned, although failure to obtain such coordination would not render a search unlawful within the meaning of Mil. R. Evid. 311. If other nonmilitary property within a foreign country is to be searched, the search should be conducted in accordance with any relevant treaty or agreement or in coordination with an appropriate representative of the foreign country, although failure to obtain such coordination or noncompliance with a treaty or agreement would not render a search unlawful within the meaning of Mil. R. Evid. 311.

(d) *Who May Authorize.* A search authorization under this rule is valid only if issued by an impartial individual in one of the categories set forth in subdivisions (d)(1) and (d)(2). An otherwise impartial authorizing official does not lose impartiality merely because he or she is present at the scene of a search or is otherwise readily available to persons who may seek the issuance of a search authorization; nor does such an official lose impartial character merely because the official previously and impartially authorized investigative activities when such previous authorization is similar in intent or function to a pretrial authorization made by the United States district courts.

(1) *Commander.* A commander or other person serving in a position designated by the Secretary concerned as either a position analogous to an officer in charge or a position of command, who has control over the place where the property or person to be searched is situated or found, or, if that place is not under military control, having control over persons subject to military law or the law of war; or

(2) *Military Judge or Magistrate.* A military judge or magistrate if authorized under regulations prescribed by the Secretary of Defense or the Secretary concerned.

(e) *Who May Search.*

(1) *Search Authorization.* Any commissioned officer, warrant officer, petty officer, noncommissioned officer, and, when in the execution of guard or police duties, any criminal investigator, member of the Air Force security forces, military police, or shore patrol, or person designated by proper authority to perform guard or police duties, or any agent of any such person, may conduct or authorize a search when a search authorization has been granted under this rule or a search would otherwise be proper under subdivision (g).

(2) *Search Warrants.* Any civilian or military criminal investigator authorized to request search warrants pursuant to applicable law or regulation is authorized to serve and execute search warrants. The execution of a search warrant affects admissibility only insofar as exclusion of evidence is required by the Constitution of the United States or an applicable federal statute.

(f) *Basis for Search Authorizations.*

(1) *Probable Cause Requirement.* A search authorization issued under this rule must be based upon probable cause.

(2) *Probable Cause Determination.* Probable cause to search exists when there is a reasonable belief that the person, property, or evidence sought is located in the place or on the person to be searched. A search authorization may be based upon hearsay evidence in whole or in part. A determination of probable cause under this rule will be based upon any or all of the following:

(A) written statements communicated to the authorizing official;

(B) oral statements communicated to the authorizing official in person, via telephone, or by other appropriate means of communication; or

(C) such information as may be known by the authorizing official that would not preclude the officer from acting in an impartial fashion. The Secretary of Defense or the Secretary concerned may prescribe additional requirements through regulation.

(g) *Exigencies.* Evidence obtained from a probable cause search is admissible without a search warrant or search authorization when there is a reasonable belief that the delay necessary to obtain a search warrant or search authorization would result in the removal, destruction, or concealment of the property or evidence sought. Military operational necessity may create an exigency by prohibiting or preventing communication with a person empowered to grant a search authorization.

Rule 316. Seizures

(a) *General rule.* Evidence obtained from reasonable seizures is admissible at trial when relevant and not otherwise inadmissible under these rules or the Constitution of the United States as applied to members of the Armed Forces.

(b) *Apprehension.* Apprehension is governed by R.C.M. 302.

(c) *Seizure of Property or Evidence.*

(1) *Based on Probable Cause.* Evidence is admissible when seized based on a reasonable belief that

the property or evidence is an unlawful weapon, contraband, evidence of crime, or might be used to resist apprehension or to escape.

(2) *Abandoned Property.* Abandoned property may be seized without probable cause and without a search warrant or search authorization. Such seizure may be made by any person.

(3) *Consent.* Property or evidence may be seized with consent consistent with the requirements applicable to consensual searches under Mil. R. Evid. 314.

(4) *Government Property.* Government property may be seized without probable cause and without a search warrant or search authorization by any person listed in subdivision (d), unless the person to whom the property is issued or assigned has a reasonable expectation of privacy therein, as provided in Mil. R. Evid. 314(d), at the time of the seizure.

(5) *Other Property.* Property or evidence not included in subdivisions (c)(1)-(4) may be seized for use in evidence by any person listed in subdivision (d) if:

(A) *Authorization.* The person is authorized to seize the property or evidence by a search warrant or a search authorization under Mil. R. Evid. 315;

(B) *Exigent Circumstances.* The person has probable cause to seize the property or evidence and under Mil. R. Evid. 315(g) a search warrant or search authorization is not required; or

(C) *Plain View.* The person while in the course of otherwise lawful activity observes in a reasonable fashion property or evidence that the person has probable cause to seize.

(6) *Temporary Detention.* Nothing in this rule prohibits temporary detention of property on less than probable cause when authorized under the Constitution of the United States.

(d) *Who May Seize.* Any commissioned officer, warrant officer, petty officer, noncommissioned officer, and, when in the execution of guard or police duties, any criminal investigator, member of the Air Force security forces, military police, or shore patrol, or individual designated by proper authority to perform guard or police duties, or any agent of any such person, may seize property pursuant to this rule.

(e) *Other Seizures.* Evidence obtained from a seizure not addressed in this rule is admissible provided that its seizure was permissible under the Constitution of the United States as applied to members of the Armed Forces.

Rule 317. Interception of wire and oral communications

(a) *General rule.* Wire or oral communications constitute evidence obtained as a result of an unlawful search or seizure within the meaning of Mil. R. Evid. 311 when such evidence must be excluded under the Fourth Amendment to the Constitution of the United States as applied to members of the Armed Forces or if such evidence must be excluded under a federal statute applicable to members of the Armed Forces.

(b) *When Authorized by Court Order* Evidence from the interception of wire or oral communications is admissible when authorized pursuant to an application to a federal judge of competent jurisdiction under the provisions of a federal statute.

Discussion

Pursuant to 18 U.S.C. §2516(1), the Attorney General, Deputy Attorney General, Associate Attorney General, or any Assistant Attorney General, any acting Assistant Attorney General, or any Deputy Assistant Attorney General or acting Deputy Assistant Attorney General in the Criminal Division or National Security Division specially designated by the Attorney General, may authorize an application to a Federal judge of competent jurisdiction for, and such judge may grant in conformity with 18 U.S.C. §2518, an order authorizing or approving the interception of wire or oral communications by the Federal Bureau of Investigation, or a Federal agency having responsibility for the investigation of the offense as to which the application is made, for purposes of obtaining evidence concerning the offenses enumerated in 18 U.S.C. §2516(1), to the extent such offenses are punishable under the Uniform Code of Military Justice.

(c) *Regulations.* Notwithstanding any other provision of these rules, evidence obtained by members of the Armed Forces or their agents through interception of wire or oral communications for law enforcement purposes is not admissible unless such interception:

(1) takes place in the United States and is authorized under subdivision (b);

(2) takes place outside the United States and is authorized under regulations issued by the Secretary of Defense or the Secretary concerned; or

(3) is authorized under regulations issued by the

Secretary of Defense or the Secretary concerned and is not unlawful under applicable federal statutes.

Rule 321. Eyewitness identification

(a) *General rule.* Testimony concerning a relevant out-of-court identification by any person is admissible, subject to an appropriate objection under this rule, if such testimony is otherwise admissible under these rules. The witness making the identification and any person who has observed the previous identification may testify concerning it. When in testimony a witness identifies the accused as being, or not being, a participant in an offense or makes any other relevant identification concerning a person in the courtroom, evidence that on a previous occasion the witness made a similar identification is admissible to corroborate the witness's testimony as to identity even if the credibility of the witness has not been attacked directly, subject to appropriate objection under this rule.

(b) *When Inadmissible.* An identification of the accused as being a participant in an offense, whether such identification is made at the trial or otherwise, is inadmissible against the accused if:

(1) The identification is the result of an unlawful lineup or other unlawful identification process, as defined in subdivision (c), conducted by the United States or other domestic authorities and the accused makes a timely motion to suppress or an objection to the evidence under this rule; or

(2) Exclusion of the evidence is required by the Due Process Clause of the Fifth Amendment to the Constitution of the United States as applied to members of the Armed Forces. Evidence other than an identification of the accused that is obtained as a result of the unlawful lineup or unlawful identification process is inadmissible against the accused if the accused makes a timely motion to suppress or an objection to the evidence under this rule and if exclusion of the evidence is required under the Constitution of the United States as applied to members of the Armed Forces.

(c) *Unlawful Lineup or Identification Process.*

(1) *Unreliable.* A lineup or other identification process is unreliable, and therefore unlawful, if the lineup or other identification process is so suggestive as to create a substantial likelihood of misidentification.

(2) *In Violation of Right to Counsel.* A lineup is unlawful if it is conducted in violation of the accused's rights to counsel.

(A) *Military Lineups.* An accused or suspect is entitled to counsel if, after preferral of charges or imposition of pretrial restraint under R.C.M. 304 for the offense under investigation, the accused is required by persons subject to the code or their agents to participate in a lineup for the purpose of identification. When a person entitled to counsel under this rule requests counsel, a judge advocate or a person certified in accordance with Article 27(b) will be provided by the United States at no expense to the accused or suspect and without regard to indigency or lack thereof before the lineup may proceed. The accused or suspect may waive the rights provided in this rule if the waiver is freely, knowingly, and intelligently made.

(B) *Nonmilitary Lineups.* When a person subject to the code is required to participate in a lineup for purposes of identification by an official or agent of the United States, of the District of Columbia, or of a State, Commonwealth, or possession of the United States, or any political subdivision of such a State, Commonwealth, or possession, and the provisions of subdivision (c)(2)(A) do not apply, the person's entitlement to counsel and the validity of any waiver of applicable rights will be determined by the principles of law generally recognized in the trial of criminal cases in the United States district courts involving similar lineups.

(d) *Motions to Suppress and Objections.*

(1) *Disclosure.* Prior to arraignment, the prosecution must disclose to the defense all evidence of, or derived from, a prior identification of the accused as a lineup or other identification process that it intends to offer into evidence against the accused at trial.

(2) *Time Requirement.* When such evidence has been disclosed, any motion to suppress or objection under this rule must be made by the defense prior to submission of a plea. In the absence of such motion or objection, the defense may not raise the issue at a later time except as permitted by the military judge for good cause shown. Failure to so move constitutes a waiver of the motion or objection.

(3) *Continuing Duty.* If the prosecution intends to offer such evidence and the evidence was not disclosed prior to arraignment, the prosecution must provide timely notice to the military judge and counsel for the accused. The defense may enter an objec-

tion at that time, and the military judge may make such orders as are required in the interests of justice.

(4) *Specificity.* The military judge may require the defense to specify the grounds upon which the defense moves to suppress or object to evidence. If defense counsel, despite the exercise of due diligence, has been unable to interview adequately those persons involved in the lineup or other identification process, the military judge may enter any order required by the interests of justice, including authorization for the defense to make a general motion to suppress or a general objection.

(5) *Defense Evidence.* The defense may present evidence relevant to the issue of the admissibility of evidence as to which there has been an appropriate motion or objection under this rule. An accused may testify for the limited purpose of contesting the legality of the lineup or identification process giving rise to the challenged evidence. Prior to the introduction of such testimony by the accused, the defense must inform the military judge that the testimony is offered under subdivision (d). When the accused testifies under subdivision (d), the accused may be cross-examined only as to the matter on which he or she testifies. Nothing said by the accused on either direct or cross-examination may be used against the accused for any purpose other than in a prosecution for perjury, false swearing, or the making of a false official statement.

(6) *Burden and Standard of Proof.* When the defense has raised a specific motion or objection under subdivision (d)(3), the burden on the prosecution extends only to the grounds upon which the defense moved to suppress or object to the evidence.

(A) *Right to Counsel.*

(i) *Initial Violation of Right to Counsel at a Lineup.* When the accused raises the right to presence of counsel under this rule, the prosecution must prove by a preponderance of the evidence that counsel was present at the lineup or that the accused, having been advised of the right to the presence of counsel, voluntarily and intelligently waived that right prior to the lineup.

(ii) *Identification Subsequent to a Lineup Conducted in Violation of the Right to Counsel.* When the military judge determines that an identification is the result of a lineup conducted without the presence of counsel or an appropriate waiver, any later identification by one present at such unlawful

lineup is also a result thereof unless the military judge determines that the contrary has been shown by clear and convincing evidence.

(B) *Unreliable Identification.*

(i) *Initial Unreliable Identification.* When an objection raises the issue of an unreliable identification, the prosecution must prove by a preponderance of the evidence that the identification was reliable under the circumstances.

(ii) *Identification Subsequent to an Unreliable Identification.* When the military judge determines that an identification is the result of an unreliable identification, a later identification may be admitted if the prosecution proves by clear and convincing evidence that the later identification is not the result of the inadmissible identification.

(7) *Rulings.* A motion to suppress or an objection to evidence made prior to plea under this rule will be ruled upon prior to plea unless the military judge, for good cause, orders that it be deferred for determination at the trial of the general issue or until after findings, but no such determination will be deferred if a party's right to appeal the ruling is affected adversely. Where factual issues are involved in ruling upon such motion or objection, the military judge will state his or her essential findings of fact on the record.

(e) *Effect of Guilty Pleas.* Except as otherwise expressly provided in R.C.M. 910(a)(2), a plea of guilty to an offense that results in a finding of guilty waives all issues under this rule with respect to that offense whether or not raised prior to the plea.

SECTION IV
RELEVANCY AND ITS LIMITS

Rule 401. Test for relevant evidence

Evidence is relevant if:

(a) it has any tendency to make a fact more or less probable than it would be without the evidence; and

(b) the fact is of consequence in determining the action.

Rule 402. General admissibility of relevant evidence

(a) Relevant evidence is admissible unless any of the following provides otherwise:

(1) the United States Constitution as it applies to members of the Armed Forces;

(2) a federal statute applicable to trial by courts-martial;

(3) these rules; or

(4) this Manual.

(b) Irrelevant evidence is not admissible.

Rule 403. Excluding relevant evidence for prejudice, confusion, waste of time, or other reasons

The military judge may exclude relevant evidence if its probative value is substantially outweighed by a danger of one or more of the following: unfair prejudice, confusing the issues, misleading the members, undue delay, wasting time, or needlessly presenting cumulative evidence.

Rule 404. Character evidence; crimes or other acts

(a) *Character Evidence.*

(1) *Prohibited Uses.* Evidence of a person's character or character trait is not admissible to prove that on a particular occasion the person acted in accordance with the character or trait.

(2) *Exceptions for an Accused or Victim*

(A) The accused may offer evidence of the accused's pertinent trait, and if the evidence is admitted, the prosecution may offer evidence to rebut it.

(B) Subject to the limitations in Mil. R. Evid. 412, the accused may offer evidence of an alleged victim's pertinent trait, and if the evidence is admitted, the prosecution may:

(i) offer evidence to rebut it; and

(ii) offer evidence of the accused's same trait; and

(C) in a homicide or assault case, the prosecution may offer evidence of the alleged victim's trait of peacefulness to rebut evidence that the victim was the first aggressor.

(3) *Exceptions for a Witness.* Evidence of a witness's character may be admitted under Mil R. Evid. 607, 608, and 609.

(b) *Crimes, Wrongs, or Other Acts.*

(1) *Prohibited Uses.* Evidence of a crime, wrong, or other act is not admissible to prove a person's character in order to show that on a particular occasion the person acted in accordance with the character.

(2) *Permitted Uses; Notice.* This evidence may be admissible for another purpose, such as proving motive, opportunity, intent, preparation, plan, knowledge, identity, absence of mistake, or lack of accident. On request by the accused, the prosecution must:

(A) provide reasonable notice of the general nature of any such evidence that the prosecution intends to offer at trial; and

(B) do so before trial – or during trial if the military judge, for good cause, excuses lack of pretrial notice.

Rule 405. Methods of proving character

(a) *By Reputation or Opinion.* When evidence of a person's character or character trait is admissible, it may be proved by testimony about the person's reputation or by testimony in the form of an opinion. On cross-examination of the character witness, the military judge may allow an inquiry into relevant specific instances of the person's conduct.

(b) *By Specific Instances of Conduct.* When a person's character or character trait is an essential element of a charge, claim, or defense, the character or trait may also be proved by relevant specific instances of the person's conduct.

(c) *By Affidavit.* The defense may introduce affidavits or other written statements of persons other than the accused concerning the character of the accused. If the defense introduces affidavits or other written statements under this subdivision, the prosecution may, in rebuttal, also introduce affidavits or other written statements regarding the character of the accused. Evidence of this type may be introduced by the defense or prosecution only if, aside from being contained in an affidavit or other written statement, it would otherwise be admissible under these rules.

(d) *Definitions.* "Reputation" means the estimation in which a person generally is held in the community in which the person lives or pursues a business or profession. "Community" in the Armed Forces includes a post, camp, ship, station, or other military organization regardless of size.

Rule 406. Habit; routine practice

Evidence of a person's habit or an organization's routine practice may be admitted to prove that on a particular occasion the person or organization acted in accordance with the habit or routine practice. The military judge may admit this evidence regardless of whether it is corroborated or whether there was an eyewitness.

Rule 407. Subsequent remedial measures

(a) When measures are taken that would have made an earlier injury or harm less likely to occur, evidence of the subsequent measures is not admissible to prove:

(1) negligence;

(2) culpable conduct;

(3) a defect in a product or its design; or

(4) a need for a warning or instruction.

(b) The military judge may admit this evidence for another purpose, such as impeachment or – if disputed – proving ownership, control, or the feasibility of precautionary measures.

Rule 408. Compromise offers and negotiations

(a) *Prohibited Uses.* Evidence of the following is not admissible – on behalf of any party – either to prove or disprove the validity or amount of a disputed claim or to impeach by a prior inconsistent statement or a contradiction:

(1) furnishing, promising, or offering – or accepting, promising to accept, or offering to accept – a valuable consideration in order to compromise the claim; and

(2) conduct or a statement made during compromise negotiations about the claim – except when the negotiations related to a claim by a public office in the exercise of its regulatory, investigative, or enforcement authority.

(b) *Exceptions.* The military judge may admit this evidence for another purpose, such as proving witness bias or prejudice, negating a contention of undue delay, or proving an effort to obstruct a criminal investigation or prosecution.

Rule 409. Offers to pay medical and similar expenses

Evidence of furnishing, promising to pay, or offering to pay medical, hospital, or similar expenses

resulting from an injury is not admissible to prove liability for the injury.

Rule 410. Pleas, plea discussions, and related statements

(a) *Prohibited Uses.* Evidence of the following is not admissible against the accused who made the plea or participated in the plea discussions:

(1) a guilty plea that was later withdrawn;

(2) a nolo contendere plea;

(3) any statement made in the course of any judicial inquiry regarding either of the foregoing pleas; or

(4) any statement made during plea discussions with the convening authority, staff judge advocate, trial counsel or other counsel for the government if the discussions did not result in a guilty plea or they resulted in a later-withdrawn guilty plea.

(b) *Exceptions.* The military judge may admit a statement described in subdivision (a)(3) or (a)(4):

(1) when another statement made during the same plea or plea discussions has been introduced, if in fairness the statements ought to be considered together; or

(2) in a proceeding for perjury or false statement, if the accused made the statement under oath, on the record, and with counsel present.

(c) *Request for Administrative Disposition.* A "statement made during plea discussions" includes a statement made by the accused solely for the purpose of requesting disposition under an authorized procedure for administrative action in lieu of trial by court-martial; "on the record" includes the written statement submitted by the accused in furtherance of such request.

Rule 411. Liability Insurance

Evidence that a person was or was not insured against liability is not admissible to prove whether the person acted negligently or otherwise wrongfully. The military judge may admit this evidence for another purpose, such as proving witness bias or prejudice or proving agency, ownership, or control.

Rule 412. Sex offense cases: The victim's sexual behavior or predisposition

(a) *Evidence generally inadmissible.* The following evidence is not admissible in any proceeding involving an alleged sexual offense except as provided in subdivisions (b) and (c):

(1) Evidence offered to prove that any alleged victim engaged in other sexual behavior.

(2) Evidence offered to prove any alleged victim's sexual predisposition.

(b) *Exceptions.*

(1) In a proceeding, the following evidence is admissible, if otherwise admissible under these rules:

(A) evidence of specific instances of sexual behavior by the alleged victim offered to prove that a person other than the accused was the source of semen, injury, or other physical evidence;

(B) evidence of specific instances of sexual behavior by the alleged victim with respect to the person accused of the sexual misconduct offered by the accused to prove consent or by the prosecution; and

(C) evidence the exclusion of which would violate the constitutional rights of the accused.

(c) *Procedure to determine admissibility.*

(1) A party intending to offer evidence under subsection (b) must—

(A) file a written motion at least 5 days prior to entry of pleas specifically describing the evidence and stating the purpose for which it is offered unless the military judge, for good cause shown, requires a different time for filing or permits filing during trial; and

(B) serve the motion on the opposing party and the military judge and notify the alleged victim or, when appropriate, the alleged victim's guardian or representative.

(2) Before admitting evidence under this rule, the military judge must conduct a hearing, which shall be closed. At this hearing, the parties may call witnesses, including the alleged victim, and offer relevant relevant evidence. The alleged victim must be afforded a reasonable opportunity to attend and be heard. In a case before a court-martial composed of a military judge and members, the military judge shall conduct the hearing outside the presence of the members pursuant to Article 39(a). The motion, related papers, and the record of the hearing must be sealed and remain under seal unless the court orders otherwise.

(3) If the military judge determines on the basis of the hearing described in paragraph (2) of this subsection that the evidence that the accused seeks to offer is relevant for a purpose under subsection (b) and that the probative value of such evidence outweighs the danger of unfair prejudice to the alleged victim's privacy, such evidence shall be admissible under this rule to the extent an order made by the military judge specifies evidence that may be offered and areas with respect to which the alleged victim may be examined or cross-examined. Such evidence is still subject to challenge under Mil. R. Evid. 403.

(d) For purposes of this rule, the term "sexual offense" includes any sexual misconduct punishable under the Uniform Code of Military Justice, federal law or state law. "Sexual behavior" includes any sexual behavior not encompassed by the alleged offense. The term "sexual predisposition" refers to an alleged victim's mode of dress, speech, or lifestyle that does not directly refer to sexual activities or thoughts but that may have a sexual connotation for the factfinder.

(e) A "nonconsensual sexual offense" is a sexual offense in which consent by the victim is an affirmative defense or in which the lack of consent is an element of the offense. This term includes rape, forcible sodomy, assault with intent to commit rape or forcible sodomy, indecent assault, and attempts to commit such offenses.

Rule 413. Similar crimes in sexual offense cases

(a) *Permitted Uses.* In a court-martial proceeding for a sexual offense, the military judge may admit evidence that the accused committed any other sexual offense. The evidence may be considered on any matter to which it is relevant.

(b) *Disclosure to the Accused.* If the prosecution intends to offer this evidence, the prosecution must disclose it to the accused, including any witnesses' statements or a summary of the expected testimony. The prosecution must do so at least 5 days prior to entry of pleas or at a later time that the military judge allows for good cause.

(c) *Effect on Other Rules.* This rule does not limit the admission or consideration of evidence under any other rule.

(d) *Definition.* As used in this rule, "sexual offense" means an offense punishable under the Uniform Code of Military Justice, or a crime under federal or state law (as "state" is defined in 18 U.S.C. § 513), involving:

(1) any conduct prohibited by Article 120;

(2) any conduct prohibited by 18 U.S.C. chapter 109A;

(3) contact, without consent, between any part of the accused's body, or an object held or controlled by the accused, and another person's genitals or anus;

(4) contact, without consent, between the accused's genitals or anus and any part of another person's body;

(5) contact with the aim of deriving sexual pleasure or gratification from inflicting death, bodily injury, or physical pain on another person; or

(6) an attempt or conspiracy to engage in conduct described in subdivisions (d)(1)-(5).

Rule 414. Similar crimes in child-molestation cases

(a) *Permitted Uses.* In a court-martial proceeding in which an accused is charged with an act of child molestation, the military judge may admit evidence that the accused committed any other offense of child molestation. The evidence may be considered on any matter to which it is relevant.

(b) *Disclosure to the Accused.* If the prosecution intends to offer this evidence, the prosecution must disclose it to the accused, including witnesses' statements or a summary of the expected testimony. The prosecution must do so at least 5 days prior to entry of pleas or at a later time that the military judge allows for good cause.

(c) *Effect on Other Rules.* This rule does not limit the admission or consideration of evidence under any other rule.

(d) *Definitions.* As used in this rule:

(1) "Child" means a person below the age of 16; and

(2) "Child molestation" means an offense punishable under the Uniform Code of Military Justice, or a crime under federal law or under state law (as "state" is defined in 18 U.S.C. § 513), that involves:

(A) any conduct prohibited by Article 120 and committed with a child;

(B) any conduct prohibited by 18 U.S.C. chapter 109A and committed with a child;

(C) any conduct prohibited by 18 U.S.C. chapter 110;

(D) contact between any part of the accused's body, or an object held or controlled by the accused, and a child's genitals or anus;

(E) contact between the accused's genitals or anus and any part of a child's body;

(F) contact with the aim of deriving sexual pleasure or gratification from inflicting death, bodily injury, or physical pain on a child; or

(G) an attempt or conspiracy to engage in conduct described in subdivisions (d)(2)(A)-(F).

SECTION V
PRIVILEGES

Rule 501. Privilege in general

(a) A person may not claim a privilege with respect to any matter except as required by or provided for in:

(1) the United States Constitution as applied to members of the Armed Forces;

(2) a federal statute applicable to trials by courts-martial;

(3) these rules;

(4) this Manual; or

(5) the principles of common law generally recognized in the trial of criminal cases in the United States district courts under rule 501 of the Federal Rules of Evidence, insofar as the application of such principles in trials by courts-martial is practicable and not contrary to or inconsistent with the Uniform Code of Military Justice, these rules, or this Manual.

(b) A claim of privilege includes, but is not limited to, the assertion by any person of a privilege to:

(1) refuse to be a witness;

(2) refuse to disclose any matter;

(3) refuse to produce any object or writing; or

(4) prevent another from being a witness or disclosing any matter or producing any object or writing.

(c) The term "person" includes an appropriate representative of the Federal Government, a State, or political subdivision thereof, or any other entity claiming to be the holder of a privilege.

(d) Notwithstanding any other provision of these rules, information not otherwise privileged does not become privileged on the basis that it was acquired by a medical officer or civilian physician in a professional capacity.

Rule 502. Lawyer-client privilege

(a) *General Rule.* A client has a privilege to refuse to disclose and to prevent any other person from disclosing confidential communications made for the purpose of facilitating the rendition of professional legal services to the client:

(1) between the client or the client's representative and the lawyer or the lawyer's representative;

(2) between the lawyer and the lawyer's representative;

(3) by the client or the client's lawyer to a lawyer representing another in a matter of common interest;

(4) between representatives of the client or between the client and a representative of the client; or

(5) between lawyers representing the client.

(b) *Definitions.* As used in this rule:

(1) "Client" means a person, public officer, corporation, association, organization, or other entity, either public or private, who receives professional legal services from a lawyer, or who consults a lawyer with a view to obtaining professional legal services from the lawyer.

(2) "Lawyer" means a person authorized, or reasonably believed by the client to be authorized, to practice law; or a member of the Armed Forces detailed, assigned, or otherwise provided to represent a person in a court-martial case or in any military investigation or proceeding. The term "lawyer" does not include a member of the Armed Forces serving in a capacity other than as a judge advocate, legal officer, or law specialist as defined in Article 1, unless the member:

(A) is detailed, assigned, or otherwise provided to represent a person in a court-martial case or in any military investigation or proceeding;

(B) is authorized by the Armed Forces, or reasonably believed by the client to be authorized, to render professional legal services to members of the Armed Forces; or

(C) is authorized to practice law and renders professional legal services during off-duty employment.

(3) "Lawyer's representative" means a person employed by or assigned to assist a lawyer in providing professional legal services.

(4) A communication is "confidential" if not intended to be disclosed to third persons other than those to whom disclosure is in furtherance of the rendition of professional legal services to the client or those reasonably necessary for the transmission of the communication.

(c) *Who May Claim the Privilege.* The privilege may be claimed by the client, the guardian or conservator of the client, the personal representative of a deceased client, or the successor, trustee, or similar representative of a corporation, association, or other organization, whether or not in existence. The lawyer or the lawyer's representative who received the communication may claim the privilege on behalf of the client. The authority of the lawyer to do so is presumed in the absence of evidence to the contrary.

(d) *Exceptions.* There is no privilege under this rule under any of the following circumstances:

(1) *Crime or Fraud.* If the communication clearly contemplated the future commission of a fraud or crime or if services of the lawyer were sought or obtained to enable or aid anyone to commit or plan to commit what the client knew or reasonably should have known to be a crime or fraud;

(2) *Claimants through Same Deceased Client.* As to a communication relevant to an issue between parties who claim through the same deceased client, regardless of whether the claims are by testate or intestate succession or by inter vivos transaction;

(3) *Breach of Duty by Lawyer or Client.* As to a communication relevant to an issue of breach of duty by the lawyer to the client or by the client to the lawyer;

(4) *Document Attested by the Lawyer.* As to a communication relevant to an issue concerning an attested document to which the lawyer is an attesting witness; or

(5) *Joint Clients.* As to a communication relevant to a matter of common interest between two or more clients if the communication was made by any of them to a lawyer retained or consulted in common, when offered in an action between any of the clients.

Rule 503. Communications to clergy

(a) *General Rule.* A person has a privilege to refuse to disclose and to prevent another from disclosing a confidential communication by the person to a clergyman or to a clergyman's assistant, if such communication is made either as a formal act of religion or as a matter of conscience.

(b) *Definitions.* As used in this rule:

(1) "Clergyman" means a minister, priest, rabbi, chaplain, or other similar functionary of a religious organization, or an individual reasonably believed to be so by the person consulting the clergyman.

(2) "Clergyman's assistant" means a person employed by or assigned to assist a clergyman in his capacity as a spiritual advisor.

(3) A communication is "confidential" if made to a clergyman in the clergyman's capacity as a spiritual adviser or to a clergyman's assistant in the assistant's official capacity and is not intended to be disclosed to third persons other than those to whom disclosure is in furtherance of the purpose of the communication or to those reasonably necessary for the transmission of the communication.

(c) *Who May Claim the Privilege.* The privilege may be claimed by the person, guardian, or conservator, or by a personal representative if the person is deceased. The clergyman or clergyman's assistant who received the communication may claim the privilege on behalf of the person. The authority of the clergyman or clergyman's assistant to do so is presumed in the absence of evidence to the contrary.

Rule 504. Husband-wife privilege

(a) *Spousal Incapacity.* A person has a privilege to refuse to testify against his or her spouse.

(b) *Confidential Communication Made During the Marriage.*

(1) *General Rule.* A person has a privilege during and after the marital relationship to refuse to disclose, and to prevent another from disclosing, any confidential communication made to the spouse of the person while they were husband and wife and not separated as provided by law.

(2) *Definition.* As used in this rule, a communication is "confidential" if made privately by any person to the spouse of the person and is not intended to be disclosed to third persons other than those reasonably necessary for transmission of the communication.

(3) *Who May Claim the Privilege.* The privilege may be claimed by the spouse who made the communication or by the other spouse on his or her behalf. The authority of the latter spouse to do so is presumed in the absence of evidence of a waiver. The privilege will not prevent disclosure of the communication at the request of the spouse to whom the communication was made if that spouse is an accused regardless of whether the spouse who made the communication objects to its disclosure.

(c) *Exceptions.*

(1) *To Spousal Incapacity Only.* There is no privilege under subdivision (a) when, at the time the testimony of one of the parties to the marriage is to be introduced in evidence against the other party, the parties are divorced or the marriage has been annulled.

(2) *To Spousal Incapacity and Confidential Communications.* There is no privilege under subdivisions (a) or (b):

(A) In proceedings in which one spouse is charged with a crime against the person or property of the other spouse or a child of either, or with a crime against the person or property of a third person committed in the course of committing a crime against the other spouse;

(B) When the marital relationship was entered into with no intention of the parties to live together as spouses, but only for the purpose of using the purported marital relationship as a sham, and with respect to the privilege in subdivision (a), the relationship remains a sham at the time the testimony or statement of one of the parties is to be introduced against the other; or with respect to the privilege in subdivision (b), the relationship was a sham at the time of the communication; or

(C) In proceedings in which a spouse is charged, in accordance with Article 133 or 134, with importing the other spouse as an alien for prostitution or other immoral purpose in violation of 18 U.S.C. §1328; with transporting the other spouse in interstate commerce for immoral purposes or other offense in violation of 18 U.S.C. §§ 2421-2424; or with violation of such other similar statutes under which such privilege may not be claimed in the trial of criminal cases in the United States district courts.

(D) Where both parties have been substantial participants in illegal activity, those communications between the spouses during the marriage regarding the illegal activity in which they have jointly participated are not marital communications for purposes of the privilege in subdivision (b) and are not entitled to protection under the privilege in subdivision (b).

(d) *Definitions.* As used in this rule:

(1) "A child of either" means a biological child, adopted child, or ward of one of the spouses and includes a child who is under the permanent or temporary physical custody of one of the spouses, regardless of the existence of a legal parent-child relationship. For purposes of this rule only, a child is:

(A) an individual under the age of 18; or

(B) an individual with a mental handicap who functions under the age of 18.

(2) "Temporary physical custody" means a parent has entrusted his or her child with another. There is no minimum amount of time necessary to establish temporary physical custody, nor is a written agreement required. Rather, the focus is on the parent's agreement with another for assuming parental responsibility for the child. For example, temporary physical custody may include instances where a parent entrusts another with the care of their child for recurring care or during absences due to temporary duty or deployments.

Rule 505. Classified information

(a) *General Rule.* Classified information must be protected and is privileged from disclosure if disclosure would be detrimental to the national security. Under no circumstances may a military judge order the release of classified information to any person not authorized to receive such information. The Secretary of Defense may prescribe security procedures for protection against the compromise of classified information submitted to courts-martial and appellate authorities.

(b) *Definitions.* As used in this rule:

(1) "Classified information" means any information or material that has been determined by the United States Government pursuant to an executive order, statute, or regulations, to require protection against unauthorized disclosure for reasons of national security, and any restricted data, as defined in 42 U.S.C. §2014(y).

(2) "National security" means the national defense and foreign relations of the United States.

(3) "In camera hearing" means a session under Article 39(a) from which the public is excluded.

(4) "In camera review" means an inspection of documents or other evidence conducted by the military judge alone in chambers and not on the record.

(5) "Ex parte" means a discussion between the military judge and either the defense counsel or prosecution, without the other party or the public present. This discussion can be on or off the record, depending on the circumstances. The military judge will grant a request for an ex parte discussion or hearing only after finding that such discussion or hearing is necessary to protect classified information or other good cause. Prior to granting a request from one party for an ex parte discussion or hearing, the military judge must provide notice to the opposing party on the record. If the ex parte discussion is conducted off the record, the military judge should later state on the record that such ex parte discussion took place and generally summarize the subject matter of the discussion, as appropriate.

(c) *Access to Evidence.* Any information admitted into evidence pursuant to any rule, procedure, or order by the military judge must be provided to the accused.

(d) *Declassification.* Trial counsel should, when practicable, seek declassification of evidence that may be used at trial, consistent with the requirements of national security. A decision not to declassify evidence under this section is not subject to review by a military judge or upon appeal.

(e) *Action Prior to Referral of Charges*

(1) Prior to referral of charges, upon a showing by the accused that the classified information sought is relevant and necessary to an element of the offense or a legally cognizable defense, the convening authority must respond in writing to a request by the accused for classified information if the privilege in this rule is claimed for such information. In response to such a request, the convening authority may:

(A) delete specified items of classified information from documents made available to the accused;

(B) substitute a portion or summary of the information for such classified documents;

(C) substitute a statement admitting relevant facts that the classified information would tend to prove;

(D) provide the document subject to conditions

that will guard against the compromise of the information disclosed to the accused; or

(E) withhold disclosure if actions under (A) through (D) cannot be taken without causing identifiable damage to the national security.

(2) An Article 32 investigating officer may not rule on any objection by the accused to the release of documents or information protected by this rule.

(3) Any objection by the accused to the withholding of information or to the conditions of disclosure must be raised through a motion for appropriate relief at a pretrial conference.

(f) *Actions after Referral of Charges.*

(1) *Pretrial Conference.* At any time after referral of charges, any party may move for a pretrial conference under Article 39(a) to consider matters relating to classified information that may arise in connection with the trial. Following such a motion, or when the military judge recognizes the need for such conference, the military judge must promptly hold a pretrial conference under Article 39(a).

(2) *Ex Parte Permissible.* Upon request by either party and with a showing of good cause, the military judge must hold such conference ex parte to the extent necessary to protect classified information from disclosure.

(3) *Matters to be Established at Pretrial Conference.*

(A) *Timing of Subsequent Actions.* At the pretrial conference, the military judge must establish the timing of:

(i) requests for discovery;

(ii) the provision of notice required by subdivision (i) of this rule; and

(iii) established by subdivision (j) of this rule.

(B) *Other Matters.* At the pretrial conference, the military judge may also consider any matter that relates to classified information or that may promote a fair and expeditious trial.

(4) *Convening Authority Notice and Action.* If a claim of privilege has been made under this rule with respect to classified information that apparently contains evidence that is relevant and necessary to an element of the offense or a legally cognizable defense and is otherwise admissible in evidence in the court-martial proceeding, the matter must be reported to the convening authority. The convening authority may:

(A) institute action to obtain the classified information for the use by the military judge in making a determination under subdivision (j);

(B) dismiss the charges;

(C) dismiss the charges or specifications or both to which the information relates; or

(D) take such other action as may be required in the interests of justice.

(5) *Remedies.* If, after a reasonable period of time, the information is not provided to the military judge in circumstances where proceeding with the case without such information would materially prejudice a substantial right of the accused, the military judge must dismiss the charges or specifications or both to which the classified information relates.

(g) *Protective Orders.* Upon motion of the trial counsel, the military judge must issue an order to protect against the disclosure of any classified information that has been disclosed by the United States to any accused in any court-martial proceeding or that has otherwise been provided to, or obtained by, any such accused in any such court-martial proceeding. The terms of any such protective order may include, but are not limited to, provisions.

(1) prohibiting the disclosure of the information except as authorized by the military judge;

(2) requiring storage of material in a manner appropriate for the level of classification assigned to the documents to be disclosed;

(3) requiring controlled access to the material during normal business hours and at other times upon reasonable notice;

(4) mandating that all persons requiring security clearances will cooperate with investigatory personnel in any investigations that are necessary to obtain a security clearance;

(5) requiring the maintenance of logs regarding access by all persons authorized by the military judge to have access to the classified information in connection with the preparation of the defense;

(6) regulating the making and handling of notes taken from material containing classified information; or

(7) requesting the convening authority to authorize the assignment of government security personnel and the provision of government storage facilities.

(h) *Discovery and Access by the Accused.*

(1) *Limitations.*

(A) *Government Claim of Privilege.* In a court-martial proceeding in which the government seeks to delete, withhold, or otherwise obtain other relief with respect to the discovery of or access to any classified information, the trial counsel must submit a declaration invoking the United States' classified information privilege and setting forth the damage to the national security that the discovery of or access to such information reasonably could be expected to cause. The declaration must be signed by the head, or designee, of the executive or military department or government agency concerned.

(B) *Standard for Discovery or Access by the Accused.* Upon the submission of a declaration under subdivision (h)(1)(A), the military judge may not authorize the discovery of or access to such classified information unless the military judge determines that such classified information would be noncumulative and relevant to a legally cognizable defense, rebuttal of the prosecution's case, or to sentencing. If the discovery of or access to such classified information is authorized, it must be addressed in accordance with the requirements of subdivision (h)(2).

(2) *Alternatives to Full Discovery.*

(A) *Substitutions and Other Alternatives.* The military judge, in assessing the accused's right to discover or access classified information under subdivision (h), may authorize the government:

(i) to delete or withhold specified items of classified information;

(ii) to substitute a summary for classified information; or

(iii) to substitute a statement admitting relevant facts that the classified information or material would tend to prove, unless the military judge determines that disclosure of the classified information itself is necessary to enable the accused to prepare for trial.

(B) *In Camera Review.* The military judge must, upon the request of the prosecution, conduct an in camera review of the prosecution's motion and any materials submitted in support thereof and must not disclose such information to the accused.

(C) *Action by Military Judge.* The military judge must grant the request of the trial counsel to substitute a summary or to substitute a statement

admitting relevant facts, or to provide other relief in accordance with subdivision (h)(2)(A), if the military judge finds that the summary, statement, or other relief would provide the accused with substantially the same ability to make a defense as would discovery of or access to the specific classified information.

(3) *Reconsideration.* An order of a military judge authorizing a request of the trial counsel to substitute, summarize, withhold, or prevent access to classified information under subdivision (h) is not subject to a motion for reconsideration by the accused, if such order was entered pursuant to an ex parte showing under subdivision (h).

(i) *Disclosure by the Accused.*

(1) *Notification to Trial Counsel and Military Judge.* If an accused reasonably expects to disclose, or to cause the disclosure of, classified information in any manner in connection with any trial or pretrial proceeding involving the prosecution of such accused, the accused must, within the time specified by the military judge or, where no time is specified, prior to arraignment of the accused, notify the trial counsel and the military judge in writing.

(2) *Content of Notice.* Such notice must include a brief description of the classified information.

(3) *Continuing Duty to Notify.* Whenever the accused learns of additional classified information the accused reasonably expects to disclose, or to cause the disclosure of, at any such proceeding, the accused must notify trial counsel and the military judge in writing as soon as possible thereafter and must include a brief description of the classified information.

(4) *Limitation on Disclosure by Accused.* The accused may not disclose, or cause the disclosure of, any information known or believed to be classified in connection with a trial or pretrial proceeding until:

(A) notice has been given under subdivision (i); and

(B) the government has been afforded a reasonable opportunity to seek a determination pursuant to the procedure set forth in subdivision (j).

(5) *Failure to comply.* If the accused fails to comply with the requirements of subdivision (i), the military judge:

(A) may preclude disclosure of any classified information not made the subject of notification; and

(B) may prohibit the examination by the accused of any witness with respect to any such information.

(j) *Procedure for Use of Classified Information in Trials and Pretrial Proceedings.*

(1) *Hearing on Use of Classified Information.*

(A) *Motion for Hearing.* Within the time specified by the military judge for the filing of a motion under this rule, either party may move for a hearing concerning the use at any proceeding of any classified information. Upon a request by either party, the military judge must conduct such a hearing and must rule prior to conducting any further proceedings.

(B) *Request for In Camera Hearing.* Any hearing held pursuant to subdivision (j) (or any portion of such hearing specified in the request of a knowledgeable United States official) must be held in camera if a knowledgeable United States official possessing authority to classify information submits to the military judge a declaration that a public proceeding may result in the disclosure of classified information.

(C) *Notice to Accused.* Before the hearing, trial counsel must provide the accused with notice of the classified information that is at issue. Such notice must identify the specific classified information at issue whenever that information previously has been made available to the accused by the United States. When the United States has not previously made the information available to the accused in connection with the case the information may be described by generic category, in such forms as the military judge may approve, rather than by identification of the specific information of concern to the United States.

(D) *Standard for Disclosure.* Classified information is not subject to disclosure under subdivision (j) unless the information is relevant and necessary to an element of the offense or a legally cognizable defense and is otherwise admissible in evidence. In presentencing proceedings, relevant and material classified information pertaining to the appropriateness of, or the appropriate degree of, punishment must be admitted only if no unclassified version of such information is available.

(E) *Written Findings.* As to each item of classified information, the military judge must set forth in writing the basis for the determination.

(2) *Alternatives to Full Disclosure.*

(A) *Motion by the Prosecution.* Upon any determination by the military judge authorizing the disclosure of specific classified information under the procedures established by subdivision (j), the trial counsel may move that, in lieu of the disclosure of such specific classified information, the military judge order:

(i) the substitution for such classified information of a statement admitting relevant facts that the specific classified information would tend to prove;

(ii) the substitution for such classified information of a summary of the specific classified information; or

(iii) any other procedure or redaction limiting the disclosure of specific classified information.

(B) *Declaration of Damage to National Security.* The trial counsel may, in connection with a motion under subdivision (j), submit to the military judge a declaration signed by the head, or designee, of the executive or military department or government agency concerned certifying that disclosure of classified information would cause identifiable damage to the national security of the United States and explaining the basis for the classification of such information. If so requested by the trial counsel, the military judge must examine such declaration during an in camera review.

(C) *Hearing.* The military judge must hold a hearing on any motion under subdivision (j). Any such hearing must be held in camera at the request of a knowledgeable United States official possessing authority to classify information.

(D) *Standard for Use of Alternatives.* The military judge must grant such a motion of the trial counsel if the military judge finds that the statement, summary, or other procedure or redaction will provide the accused with substantially the same ability to make his or her defense as would disclosure of the specific classified information.

(3) *Sealing of Records of In Camera Hearings.* If at the close of an in camera hearing under subdivision (j) (or any portion of a hearing under subdivision (j) that is held in camera), the military judge determines that the classified information at issue may not be disclosed or elicited at the trial or pretrial proceeding, the record of such in camera hearing must be sealed in accordance with R.C.M. 1103A and preserved for use in the event of an appeal. The accused may seek reconsideration of the

military judge's determination prior to or during trial.

(4) *Remedies.*

(A) If the military judge determines that alternatives to full disclosure may not be used and the prosecution continues to object to disclosure of the information, the military judge must issue any order that the interests of justice require, including but not limited to, an order:

(i) striking or precluding all or part of the testimony of a witness;

(ii) declaring a mistrial;

(iii) finding against the government on any issue as to which the evidence is relevant and material to the defense;

(iv) dismissing the charges, with or without prejudice; or

(v) dismissing the charges or specifications or both to which the information relates.

(B) The government may avoid the sanction for nondisclosure by permitting the accused to disclose the information at the pertinent court-martial proceeding.

(5) *Disclosure of Rebuttal Information.* Whenever the military judge determines that classified information may be disclosed in connection with a trial or pretrial proceeding, the military judge must, unless the interests of fairness do not so require, order the prosecution to provide the accused with the information it expects to use to rebut the classified information.

(A) *Continuing Duty.* The military judge may place the prosecution under a continuing duty to disclose such rebuttal information.

(B) *Sanction for Failure to Comply.* If the prosecution fails to comply with its obligation under subdivision (j), the military judge:

(i) may exclude any evidence not made the subject of a required disclosure; and

(ii) may prohibit the examination by the prosecution of any witness with respect to such information.

(6) *Disclosure at Trial of Previous Statements by a Witness.*

(A) *Motion for Production of Statements in Possession of the Prosecution.* After a witness called by the trial counsel has testified on direct examination, the military judge, on motion of the accused, may order production of statements of the witness in the possession of the prosecution that relate to the subject matter as to which the witness has testified. This paragraph does not preclude discovery or assertion of a privilege otherwise authorized.

(B) *Invocation of Privilege by the Government.* If the government invokes a privilege, the trial counsel may provide the prior statements of the witness to the military judge for in camera review to the extent necessary to protect classified information from disclosure.

(C) *Action by Military Judge.* If the military judge finds that disclosure of any portion of the statement identified by the government as classified would be detrimental to the national security in the degree required to warrant classification under the applicable Executive Order, statute, or regulation, that such portion of the statement is consistent with the testimony of the witness, and that the disclosure of such portion is not necessary to afford the accused a fair trial, the military judge must excise that portion from the statement. If the military judge finds that such portion of the statement is inconsistent with the testimony of the witness or that its disclosure is necessary to afford the accused a fair trial, the military judge must, upon the request of the trial counsel, consider alternatives to disclosure in accordance with subdivision (j)(2).

(k) *Introduction into Evidence of Classified Information.*

(1) *Preservation of Classification Status.* Writings, recordings, and photographs containing classified information may be admitted into evidence in court-martial proceedings under this rule without change in their classification status.

(A) *Precautions.* The military judge in a trial by court-martial, in order to prevent unnecessary disclosure of classified information, may order admission into evidence of only part of a writing, recording, or photograph, or may order admission into evidence of the whole writing, recording, or photograph with excision of some or all of the classified information contained therein, unless the whole ought in fairness be considered.

(B) *Classified Information Kept Under Seal.* The military judge must allow classified information offered or accepted into evidence to remain under seal during the trial, even if such evidence is disclosed in the court-martial proceeding, and may, upon motion by the government, seal exhibits containing classified information in accordance with R.C.M. 1103A for any period after trial as necessary to prevent a disclosure of classified information when a knowledgeable United States official possessing authority to classify information submits to the military judge a declaration setting forth the damage to the national security that the disclosure of such information reasonably could be expected to cause.

(2) *Testimony.*

(A) *Objection by Trial Counsel.* During the examination of a witness, trial counsel may object to any question or line of inquiry that may require the witness to disclose classified information not previously found to be admissible.

(B) *Action by Military Judge.* Following an objection under subdivision (k), the military judge must take such suitable action to determine whether the response is admissible as will safeguard against the compromise of any classified information. Such action may include requiring trial counsel to provide the military judge with a proffer of the witness's response to the question or line of inquiry and requiring the accused to provide the military judge with a proffer of the nature of the information sought to be elicited by the accused. Upon request, the military judge may accept an ex parte proffer by trial counsel to the extent necessary to protect classified information from disclosure.

(3) *Closed session.* The military judge may, subject to the requirements of the United States Constitution, exclude the public during that portion of the presentation of evidence that discloses classified information.

(l) *Record of Trial.* If under this rule any information is withheld from the accused, the accused objects to such withholding, and the trial is continued to an adjudication of guilt of the accused, the entire unaltered text of the relevant documents as well as the prosecution's motion and any materials submitted in support thereof must be sealed in accordance with R.C.M. 1103A and attached to the record of trial as an appellate exhibit. Such material must be made available to reviewing authorities in closed proceedings for the purpose of reviewing the determination of the military judge. The record of trial with respect to any classified matter will be prepared under R.C.M. 1103(h) and 1104(b)(1)(D).

Discussion

In addition to the Sixth Amendment right of an accused to a public trial, the Supreme Court has held that the press and general public have a constitutional right under the First Amendment to access to criminal trials. *United States v. Hershey*, 20 M.J. 433, 436 (C.M.A. 1985) (citing *Richmond Newspapers, Inc. v. Virginia*, 448 U.S. 555 (1980)). The test that must be met before closure of a criminal trial to the public is set out in *Press-Enterprise Co. v. Superior Court*, 464 U.S. 501 (1984), to wit: the presumption of openness "may be overcome by an overriding interest based on findings that closure is essential to preserve higher values and is narrowly tailored to serve that interest. The military judge must consider reasonable alternatives to closure and must make adequate findings supporting the closure to aid in review.

Rule 506. Government information other than classified information

(a) *Protection of Government Information.* Except where disclosure is required by a federal statute, government information is privileged from disclosure if disclosure would be detrimental to the public interest.

(b) *Scope.* "Government information" includes official communication and documents and other information within the custody or control of the Federal Government. This rule does not apply to classified information (Mil. R. Evid. 505) or to the identity of an informant (Mil. R. Evid. 507).

(c) *Definitions.* As used in this rule:

(1) "In camera hearing" means a session under Article 39(a) from which the public is excluded.

(2) "In camera review" means an inspection of documents or other evidence conducted by the military judge alone in chambers and not on the record.

(3) "Ex parte" means a discussion between the military judge and either the defense counsel or prosecution, without the other party or the public present. This discussion can be on or off the record, depending on the circumstances. The military judge will grant a request for an ex parte discussion or hearing only after finding that such discussion or hearing is necessary to protect government information or other good cause. Prior to granting a request from one party for an ex parte discussion or hearing, the military judge must provide notice to the opposing party on the record. If the ex parte discussion is conducted off the record, the military judge should later state on the record that such ex parte discussion took place and generally summarize the subject matter of the discussion, as appropriate.

(d) *Who May Claim the Privilege.* The privilege may be claimed by the head, or designee, of the executive or military department or government agency concerned. The privilege for records and information of the Inspector General may be claimed by the immediate superior of the inspector general officer responsible for creation of the records or information, the Inspector General, or any other superior authority. A person who may claim the privilege may authorize a witness or the trial counsel to claim the privilege on his or her behalf. The authority of a witness or the trial counsel to do so is presumed in the absence of evidence to the contrary.

(e) *Action Prior to Referral of Charges.*

(1) Prior to referral of charges, upon a showing by the accused that the government information sought is relevant and necessary to an element of the offense or a legally cognizable defense, the convening authority must respond in writing to a request by the accused for government information if the privilege in this rule is claimed for such information. In response to such a request, the convening authority may:

(A) delete specified items of government information claimed to be privileged from documents made available to the accused;

(B) substitute a portion or summary of the information for such documents;

(C) substitute a statement admitting relevant facts that the government information would tend to prove;

(D) provide the document subject to conditions similar to those set forth in subdivision (g) of this rule; or

(E) withhold disclosure if actions under subdivisions (e)(1)(1)-(4) cannot be taken without causing identifiable damage to the public interest.

(2) Any objection by the accused to withholding of information or to the conditions of disclosure must be raised through a motion for appropriate relief at a pretrial conference.

(f) *Action After Referral of Charges.*

(1) *Pretrial Conference.* At any time after referral of charges, any party may move for a pretrial conference under Article 39(a) to consider matters relating to government information that may arise in connection with the trial. Following such a motion, or when the military judge recognizes the need for such conference, the military judge must promptly hold a pretrial conference under Article 39(a).

(2) *Ex Parte Permissible.* Upon request by either party and with a showing of good cause, the military judge must hold such conference ex parte to the extent necessary to protect government information from disclosure.

(3) *Matters to be Established at Pretrial Conference.*

(A) *Timing of Subsequent Actions.* At the pretrial conference, the military judge must establish the timing of:

(i) requests for discovery;

(ii) the provision of notice required by subdivision (i) of this rule; and

(iii) the initiation of the procedure established by subdivision (j) of this rule.

(B) *Other Matters.* At the pretrial conference, the military judge may also consider any matter which relates to government information or which may promote a fair and expeditious trial.

(4) *Convening Authority Notice and Action.* If a claim of privilege has been made under this rule with respect to government information that apparently contains evidence that is relevant and necessary to an element of the offense or a legally cognizable defense and is otherwise admissible in evidence in the court-martial proceeding, the matter must be reported to the convening authority. The convening authority may:

(A) institute action to obtain the information for use by the military judge in making a determination under subdivision (j);

(B) dismiss the charges;

(C) dismiss the charges or specifications or both to which the information relates; or

(D) take such other action as may be required in the interests of justice.

(5) *Remedies.* If after a reasonable period of time the information is not provided to the military judge in circumstances where proceeding with the case without such information would materially prejudice a substantial right of the accused, the military judge must dismiss the charges or specifications or both to which the information relates.

(g) *Protective Orders.* Upon motion of the trial counsel, the military judge must issue an order to protect against the disclosure of any government information that has been disclosed by the United States to any accused in any court-martial proceeding or that has otherwise been provided to, or obtained by, any such accused in any such court-martial proceeding. The terms of any such protective order may include, but are not limited to, provisions:

(1) prohibiting the disclosure of the information except as authorized by the military judge;

(2) requiring storage of the material in a manner appropriate for the nature of the material to be disclosed;

(3) requiring controlled access to the material during normal business hours and at other times upon reasonable notice;

(4) requiring the maintenance of logs recording access by persons authorized by the military judge to have access to the government information in connection with the preparation of the defense;

(5) regulating the making and handling of notes taken from material containing government information; or

(6) requesting the convening authority to authorize the assignment of government security personnel and the provision of government storage facilities.

(h) *Discovery and Access by the Accused.*

(1) *Limitations.*

(A) *Government Claim of Privilege.* In a court-martial proceeding in which the government seeks to delete, withhold, or otherwise obtain other relief with respect to the discovery of or access to any government information subject to a claim of privilege, the trial counsel must submit a declaration invoking the United States' government information privilege and setting forth the detriment to the public interest that the discovery of or access to such information reasonably could be expected to cause. The declaration must be signed by a knowledgeable United States official as described in subdivision (d) of this rule.

(B) *Standard for Discovery or Access by the Accused.* Upon the submission of a declaration under subdivision (h)(1)(A), the military judge may not authorize the discovery of or access to such government information unless the military judge determines that such government information would be noncumulative, relevant, and helpful to a legally cognizable defense, rebuttal of the prosecution's case, or to sentencing. If the discovery of or access to such government information is authorized, it

must be addressed in accordance with the requirements of subdivision (h)(2).

(2) *Alternatives to Full Disclosure.*

(A) *Substitutions and Other Alternatives.* The military judge, in assessing the accused's right to discover or access government information under subdivision (h), may authorize the government:

(i) to delete or withhold specified items of government information;

(ii) to substitute a summary for government information; or

(iii) to substitute a statement admitting relevant facts that the government information or material would tend to prove, unless the military judge determines that disclosure of the government information itself is necessary to enable the accused to prepare for trial.

(B) *In Camera Review.* The military judge must, upon the request of the prosecution, conduct an in camera review of the prosecution's motion and any materials submitted in support thereof and must not disclose such information to the accused.

(C) *Action by Military Judge.* The military judge must grant the request of the trial counsel to substitute a summary or to substitute a statement admitting relevant facts, or to provide other relief in accordance with subdivision (h)(2)(A), if the military judge finds that the summary, statement, or other relief would provide the accused with substantially the same ability to make a defense as would discovery of or access to the specific government information.

(i) *Disclosure by the Accused.*

(1) *Notification to Trial Counsel and Military Judge.* If an accused reasonably expects to disclose, or to cause the disclosure of, government information subject to a claim of privilege in any manner in connection with any trial or pretrial proceeding involving the prosecution of such accused, the accused must, within the time specified by the military judge or, where no time is specified, prior to arraignment of the accused, notify the trial counsel and the military judge in writing.

(2) *Content of Notice.* Such notice must include a brief description of the government information.

(3) *Continuing Duty to Notify.* Whenever the accused learns of additional government information the accused reasonably expects to disclose, or to cause the disclosure of, at any such proceeding, the

accused must notify trial counsel and the military judge in writing as soon as possible thereafter and must include a brief description of the government information.

(4) *Limitation on Disclosure by Accused.* The accused may not disclose, or cause the disclosure of, any information known or believed to be subject to a claim of privilege in connection with a trial or pre-trial proceeding until:

(A) notice has been given under subdivision (i); and

(B) the government has been afforded a reasonable opportunity to seek a determination pursuant to the procedure set forth in subdivision (j).

(5) *Failure to Comply.* If the accused fails to comply with the requirements of subdivision (i), the military judge:

(A) may preclude disclosure of any government information not made the subject of notification; and

(B) may prohibit the examination by the accused of any witness with respect to any such information.

(j) *Procedure for Use of Government Information Subject to a Claim of Privilege in Trials and Pretrial Proceedings.*

(1) *Hearing on Use of Government Information.*

(A) *Motion for Hearing.* Within the time specified by the military judge for the filing of a motion under this rule, either party may move for an in camera hearing concerning the use at any proceeding of any government information that may be subject to a claim of privilege. Upon a request by either party, the military judge must conduct such a hearing and must rule prior to conducting any further proceedings.

(B) *Request for In Camera Hearing.* Any hearing held pursuant to subdivision (j) must be held in camera if a knowledgeable United States official described in subdivision (d) of this rule submits to the military judge a declaration that disclosure of the information reasonably could be expected to cause identifiable damage to the public interest.

(C) *Notice to Accused.* Subject to subdivision (j)(2) below, the prosecution must disclose government information claimed to be privileged under this rule for the limited purpose of litigating, in camera, the admissibility of the information at trial. The mil-

itary judge must enter an appropriate protective order to the accused and all other appropriate trial participants concerning the disclosure of the information according to subdivision (g), above. The accused may not disclose any information provided under subdivision (j) unless, and until, such information has been admitted into evidence by the military judge. In the in camera hearing, both parties may have the opportunity to brief and argue the admissibility of the government information at trial.

(D) *Standard for Disclosure.* Government information is subject to disclosure at the court-martial proceeding under subdivision (j) if the party making the request demonstrates a specific need for information containing evidence that is relevant to the guilt or innocence or to punishment of the accused, and is otherwise admissible in the court-martial proceeding.

(E) *Written Findings.* As to each item of government information, the military judge must set forth in writing the basis for the determination.

(2) *Alternatives to Full Disclosure.*

(A) *Motion by the Prosecution.* Upon any determination by the military judge authorizing disclosure of specific government information under the procedures established by subdivision (j), the prosecution may move that, in lieu of the disclosure of such information, the military judge order:

(i) the substitution for such government information of a statement admitting relevant facts that the specific government information would tend to prove;

(ii) the substitution for such government information of a summary of the specific government information; or

(iii) any other procedure or redaction limiting the disclosure of specific government information.

(B) *Hearing.* The military judge must hold a hearing on any motion under subdivision (j). At the request of the trial counsel, the military judge will conduct an in camera hearing.

(C) *Standard for Use of Alternatives.* The military judge must grant such a motion of the trial counsel if the military judge finds that the statement, summary, or other procedure or redaction will provide the accused with substantially the same ability to make his or her defense as would disclosure of the specific government information.

(3) *Sealing of Records of In Camera Hearings.* If

at the close of an in camera hearing under subdivision (j) (or any portion of a hearing under subdivision (j) that is held in camera), the military judge determines that the government information at issue may not be disclosed or elicited at the trial or pretrial proceeding, the record of such in camera hearing must be sealed in accordance with R.C.M. 1103A and preserved for use in the event of an appeal. The accused may seek reconsideration of the military judge's determination prior to or during trial.

(4) *Remedies.*

(A) If the military judge determines that alternatives to full disclosure may not be used and the prosecution continues to object to disclosure of the information, the military judge must issue any order that the interests of justice require, including but not limited to, an order:

(i) striking or precluding all or part of the testimony of a witness;

(ii) declaring a mistrial;

(iii) finding against the government on any issue as to which the evidence is relevant and necessary to the defense;

(iv) dismissing the charges, with or without prejudice; or

(v) dismissing the charges or specifications or both to which the information relates.

(B) The government may avoid the sanction for nondisclosure by permitting the accused to disclose the information at the pertinent court-martial proceeding.

(5) *Disclosure of Rebuttal Information.* Whenever the military judge determines that government information may be disclosed in connection with a trial or pretrial proceeding, the military judge must, unless the interests of fairness do not so require, order the prosecution to provide the accused with the information it expects to use to rebut the government information.

(A) *Continuing Duty.* The military judge may place the prosecution under a continuing duty to disclose such rebuttal information.

(B) *Sanction for Failure to Comply.* If the prosecution fails to comply with its obligation under subdivision (j), the military judge may make such ruling as the interests of justice require, to include:

(i) excluding any evidence not made the subject of a required disclosure; and

(ii) prohibiting the examination by the prosecution of any witness with respect to such information.

(k) *Appeals of Orders and Rulings.* In a court-martial in which a punitive discharge may be adjudged, the government may appeal an order or ruling of the military judge that terminates the proceedings with respect to a charge or specification, directs the disclosure of government information, or imposes sanctions for nondisclosure of government information. The government may also appeal an order or ruling in which the military judge refuses to issue a protective order sought by the United States to prevent the disclosure of government information, or to enforce such an order previously issued by appropriate authority. The government may not appeal an order or ruling that is, or amounts to, a finding of not guilty with respect to the charge or specification.

(l) *Introduction into Evidence of Government Information Subject to a Claim of Privilege.*

(1) *Precautions.* The military judge in a trial by court-martial, in order to prevent unnecessary disclosure of government information after there has been a claim of privilege under this rule, may order admission into evidence of only part of a writing, recording, or photograph or admit into evidence the whole writing, recording, or photograph with excision of some or all of the government information contained therein, unless the whole ought in fairness to be considered.

(2) *Government Information Kept Under Seal.* The military judge must allow government information offered or accepted into evidence to remain under seal during the trial, even if such evidence is disclosed in the court-martial proceeding, and may, upon motion by the prosecution, seal exhibits containing government information in accordance with R.C.M. 1103A for any period after trial as necessary to prevent a disclosure of government information when a knowledgeable United States official described in subdivision (d) submits to the military judge a declaration setting forth the detriment to the public interest that the disclosure of such information reasonably could be expected to cause.

(3) *Testimony.*

(A) *Objection by Trial Counsel.* During examination of a witness, trial counsel may object to any question or line of inquiry that may require the witness to disclose government information not previously found admissible if such information has been or is reasonably likely to be the subject of a claim of privilege under this rule.

(B) *Action by Military Judge.* Following such an objection, the military judge must take such suitable action to determine whether the response is admissible as will safeguard against the compromise of any government information. Such action may include requiring trial counsel to provide the military judge with a proffer of the witness's response to the question or line of inquiry and requiring the accused to provide the military judge with a proffer of the nature of the information sought to be elicited by the accused. Upon request, the military judge may accept an ex parte proffer by trial counsel to the extent necessary to protect government information from disclosure.

(m) *Record of Trial.* If under this rule any information is withheld from the accused, the accused objects to such withholding, and the trial is continued to an adjudication of guilt of the accused, the entire unaltered text of the relevant documents as well as the prosecution's motion and any materials submitted in support thereof must be sealed in accordance with R.C.M. 1103A and attached to the record of trial as an appellate exhibit. Such material must be made available to reviewing authorities in closed proceedings for the purpose of reviewing the determination of the military judge.

Rule 507. Identity of informants

(a) *General Rule.* The United States or a State or subdivision thereof has a privilege to refuse to disclose the identity of an informant. Unless otherwise privileged under these rules, the communications of an informant are not privileged except to the extent necessary to prevent the disclosure of the informant's identity.

(b) *Definitions.* As used in this rule:

(1) "Informant" means a person who has furnished information relating to or assisting in an investigation of a possible violation of law to a person whose official duties include the discovery, investigation, or prosecution of crime.

(2) "In camera review" means an inspection of documents or other evidence conducted by the military judge alone in chambers and not on the record.

(c) *Who May Claim the Privilege.* The privilege may be claimed by an appropriate representative of the United States, regardless of whether information was furnished to an officer of the United States or a State or subdivision thereof. The privilege may be claimed by an appropriate representative of a State or subdivision if the information was furnished to an officer thereof, except the privilege will not be allowed if the prosecution objects.

(d) *Exceptions.*

(1) *Voluntary Disclosures; Informant as a Prosecution Witness.* No privilege exists under this rule:

(A) if the identity of the informant has been disclosed to those who would have cause to resent the communication by a holder of the privilege or by the informant's own action; or

(B) if the informant appears as a witness for the prosecution.

(2) *Informant as a Defense Witness.* If a claim of privilege has been made under this rule, the military judge must, upon motion by the accused, determine whether disclosure of the identity of the informant is necessary to the accused's defense on the issue of guilt or innocence. Whether such a necessity exists will depend on the particular circumstances of each case, taking into consideration the offense charged, the possible defense, the possible significance of the informant's testimony, and other relevant factors. If it appears from the evidence in the case or from other showing by a party that an informant may be able to give testimony necessary to the accused's defense on the issue of guilt or innocence, the military judge may make any order required by the interests of justice.

(3) *Informant as a Witness regarding a Motion to Suppress Evidence.* If a claim of privilege has been made under this rule with respect to a motion under Mil. R. Evid. 311, the military judge must, upon motion of the accused, determine whether disclosure of the identity of the informant is required by the United States Constitution as applied to members of the Armed Forces. In making this determination, the military judge may make any order required by the interests of justice.

(e) *Procedures.*

(1) *In Camera Review.* If the accused has articulated a basis for disclosure under the standards set forth in this rule, the prosecution may ask the mili-

tary judge to conduct an in camera review of affidavits or other evidence relevant to disclosure.

(2) *Order by the Military Judge.* If a claim of privilege has been made under this rule, the military judge may make any order required by the interests of justice.

(3) *Action by the Convening Authority.* If the military judge determines that disclosure of the identity of the informant is required under the standards set forth in this rule, and the prosecution elects not to disclose the identity of the informant, the matter must be reported to the convening authority. The convening authority may institute action to secure disclosure of the identity of the informant, terminate the proceedings, or take such other action as may be appropriate under the circumstances.

(4) *Remedies.* If, after a reasonable period of time disclosure is not made, the military judge, sua sponte or upon motion of either counsel and after a hearing if requested by either party, may dismiss the charge or specifications or both to which the information regarding the informant would relate if the military judge determines that further proceedings would materially prejudice a substantial right of the accused.

Rule 508. Political vote

A person has a privilege to refuse to disclose the tenor of the person's vote at a political election conducted by secret ballot unless the vote was cast illegally.

Rule 509. Deliberations of courts and juries

Except as provided in Mil. R. Evid. 606, the deliberations of courts, courts-martial, military judges, and grand and petit juries are privileged to the extent that such matters are privileged in trial of criminal cases in the United States district courts, but the results of the deliberations are not privileged.

Rule 510. Waiver of privilege by voluntary disclosure

(a) A person upon whom these rules confer a privilege against disclosure of a confidential matter or communication waives the privilege if the person or the person's predecessor while holder of the privilege voluntarily discloses or consents to disclosure of any significant part of the matter or communica-

tion under such circumstances that it would be inappropriate to allow the claim of privilege. This rule does not apply if the disclosure is itself a privileged communication.

(b) Unless testifying voluntarily concerning a privileged matter or communication, an accused who testifies in his or her own behalf or a person who testifies under a grant or promise of immunity does not, merely by reason of testifying, waive a privilege to which he or she may be entitled pertaining to the confidential matter or communication.

Rule 511. Privileged matter disclosed under compulsion or without opportunity to claim privilege

(a) *General Rule.* Evidence of a statement or other disclosure of privileged matter is not admissible against the holder of the privilege if disclosure was compelled erroneously or was made without an opportunity for the holder of the privilege to claim the privilege.

(b) *Use of Communications Media.* The telephonic transmission of information otherwise privileged under these rules does not affect its privileged character. Use of electronic means of communication other than the telephone for transmission of information otherwise privileged under these rules does not affect the privileged character of such information if use of such means of communication is necessary and in furtherance of the communication.

Rule 512. Comment upon or inference from claim of privilege; instruction

(a) *Comment or Inference Not Permitted.*

(1) The claim of a privilege by the accused whether in the present proceeding or upon a prior occasion is not a proper subject of comment by the military judge or counsel for any party. No inference may be drawn therefrom.

(2) The claim of a privilege by a person other than the accused whether in the present proceeding or upon a prior occasion normally is not a proper subject of comment by the military judge or counsel for any party. An adverse inference may not be drawn there from except when determined by the military judge to be required by the interests of justice.

(b) *Claiming a Privilege Without the Knowledge of the Members.* In a trial before a court-martial with members, proceedings must be conducted, to the extent practicable, so as to facilitate the making of claims of privilege without the knowledge of the members. Subdivision (b) does not apply to a special court-martial without a military judge.

(c) *Instruction.* Upon request, any party against whom the members might draw an adverse inference from a claim of privilege is entitled to an instruction that no inference may be drawn there from except as provided in subdivision (a)(2).

Rule 513. Psychotherapist—patient privilege

(a) *General Rule.* A patient has a privilege to refuse to disclose and to prevent any other person from disclosing a confidential communication made between the patient and a psychotherapist or an assistant to the psychotherapist, in a case arising under the Uniform Code of Military Justice, if such communication was made for the purpose of facilitating diagnosis or treatment of the patient's mental or emotional condition.

(b) *Definitions.* As used in this rule:

(1) "Patient" means a person who consults with or is examined or interviewed by a psychotherapist for purposes of advice, diagnosis, or treatment of a mental or emotional condition.

(2) "Psychotherapist" means a psychiatrist, clinical psychologist, or clinical social worker who is licensed in any State, territory, possession, the District of Columbia or Puerto Rico to perform professional services as such, or who holds credentials to provide such services from any military health care facility, or is a person reasonably believed by the patient to have such license or credentials.

(3) "Assistant to a psychotherapist" means a person directed by or assigned to assist a psychotherapist in providing professional services, or is reasonably believed by the patient to be such.

(4) A communication is "confidential" if not intended to be disclosed to third persons other than those to whom disclosure is in furtherance of the rendition of professional services to the patient or those reasonably necessary for such transmission of the communication.

(5) "Evidence of a patient's records or communications" means testimony of a psychotherapist, or assistant to the same, or patient records that pertain to communications by a patient to a psychotherapist, or assistant to the same, for the purposes of diagnosis or treatment of the patient's mental or emotional condition.

(c) *Who May Claim the Privilege.* The privilege may be claimed by the patient or the guardian or conservator of the patient. A person who may claim the privilege may authorize trial counsel or defense counsel to claim the privilege on his or her behalf. The psychotherapist or assistant to the psychotherapist who received the communication may claim the privilege on behalf of the patient. The authority of such a psychotherapist, assistant, guardian, or conservator to so assert the privilege is presumed in the absence of evidence to the contrary.

(d) *Exceptions.* There is no privilege under this rule:

(1) when the patient is dead;

(2) when the communication is evidence of child abuse or of neglect, or in a proceeding in which one spouse is charged with a crime against a child of either spouse;

(3) when federal law, state law, or service regulation imposes a duty to report information contained in a communication;

(4) when a psychotherapist or assistant to a psychotherapist believes that a patient's mental or emotional condition makes the patient a danger to any person, including the patient;

(5) if the communication clearly contemplated the future commission of a fraud or crime or if the services of the psychotherapist are sought or obtained to enable or aid anyone to commit or plan to commit what the patient knew or reasonably should have known to be a crime or fraud;

(6) when necessary to ensure the safety and security of military personnel, military dependents, military property, classified information, or the accomplishment of a military mission;

(7) when an accused offers statements or other evidence concerning his mental condition in defense, extenuation, or mitigation, under circumstances not covered by R.C.M. 706 or Mil. R. Evid. 302. In such situations, the military judge may, upon motion, order disclosure of any statement made by the accused to a psychotherapist as may be necessary in the interests of justice; or

(8) when admission or disclosure of a communication is constitutionally required.

(e) *Procedure to Determine Admissibility of Patient Records or Communications.*

(1) In any case in which the production or admis-

sion of records or communications of a patient other than the accused is a matter in dispute, a party may seek an interlocutory ruling by the military judge. In order to obtain such a ruling, the party must:

(A) file a written motion at least 5 days prior to entry of pleas specifically describing the evidence and stating the purpose for which it is sought or offered, or objected to, unless the military judge, for good cause shown, requires a different time for filing or permits filing during trial; and

(B) serve the motion on the opposing party, the military judge and, if practical, notify the patient or the patient's guardian, conservator, or representative that the motion has been filed and that the patient has an opportunity to be heard as set forth in subdivision (e)(2).

(2) Before ordering the production or admission of evidence of a patient's records or communication, the military judge must conduct a hearing. Upon the motion of counsel for either party and upon good cause shown, the military judge may order the hearing closed. At the hearing, the parties may call witnesses, including the patient, and offer other relevant evidence. The patient must be afforded a reasonable opportunity to attend the hearing and be heard at the patient's own expense unless the patient has been otherwise subpoenaed or ordered to appear at the hearing. However, the proceedings may not be unduly delayed for this purpose. In a case before a court-martial composed of a military judge and members, the military judge must conduct the hearing outside the presence of the members.

(3) The military judge may examine the evidence or a proffer thereof in camera, if such examination is necessary to rule on the motion.

(4) To prevent unnecessary disclosure of evidence of a patient's records or communications, the military judge may issue protective orders or may admit only portions of the evidence.

(5) The motion, related papers, and the record of the hearing must be sealed in accordance with R.C.M. 1103A and must remain under seal unless the military judge or an appellate court orders otherwise.

Rule 514. Victim advocate—victim privilege

(a) *General Rule.* A victim has a privilege to refuse to disclose and to prevent any other person from disclosing a confidential communication made between the alleged victim and a victim advocate, in a case arising under the Uniform Code of Military Justice, if such communication was made for the purpose of facilitating advice or supportive assistance to the alleged victim.

(b) *Definitions.* As used in this rule:

(1) "Victim" means any person who is alleged to have suffered direct physical or emotional harm as the result of a sexual or violent offense.

(2) "Victim advocate" means a person who:

(A) is designated in writing as a victim advocate in accordance with service regulation;

(B) is authorized to perform victim advocate duties in accordance with service regulation and is acting in the performance of those duties; or

(C) is certified as a victim advocate pursuant to federal or state requirements.

(3) A communication is "confidential" if made in the course of the victim advocate – victim relationship and not intended to be disclosed to third persons other than those to whom disclosure is made in furtherance of the rendition of advice or assistance to the alleged victim or those reasonably necessary for such transmission of the communication.

(4) "Evidence of a victim's records or communications" means testimony of a victim advocate, or records that pertain to communications by a victim to a victim advocate, for the purposes of advising or providing supportive assistance to the victim.

(c) *Who May Claim the Privilege.* The privilege may be claimed by the victim or the guardian or conservator of the victim. A person who may claim the privilege may authorize trial counsel or a defense counsel representing the victim to claim the privilege on his or her behalf. The victim advocate who received the communication may claim the privilege on behalf of the victim. The authority of such a victim advocate, guardian, conservator, or a defense counsel representing the victim to so assert the privilege is presumed in the absence of evidence to the contrary.

(d) *Exceptions.* There is no privilege under this rule:

(1) when the victim is dead;

(2) when federal law, state law, or service regulation imposes a duty to report information contained in a communication;

(3) when a victim advocate believes that a vic-

tim's mental or emotional condition makes the victim a danger to any person, including the victim;

(4) if the communication clearly contemplated the future commission of a fraud or crime, or if the services of the victim advocate are sought or obtained to enable or aid anyone to commit or plan to commit what the victim knew or reasonably should have known to be a crime or fraud;

(5) when necessary to ensure the safety and security of military personnel, military dependents, military property, classified information, or the accomplishment of a military mission; or

(6) when admission or disclosure of a communication is constitutionally required.

(e) *Procedure to Determine Admissibility of Victim Records or Communications.*

(1) In any case in which the production or admission of records or communications of a victim is a matter in dispute, a party may seek an interlocutory ruling by the military judge. In order to obtain such a ruling, the party must:

(A) file a written motion at least 5 days prior to entry of pleas specifically describing the evidence and stating the purpose for which it is sought or offered, or objected to, unless the military judge, for good cause shown, requires a different time for filing or permits filing during trial; and

(B) serve the motion on the opposing party, the military judge and, if practicable, notify the victim or the victim's guardian, conservator, or representative that the motion has been filed and that the victim has an opportunity to be heard as set forth in subdivision (e)(2).

(2) Before ordering the production or admission of evidence of a victim's records or communication, the military judge must conduct a hearing. Upon the motion of counsel for either party and upon good cause shown, the military judge may order the hearing closed. At the hearing, the parties may call witnesses, including the victim, and offer other relevant evidence. The victim must be afforded a reasonable opportunity to attend the hearing and be heard at the victim's own expense unless the victim has been otherwise subpoenaed or ordered to appear at the hearing. However, the proceedings may not be unduly delayed for this purpose. In a case before a court-martial composed of a military judge and members, the military judge must conduct the hearing outside the presence of the members.

(3) The military judge may examine the evidence or a proffer thereof in camera, if such examination is necessary to rule on the motion.

(4) To prevent unnecessary disclosure of evidence of a victim's records or communications, the military judge may issue protective orders or may admit only portions of the evidence.

(5) The motion, related papers, and the record of the hearing must be sealed in accordance with R.C.M. 1103A and must remain under seal unless the military judge or an appellate court orders otherwise.

SECTION VI
WITNESSES

Rule 601. Competency to testify in general

Every person is competent to be a witness unless these rules provide otherwise.

Rule 602. Need for personal knowledge

A witness may testify to a matter only if evidence is introduced sufficient to support a finding that the witness has personal knowledge of the matter. Evidence to prove personal knowledge may consist of the witness's own testimony. This rule does not apply to a witness's expert testimony under Mil. R. Evid. 703.

Rule 603. Oath or affirmation to testify truthfully

Before testifying, a witness must give an oath or affirmation to testify truthfully. It must be in a form designed to impress that duty on the witness's conscience.

Rule 604. Interpreter

An interpreter must be qualified and must give an oath or affirmation to make a true translation.

Rule 605. Military judge's competency as a witness

(a) The presiding military judge may not testify as a witness at any proceeding of that court-martial. A party need not object to preserve the issue.

(b) This rule does not preclude the military judge

from placing on the record matters concerning docketing of the case.

Rule 606. Member's competency as a witness

(a) *At the Trial by Court-Martial.* A member of a court-martial may not testify as a witness before the other members at any proceeding of that court-martial. If a member is called to testify, the military judge must – except in a special court-martial without a military judge – give the opposing party an opportunity to object outside the presence of the members.

(b) *During an Inquiry into the Validity of a Finding or Sentence.*

(1) *Prohibited Testimony or Other Evidence.* During an inquiry into the validity of a finding or sentence, a member of a court-martial may not testify about any statement made or incident that occurred during the deliberations of that court-martial; the effect of anything on that member's or another member's vote; or any member's mental processes concerning the finding or sentence. The military judge may not receive a member's affidavit or evidence of a member's statement on these matters.

(2) *Exceptions.* A member may testify about whether:

(A) extraneous prejudicial information was improperly brought to the members' attention;

(B) unlawful command influence or any other outside influence was improperly brought to bear on any member; or

(C) a mistake was made in entering the finding or sentence on the finding or sentence forms.

Rule 607. Who may impeach a witness

Any party, including the party that called the witness, may attack the witness's credibility.

Rule 608. A witness's character for truthfulness or untruthfulness

(a) *Reputation or Opinion Evidence.* A witness's credibility may be attacked or supported by testimony about the witness's reputation for having a character for truthfulness or untruthfulness, or by testimony in the form of an opinion about that character. Evidence of truthful character is admissible only after the witness's character for truthfulness has been attacked.

(b) *Specific Instances of Conduct.* Except for a criminal conviction under Mil. R. Evid. 609, extrinsic evidence is not admissible to prove specific instances of a witness's conduct in order to attack or support the witness's character for truthfulness. The military judge may, on cross-examination, allow them to be inquired into if they are probative of the character for truthfulness or untruthfulness of:

(1) the witness; or

(2) another witness whose character the witness being cross-examined has testified about. By testifying on another matter, a witness does not waive any privilege against self-incrimination for testimony that relates only to the witness's character for truthfulness.

(c) *Evidence of Bias.* Bias, prejudice, or any motive to misrepresent may be shown to impeach the witness either by examination of the witness or by evidence otherwise adduced.

Rule 609. Impeachment by evidence of a criminal conviction

(a) *In General.* The following rules apply to attacking a witness's character for truthfulness by evidence of a criminal conviction:

(1) For a crime that, in the convicting jurisdiction, was punishable by death, dishonorable discharge, or by imprisonment for more than one year, the evidence:

(A) must be admitted, subject to Mil. R. Evid. 403, in a court-martial in which the witness is not the accused; and

(B) must be admitted in a court-martial in which the witness is the accused, if the probative value of the evidence outweighs its prejudicial effect to that accused; and

(2) For any crime regardless of the punishment, the evidence must be admitted if the court can readily determine that establishing the elements of the crime required proving – or the witness's admitting – a dishonest act or false statement.

(3) In determining whether a crime tried by court-martial was punishable by death, dishonorable discharge, or imprisonment in excess of one year, the maximum punishment prescribed by the President under Article 56 at the time of the conviction applies

without regard to whether the case was tried by general, special, or summary court-martial.

(b) *Limit on Using the Evidence After 10 Years.* Subdivision (b) applies if more than 10 years have passed since the witness's conviction or release from confinement for it, whichever is later. Evidence of the conviction is admissible only if:

(1) its probative value, supported by specific facts and circumstances, substantially outweighs its prejudicial effect; and

(2) the proponent gives an adverse party reasonable written notice of the intent to use it so that the party has a fair opportunity to contest its use.

(c) *Effect of a Pardon, Annulment, or Certificate of Rehabilitation.* Evidence of a conviction is not admissible if:

(1) the conviction has been the subject of a pardon, annulment, certificate of rehabilitation, or other equivalent procedure based on a finding that the person has been rehabilitated, and the person has not been convicted of a later crime punishable by death, dishonorable discharge, or imprisonment for more than one year; or

(2) the conviction has been the subject of a pardon, annulment, or other equivalent procedure based on a finding of innocence.

(d) *Juvenile Adjudications.* Evidence of a juvenile adjudication is admissible under this rule only if:

(1) the adjudication was of a witness other than the accused;

(2) an adult's conviction for that offense would be admissible to attack the adult's credibility; and

(3) admitting the evidence is necessary to fairly determine guilt or innocence.

(e) *Pendency of an Appeal.* A conviction that satisfies this rule is admissible even if an appeal is pending, except that a conviction by summary court-martial or special court-martial without a military judge may not be used for purposes of impeachment until review has been completed under Article 64 or Article 66, if applicable. Evidence of the pendency is also admissible.

(f) *Definition.* For purposes of this rule, there is a "conviction" in a court-martial case when a sentence has been adjudged.

Rule 610. Religious beliefs or opinions

Evidence of a witness's religious beliefs or opinions is not admissible to attack or support the witness's credibility.

Rule 611. Mode and order of examining witnesses and presenting evidence

(a) *Control by the Military Judge; Purposes.* The military judge should exercise reasonable control over the mode and order of examining witnesses and presenting evidence so as to:

(1) make those procedures effective for determining the truth;

(2) avoid wasting time; and

(3) protect witnesses from harassment or undue embarrassment.

(b) *Scope of Cross-Examination.* Cross-examination should not go beyond the subject matter of the direct examination and matters affecting the witness's credibility. The military judge may allow inquiry into additional matters as if on direct examination.

(c) *Leading Questions.* Leading questions should not be used on direct examination except as necessary to develop the witness's testimony. Ordinarily, the military judge should allow leading questions:

(1) on cross-examination; and

(2) when a party calls a hostile witness or a witness identified with an adverse party.

(d) *Remote live testimony of a child.*

(1) In a case involving domestic violence or the abuse of a child, the military judge must, subject to the requirements of subdivision (d)(3) of this rule, allow a child victim or witness to testify from an area outside the courtroom as prescribed in R.C.M. 914A.

(2) *Definitions.* As used in this rule:

(A) "Child" means a person who is under the age of 16 at the time of his or her testimony.

(B) "Abuse of a child" means the physical or mental injury, sexual abuse or exploitation, or negligent treatment of a child.

(C) "Exploitation" means child pornography or child prostitution.

(D) "Negligent treatment" means the failure to provide, for reasons other than poverty, adequate food, clothing, shelter, or medical care so as to endanger seriously the physical health of the child.

(E) "Domestic violence" means an offense that has as an element the use, or attempted or threatened use of physical force against a person by a current or former spouse, parent, or guardian of the victim; by a person with whom the victim shares a child in common; by a person who is cohabiting with or has cohabited with the victim as a spouse, parent, or guardian; or by a person similarly situated to a spouse, parent, or guardian of the victim.

(3) Remote live testimony will be used only where the military judge makes the following three findings on the record:

(A) that it is necessary to protect the welfare of the particular child witness;

(B) that the child witness would be traumatized, not by the courtroom generally, but by the presence of the defendant; and

(C) that the emotional distress suffered by the child witness in the presence of the defendant is more than *de minimis*.

(4) Remote live testimony of a child will not be used when the accused elects to absent himself from the courtroom in accordance with R.C.M. 804(d).

(5) In making a determination under subdivision (d)(3), the military judge may question the child in chambers, or at some comfortable place other than the courtroom, on the record for a reasonable period of time, in the presence of the child, a representative of the prosecution, a representative of the defense, and the child's attorney or guardian ad litem.

Rule 612. Writing used to refresh a witness's memory

(a) *Scope.* This rule gives an adverse party certain options when a witness uses a writing to refresh memory:

(1) while testifying; or

(2) before testifying, if the military judge decides that justice requires the party to have those options.

(b) *Adverse Party's Options; Deleting Unrelated Matter.* An adverse party is entitled to have the writing produced at the hearing, to inspect it, to cross-examine the witness about it, and to introduce in evidence any portion that relates to the witness's testimony. If the producing party claims that the writing includes unrelated or privileged matter, the military judge must examine the writing in camera, delete any unrelated or privileged portion, and order that the rest be delivered to the adverse party. Any portion deleted over objection must be preserved for the record.

(c) *Failure to Produce or Deliver the Writing.* If a writing is not produced or is not delivered as ordered, the military judge may issue any appropriate order. If the prosecution does not comply, the military judge must strike the witness's testimony or – if justice so requires – declare a mistrial.

(d) *No Effect on Other Disclosure Requirements.* This rule does not preclude disclosure of information required to be disclosed under other provisions of these rules or this Manual.

Rule 613. Witness's prior statement

(a) *Showing or Disclosing the Statement During Examination.* When examining a witness about the witness's prior statement, a party need not show it or disclose its contents to the witness. The party must, on request, show it or disclose its contents to an adverse party's attorney.

(b) *Extrinsic Evidence of a Prior Inconsistent Statement.* Extrinsic evidence of a witness's prior inconsistent statement is admissible only if the witness is given an opportunity to explain or deny the statement and an adverse party is given an opportunity to examine the witness about it, or if justice so requires. Subdivision (b) does not apply to an opposing party's statement under Mil R. Evid. 801(d)(2).

Rule 614. Court-martial's calling or examining a witness

(a) *Calling.* The military judge may – sua sponte or at the request of the members or the suggestion of a party – call a witness. Each party is entitled to cross-examine the witness. When the members wish to call or recall a witness, the military judge must determine whether the testimony would be relevant and not barred by any rule or provision of this Manual.

(b) *Examining.* The military judge or members may examine a witness regardless of who calls the witness. Members must submit their questions to the military judge in writing. Following the opportunity for review by both parties, the military judge must rule on the propriety of the questions, and ask the questions in an acceptable form on behalf of the members. When the military judge or the members call a witness who has not previously testified, the military judge may conduct the direct examination or may assign the responsibility to counsel for any party.

(c) *Objections.* Objections to the calling of witnesses by the military judge or the members or to the interrogation by the military judge or the members may be made at the time or at the next available opportunity when the members are not present.

Rule 615. Excluding witnesses

At a party's request, the military judge must order witnesses excluded so that they cannot hear other witnesses' testimony, or the military judge may do so *sua sponte.* This rule does not authorize excluding:

(a) the accused;

(b) a member of an Armed service or an employee of the United States after being designated as a representative of the United States by the trial counsel;

(c) a person whose presence a party shows to be essential to presenting the party's case;

(d) a person authorized by statute to be present; or

(e) a victim of an offense from the trial of an accused for that offense, when the sole basis for exclusion would be that the victim may testify or present information during the presentencing phase of the trial.

SECTION VII
OPINIONS AND EXPERT TESTIMONY

Rule 701. Opinion testimony by lay witnesses

If a witness is not testifying as an expert, testimony in the form of an opinion is limited to one that is:

(a) rationally based on the witness's perception;

(b) helpful to clearly understanding the witness's testimony or to determining a fact in issue; and

(c) not based on scientific, technical, or other specialized knowledge within the scope of Mil. R. Evid. 702.

Rule 702. Testimony by expert witnesses

A witness who is qualified as an expert by knowledge, skill, experience, training, or education may testify in the form of an opinion or otherwise if:

(a) the expert's scientific, technical, or other specialized knowledge will help the trier of fact to understand the evidence or to determine a fact in issue;

(b) the testimony is based on sufficient facts or data;

(c) the testimony is the product of reliable principles and methods; and

(d) the expert has reliably applied the principles and methods to the facts of the case.

Rule 703. Bases of an expert's opinion testimony

An expert may base an opinion on facts or data in the case that the expert has been made aware of or personally observed. If experts in the particular field would reasonably rely on those kinds of facts or data in forming an opinion on the subject, they need not be admissible for the opinion to be admitted. If the facts or data would otherwise be inadmissible, the proponent of the opinion may disclose them to the members of a court-martial only if the military judge finds that their probative value in helping the members evaluate the opinion substantially outweighs their prejudicial effect.

Rule 704. Opinion on an ultimate issue

An opinion is not objectionable just because it embraces an ultimate issue.

Rule 705. Disclosing the facts or data underlying an expert's opinion

Unless the military judge orders otherwise, an expert may state an opinion – and give the reasons for it – without first testifying to the underlying facts or data. The expert may be required to disclose those facts or data on cross-examination.

Rule 706. Court-appointed expert witnesses

(a) *Appointment Process.* The trial counsel, the defense counsel, and the court-martial have equal opportunity to obtain expert witnesses under Article 46 and R.C.M. 703.

(b) *Compensation.* The compensation of expert witnesses is governed by R.C.M. 703.

(c) *Accused's Choice of Experts.* This rule does not limit an accused in calling any expert at the accused's own expense.

Rule 707. Polygraph examinations

(a) *Prohibitions.* Notwithstanding any other provision of law, the result of a polygraph examination, the polygraph examiner's opinion, or any reference to an offer to take, failure to take, or taking of a polygraph examination is not admissible.

(b) *Statements Made During a Polygraph Examination.* This rule does not prohibit admission of an otherwise admissible statement made during a polygraph examination.

SECTION VIII
HEARSAY

Rule 801. Definitions that apply to this section; exclusions from hearsay

(a) *Statement.* "Statement" means a person's oral assertion, written assertion, or nonverbal conduct, if the person intended it as an assertion.

(b) *Declarant.* "Declarant" means the person who made the statement.

(c) *Hearsay.* "Hearsay" means a statement that:

(1) the declarant does not make while testifying at the current trial or hearing; and

(2) a party offers in evidence to prove the truth of the matter asserted in the statement.

(d) *Statements that Are Not Hearsay.* A statement that meets the following conditions is not hearsay:

(1) *A Declarant-Witness's Prior Statement.* The declarant testifies and is subject to cross-examination about a prior statement, and the statement:

(A) is inconsistent with the declarant's testimony and was given under penalty of perjury at a trial, hearing, or other proceeding or in a deposition;

(B) is consistent with the declarant's testimony and is offered to rebut an express or implied charge that the declarant recently fabricated it or acted from a recent improper influence or motive in so testifying; or

(C) identifies a person as someone the declarant perceived earlier.

(2) *An Opposing Party's Statement.* The statement is offered against an opposing party and:

(A) was made by the party in an individual or representative capacity;

(B) is one the party manifested that it adopted or believed to be true;

(C) was made by a person whom the party authorized to make a statement on the subject;

(D) was made by the party's agent or employee on a matter within the scope of that relationship and while it existed; or

(E) was made by the party's co-conspirator during and in furtherance of the conspiracy.

The statement must be considered but does not by itself establish the declarant's authority under (C); the existence or scope of the relationship under (D); or the existence of the conspiracy or participation in it under (E).

Rule 802. The rule against hearsay

Hearsay is not admissible unless any of the following provides otherwise:

(a) a federal statute applicable in trial by courts-martial; or

(b) these rules.

Rule 803. Exceptions to the rule against hearsay – regardless of whether the declarant is available as a witness

The following are not excluded by the rule against hearsay, regardless of whether the declarant is available as a witness:

(1) *Present Sense Impression.* A statement describing or explaining an event or condition, made while or immediately after the declarant perceived it.

(2) *Excited Utterance.* A statement relating to a startling event or condition, made while the declarant was under the stress of excitement that it caused.

(3) *Then-Existing Mental, Emotional, or Physical Condition.* A statement of the declarant's then-existing state of mind (such as motive, intent, or plan) or emotional, sensory, or physical condition (such as mental feeling, pain, or bodily health), but not including a statement of memory or belief to prove the fact remembered or believed unless it relates to the validity or terms of the declarant's will.

(4) *Statement Made for Medical Diagnosis or Treatment.* A statement that -

(A) is made for – and is reasonably pertinent to – medical diagnosis or treatment; and

(B) describes medical history; past or present symptoms or sensations; their inception; or their general cause.

(5) *Recorded Recollection.* A record that:

(A) is on a matter the witness once knew about

but now cannot recall well enough to testify fully and accurately;

(B) was made or adopted by the witness when the matter was fresh in the witness's memory; and

(C) accurately reflects the witness's knowledge. If admitted, the record may be read into evidence but may be received as an exhibit only if offered by an adverse party.

(6) *Records of a Regularly Conducted Activity.* A record of an act, event, condition, opinion, or diagnosis if:

(A) the record was made at or near the time by – or from information transmitted by – someone with knowledge;

(B) the record was kept in the course of a regularly conducted activity of a uniformed service, business, institution, association, profession, organization, occupation, or calling of any kind, whether or not conducted for profit;

(C) making the record was a regular practice of that activity;

(D) all these conditions are shown by the testimony of the custodian or another qualified witness, or by a certification that complies with Mil. R. Evid. 902(11) or with a statute permitting certification in a criminal proceeding in a court of the United States; and

(E) neither the source of information nor the method or circumstances of preparation indicate a lack of trustworthiness. Records of regularly conducted activities include, but are not limited to, enlistment papers, physical examination papers, fingerprint cards, forensic laboratory reports, chain of custody documents, morning reports and other personnel accountability documents, service records, officer and enlisted qualification records, logs, unit personnel diaries, individual equipment records, daily strength records of prisoners, and rosters of prisoners.

(7) *Absence of a Record of a Regularly Conducted Activity.* Evidence that a matter is not included in a record described in paragraph (6) if:

(A) the evidence is admitted to prove that the matter did not occur or exist;

(B) a record was regularly kept for a matter of that kind; and

(C) neither the possible source of the information nor other circumstances indicate a lack of trustworthiness.

(8) *Public Records.* A record or statement of a public office if:

(A) it sets out:

(i) the office's activities;

(ii) a matter observed while under a legal duty to report, but not including a matter observed by law-enforcement personnel and other personnel acting in a law enforcement capacity; or

(iii) against the government, factual findings from a legally authorized investigation; and

(B) neither the source of information nor other circumstances indicate a lack of trustworthiness. Notwithstanding subdivision (8)(A)(ii), the following are admissible as a record of a fact or event if made by a person within the scope of the person's official duties and those duties included a duty to know or to ascertain through appropriate and trustworthy channels of information the truth of the fact or event and to record such fact or event: enlistment papers, physical examination papers, fingerprint cards, forensic laboratory reports, chain of custody documents, morning reports and other personnel accountability documents, service records, officer and enlisted qualification records, court-martial conviction records, logs, unit personnel diaries, individual equipment records, daily strength records of prisoners, and rosters of prisoners.

(9) *Public Records of Vital Statistics.* A record of a birth, death, or marriage, if reported to a public office in accordance with a legal duty.

(10) *Absence of a Public Record.* Testimony – or a certification under Mil. R. Evid. 902 – that a diligent search failed to disclose a public record or statement if the testimony or certification is admitted to prove that:

(A) the record or statement does not exist; or

(B) a matter did not occur or exist, if a public office regularly kept a record or statement for a matter of that kind.

(11) *Records of Religious Organizations Concerning Personal or Family History.* A statement of birth, legitimacy, ancestry, marriage, divorce, death, relationship by blood or marriage, or similar facts of personal or family history, contained in a regularly kept record of a religious organization.

(12) *Certificates of Marriage, Baptism, and Similar*

Ceremonies. A statement of fact contained in a certificate:

(A) made by a person who is authorized by a religious organization or by law to perform the act certified;

(B) attesting that the person performed a marriage or similar ceremony or administered a sacrament; and

(C) purporting to have been issued at the time of the act or within a reasonable time after it.

(13) *Family Records.* A statement of fact about personal or family history contained in a family record, such as a Bible, genealogy, chart, engraving on a ring, inscription on a portrait, or engraving on an urn or burial marker.

(14) *Records of Documents that Affect an Interest in Property.* The record of a document that purports to establish or affect an interest in property if:

(A) the record is admitted to prove the content of the original recorded document, along with its signing and its delivery by each person who purports to have signed it;

(B) the record is kept in a public office; and

(C) a statute authorizes recording documents of that kind in that office.

(15) *Statements in Documents that Affect an Interest in Property.* A statement contained in a document that purports to establish or affect an interest in property if the matter stated was relevant to the document's purpose unless later dealings with the property are inconsistent with the truth of the statement or the purport of the document.

(16) *Statements in Ancient Documents.* A statement in a document that is at least 20 years old and whose authenticity is established.

(17) *Market Reports and Similar Commercial Publications.* Market quotations, lists (including government price lists), directories, or other compilations that are generally relied on by the public or by persons in particular occupations.

(18) *Statements in Learned Treatises, Periodicals, or Pamphlets.* A statement contained in a treatise, periodical, or pamphlet if:

(A) the statement is called to the attention of an expert witness on cross-examination or relied on by the expert on direct examination; and

(B) the publication is established as a reliable authority by the expert's admission or testimony, by another expert's testimony, or by judicial notice. If admitted, the statement may be read into evidence but not received as an exhibit.

(19) *Reputation Concerning Personal or Family History.* A reputation among a person's family by blood, adoption, or marriage – or among a person's associates or in the community – concerning the person's birth, adoption, legitimacy, ancestry, marriage, divorce, death, relationship by blood, adoption, or marriage, or similar facts of personal or family history, age, ancestry, or other similar fact of the person's personal or family history.

(20) *Reputation Concerning Boundaries or General History.* A reputation in a community – arising before the controversy – concerning boundaries of land in the community or customs that affect the land, or concerning general historical events important to that community, State, or nation.

(21) *Reputation Concerning Character.* A reputation among a person's associates or in the community concerning the person's character.

(22) *Judgment of a Previous Conviction.* Evidence of a final judgment of conviction if:

(A) the judgment was entered after a trial or guilty plea, but not a nolo contendere plea;

(B) the conviction was for a crime punishable by death, dishonorable discharge, or by imprisonment for more than a year;

(C) the evidence is admitted to prove any fact essential to the judgment; and

(D) when offered by the prosecution for a purpose other than impeachment, the judgment was against the accused.

The pendency of an appeal may be shown but does not affect admissibility. In determining whether a crime tried by court-martial was punishable by death, dishonorable discharge, or imprisonment for more than one year, the maximum punishment prescribed by the President under Article 56 of the Uniform of Military Justice at the time of the conviction applies without regard to whether the case was tried by general, special, or summary court-martial.

(23) *Judgments Involving Personal, Family, or General History, or a Boundary.* A judgment that is admitted to prove a matter of personal, family, or general history, or boundaries, if the matter:

(A) was essential to the judgment; and

(B) could be proved by evidence of reputation.

Rule 804. Exceptions to the rule against hearsay – when the declarant Is unavailable as a witness

(a) *Criteria for Being Unavailable.* A declarant is considered to be unavailable as a witness if the declarant:

(1) is exempted from testifying about the subject matter of the declarant's statement because the military judge rules that a privilege applies;

(2) refuses to testify about the subject matter despite the military judge's order to do so;

(3) testifies to not remembering the subject matter;

(4) cannot be present or testify at the trial or hearing because of death or a then-existing infirmity, physical illness, or mental illness; or

(5) is absent from the trial or hearing and the statement's proponent has not been able, by process or other reasonable means, to procure:

(A) the declarant's attendance, in the case of a hearsay exception under subdivision (b)(1) or (b)(5);

(B) the declarant's attendance or testimony, in the case of a hearsay exception under subdivision (b)(2), (b)(3), or (b)(4); or

(6) is unavailable within the meaning of Article 49(d)(2).

Subdivision (a) does not apply if the statement's proponent procured or wrongfully caused the declarant's unavailability as a witness in order to prevent the declarant from attending or testifying.

(b) *The Exceptions.* The following are exceptions to the rule against hearsay, and are not excluded by that rule if the declarant is unavailable as a witness:

(1) *Former Testimony.* Testimony that:

(A) was given by a witness at a trial, hearing, or lawful deposition, whether given during the current proceeding or a different one; and

(B) is now offered against a party who had an opportunity and similar motive to develop it by direct, cross-, or redirect examination.

Subject to the limitations in Articles 49 and 50, a record of testimony given before a court-martial, court of inquiry, military commission, other military tribunal, or pretrial investigation under Article 32 is admissible under subdivision (b)(1) if the record of the testimony is a verbatim record.

(2) *Statement under the Belief of Imminent Death.* In a prosecution for any offense resulting in the death of the alleged victim, a statement that the declarant, while believing the declarant's death to be imminent, made about its cause or circumstances.

(3) *Statement against Interest.* A statement that:

(A) a reasonable person in the declarant's position would have made only if the person believed it to be true because, when made, it was so contrary to the declarant's proprietary or pecuniary interest or had so great a tendency to invalidate the declarant's claim against someone else or to expose the declarant to civil or criminal liability; and

(B) is supported by corroborating circumstances that clearly indicate its trustworthiness, if it tends to expose the declarant to criminal liability and is offered to exculpate the accused.

(4) *Statement of Personal or Family History.* A statement about:

(A) the declarant's own birth, adoption, legitimacy, ancestry, marriage, divorce, relationship by blood or marriage, or similar facts of personal or family history, even though the declarant had no way of acquiring personal knowledge about that fact; or

(B) another person concerning any of these facts, as well as death, if the declarant was related to the person by blood, adoption, or marriage or was so intimately associated with the person's family that the declarant's information is likely to be accurate.

(5) *Other Exceptions.* [Transferred to Mil.R.Evid. 807]

(6) *Statement Offered against a Party that Wrongfully Caused the Declarant's Unavailability.* A statement offered against a party that wrongfully caused or acquiesced in wrongfully causing the declarant's unavailability as a witness, and did so intending that result.

Rule 805. Hearsay within hearsay

Hearsay within hearsay is not excluded by the rule against hearsay if each part of the combined statements conforms with an exception or exclusion to the rule.

Rule 806. Attacking and supporting the declarant's credibility

When a hearsay statement – or a statement described in Mil. R. Evid. 801(d)(2)(C), (D), or (E) – has been admitted in evidence, the declarant's credibility may be attacked, and then supported, by any evidence that would be admissible for those purposes if the declarant had testified as a witness. The military judge may admit evidence of the declarant's inconsistent statement or conduct, regardless of when it occurred or whether the declarant had an opportunity to explain or deny it. If the party against whom the statement was admitted calls the declarant as a witness, the party may examine the declarant on the statement as if on cross-examination.

Rule 807. Residual exception.

(a) *In General.* Under the following circumstances, a hearsay statement is not excluded by the rule against hearsay even if the statement is not specifically covered by a hearsay exception in Mil. R. Evid. 803 or 804:

(1) the statement has equivalent circumstantial guarantees of trustworthiness;

(2) it is offered as evidence of a material fact;

(3) it is more probative on the point for which it is offered than any other evidence that the proponent can obtain through reasonable efforts; and

(4) admitting it will best serve the purposes of these rules and the interests of justice.

(b) *Notice.* The statement is admissible only if, before the trial or hearing, the proponent gives an adverse party reasonable notice of the intent to offer the statement and its particulars, including the declarant's name and address, so that the party has a fair opportunity to meet it.

SECTION IX
AUTHENTICATION AND IDENTIFICATION

Rule 901. Authenticating or identifying evidence

(a) *In General.* To satisfy the requirement of authenticating or identifying an item of evidence, the proponent must produce evidence sufficient to support a finding that the item is what the proponent claims it is.

(b) *Examples.* The following are examples only – not a complete list – of evidence that satisfies the requirement:

(1) *Testimony of a Witness with Knowledge.* Testimony that an item is what it is claimed to be.

(2) *Nonexpert Opinion about Handwriting.* A nonexpert's opinion that handwriting is genuine, based on a familiarity with it that was not acquired for the current litigation.

(3) *Comparison by an Expert Witness or the Trier of Fact.* A comparison with an authenticated specimen by an expert witness or the trier of fact.

(4) *Distinctive Characteristics and the Like.* The appearance, contents, substance, internal patterns, or other distinctive characteristics of the item, taken together with all the circumstances.

(5) *Opinion about a Voice.* An opinion identifying a person's voice – whether heard firsthand or through mechanical or electronic transmission or recording – based on hearing the voice at any time under circumstances that connect it with the alleged speaker.

(6) *Evidence about a Telephone Conversation.* For a telephone conversation, evidence that a call was made to the number assigned at the time to:

(A) a particular person, if circumstances, including self-identification, show that the person answering was the one called; or

(B) a particular business, if the call was made to a business and the call related to business reasonably transacted over the telephone.

(7) *Evidence about Public Records.* Evidence that:

(A) a document was recorded or filed in a public office as authorized by law; or

(B) a purported public record or statement is from the office where items of this kind are kept.

(8) *Evidence about Ancient Documents or Data Compilations.* For a document or data compilation, evidence that it:

(A) is in a condition that creates no suspicion about its authenticity;

(B) was in a place where, if authentic, it would likely be; and

(C) is at least 20 years old when offered.

(9) *Evidence about a Process or System.* Evidence describing a process or system and showing that it produces an accurate result.

(10) *Methods Provided by a Statute or Rule.* Any

method of authentication or identification allowed by a federal statute, a rule prescribed by the Supreme Court, or an applicable regulation prescribed pursuant to statutory authority.

Rule 902. Evidence that is self-authenticating

The following items of evidence are self-authenticating; they require no extrinsic evidence of authenticity in order to be admitted:

(1) *Domestic Public Documents that are Sealed and Signed.* A document that bears:

(A) a seal purporting to be that of the United States; any State, district, Commonwealth, territory, or insular possession of the United States; the former Panama Canal Zone; the Trust Territory of the Pacific Islands; a political subdivision of any of these entities; or a department, agency, or officer of any entity named above; and

(B) a signature purporting to be an execution or attestation.

(2) *Domestic Public Documents that are Not Sealed but are Signed and Certified.* A document that bears no seal if:

(A) it bears the signature of an officer or employee of an entity named in subdivision (1)(A) above; and

(B) another public officer who has a seal and official duties within that same entity certifies under seal – or its equivalent – that the signer has the official capacity and that the signature is genuine.

(3) *Foreign Public Documents.* A document that purports to be signed or attested by a person who is authorized by a foreign country's law to do so. The document must be accompanied by a final certification that certifies the genuineness of the signature and official position of the signer or attester – or of any foreign official whose certificate of genuineness relates to the signature or attestation or is in a chain of certificates of genuineness relating to the signature or attestation. The certification may be made by a secretary of a United States embassy or legation; by a consul general, vice consul, or consular agent of the United States; or by a diplomatic or consular official of the foreign country assigned or accredited to the United States. If all parties have been given a reasonable opportunity to investigate the document's

authenticity and accuracy, the military judge may, for good cause, either:

(A) order that it be treated as presumptively authentic without final certification; or

(B) allow it to be evidenced by an attested summary with or without final certification.

(4) *Certified Copies of Public Records.* A copy of an official record – or a copy of a document that was recorded or filed in a public office as authorized by law – if the copy is certified as correct by:

(A) the custodian or another person authorized to make the certification; or

(B) a certificate that complies with subdivision (1), (2), or (3) above, a federal statute, a rule prescribed by the Supreme Court, or an applicable regulation prescribed pursuant to statutory authority.

(4a) *Documents or Records of the United States Accompanied by Attesting Certificates.* Documents or records kept under the authority of the United States by any department, bureau, agency, office, or court thereof when attached to or accompanied by an attesting certificate of the custodian of the document or record without further authentication.

(5) *Official Publications.* A book, pamphlet, or other publication purporting to be issued by a public authority.

(6) *Newspapers and Periodicals.* Printed material purporting to be a newspaper or periodical.

(7) *Trade Inscriptions and the Like.* An inscription, sign, tag, or label purporting to have been affixed in the course of business and indicating origin, ownership, or control.

(8) *Acknowledged Documents.* A document accompanied by a certificate of acknowledgment that is lawfully executed by a notary public or another officer who is authorized to take acknowledgments.

(9) *Commercial Paper and Related Documents.* Commercial paper, a signature on it, and related documents, to the extent allowed by general commercial law.

(10) *Presumptions under a Federal Statute or Regulation.* A signature, document, or anything else that a federal statute, or an applicable regulation prescribed pursuant to statutory authority, declares to be presumptively or prima facie genuine or authentic.

(11) *Certified Domestic Records of a Regularly Conducted Activity.* The original or a copy of a domestic record that meets the requirements of Mil.

R. Evid. 803(6)(A)-(C), as shown by a certification of the custodian or another qualified person that complies with a federal statute or a rule prescribed by the Supreme Court. Before the trial or hearing, or at a later time that the military judge allows for good cause, the proponent must give an adverse party reasonable written notice of the intent to offer the record and must make the record and certification available for inspection so that the party has a fair opportunity to challenge them.

Rule 903. Subscribing witness's testimony

A subscribing witness's testimony is necessary to authenticate a writing only if required by the law of the jurisdiction that governs its validity.

SECTION X
CONTENTS OF WRITINGS, RECORDINGS, AND PHOTOGRAPHS

Rule 1001. Definitions that apply to this section

In this section:

(a) A "writing" consists of letters, words, numbers, or their equivalent set down in any form.

(b) A "recording" consists of letters, words, numbers, or their equivalent recorded in any manner.

(c) A "photograph" means a photolineart image or its equivalent stored in any form.

(d) An "original" of a writing or recording means the writing or recording itself or any counterpart intended to have the same effect by the person who executed or issued it. For electronically stored information, "original" means any printout or other output readable by sight if it accurately reflects the information. An "original" of a photograph includes the negative or a print from it.

(e) A "duplicate" means a counterpart produced by a mechanical, photolineart, chemical, electronic, or other equivalent process or technique that accurately reproduces the original.

Rule 1002. Requirement of the original

An original writing, recording, or photograph is required in order to prove its content unless these rules, this Manual, or a federal statute provides otherwise.

Rule 1003. Admissibility of duplicates

A duplicate is admissible to the same extent as the original unless a genuine question is raised about the original's authenticity or the circumstances make it unfair to admit the duplicate.

Rule 1004. Admissibility of other evidence of content

An original is not required and other evidence of the content of a writing, recording, or photograph is admissible if:

(a) *Originals lost or destroyed.* all the originals are lost or destroyed, and not by the proponent acting in bad faith;

(b) *Original not obtainable.* an original cannot be obtained by any available judicial process;

(c) *Original in possession of opponent.* the party against whom the original would be offered had control of the original; was at that time put on notice, by pleadings or otherwise, that the original would be a subject of proof at the trial or hearing; and fails to produce it at the trial or hearing; or

(d) *Collateral matters.* the writing, recording, or photograph is not closely related to a controlling issue.

Rule 1005. Copies of public records to prove content

The proponent may use a copy to prove the content of an official record – or of a document that was recorded or filed in a public office as authorized by law – if these conditions are met: the record or document is otherwise admissible; and the copy is certified as correct in accordance with Mil. R. Evid. 902(4) or is testified to be correct by a witness who has compared it with the original. If no such copy can be obtained by reasonable diligence, then the proponent may use other evidence to prove the content.

Rule 1006. Summaries to prove content

The proponent may use a summary, chart, or calculation to prove the content of voluminous writings, recordings, or photographs that cannot be conveniently examined in court. The proponent must make the originals or duplicates available for examination or copying, or both, by other parties at a reasonable time or place. The military judge may order the proponent to produce them in court.

Rule 1007. Testimony or statement of a party to prove content

The proponent may prove the content of a writing, recording, or photograph by the testimony, deposition, or written statement of the party against whom the evidence is offered. The proponent need not account for the original.

Rule 1008. Functions of the military judge and the members

Ordinarily, the military judge determines whether the proponent has fulfilled the factual conditions for admitting other evidence of the content of a writing, recording, or photograph under Mil. R. Evid. 1004 or 1005. When a court-martial is composed of a military judge and members, the members determine – in accordance with Mil. R. Evid. 104(b) – any issue about whether:

(a) an asserted writing, recording, or photograph ever existed;

(b) another one produced at the trial or hearing is the original; or

(c) other evidence of content accurately reflects the content.

SECTION XI
MISCELLANEOUS RULES

Rule 1101. Applicability of these rules

(a) *In General.* Except as otherwise provided in this Manual, these rules apply generally to all courts-martial, including summary courts-martial, Article 39(a) sessions, limited factfinding proceedings ordered on review, proceedings in revision, and con-

tempt proceedings other than contempt proceedings in which the judge may act summarily.

(b) *Rules Relaxed.* The application of these rules may be relaxed in presentencing proceedings as provided under R.C.M. 1001 and otherwise as provided in this Manual.

(c) *Rules on Privilege.* The rules on privilege apply at all stages of a case or proceeding.

(d) *Exceptions.* These rules – except for Mil. R. Evid. 412 and those on privilege – do not apply to the following:

(1) the military judge's determination, under Rule 104(a), on a preliminary question of fact governing admissibility;

(2) pretrial investigations under Article 32;

(3) proceedings for vacation of suspension of sentence under Article 72; and

(4) miscellaneous actions and proceedings related to search authorizations, pretrial restraint, pretrial confinement, or other proceedings authorized under the Uniform Code of Military Justice or this Manual that are not listed in subdivision (a).

Rule 1102. Amendments

(a) *General Rule.* Amendments to the Federal Rules of Evidence – other than Articles III and V – will amend parallel provisions of the Military Rules of Evidence by operation of law 18 months after the effective date of such amendments, unless action to the contrary is taken by the President.

(b) *Rules Determined Not to Apply.* The President has determined that the following Federal Rules of Evidence do not apply to the Military Rules of Evidence: Rules 301, 302, 415, and 902(12).

Rule 1103. Title

These rules may be cited as the Military Rules of Evidence.

APPENDIX 22
ANALYSIS OF THE MILITARY RULES OF EVIDENCE

The Military Rules of Evidence, promulgated in 1980 as Chapter XXVII of the Manual for Courts-Martial, United States, 1969 (Rev. ed.), were the product of a two year effort participated in by the General Counsel of the Department of Defense, the United States Court of Military Appeals, the Military Departments, and the Department of Transportation (the Department under which the Coast Guard was operating at that time). The Rules were drafted by the Evidence Working Group of the Joint Service Committee on Military Justice, which consisted of Commander James Pinnell, JAGC, U.S. Navy, then Major John Bozeman, JAGC, U.S. Army (from April 1978 until July 1978), Major Fredric Lederer, JAGC, U.S. Army (from August 1978), Major James Potuk, U.S. Air Force, Lieutenant Commander Tom Snook, U.S. Coast Guard, and Mr. Robert Mueller and Ms. Carol Wild Scott of the United States Court of Military Appeals. Mr. Andrew Effron represented the Office of the General Counsel of the Department of Defense on the Committee. The draft rules were reviewed and, as modified, approved by the Joint Service Committee on Military Justice. Aspects of the Rules were reviewed by the Code Committee as well. *See* Article 67(g). The Rules were approved by the General Counsel of the Department of Defense and forwarded to the White House via the Office of Management and Budget which circulated the Rules to the Departments of Justice and Transportation.

The original Analysis was prepared primarily by Major Fredric Lederer, U.S. Army, of the Evidence Working Group of the Joint Service Committee on Military Justice and was approved by the Joint Service Committee on Military Justice and reviewed in the Office of the General Counsel of the Department of Defense. The Analysis presents the intent of the drafting committee; seeks to indicate the source of the various changes to the Manual, and generally notes when substantial changes to military law result from the amendments. This Analysis is not, however, part of the Executive Order modifying the present Manual nor does it constitute the official views of the Department of Defense, the Department of Homeland Security, the Military Departments, or of the United States Court of Military Appeals.

The Analysis does not identify technical changes made to adapt the Federal Rules of Evidence to military use. Accordingly, the Analysis does not identify changes made to make the Rules gender neutral or to adapt the Federal Rules to military terminology by substituting, for example, "court members" for "jury" and "military judge" for "court." References within the Analysis to "the 1969 Manual" and "MCM, 1969 (Rev.)" refer to the Manual for Courts-Martial, 1969 (Rev. ed.) (Executive Order 11,476, as amended by Executive Order 11,835 and Executive Order 12,018) as it existed prior to the effective date of the 1980 amendments. References to "the prior law" and "the prior rule" refer to the state of the law as it existed prior to the effective date of the 1980 amendments. References to the "Federal Rules of Evidence Advisory Committee" refer to the Advisory Committee on the Rules of Evidence appointed by the Supreme Court, which prepared the original draft of the Federal Rules of Evidence.

During the Manual revision project that culminated in promulgation of the Manual for Courts-Martial, 1984 (Executive Order 12473), several changes were made in the Military Rules of Evidence, and the analysis of those changes was placed in Appendix 21. Thus, it was intended that this Appendix would remain static. In 1985, however, it was decided that changes in the analysis of the Military Rules of Evidence would be incorporated into this Appendix as those changes are made so that the reader need consult only one document to determine the drafters' intent regarding the current rules. Changes are made to the Analysis only when a rule is amended. Changes to the Analysis are clearly marked, but the original Analysis is not changed. Consequently, the Analysis of some rules contains analysis of language subsequently deleted or amended.

In addition, because this Analysis expresses the intent of the drafters, certain legal doctrines stated in this Analysis may have been overturned by subsequent case law. This Analysis does not substitute for research about current legal rules.

Several changes were made for uniformity of style with the remainder of the Manual. Only the first word in the title of a rule is capitalized. The word "rule" when used in text to refer to another rule, was changed to "Mil. R. Evid." to avoid confusion with the Rules for Courts-Martial. "Code" is used in place of Uniform Code of Military Justice. "Commander" is substituted for "commanding officer" and "officer in charge." *See* R.C.M. 103(5). Citations to the United States Code were changed to conform to the style used elsewhere. "Government" is capitalized when used as a noun to refer to the United States Government. In addition, several cross-references to paragraphs in MCM, 1969 (Rev.) were changed to indicate appropriate provisions in this Manual.

With these exceptions, however, the Military Rules of Evidence were not redrafted. Consequently, there are minor variations in style or terminology between the Military Rules of Evidence and other parts of the Manual. Where the same subject is treated in similar but not identical terms in the Military Rules of Evidence and elsewhere, a different meaning or purpose should not be inferred in the absence of a clear indication in the text or the analysis that this was intended.

2013 Amendment. On December 1, 2011, the Federal Rules of Evidence (Fed. R. Evid.) were amended by restyling the rules to make them simpler to understand and use, without changing the substantive meaning of any rule.

After considering these changes to the Federal Rules, the Joint Service Committee on Military Justice (hereinafter "the committee") made significant changes to the Military Rules of Evidence (Mil. R. Evid.) in 2012. This rewrite was implemented by Executive Order 13638 on 15 May 2013. In addition to making stylistic changes to harmonize these rules with the Federal Rules, the committee also made changes to ensure that the rules addressed the admissibility of evidence, rather than the conduct of the individual actors. Like the Federal Rules of Evidence, these rules ultimately dictate whether evidence is admissible at courts-martial and, therefore, it is appropriate to phrase the rules with admissibility as the focus, rather than a focus on the actor (i.e., the commanding officer, military judge, accused, etc.).

The rules were also reformatted to achieve clearer presentation. The committee used indented paragraphs with headings and hanging indents to allow the practitioner to distinguish between different subsections of the rules. The restyled rules also reduce the use of inconsistent terms that are intended to mean the same thing but may, because of the inconsistent use, be misconstrued by the practitioner to mean something different.

With most changes, the committee made special effort to avoid any style improvement that might result in a substantive change in the application of the rule. However, in some rules, the committee rewrote the rule with the express purpose to change the substantive content of the rule in order to affect the application of the rule in practice. In the analysis of each rule, the committee clearly indicates whether the changes are substantive or merely stylistic. The reader is encouraged to consult the analysis of each rule if he or she has questions as to whether the committee intended that a change to the rule have an effect on a ruling of admissibility.

SECTION I
General Provisions

Rule 101 Scope

(a) *Applicability.* Rule 101(a) is taken generally from Federal Rule of Evidence 101. It emphasizes that these Rules are applicable to summary as well as to special and general courts-martial. *See* "Rule of Construction." Rule 101(c), *infra.* Rule 1101 expressly indicates that the rules of evidence are inapplicable to investigative hearings under Article 32, proceedings for pretrial advice, search authorization proceedings, vacation proceedings, and certain other proceedings. Although the Rules apply to sentencing, they may be "relaxed" under Rule 1101(c) and R.C.M. 1001(c)(3).

The limitation in subdivision (a) applying the Rules to courts-martial is intended expressly to recognize that these Rules are not applicable to military commissions, provost courts, and courts of inquiry unless otherwise required by competent authority. *See* Part I, Para. 2 of the Manual. The Rules, however, serve as a "guide" for such tribunals. *Id.*

The Military Rules of Evidence are inapplicable to proceedings conducted pursuant to Article 15 of the Uniform Code of Military Justice.

The decisions of the United States Court of Appeals for the Armed Forces and of the Courts of Criminal Appeals must be utilized in interpreting these Rules. While specific decisions of the Article III courts involving rules which are common both to the Military Rules and the Federal Rules should be considered very persuasive, they are not binding; *see* Article 36 of the Uniform Code of Military Justice. It should be noted, however, that a significant policy consideration in adopting the Federal Rules of Evidence was to ensure, where possible, common evidentiary law.

(b) *Secondary sources.* Rule 101(b) is taken from Para. 137 of MCM, 1969 (Rev.) which had its origins in Article 36 of the Uniform Code of Military Justice. Rule 101(a) makes it clear that the Military Rules of Evidence are the primary source of evidentiary law for military practice. Notwithstanding their wide scope, however, Rule 101(b) recognizes that recourse to secondary sources may occasionally be necessary. Rule 101(b) prescribes the sequence in which such sources shall be utilized.

Rule 101(b)(1) requires that the first such source be the "rules of evidence generally recognized in the trial of criminal cases in the United States District courts." To the extent that a Military Rule of Evidence reflects an express modification of a Federal Rule of Evidence or a federal evidentiary procedure, the President has determined that the unmodified Federal Rule or procedure is, within the meaning of Article 36(a), either not "practicable" or is "contrary to or inconsistent with" the Uniform Code of Military Justice. Consequently, to the extent to which the Military Rules do not dispose of an issue, the Article III Federal practice when practicable and not inconsistent or contrary to the Military Rules shall be applied. In determining whether there is a rule of evidence "generally recognized," it is anticipated that ordinary legal research shall be involved with primary emphasis being placed upon the published decisions of the three levels of the Article III courts.

Under Rule 1102, which concerns amendments to the Federal Rules of Evidence, no amendment to the Federal Rules shall be applicable to courts-martial until 180 days after the amendment's effective date unless the President shall direct its earlier adoption. Thus, such an amendment cannot be utilized as a secondary source until 180 days has passed since its effective date or until the President had directed its adoption, whichever occurs first. An amendment will not be applicable at any time if the President so directs.

It is the intent of the Committee that the expression, "common law" found within Rule 101(b)(2) be construed in its broadest possible sense. It should include the federal common law and what may be denominated military common law. Prior military cases may be cited as authority under Rule 101(b)(2) to the extent that they are based upon a present Manual provision which has been retained in the Military Rules of Evidence or to the extent that they are not inconsistent with the "rules of evidence generally recognized in the trial of criminal cases in the United States District courts," deal with matters "not otherwise prescribed in this Manual or these rules," and are "practicable and not inconsistent with or contrary to the Uniform Code of Military justice or this Manual."

(c) *Rule of construction.* Rule 101(c) is intended to avoid unnecessary repetition of the expressions, "president of a special court-martial without a military judge" and "summary court-martial officer." "Summary court-martial officer" is used instead of "summary court-martial" for purposes of clarity. A summary court-martial is considered to function in the same role as a military judge notwithstanding possible lack of legal training. As previously noted in Para. 137, MCM, 1969 (Rev.), "a summary court-martial has the same discretionary power as a military judge concerning the reception of evidence." Where the application of these Rules in a summary court-martial or a special court-martial without a military judge is different from the application of the Rules in a court-martial with a military judge, specific reference has been made.

Disposition of present Manual. That part of Para. 137, MCM, 1969 (Rev.), not reflected in Rule 101 is found in other rules, *see, e.g.,* Rules 104, 401, 403. The reference in Para. 137 to privileges arising out of treaty or executive agreement was deleted as being unnecessary. *See generally* Rule 501.

2013 Amendment. In subsection (a), the phrase "including summary courts-martial" was removed because Rule 1101 already addresses the applicability of these rules to summary courts-martial. In subsection (b), the word "shall" was changed to "will" because the committee agreed with the approach of the Advisory

Committee on Evidence Rules to minimize the use of words such as "shall" and "should" because of the potential disparity in application and interpretation of whether the word is precatory or proscriptive. *See* Fed. R. Evid. 101, Restyled Rules Committee Note. In making this change, the committee did not intend to change any result in any ruling on evidence admissibility.

The discussion section was added to this rule to alert the practitioner that discussion sections, which previously did not appear in Part III of the Manual, are included in this edition to elucidate the committee's understanding of the rules. The discussion sections do not have the force of law and may be changed by the committee without an Executive Order, as warranted by changes in applicable case law. The discussion sections should be considered treatise material and are non-binding on the practitioner.

The committee also revised this rule for stylistic reasons and to align it with the Federal Rules of Evidence but in doing so did not intend to change any result in any ruling on evidence admissibility.

Rule 102 Purpose and construction

Rule 102 is taken without change from Federal Rule of Evidence 102 and is without counterpart in MCM, 1969 (Rev.). It provides a set of general guidelines to be used in construing the Military Rules of Evidence. It is, however, only a rule of construction and not a license to disregard the Rules in order to reach a desired result.

Rule 103 Rulings on evidence

(a) *Effect of erroneous ruling.* Rule 103(a) is taken from the Federal Rule with a number of changes. The first, the use of the language, "the ruling materially prejudices a substantial right of a party" in place of the Federal Rule's "a substantial right of party is affected" is required by Article 59(a) of the Uniform Code of Military Justice. Rule 103(a) comports with present military practice.

The second significant change is the addition of material relating to constitutional requirements and explicitly states that errors of constitutional magnitude may require a higher standard than the general one required by Rule 103(a). For example, the harmless error rule, when applicable to an error of constitutional dimensions, prevails over the general rule of Rule 103(a). Because Section III of these Rules embodies constitutional rights, two standards of error may be at issue; one involving the Military Rules of Evidence, and one involving the underlying constitutional rule. In such a case, the standard of error more advantageous to the accused will apply.

Rule 103(a)(1) requires that a timely motion or objection generally be made in order to preserve a claim of error. This is similar to but more specific than prior practice. In making such a motion or objection, the party has a right to state the specific grounds of the objection to the evidence. Failure to make a timely and sufficiently specific objection may waive the objection for purposes of both trial and appeal. In applying Federal Rule 103(a), the Article III courts have interpreted the Rule strictly and held the defense to an extremely high level of specificity. *See, e.g., United States v. Rubin*, 609 F.2d 51, 61-63 (2d Cir. 1979) (objection to form of witness's testimony did not raise or preserve an appropriate hearsay objection); *United States v. O'Brien*, 601

F.2d 1067 (9th Cir. 1979) (objection that prosecution witness was testifying from material not in evidence held inadequate to raise or preserve an objection under Rule 1006). As indicated in the Analysis of Rule 802, Rule 103 significantly changed military law insofar as hearsay is concerned. Unlike present law under which hearsay is absolutely incompetent, the Military Rules of Evidence simply treat hearsay as being inadmissible upon adequate objection; *see* Rules 803, 103(a). Note in the context of Rule 103(a) that R.C.M. 801(a)(3) (Discussion) states: "The parties are entitled to reasonable opportunity to properly present and support their contentions on any relevant matter."

An "offer of proof" is a concise statement by counsel setting forth the substance of the expected testimony or other evidence.

Rule 103(a) prescribes a standard by which errors will be tested on appeal. Although counsel at trial need not indicate how an alleged error will "materially prejudice a substantial right" in order to preserve error, such a showing, during or after the objection or offer, may be advisable as a matter of trial practice to further illuminate the issue for both the trial and appellate bench.

2004 Amendment: Subdivision (a)(2) was modified based on the amendment to Fed. R. Evid. 103(a)(2), effective 1 December 2000, and is virtually identical to its Federal Rule counterpart. It is intended to provide that where an advance ruling is definitive, a party need not renew an objection or offer of proof at trial; otherwise, renewal is required.

(b) *Record of offer,* and (c) *Hearing of members*— Rule 103(b) and (c) are taken from the Federal Rules with minor changes in terminology to adapt them to military procedure.

(d) *Plain error*— Rule 103(d) is taken from the Federal Rule with a minor change of terminology to adapt it to military practice and the substitution of "materially prejudices" substantial rights of "affecting" substantial rights to conform it to Article 59(a) of the Uniform Code of Military Justice.

2013 Amendment. The committee revised this rule for stylistic reasons and to align it with the Federal Rules of Evidence but in doing so did not intend to change any result in any ruling on evidence admissibility.

Rule 104 Preliminary questions

(a) *Questions of admissibility generally.* Rule 104(a) is taken generally from the Federal Rule. Language in the Federal Rule requiring that admissibility shall be determined by the "court, subject to the provisions of subdivision (b)" has been struck to ensure that, subject to Rule 1008, questions of admissibility are solely for the military judge and not for the court-members. The deletion of the language is not intended, however, to negate the general interrelationship between subdivisions (a) and (b). When relevancy is conditioned on the fulfillment of a condition of fact, the military judge shall "admit it upon, or subject to, the introduction of evidence sufficient to support a finding of the fulfillment of the condition."

Pursuant to language taken from Federal Rule of Evidence 104(a), the rules of evidence, other than those with respect to privileges, are inapplicable to "preliminary questions concerning the qualification of a person to be a witness, the existence of a privilege, the admissibility of evidence...." These exceptions are new to military law and may substantially change military practice. The Federal Rule has been modified, however, by inserting language relating to applications for continuances and determinations of witness availability. The change, taken from MCM, 1969 (Rev.), Para. 137, is required by the worldwide disposition of the armed forces which makes matters relating to continuances and witness availability particularly difficult, if not impossible, to resolve under the normal rules of evidence— particularly the hearsay rule.

A significant and unresolved issue stemming from the language of Rule 104(a) is whether the rules of evidence shall be applicable to evidentiary questions involving constitutional or statutory issues such as those arising under Article 31. Thus it is unclear, for example, whether the rules of evidence are applicable to a determination of the voluntariness of an accused's statement. While the Rule strongly suggests that rules of evidence are not applicable to admissibility determinations involving constitutional issues, the issue is unresolved at present.

(b) *Relevancy conditioned on fact.* Rule 104(b) is taken from the Federal Rule except that the following language had been added: "A ruling on the sufficiency of evidence to support a finding of fulfillment of a condition of fact is the sole responsibility of the military judge." This material was added in order to clarify the rule and to explicitly preserve contemporary military procedure, Para. 57, MCM, 1969 (Rev.). Under the Federal Rule, it is unclear whether and to what extent evidentiary questions are to be submitted to the jury as questions of admissibility. Rule 104(b) has thus been clarified to eliminate any possibility, except as required by Rule 1008, that the court members will make an admissibility determination. Failure to clarify the rule would produce unnecessary confusion in the minds of the court members and unnecessarily prolong trials. Accordingly, adoption of the language of the Federal Rules without modification is impracticable in the armed forces.

(c) *Hearing of members.* Rule 104(c) is taken generally from the Federal Rule. Introductory material has been added because of the impossibility of conducting a hearing out of the presence of the members in a special court-martial without a military judge. "Statements of an accused" has been used in lieu of "confessions" because of the phrasing of Article 31 of the Uniform Code of Military Justice, which has been followed in Rules 301–306.

(d) *Testimony by accused.* Rule 104(d) is taken without change from the Federal Rule. Application of this rule in specific circumstances is set forth in Rule 304(f), 311(f) and 321(e).

(e) *Weight and credibility.* Rule 104(e) is taken without change from the Federal Rule.

2013 Amendment. The committee revised this rule for stylistic reasons and to align it with the Federal Rules of Evidence but in doing so did not intend to change any result in any ruling on evidence admissibility.

Rule 105 Limiting Evidence that is Not Admissible Against Other Parties or for Other Purposes

Rule 105 is taken without change from the Federal Rule. In view of its requirement that the military judge restrict evidence to its proper scope "upon request," it overrules *United States v. Grunden,* 2 M.J. 116 (C.M.A. 1977) (holding that the military judge must *sua sponte* instruct the members as to use of evidence of uncharged misconduct) and related cases insofar as they *require* the military judge to *sua sponte* instruct the members. *See*

e.g., S. SALTZBURG & K. REDDEN, *FEDERAL RULES OF EVIDENCE MANUAL* 50 (2d ed. 1977); *United States v. Sangrey,* 586 F.2d 1315 (9th Cir. 1978); *United States v. Barnes,* 586 F.2d 1052 (5th Cir. 1978); *United States v. Bridwell,* 583 F.2d 1135 (10th Cir. 1978); *but see United States v. Ragghianti,* 560 F.2d 1376 (9th Cir. 1977). This is compatible with the general intent of both the Federal and Military Rules in that they place primary if not full responsibility upon counsel for objecting to or limiting evidence. Note that the Rule 306, dealing with statements of co-accused, is more restrictive and protective than Rule 105. The military judge may, of course, choose to instruct *sua sponte* but need not do so. Failure to instruct *sua sponte* could potentially require a reversal only if such failure could be considered "plain error" within the meaning of Rule 103(d). Most failures to instruct *sua sponte,* or to instruct, cannot be so considered in light of current case law.

2013 Amendment. The committee revised this rule for stylistic reasons and to align it with the Federal Rules of Evidence but in doing so did not intend to change any result in any ruling on evidence admissibility.

Rule 106 Remainder of or related writings or recorded statements

Rule 106 is taken from the Federal Rule without change. In view of the tendency of fact-finders to give considerable evidentiary weight to written matters, the Rule is intended to preclude the misleading situation that can occur if a party presents only part of a writing or recorded statement. In contrast to Para. 140 *a,* MCM, 1969 (Rev.), which applies only to statements by an accused, the new Rule is far more expansive and permits a party to require the opposing party to introduce evidence. That aspect of Para. 140 *a*(b) survives as Rule 304(h)(2) and allows the defense to complete an alleged confession or admission offered by the prosecution. When a confession or admission is involved, the defense may employ both Rules 106 and 304(h)(2), as appropriate.

2013 Amendment. The committee revised this rule for stylistic reasons and to align it with the Federal Rules of Evidence but in doing so did not intend to change any result in any ruling on evidence admissibility.

SECTION II
JUDICIAL NOTICE

Rule 201 Judicial notice of adjudicative facts

(a) *Scope of Rule.* Rule 201(a) provides that Rule 201 governs judicial notice of adjudicative facts. In so doing, the Rule replaced MCM, 1969 (Rev.), Para. 147 *a.* The Federal Rules of Evidence Advisory Committee defined adjudicative facts as "simply the facts of the particular case" and distinguished them from legislative facts which it defined as "those which have relevance to legal reasoning and the lawmaking process, whether in the formulation of a legal principle or ruling by a judge or court or in the enactment of a legislative body," reprinted in S. SALTZBURG & K. REDDEN, *FEDERAL RULES OF EVIDENCE MANUAL* 63 (2d ed. 1977). The distinction between the two types of facts, originated by Professor Kenneth Davis, can on occasion be highly confusing in practice and resort to any of the usual treatises may be helpful.

(b) *Kinds of facts.* Rule 201(b) was taken generally from the Federal Rule. The limitation with FED. R. EVID. 201(b)(1) to facts known "within the territorial jurisdiction of the trial court" was replaced, however, by the expression, "generally known universally, locally, or in the area, pertinent to the event." The worldwide disposition of the armed forces rendered the original language inapplicable and impracticable within the military environment. Notice of signatures, appropriate under Para. 147 *a*, MCM, 1969 (Rev.), will normally be inappropriate under this Rule. Rule 902(4) & (10) will, however, usually yield the same result as under Para. 147 *a.*

When they qualify as adjudicative facts under Rule 201, the following are examples of matters of which judicial notice may be taken:

The ordinary division of time into years, months, weeks and other periods; general facts and laws of nature, including their ordinary operations and effects; general facts of history; generally known geolineartal facts; such specific facts and propositions of generalized knowledge as are so universally known that they cannot reasonably be the subject of dispute; such facts as are so generally known or are of such common notoriety in the area in which the trial is held that they cannot reasonably be the subject of dispute; and specific facts and propositions of generalized knowledge which are capable of immediate and accurate determination by resort to easily accessible sources of reasonable indisputable accuracy.

(c) *When discretionary.* While the first sentence of the subdivision is taken from the Federal Rule, the second sentence is new and is included as a result of the clear implication of subdivision (e) and of the holding in *Garner v. Louisiana,* 368 U.S. 157, 173-74 (1961). In *Garner,* the Supreme Court rejected the contention of the State of Louisiana that the trial judge had taken judicial notice of certain evidence stating that:

There is nothing in the records to indicate that the trial judge did in fact take judicial notice of anything. To extend the doctrine of judicial notice ... would require us to allow the prosecution to do through argument to this Court what it is required by due process to do at the trial, and would be to turn the doctrine into a pretext for dispensing with a trial of the facts of which the court is taking judicial notice, not only does he not know upon what evidence he is being convicted, but, in addition, he is deprived of any opportunity to challenge the deductions drawn from such notice or to dispute the notoriety or truth of the facts allegedly relied upon. 368 U.S. at 173

(d) *When mandatory.* Rule 201(d) provides that the military judge shall take notice when requested to do so by a party who supplies the military judge with the necessary information. The military judge must take judicial notice only when the evidence is properly within this Rule, is relevant under Rule 401, and is not inadmissible under these Rules.

(e) *Opportunity to be heard; Time of taking notice; Instructing Members.* Subdivisions (e), (f) and (g) of Rule 201 are taken from the Federal Rule without change.

2013 Amendment. The committee revised this rule for stylistic reasons and to align it with the Federal Rules of Evidence. Former subsection (d) was subsumed into subsection (c) and the remaining subsections were renumbered accordingly. In making these changes, the committee did not intend to change any result in any ruling on evidence admissibility.

Rule 202 Judicial notice of law

In general. Rule 201A is new. Not addressed by the Federal Rules of Evidence, the subject matter of the Rule is treated as a procedural matter in the Article III courts; *see e.g.,* FED R. CRIM. P. 26.1. Adoption of a new evidentiary rule was thus required. Rule 201A is generally consistent in principle with Para. 147 *a,* MCM, 1969 (Rev.).

Domestic law. Rule 201A(a) recognizes that law may constitute the adjudicative fact within the meaning of Rule 201(a) and requires that when that is the case, *i.e.,* insofar as a domestic law is a fact that is of consequence to the determination of the action, the procedural requirements of Rule 201 must be applied. When domestic law constitutes only a legislative fact, *see* the Analysis to Rule 201(a), the procedural requirements of Rule 201 may be utilized as a matter of discretion. For purposes of this Rule, it is intended that "domestic law" include: treaties of the United States; executive agreements between the United States and any State thereof, foreign country or international organization or agency; the laws and regulations pursuant thereto of the United States, of the District of Columbia, and of a State, Commonwealth, or possession; international law, including the laws of war, general maritime law and the law of air and space; and the common law. This definition is taken without change from Para. 147 *a* except that references to the law of space have been added. "Regulations" of the United States include regulations of the armed forces.

When a party requests that domestic law be noticed, or when the military judge *sua sponte* takes such notice, a copy of the applicable law should be attached to the record of trial unless the law in question can reasonably be anticipated to be easily available to any possible reviewing authority.

1984 Amendment: Subsection (a) was modified in 1984 to clarify that the requirements of Mil. R. Evid. 201(g) do not apply when judicial notice of domestic law is taken. Without this clarification, Mil. R. Evid. 201A could be construed to require the military judge to instruct the members that they could disregard a law which had been judicially noticed. This problem was discussed in *United States v. Mead,* 16 M.J. 270 (C.M.A.1983).

Foreign law. Rule 201A(b) is taken without significant change from FED R. CRIM. P 26.1 and recognizes that notice of foreign law may require recourse to additional evidence including testimony of witnesses. For purposes of this Rule, it is intended that "foreign law" include the laws and regulations of foreign countries and their political subdivisions and of international organizations and agencies. Any material or source received by the military judge for use in determining foreign law, or pertinent extracts therefrom, should be included in the record of trial as an exhibit.

2013 Amendment. Former Rule 201A was renumbered so that it now appears as Rule 202. In previous editions, Rule 202 did not exist and therefore no other rules were renumbered as a result of this change. The phrase "in accordance with Mil. R. Evid. 104" was added to subsection (b) to clarify that Rule 104 controls the military judge's relevancy determination.

The committee also revised this rule for stylistic reasons but in doing so did not intend to change any result in any ruling on evidence admissibility.

SECTION III

EXCLUSIONARY RULES AND RELATED MATTERS CONCERNING SELF-INCRIMINATION, SEARCH AND SEIZURE, AND EYEWITNESS IDENTIFICATION

Military Rules of Evidence 301–306, 311–317, and 321 were new in 1980 and have no equivalent in the Federal Rules of Evidence. They represent a partial codification of the law relating to self-incrimination, confessions and admissions, search and seizure, and eye-witness identification. They are often rules of criminal procedure as well as evidence and have been located in this section due to their evidentiary significance. They replace Federal Rules of Evidence 301 and 302 which deal with civil matters exclusively.

The Committee believed it imperative to codify the material treated in Section III because of the large numbers of lay personnel who hold important roles within the military criminal legal system. Non-lawyer legal officers aboard ship, for example, do not have access to attorneys and law libraries. In all cases, the Rules represent a judgement that it would be impracticable to operate without them. *See* Article 36. The Rules represent a compromise between specificity, intended to ensure stability and uniformity with the armed forces, and generality, intended usually to allow change via case law. In some instances they significantly change present procedure. *See, e.g.,* Rule 304(d) (procedure for suppression motions relating to confessions and admissions).

Rule 301 Privilege concerning compulsory self-incrimination

(a) *General rule.* Rule 301(a) is consistent with the rule expressed in the first paragraph, Para. 150 *b* of MCM, 1969 (Rev.), but omits the phrasing of the privileges and explicitly states that, as both variations apply, the accused or witness receives the protection of whichever privilege may be the more beneficial. The fact that the privilege extends to a witness as well as an accused is inherent within the new phrasing which does not distinguish between the two.

The Rule states that the privileges are applicable only "to evidence of a testimonial or communicative nature," *Schmerber v. California*, 384 U.S. 757, 761 (1966). The meaning of "testimonial or communicative" for the purpose of Article 31 of the Uniform Code of Military Justice is not fully settled. Past decisions of the Court of Military Appeals have extended the Article 31 privilege against self-incrimination to voice and handwriting exemplars and perhaps under certain conditions to bodily fluids. *United States v. Ruiz*, 23 U.S.C.M.A. 181, 48 C.M.R. 797 (1974). Because of the unsettled law in the area of bodily fluids, it is not the intent of the Committee to adopt any particular definition of "testimonial or communicative." It is believed, however, that the decisions of the United States Supreme Court construing the Fifth Amendment, *e.g., Schmerber v. California*, 384 U.S. 757 (1966), should be persuasive in this area. Although the right against self-incrimination has a number of varied justifications, its primary purposes are to shield the individual's thought processes from Government inquiry and to permit an individual to refuse to

create evidence to be used against him. Taking a bodily fluid sample from the person of an individual fails to involve either concern. The fluid in question already exists; the individual's actions are irrelevant to its seizure except insofar as the health and privacy of the individual can be further protected through his or her cooperation. No persuasive reason exists for Article 31 to be extended to bodily fluids. To the extent that due process issues are involved in bodily fluid extractions, Rule 312 provides adequate protections.

The privilege against self-incrimination does not protect a person from being compelled by an order or forced to exhibit his or her body or other physical characteristics as evidence. Similarly, the privilege is not violated by taking the fingerprints of an individual, in exhibiting or requiring that a scar on the body be exhibited, in placing an individual's feet in tracks, or by trying shoes or clothing on a person or in requiring the person to do so, or by compelling a person to place a hand, arm, or other part of the body under the ultra-violet light for identification or other purposes.

The privilege is not violated by the use of compulsion in requiring a person to produce a record or writing under his or her control containing or disclosing incriminating matter when the record or writing is under control in a representative rather than a personal capacity as, for example, when it is in his or her control as the custodian for a non-appropriated fund. *See, e.g.,* Para. 150 *b* of MCM, 1969 (Rev.); *United States v. Sellers*, 12 U.S.C.M.A. 262, 30 C.M.R. 262 (1961); *United States v. Haskins*, 11 U.S.C.M.A. 365, 29 C.M.R. 181 (1960).

(b) *Standing.*

(1) *In general.* Rule 301(b)(1) recites the first part of the third paragraph of Para. 150 *b*, MCM, 1969 (Rev.) without change except that the present language indicating that neither counsel nor the court may object to a self-incriminating question put to the witness has been deleted as being unnecessary.

(2) *Judicial advice.* A clarified version of the military judge's responsibility under Para. 150 *b* of MCM, 1969 (Rev.) to warn an uninformed witness of the right against self-incrimination has been placed in Rule 301(b)(2). The revised procedure precludes counsel asking in open court that a witness be advised of his or her rights, a practice which the Committee deemed of doubtful propriety.

(c) *Exercise of the privilege.* The first sentence of Rule 301(c) restates generally the first sentence of the second paragraph of Para. 150 *b*, MCM, 1969 (Rev.). The language "unless it clearly appears to the military judge" was deleted. The test involved is purely objective.

The second sentence of Rule 301(c) is similar to the second and third sentences of the second paragraph of Para. 150 *b* but the language has been rephrased. The present Manual's language states that the witness can be required to answer if for "any other reason, he can successfully object to being tried for any offense as to which the answer may supply information to incriminate him . . ." Rule 301(c) provides: "A witness may not assert the privilege if the witness is not subject to criminal penalty as a result of an answer by reason of immunity, running of the statute of limitations, or similar reason." It is believed that the new language is simpler and more accurate as the privilege is properly defined in terms of consequence rather than in terms of "being tried." In the absence of a possible criminal penalty, to include the mere fact of conviction, there is no risk of self-incrimination. It is not the intent of the Committee to adopt any particular definition of "criminal penalty." It should be noted, however, that the courts have occasionally found that certain consequences that are technically non-criminal are so similar in effect that the privilege should be construed to apply. *See e.g., Spevack v. Klein*, 385 U.S. 511 (1967); *United States v. Ruiz*, 23 U.S.C.M.A. 181, 48 C.M.R. 797 (1974). Thus, the definition of "criminal penalty" may depend upon the facts of a given case as well as the applicable case law.

It should be emphasized that an accused, unlike a witness, need not take the stand to claim the privilege.

(1) *Immunity generally.* Rule 301(c)(1) recognizes that "testimonial" or "use plus fruits" immunity is sufficient to overcome the privilege against self-incrimination, *cf., United States v. Rivera*, 1 M.J. 107 (C.M.A. 1975), *reversing on other grounds,* 49 C.M.R. 259 (A.C.M.R. 1974), and declares that such immunity is adequate for purposes of the Manual. The Rule recognizes that immunity may be granted under federal statutes as well as under provisions of the Manual.

(2) *Notification of immunity or leniency.* The basic disclosure provision of Rule 301(c)(2) is taken from *United States v. Webster*, 1 M.J. 216 (C.M.A. 1975). Disclosure should take place prior to arraignment in order to conform with the timing requirements of Rule 304 and to ensure efficient trial procedure.

(d) *Waiver by a witness.* The first sentence of Rule 301(d) repeats without change the third sentence of the third paragraph of Para. 150 *b* of MCM, 1969 (Rev.).

The second sentence of the Rule restates the second section of the present rule but with a minor change of wording. The present text reads: "The witness may be considered to have waived the privilege to this extent by having made the answer, but such a waiver will not extend to a rehearing or new or other trial," while the new language is: "This limited waiver of the privilege applies only at the trial at which the answer is given, does not extend to a rehearing or new or other trial, and is subject to Rule 608(b)."

(e) *Waiver by the accused.* Except for the reference to Rule 608(b), Rule 301 (e) generally restates the fourth sentence of the third rule of Para. 149 *b*(1), MCM, 1969 (Rev.). "Matters" was substituted for "issues" for purposes of clarity.

The mere act of taking the stand does not waive the privilege. If an accused testifies on direct examination only as to matters not bearing upon the issue of guilt or innocence of any offense for which the accused is being tried, as in Rule 304 (f), the accused may not be cross-examined on the issue of guilt or innocence at all. *See* Para. 149 *b* (1), MCM, 1969 (Rev.) and Rule 608(b).

The last sentence of the third rule of Para. 149 *b*(1), MCM, 1969 (Rev.) has been deleted as unnecessary. The Analysis statement above, "The mere act of taking the stand does not waive the privilege," reinforces the fact that waiver depends upon the actual content of the accused's testimony.

The last sentence of Rule 301(e) restates without significant change the sixth sentence of the third rule of Para. 149 *b*(1), MCM, 1969 (Rev.).

(f) *Effect of claiming the privilege.*

(1) *Generally.* Rule 301(f)(1) is taken without change from the fourth rule of Para. 150 *b*, MCM, 1969 (Rev.). It should be noted that it is ethically improper to call a witness with the intent of having the witness claim a valid privilege against self-incrimination in open court, *see, e.g.,* ABA STANDARDS RELATING TO THE ADMINISTRATION OF CRIMINAL JUSTICE, STANDARDS RELATING TO THE PROSECUTION FUNCTION AND THE DEFENSE FUNCTION, Prosecution Standard 3–5.7(c); Defense Standard 4–7.6(c) (Approved draft 1979).

Whether and to what extent a military judge may permit comment on the refusal of a witness to testify after his or her claimed reliance on the privilege against self-incrimination has been determined by the judge to be invalid is a question not dealt with by the Rule and one which is left to future decisions for resolution.

(2) *On cross-examination.* This provision is new and is intended to clarify the situation in which a witness who has testified fully on direct examination asserts the privilege against self-incrimination on cross-examination. It incorporates the prevailing civilian rule, which has also been discussed in military cases. *See e.g., United States v. Colon-Atienza*, 22 U.S.C.M.A. 399, 47 C.M.R. 336 (1973); *United States v. Rivas*, 3 M.J. 282 (C.M.A. 1977). Where the assertion shields only "collateral" matters—*i.e.*, evidence of minimal importance (usually dealing with a rather distant fact solicited for impeachment purposes)—it is not appropriate to strike direct testimony. A matter is collateral when sheltering it would create little danger of prejudice to the accused. Where the privilege reaches the core of the direct testimony or prevents a full inquiry into the credibility of the witness, however, striking of the direct testimony would appear mandated. Cross-examination includes for the purpose of Rule 301 the testimony of a hostile witness called as if on cross-examination. *See* Rule 607. Depending upon the circumstances of the case, a refusal to strike the testimony of a Government witness who refuses to answer defense questions calculated to impeach the credibility of the witness may constitute prejudicial limitation of the accused's right to cross-examine the witness.

(3) *Pretrial.* Rule 301(f)(3) is taken generally from Para. 140 *a* (4), MCM, 1969 (Rev.) and follows the decisions of the United States Supreme Court in *United States v. Hale*, 422 U.S. 171 (1975) and *Doyle v. Ohio*, 426 U.S. 610 (1976). *See also United States v. Brooks*, 12 U.S.C.M.A. 423, 31 C.M.R. 9 (1961); *United States v. McBride*, 50 C.M.R. 126 (A.F.C.M.R. 1975). The prior Manual provision has been expanded to include a request to terminate questioning.

(g) *Instructions.* Rule 301(g) has no counterpart in the 1969 Manual. It is designed to address the potential for prejudice that may occur when an accused exercises his or her right to remain silent. Traditionally, the court members have been instructed to disregard the accused's silence and not to draw any adverse inference from it. However, counsel for the accused may determine that this very instruction may emphasize the accused's silence, creating a prejudicial effect. Although the Supreme Court has held that it is not unconstitutional for a judge to instruct a jury over the objection of the accused to disregard the accused's silence, it has also stated: "It may be wise for a trial judge not to give such a cautionary instruction over a defendant's objection." *Lakeside v. Oregon*, 435 U.S. 333, 340-41 (1978). Rule 301(g) recognizes that the decision to ask for a cautionary instruction is one of great tactical importance for the defense and generally leaves that decision solely within the hands of the defense. Although the military judge may give the instruction when it is necessary in the interests of justice, the intent of the Committee is to leave the decision in the hands of the defense in all but the most unusual cases. *See also* Rule 105. The military judge may determine the content of any instruction that is requested to be given.

(h) *Miscellaneous.* The last portion of paragraph 150 *b*, MCM, 1969 (Rev.), dealing with exclusion of evidence obtained in violation of due process, has been deleted and its content placed in the new Rules on search and seizure. *See e.g.,* Rule 312, Bodily Views and Intrusions. The exclusionary rule previously found in the last rule of Para. 150 *b* was deleted as being unnecessary in view of the general exclusionary rule in Rule 304.

2013 Amendment. In subsection (c), the phrase "concerning the issue of guilt or innocence" was removed because this subsection applies to the presentencing phase of the trial as well as the merits phase. The use of the term "concerning the issue of guilt or innocence" incorrectly implied that the subsection only referred to the merits phase. The rule was renamed "Limited Waiver," changed from "Waiver by the accused," to indicate that when an accused who is on trial for two or more offenses testifies on direct as to only one of the offenses, he has only waived his rights with respect to that offense and no other. Also, the committee moved this subsection up in the rule and renumbered it in order to address the issue of limited waivers earlier because of the importance of preserving the accused's right against self-incrimination.

In subsection (d), the committee intends that the word "answer" be defined as "a witness's response to a question posed." *Black's Law Dictionary* 100 (8th ed. 2004). Subsection (d) only applies when the witness's response to the question posed may be incriminating. It does not apply when the witness desires to make a statement that is unresponsive to the question asked for the purpose of gaining protection from the privilege.

Former subsections (d) and (f)(2) were combined for ease of use. The issues typically arise chronologically in the course of a trial, because a witness often testifies on direct without asserting the privilege and then, during the ensuing cross-examination, asserts the privilege.

Former subsection (b)(2) was moved to a discussion section because it addresses conduct rather than the admissibility of evidence. *See supra*, General Provisions Analysis. Also, the committee changed the word "should" to "may" in light of CAAF's holding in *United States v. Bell*, 44 M.J. 403 (C.A.A.F. 2006). In that case, CAAF held that Congress did not intend for Article 31(b) warnings to apply at trial, and noted that courts have the discretion, but not an obligation, to warn witnesses on the stand. *Bell*, 44 M.J. at 405. If a member testifies at an Article 32 hearing or court-martial without receiving Article 31(b) warnings, his Fifth Amendment rights have not been violated and those statements can be used against him at subsequent proceedings. *Id.* at 405-06.

As a result of the various changes, the committee renumbered the remaining subsections accordingly. The committee also revised this rule for stylistic reasons but in doing so did not intend to change any result in any ruling on evidence admissibility.

Rule 302 Privilege concerning mental examination of an accused

Introduction. The difficulty giving rise to Rule 302 and its

conforming changes is a natural consequence of the tension between the right against self-incrimination and the favored position occupied by the insanity defense. If an accused could place a defense expert on the stand to testify to his lack of mental responsibility and yet refuse to cooperate with a Government expert, it would place the prosecution in a disadvantageous position. The courts have attempted to balance the competing needs and have arrived at what is usually, although not always, an adequate compromise; when an accused has raised a defense of insanity through expert testimony, the prosecution may compel the accused to submit to Government psychiatric examination on pain of being prevented from presenting any defense expert testimony (or of striking what expert testimony has already presented). However, at trial the expert may testify *only* as to his or her conclusions and their basis and not as to the contents of any statements made by the accused during the examination. *See e.g., United States v. Albright*, 388 F.2d 719 (4th Cir. 1968); *United States v. Babbidge*, 18 U.S.C.M.A. 327, 40 C.M.R. 39 (1969). *See generally,* Frederic Lederer, *Rights Warnings in the Armed Services,* 72 Mil. L. Rev. 1 (1976); Don Holladay, *Pretrial Mental Examinations Under Military Law: A Re-Examination*, 16 A.F. L. Rev. 14 (1974). This compromise, which originally was a product of case law, is based on the premise that raising an insanity defense is an implied partial waiver of the privilege against self-incrimination and has since been codified in the Federal Rules of Criminal Procedure, Fed. R. Crim. P. 12-2, and MCM, 1969 (Rev.). Para. 140 *a*, 122 *b*, 150 *b*. The compromise, however, does not fully deal with the problem in the military.

In contrast to the civilian accused who is more likely to have access to a civilian doctor as an expert witness for the defense—a witness with no governmental status— the military accused normally must rely upon the military doctors assigned to the local installation. In the absence of a doctor-patient privilege, anything said can be expected to enter usual Government medical channels. Once in those channels there is nothing in the present Manual that prevents the actual psychiatric report from reaching the prosecution and release of such information appears to be common in contemporary practice. As a result, even when the actual communications made by the accused are not revealed by the expert witness in open court, under the 1969 Manual they may be studied by the prosecution and could be used to discover other evidence later admitted against the accused. This raises significant derivative evidence problems, *cf. United States v. Rivera*, 23 U.S.C.M.A. 430, 50 C.M.R. 389 (1975). One military judge's attempt to deal with this problem by issuing a protective order was commended by the Court of Military Appeals in an opinion that contained a caveat from Judge Duncan that the trial judge may have exceeded his authority in issuing the order, *United States v. Johnson*, 22 U.S.C.M.A. 424, 47 C.M.R. 401 (1973).

Further complicating this picture is the literal language of Article 31(b) which states, in part, that "No person subject to this chapter may ... request a statement from, an accused or a person suspected of an offense without first informing him ..." [of his rights]. Accordingly, a psychiatrist who complies with the literal meaning of Article 31(b) may effectively and inappropriately destroy the very protections created by *Babbidge* and related cases, while hindering the examination itself. At the same time, the validity of warnings and any consequent "waiver" under such circumstances is most questionable because *Babbidge* never considered the case of an accused forced to choose between a waiver and a prohibited or limited insanity defense. Also left open by the present compromise is the question of what circumstances, if any, will permit a prosecutor to solicit the actual statements made by the suspect during the mental examination. In *United States v. Frederick*, 3 M.J. 230 (C.M.A. 1977), the Court of Military Appeals held that the defense counsel had opened the door via his questioning of the witness and thus allowed the prosecution a broader examination of the expert witness than would otherwise have been allowed. At present, what constitutes "opening the door" is unclear. An informed defense counsel must proceed with the greatest of caution being always concerned that what may be an innocent question may be considered to be an "open sesame."

Under the 1969 Manual interpretation of *Babbidge, supra*, the accused could refuse to submit to a Government examination until after the actual presentation of defense expert testimony on the insanity issue. Thus, trial might have to be adjourned for a substantial period in the midst of the defense case. This was conducive to neither justice nor efficiency.

A twofold solution to these problems was developed. Rule 302 provides a form of testimonial immunity intended to protect an accused from use of anything he might say during a mental examination ordered pursuant to Para. 121, MCM, 1969 (Rev.) (now R.C.M. 706, MCM, 1984). Paragraph 121 was modified to sharply limit actual disclosure of information obtained from the accused during the examination. Together, these provisions would adequately protect the accused from disclosure of any statements made during the examination. This would encourage the accused to cooperate fully in the examination while protecting the Fifth Amendment and Article 31 rights of the accused.

Paragraph 121 was retitled to eliminate "Before Trial" and was thus made applicable before and during trial. Pursuant to paragraph 121, an individual's belief or observations, reflecting possible need for a mental examination of the accused, should have been submitted to the convening authority with immediate responsibility for the disposition of the charges or, after referral, to the military judge or president of a special court-martial without a military judge. The submission could, but needed not, be accompanied by a formal application for a mental examination. While the convening authority could act on a submission under paragraph 121 after referral, he or she might do so only when a military judge was not reasonably available.

Paragraph 121 was revised to reflect the new test for insanity set forth in *United States v. Frederick*, 3 M.J. 230 (C.M.A. 1977), and to require sufficient information for the fact finder to be able to make an intelligent decision rather than necessarily relying solely upon an expert's conclusion. Further questions, tailored to the individual case, could also be propounded. Thus, in an appropriate case, the following might be asked:

Did the accused, at the time of the alleged offense and as a result of such mental disease or defect, lack substantial capacity to (possess actual knowledge), (entertain a specific intent), (premeditate a design to kill)?

What is the accused's intelligence level?

Was the accused under the influence of alcohol or other drugs at the time of the offense? If so, what was the degree of intoxication and was it voluntary? Does the diagnosis of alcoholism, alcohol or drug induced organic brain syndrome, or pathologic intoxication apply?

As the purpose of the revision of paragraph 121 and the creation of Rule 302 was purely to protect the privilege against self-incrimination of an accused undergoing a mental examination related to a criminal case, both paragraph 121 and Rule 302 were inapplicable to proceedings not involving criminal consequences.

The order to the sanity board required by paragraph 121 affects only members of the board and other medical personnel. Upon request by a commanding officer of the accused, that officer shall be furnished a copy of the board's full report. The commander may then make such use of the report as may be appropriate (including consultation with a judge advocate) subject only to the restriction on release to the trial counsel and to Rule 302. The restriction is fully applicable to all persons subject to the Uniform Code of Military Justice. Thus, it is intended that the trial counsel receive only the board's conclusions unless the defense should choose to disclose specific matter. The report itself shall be released to the trial counsel, minus any statements made by the accused, when the defense raises a sanity issue at trial and utilizes an expert witness in its presentation. Rule 302(c).

Although Rule 302(c) does not apply to determinations of the competency of the accused to stand trial, paragraph 121 did prohibit access to the sanity board report by the trial counsel except as specifically authorized. In the event that the competency of an accused to stand trial was at issue, the trial counsel could request, pursuant to paragraph 121, that the military judge disclose the sanity board report to the prosecution. In such a case, the trial counsel who had read the report would be disqualified from prosecuting the case in chief if Rule 302(a) were applicable.

As indicated above, paragraph 121 required that the sanity board report be kept within medical channels except insofar as it would be released to the defense and, upon request, to the commanding officer of the accused. The paragraph expressly prohibited any person from supplying the trial counsel with information relating to the contents of the report. Care should be taken not to misconstrue the intent of the provision. The trial counsel is dealt with specifically because in the normal case it is only the trial counsel who is involved in the preparation of the case at the stage at which a sanity inquiry is likely to take place. Exclusion of evidence will result, however, even if the information is provided to persons other than trial counsel if such information is the source of derivative evidence. Rule 302 explicitly allows suppression of any evidence resulting from the accused's statement to the sanity board, and evidence derivative thereof, with limited exceptions as found in Rule 302. This is consistent with the theory behind the revisions which treats the accused's communication to the sanity board as a form of coerced statement required under a form of testimonial immunity. For example, a commander who has obtained the sanity board's report may obtain legal advice from a judge advocate, including the staff judge advocate, concerning the content of the sanity board's report. If the judge advocate uses the information in order to obtain evidence against the accused or provides it to another person who used it to obtain evidence to be used in the case, Rule 302 authorizes exclusion. Commanders must take great care when discussing the sanity board report with others, and judge advocates exposed to the report must also take great care to operate within the Rule.

(a) *General Rule.* Rule 302(a) provides that, absent defense offer, neither a statement made by the accused at a mental examination ordered under paragraph 121 nor derivative evidence thereof shall be received into evidence against the accused at trial on the merits or during sentencing when the Rule is applicable. This should be treated as a question of testimonial immunity for the purpose of determining the applicability of the exclusionary rule in the area. The Committee does not express an opinion as to whether statements made at such a mental examination or derivative evidence thereof may be used in making an adverse determination as to the disposition of the charges against the accused.

Subject to Rule 302(b), Rule 302(a) makes statements made by an accused at a paragraph 121 examination (now in R.C.M. 706(c), MCM 1984) inadmissible even if Article 31 (b) and counsel warnings have been given. This is intended to resolve problems arising from the literal interpretation of Article 31 discussed above. It protects the accused and enhances the validity of the examination.

(b) *Exceptions.* Rule 301(b) is taken from prior law; *see* Para. 122 *b*, MCM 1969 (Rev.). The waiver provision of Rule 302(b)(1) applies only when the defense makes explicit use of statements made by the accused to a sanity board or derivative evidence thereof. The use of lay testimony to present an insanity defense is not derivative evidence when the witness has not read the report.

(c) *Release of evidence.* Rule 302(c) is new and is intended to provide the trial counsel with sufficient information to reply to an insanity defense raised via expert testimony. The Rule is so structured as to permit the defense to choose how much information will be available to the prosecution by determining the nature of the defense to be made. If the accused fails to present an insanity defense or does so only through lay testimony, for example, the trial counsel will not receive access to the report. If the accused presents a defense, however, which includes specific incriminating statements made by the accused to the sanity board, the military judge may order disclosure to the trial counsel of "such statement. . . as may be necessary in the interest of justice."

Inasmuch as the revision of paragraph 121 and the creation of Rule 302 were intended primarily to deal with the situation in which the accused denies committing an offense and only raises an insanity defense as an alternative defense, the defense may consider that it is appropriate to disclose the entire sanity report to the trial counsel in a case in which the defense concedes the commission of the offense but is raising as its sole defense the mental state of the accused.

(d) *Non-compliance by the accused.* Rule 302(d) restates prior law and is in addition to any other lawful sanctions. As Rule 302 and the revised paragraph 121 adequately protect the accused's right against self-incrimination at a sanity board, sanctions other than that found in Rule 302(d) should be statutorily and constitutionally possible. In an unusal case these sanctions might include prosecution of an accused for disobedience of a lawful order to cooperate with the sanity board.

(e) *Procedure.* Rule 302(e) recognizes that a violation of paragraph 121 or Rule 302 is in effect a misuse of immunized testimony—the coerced testimony of the accused at the sanity board—and thus results in an involuntary statement which may be challenged under Rule 304.

2013 Amendment. The committee revised this rule for stylistic reasons but in doing so did not intend to change any result in any

ruling on evidence admissibility.

Rule 303 Degrading questions

Rule 303 restates Article 31(c). The content of Para. 150 *a*, MCM, 1969 (Rev.) has been omitted.

A specific application of Rule 303 is in the area of sexual offenses. Under prior law, the victims of such offenses were often subjected to a probing and degrading cross-examination related to past sexual history— an examination usually of limited relevance at best. Rule 412 of the Military Rules of Evidence now prohibits such questioning, but Rule 412 is, however, not applicable to Article 32 hearings as it is only a rule of evidence; *see* Rule 1101. Rule 303 and Article 31(c) on the other hand, are rules of privilege applicable to all persons, military or civilian, and are thus fully applicable to Article 32 proceedings. Although Rule 303 (Article 31(c)) applies only to "military tribunals," it is apparent that Article 31(c) was intended to apply to courts-of-inquiry, and implicitly to Article 32 hearings. *The Uniform Code of Military Justice, Hearings on H.R. 2498 Before a Subcomm. of the House Comm. on Armed Services,* 81st Cong., 1st Sess. 975 (1949). The Committee intends that the expression "military tribunals" in Rule 303 includes Article 32 hearings.

Congress found the information now safeguarded by Rule 412 to be degrading. *See e.g.,* Cong. Rec. H119944-45 (Daily ed. Oct. 10, 1978) (Remarks of Rep. Mann). As the material within the constitutional scope of Rule 412 is inadmissible at trial, it is thus not relevant let alone "material." Consequently that data within the lawful coverage of Rule 412 is both immaterial and degrading and thus is within the ambit of Rule 303 (Article 31(c)).

Rule 303 is therefore the means by which the substance of Rule 412 applies to Article 32 proceedings, and no person may be compelled to answer a question that would be prohibited by Rule 412. As Rule 412 permits a victim to refuse to supply irrelevant and misleading sexual information at trial, so too does the substance of Rule 412 through Rule 303 permit the victim to refuse to supply such degrading information at an Article 32 for use by the defense or the convening authority. *See generally* Rule 412 and the Analysis thereto. It should also be noted that it would clearly be unreasonable to suggest that Congress in protecting the victims of sexual offenses from the degrading and irrelevant cross-examination formerly typical of sexual cases would have intended to permit the identical examination at a military preliminary hearing that is not even presided over by a legally trained individual. Thus public policy fully supports the application of Article 31(c) in this case.

1993 Amendment: R.C.M. 405(i) and Mil. R. Evid. 1101(d) were amended to make the provisions of Mil. R. Evid. 412 applicable at pretrial investigations. These changes ensure that the same protections afforded victims of nonconsensual sex offenses at trial are available at pretrial hearings. *See* Criminal Justice Subcommittee of House Judiciary Committee Report, 94th Cong., 2d Session, July 29, 1976. Pursuant to these amendments, Mil. R. Evid. 412 should be applied in conjunction with Mil. R. Evid. 303. As such, no witness may be compelled to answer a question calling for a personally degrading response prohibited by Rule 303. Mil. R. Evid. 412, however, protects the victim even if the victim does not testify. Accordingly, Rule 412 will prevent questioning of the victim or other witness if the questions call for responses prohibited by Rule 412.

2013 Amendment. The committee revised this rule for stylistic reasons and to ensure that it addressed admissibility rather than conduct. *See supra*, General Provisions Analysis. In doing so, the committee did not intend to change any result in any ruling on evidence admissibility.

Rule 304 Confessions and admissions

(a) *General rule.* The exclusionary rule found in Rule 304(a) is applicable to Rules 301–305, and basically restates prior law which appeared in paragraphs 140 *a*(6) and 150 *b*, MCM, 1969 (Rev.). Rule 304(b) does permit, however, limited impeachment use of evidence that is excludable on the merits. A statement that is not involuntary within the meaning of Rule 304(c)(3), Rule 305(a) or Rule 302(a) is voluntary and will not be excluded under this Rule.

The seventh paragraph of Para. 150 *b* of the 1969 Manual attempts to limit the derivative evidence rule to *statements* obtained through *compulsion* that is "applied by, or at the instigation or with the participation of, an *official or agent of the United States, or any State thereof or political subdivision of either, who was acting in a governmental capacity.* . ." (emphasis added). Rule 304, however, makes all derivative evidence inadmissible. Although some support for the 1969 Manual limitations can be found in the literal phrasing of Article 31(d), the intent of the Article as indicated in the commentary presented during the House hearings, *The Uniform Code of Military Justice, Hearing on H.R. 2498 Before a Subcomm. of the House Comm. on Armed Services,* 81st Cong., 1st Sess. 984 (1949), was to exclude "evidence" rather than just "statements." Attempting to allow admission of evidence obtained from statements which were the product of coercion, unlawful influence, or unlawful inducement would appear to be both against public policy and unnecessarily complicated. Similarly, the 1969 Manual's attempt to limit the exclusion of derivative evidence to that obtained through compulsion caused by "Government agents" has been deleted in favor of the simpler exclusion of all derivative evidence. This change, however, does not affect the limitation, as expressed in current case law, that the warning requirements apply only when the interrogating individual is either a civilian law enforcement officer or an individual subject to the Uniform Code of Military Justice acting in an official disciplinary capacity or in a position of authority over a suspect or accused. The House hearings indicate that all evidence obtained in violation of Article 31 was to be excluded and all persons subject to the Uniform Code of Military Justice may violate Article 31(a). Consequently, the attempted 1969 Manual restriction could affect at most only derivative evidence obtained from involuntary statements compelled by private citizens. Public policy demands that private citizens not be encouraged to take the law into their own hands and that law enforcement agents not be encouraged to attempt to circumvent an accused's rights via proxy interrogation.

It is clear that truly spontaneous statements are admissible as they are not "obtained" from an accused or suspect. An apparently volunteered statement which is actually the result of coercive circumstances intentionally created or used by interrogators will be involuntary. *Cf. Brewer v. Williams,* 430 U.S. 387 (1977), Rule 305(b)(2). Manual language dealing with this area has been deleted as being unnecessary.

(b) *Exceptions.* Rule 304(b)(1) adopts *Harris v. New York,* 401 U.S. 222 (1971) insofar as it would allow use for impeachment or at a later trial for perjury, false swearing, or the making of a false official statement, or statements taken in violation of the counsel warnings required under Rule 305(d)-(e). Under Paras. 140 *a*(2) and 153b, MCM, 1969 (Rev.), use of such statements was not permissible. *United States v. Girard,* 23 U.S.C.M.A. 263, 49 C.M.R. 438 (1975); *United States v. Jordan,* 20 U.S.C.M.A. 614, 44 C.M.R. 44 (1971). The Court of Military Appeals has recognized expressly the authority of the President to adopt the holding in *Harris* on impeachment. *Jordan, supra,* 20 U.S.C.M.A. 614, 617, 44 C.M.R. 44, 47, and Rule 304(b) adopts Harris to military law. A statement obtained in violation of Article 31(b), however, remains inadmissible for all purposes, as is a statement that is otherwise involuntary under Rules 302, 304(b)(3), or 305(a). It was the intent of the Committee to permit use of a statement which is involuntary because the *waiver of counsel* rights under Rule 305(g) was absent or improper which is implicit in Rule 304(b)'s reference to Rule 305(d).

1986 Amendment: Rule 304(b)(2) was added to incorporate the "inevitable discovery" exception to the exclusionary rule based on *Nix v. Williams,* 467 U.S. 431, 104 S.Ct. 2501 (1984); *see also United States v. Kozak,* 12 M.J. 389 (C.M.A. 1982); Analysis of Rule 311(b)(2).

1990 Amendment: Subsection (b)(1) was amended by adding "the requirements of Mil. R. Evid. 305(c) and 305(f), or." This language expands the scope of the exception and thereby permits statements obtained in violation of Article 31(b), UCMJ, and Mil. R. Evid. 305(c) and (f) to be used for impeachment purposes or at a later trial for perjury, false swearing, or the making of a false official statement. *See Harris v. New York,* 401 U.S. 222 (1971); *cf. United States v. Williams,* 23 M.J. 362 (C.M.A. 1987). An accused cannot pervert the procedural safeguards of Article 31(b) into a license to testify perjuriously in reliance on the Government's disability to challenge credibility utilizing the traditional truth-testing devices of the adversary process. *See Walder v. United States,* 347 U.S. 62 (1954); *United States v. Knox,* 396 U.S. 77 (1969). Similarly, when the procedural protections of Mil. R. Evid. 305(f) and *Edwards v. Arizona,* 451 U.S. 477 (1981), are violated, the deterrent effect of excluding the unlawfully obtained evidence is fully vindicated by preventing its use in the Government's case-in-chief, but permitting its collateral use to impeach an accused who testifies inconsistently or perjuriously. *See Oregon v. Hass,* 420 U.S. 714 (1975). Statements which are not the product of free and rational choice, *Greenwald v. Wisconsin ,* 390 U.S. 519 (1968), or are the result of coercion, unlawful influence, or unlawful inducements are involuntary and thus inadmissible, because of their untrustworthiness, even as impeachment evidence. *See Mincey v. Arizona,* 437 U.S. 385 (1978).

1994 Amendment: Rule 304(b)(1) adopts *Harris v. New York,* 401 U.S. 222 (1971), insofar as it would allow use for impeachment or at a later trial for perjury, false swearing, or the making of a false official statement, statements taken in violation of the counsel warnings required under Mil R. Evid. 305(d)-(e). Under paragraphs 140a(2) and 153b, MCM, 1969 (Rev.), use of such statements was not permissible. *United States v. Girard,* 23 U.S.C.M.A. 263, 49 C.M.R. 438 (1975); *United States v. Jordan,* 20 U.S.C.M.A. 614, 44 C.M.R. 44 (1971). The Court of Military Appeals has recognized expressly the authority of the President to adopt the holding in *Harris* on impeachment. *Jordan,* 20 U.S.C.M.A. at 617, 44 C.M.R. at 47, and Mil R. Evid. 304(b) adopts *Harris* in military law. Subsequently, in *Michigan v. Har-*

vey, 494 U.S. 344 (1990), the Supreme Court held that statements taken in violation of *Michigan v. Jackson*, 475 U.S. 625 (1986), could also be used to impeach a defendant's false and inconsistent testimony. In so doing, the Court extended the Fifth Amendment rationale of *Harris* to Sixth Amendment violations of the right to counsel.

(c) *Definitions*.

(1) *Confession and admission*. Rules 304(c)(1) and (2) express without change the definitions found in Para. 140 *a*(1), MCM, 1969 (Rev.). Silence may constitute an admission when it does not involve a reliance on the privilege against self-incrimination or related rights. Rule 301(f)(3). For example, if an imputation against a person comes to his or her attention under circumstances that would reasonably call for a denial of its accuracy if the imputation were not true, a failure to utter such a denial could possibly constitute an admission by silence. Note, however, in this regard, Rule 304(h)(3), and Rule 801(a)(2).

(2) *Involuntary*. The definition of "involuntary" in Rule 304(c)(3) summarizes the prior definition of "not voluntary" as found in Para. 140 *a*(2), MCM, 1969 (Rev.). The examples in Para. 140 *a*(2) are set forth in this paragraph. A statement obtained in violation of the warning and waiver requirements of Rule 305 is "involuntary." Rule 305(a).

The language governing statements obtained through the use of "coercion, unlawful influence, and unlawful inducement," found in Article 31(d) makes it clear that a statement obtained by any person, regardless of status, that is the product of such conduct is involuntary. Although it is unlikely that a private citizen may run afoul of the prohibition of unlawful influence or inducement, such a person clearly may coerce a statement and such coercion will yield an involuntary statement.

A statement made by the accused during a mental examination ordered under Para. 121, MCM, 1969 (Rev.) (now R.C.M. 706, MCM, 1984) is treated as an involuntary statement under Rule 304. *See* Rule 302(a). The basis for this rule is that Para. 121 and Rule 302 compel the accused to participate in the Government examination or face a judicial order prohibiting the accused from presenting any expert testimony on the issue of mental responsibility.

Insofar as Rule 304(c)(3) is concerned, some examples which may by themselves or in conjunction with others constitute coercion, unlawful influence, or unlawful inducement in obtaining a confession or admission are:

Infliction of bodily harm including questioning accompanied by deprivation of the necessities of life such as food, sleep, or adequate clothing;

Threats of bodily harm;

Imposition of confinement or deprivation of privileges or necessities because a statement was not made by the accused, or threats thereof if a statement is not made;

Promises of immunity or clemency as to any offense allegedly committed by the accused;

Promises of reward or benefit, or threats of disadvantage likely to induce the accused to make the confession or admission.

There is no change in the principle, set forth in the fifth paragraph of Para. 140 *a*(2), MCM, 1969 (Rev.), that a statement obtained "in an interrogation conducted in accordance with all applicable rules is not involuntary because the interrogation was preceded by one that was not so conducted, if it clearly appears

that all improper influences of the preceding interrogations had ceased to operate on the mind of the accused or suspect at the time that he or she made the statement." In such a case, the effect of the involuntary statement is sufficiently attenuated to permit a determination that the latter statement was not "*obtained* in violation of" the rights and privileges found in Rule 304(c)(3) and 305(a) (emphasis added).

(d) *Procedure*. Rule 304(d) makes a significant change in prior procedure. Under Para. 140 *a*(2), MCM, 1969 (Rev.), the prosecution was required to prove a statement to be voluntary before it could be admitted in evidence absent explicit defense waiver. Rule 304(d) is intended to reduce the number of unnecessary objections to evidence on voluntariness grounds and to narrow what litigation remains by requiring the defense to move to suppress or to object to evidence covered by this Rule. Failure to so move or object constitutes a waiver of the motion or objection. This follows civilian procedure in which the accused is provided an opportunity to assert privilege against self-incrimination and related rights but may waive any objection to evidence obtained in violation of the privilege through failure to object.

(1) *Disclosure*. Prior procedure (Para. 121, MCM, 1969 (Rev.)) is changed to assist the defense in formulating its challenges. The prosecution is required to disclose prior to arraignment all statements by the accused known to the prosecution which are relevant to the case (including matters likely to be relevant in rebuttal and sentencing) and within military control. Disclosure should be made in writing in order to prove compliance with the Rule and to prevent misunderstandings. As a general matter, the trial counsel is not authorized to obtain statements made by the accused at a sanity board, with limited exceptions. If the trial counsel has knowledge of such statements, they must be disclosed. Regardless of trial counsel's knowledge, the defense is entitled to receive the full report of the sanity board.

(2) *Motions and objections*. The defense is required under Rule 304(d)(2) to challenge evidence disclosed prior to arraignment under Rule 304(d)(1) prior to submission of plea. In the absence of a motion or objection prior to plea, the defense may not raise the issue at a later time except as permitted by the military judge for good cause shown. Failure to challenge disclosed evidence waives the objection. This is a change from prior law under which objection traditionally has been made after plea but may be made, at the discretion of the military judge, prior to plea. This change brings military law into line with civilian federal procedure and resolves what is presently a variable and uncertain procedure.

Litigation of a defense motion to suppress or an objection to a statement made by the accused or to any derivative evidence should take place at a hearing held outside the presence of the court members. *See, e.g.,* Rule 104(c).

(3) *Specificity*. Rule 304(d)(3) permits the military judge to require the defense to specify the grounds for an objection under Rule 304, but if the defense has not had adequate opportunity to interview those persons present at the taking of a statement, the military judge may issue an appropriate order including granting a continuance for purposes of interview or permitting a general objection. In view of the waiver that results in the event of failure to object, defense counsel must have sufficient information in order to decide whether to object to the admissibility of a statement by the accused. Although telephone or other long distance

communications may be sufficient to allow a counsel to make an informed decision, counsel may consider a personal interview to be essential in this area and in such a case counsel is entitled to personally interview the witnesses to the taking of a statement before specificity can be required. When such an interview is desired but despite due diligence counsel has been unable to interview adequately those persons included in the taking of a statement, the military judge has authority to resolve the situation. Normally this would include the granting of a continuance for interviews, or other appropriate relief. If an adequate opportunity to interview is absent, even if this results solely from the witness' unwillingness to speak to the defense, then the specificity requirement does not apply. Lacking adequate opportunity to interview, the defense may be authorized to enter a general objection to the evidence. If a general objection has been authorized, the prosecution must present evidence to show affirmatively that the statement was voluntary in the same manner as it would be required to do under prior law. Defense counsel is not required to meet the requirements of Para. 115, MCM, 1969 (Rev.), in order to demonstrate "due diligence" under the Rule. Nor shall the defense be required to present evidence to raise a matter under the Rule. The defense shall present its motion by offer of proof, but it may be required to present evidence in support of the motion should the prosecution first present evidence in opposition to the motion.

If a general objection to the prosecution evidence is not authorized, the defense may be required by Rule 304(d)(3) to make specific objection to prosecution evidence. It is not the intent of the Committee to require extremely technical pleading, but enough specificity to reasonably narrow the issue is desirable. Examples of defense objections include but are not limited to one or more of the following non-exclusive examples:

That the accused was a suspect but not given Article 31(b) or Rule 305(c) warnings prior to interrogation.

That although 31(b) or Rule 305(c) warnings were given, counsel warnings under Rule 305(d) were necessary and not given (or given improperly). (Rule 305(d); *United States v. Tempia*, 16 U.S.C.M.A. 629, 37 C.M.R. 249 (1967).)

That despite the accused's express refusal to make a statement, she was questioned and made an admission. (*see e.g.*, Rule 305(f); *Michigan v. Mosely*, 423 U.S. 96 (1975); *United States v. Westmore*, 17 U.S.C.M.A. 406, 38 C.M.R. 204 (1968).)

That the accused requested counsel but was interrogated by the military police without having seen counsel. (*see e.g.*, Rule 305(a) and (d); *United States v. Gaines*, 21 U.S.C.M.A. 236, 45 C.M.R. 10 (1972).)

That the accused was induced to make a statement by a promise of leniency by his squadron commander. (*see e.g.*, Rule 304(b)(3), Manual for Courts-Martial, United States, 1969 (Rev. ed.), Para 140a(2); *People v. Pineda*, 182 Colo. 388, 513 P.2d 452 (1973).)

That an accused was threatened with prosecution of her husband if she failed to make a statement. (*see e.g.*, Rule 304(b)(3), *Jarriel v. State*, 317 So. 2d 141 (Fla. App. 1975).)

That the accused was held incommunicado and beaten until she confessed. (*see e.g.*, Rule 304(b)(3); *Payne v. Arkansas*, 356 U.S. 560 (1958).)

That the accused made the statement in question only because he had previously given a statement to his division officer which was involuntary because he was improperly warned. (*see*

e.g., Rule 304(b)(3); *United States v. Seay*, 1 M.J. 201 (C.M.A. 1978).)

Although the prosecution retains at all times the burden of proof in this area, a specific defense objection under this Rule must include enough facts to enable the military judge to determine whether the objection is appropriate. These facts will be brought before the court via recital by counsel; the defense will not be required to offer evidence in order to raise the issue. If the prosecution concurs with the defense recital, the facts involved will be taken as true for purposes of the motion and evidence need not be presented. If the prosecution does not concur and the defense facts would justify relief if taken as true, the prosecution will present its evidence and the defense will then present its evidence. The general intent of this provision is to narrow the litigation as much as may be possible without affecting the prosecution's burden.

In view of the Committee's intent to narrow litigation in this area, it has adopted a basic structure in which the defense, when required by the military judge to object with specificity, has total responsibility in terms of what objection, if any, to raise under this Rule.

(4) *Rulings.* Rule 304(d)(4) is taken without significant change from Federal Rule of Criminal Procedure 12(e). As a plea of guilty waives all self-incrimination or voluntariness objections, Rule 304(d)(5), it is contemplated that litigation of confession issues raised before the plea will be fully concluded prior to plea. Cases involving trials by military judge alone in which the accused will enter a plea of not guilty are likely to be the only ones in which deferral of ruling is even theoretically possible. If the prosecution does not intend to use against the accused a statement challenged by the accused under this Rule but is unwilling to abandon any potential use of such statement, two options exist. First, the matter can be litigated before plea, or second, if the accused clearly intends to plead not guilty regardless of the military judge's ruling as to the admissibility of the statements in question, the matter may be deferred until such time as the prosecution indicates a desire to use the statements.

(5) *Effect of guilty plea.* Rule 304(d)(5) restates prior law; *see, e.g., United States v. Dusenberry*, 23 U.S.C.M.A. 287, 49 C.M.R. 536 (1975).

(e) *Burden of proof.* Rule 304(e) substantially changes military law. Under the prior system, the armed forces did not follow the rule applied in the civilian federal courts. Instead, MCM, 1969 (Rev.) utilized the minority "Massachusetts Rule," sometimes known as the "Two Bite Rule." Under this procedure the defense first raises a confession or admission issue before the military judge who determines it on a preponderance basis: if the judge determines the issue adversely to the accused, the defense may raise the issue again before the members. In such a case, the members must be instructed not to consider the evidence in question unless they find it to have been voluntary beyond a reasonable doubt. The Committee determined that this bifurcated system unnecessarily complicated the final instructions to the members to such an extent as to substantially confuse the important matters before them. In view of the preference expressed in Article 36 for the procedure used in the trial of criminal cases in the United States district courts, the Committee adopted the majority "Orthodox Rule" as used in Article III courts. Pursuant to this procedure, the military judge determines the admissibility of confessions or admissions using a preponderance basis. No recourse exists to the court members on the question of admissibility. In the event of a ruling on admissibility adverse to the accused, the accused may present evidence to the members as to voluntariness for their consideration in determining what weight to give to the statements in question.

It should be noted that under the Rules the prosecution's burden extends only to the specific issue raised by the defense under Rule 304(d), should specificity have been required pursuant to Rule 304(d)(3).

(1) *In general.* Rule 304(e)(1) requires that the military judge find by a preponderance that a statement challenged under this rule was made voluntarily. When a trial is before a special court-martial without a military judge, the ruling of the President of the court is subject to objection by any member. The President's decision may be overruled. The Committee authorized use of this procedure in view of the importance of the issue and the absence of a legally trained presiding officer.

(2) *Weight of the evidence.* Rule 304(e)(2) allows the defense to present evidence with respect to voluntariness to the members for the purpose of determining what weight to give the statement. When trial is by judge alone, the evidence received by the military judge on the question of admissibility also shall be considered by the military judge on the question of weight without the necessity of a formal request to do so by counsel. Additional evidence may, however, be presented to the military judge on the matter of weight if counsel chooses to do so.

(3) *Derivative evidence.* Rule 304(e)(3) recognizes that derivative evidence is distinct from the primary evidence dealt with by Rule 304, *i.e.,* statements. The prosecution may prove that notwithstanding an involuntary statement, the evidence in question was not "obtained by use of" it and is not derivative.

February 1986 Amendment: Because of the 1986 addition of Rule 304(b)(2), the prosecution may prove that, notwithstanding an involuntary statement, derivative evidence is admissible under the "inevitable discovery" exception. The standard of proof is a preponderance of the evidence (*Nix v. Williams*, 467 U.S. 431, 104 S.Ct. 2501 (1984)).

(f) *Defense evidence.* Rule 304(f) generally restates prior law as found in Para. 140 *a*(3) & (6), MCM, 1969 (Rev.). Under this Rule, the defense must specify that the accused plans to take the stand under this subdivision. This is already normal practice and is intended to prevent confusion. Testimony given under this subdivision may not be used at the same trial at which it is given for any other purpose to include impeachment. The language, "the accused may be cross-examined only as to matter on which he or she so testifies" permits otherwise proper and relevant impeachment of the accused. *See, e.g.,* Rule 607–609; 613.

(g) *Corroboration.* Rule 304(g) restates the prior law of corroboration with one major procedural change. Previously, no instruction on the requirement of corroboration was required unless the evidence was substantially conflicting, self-contradictory, uncertain, or improbable and there was a defense request for such an instruction. *United States v. Seigle,* 22 U.S.C.M.A. 403, 47 C.M.R. 340 (1973). The holding in *Seigle* in consistent with the 1969 Manual's view that the issue of admissibility may be decided by the members, but it is inconsistent with the position taken in Rule 304(d) that admissibility is the sole responsibility of

the military judge. Inasmuch as the Rule requires corroborating evidence as a condition precedent to admission of the statement, submission of the issue to the members would seem to be both unnecessary and confusing. Consequently, the Rule does not follow *Seigle* insofar as the case allows the issue to be submitted to the members. The members must still weigh the evidence when determining the guilt or innocence of the accused, and the nature of any corroborating evidence is an appropriate matter for the members to consider when weighing the statement before them.

The corroboration rule requires only that evidence be admitted which would support an inference that the essential facts admitted in the statement are true. For example, presume that an accused charged with premeditated murder has voluntarily confessed that, intending to kill the alleged victim, she concealed herself so that she might surprise the victim at a certain place and that when the victim passed by, she plunged a knife in his back. At trial, the prosecution introduces independent evidence that the victim was found dead as a result of a knife wound in his back at the place where, according to the confession, the incident occurred. This fact would corroborate the confession because it would support an inference of the truth of the essential facts admitted in the confession.

(h) *Miscellaneous.*

(1) *Oral statements.* Rule 304(h)(1) is taken verbatim from 1969 Manual paragraph 140 *a*(6). It recognizes that although an oral statement may be transcribed, the oral statement is separate and distinct from the transcription and that accordingly the oral statement may be received into evidence without violation of the best evidence rule unless the specific writing is in question, *see* Rule 1002. So long as the oral statement is complete, no specific rule would require the prosecution to offer the transcription. The defense could of course offer the writing when it would constitute impeachment.

(2) *Completeness.* Rule 304(h)(2) is taken without significant change from 1969 Manual paragraph 140 *a*(6). Although Rule 106 allows a party to require an adverse party to complete an otherwise incomplete written statement in an appropriate case, Rule 304(h)(2) allows the defense to complete an incomplete statement regardless of whether the statement is oral or in writing. As Rule 304(h)(2) does not by its terms deal only with oral statements, it provides the defense in this area with the option of using Rule 106 or 304(h)(2) to complete a written statement.

(3) *Certain admission by silence.* Rule 304(h)(3) is taken from Para. 140 *a*(4) of the 1969 Manual. That part of the remainder of Para. 140 *a*(4) dealing with the existence of the privilege against self-incrimination is now set forth in Rule 301(f)(3). The remainder of Para. 140 *a*(4) has been set forth in the Analysis to subdivision (d)(2), dealing with an admission by silence, or has been omitted as being unnecessary.

1986 Amendment: Mil. R. Evid. 304(h)(4) was added to make clear that evidence of a refusal to obey a lawful order to submit to a chemical analysis of body substances is admissible evidence when relevant either to a violation of such order or an offense which the test results would have been offered to prove. The Supreme Court in *South Dakota v. Neville,* 459 U.S. 553 (1983) held that where the government may compel an individual to submit to a test of a body substance, evidence of a refusal to submit to the test is constitutionally admissible. Since the results of tests of body substances are non-testimonial, a servicemember has no Fifth Amendment or Article 31 right to refuse to submit to such a test. *United States v. Armstrong*, 9 M.J. 374 (C.M.A. 1980); *Schmerber v. State of California*, 384 U.S. 757 (1966). A test of body substances in various circumstances, such as search incident to arrest, probable cause and exigent circumstances, and inspection or random testing programs, among others, is a reasonable search and seizure in the military. *Murray v. Haldeman*, 16 M.J. 74 (C.M.A. 1983); Mil. R. Evid. 312; Mil. R. Evid. 313. Under the Uniform Code of Military Justice, a military order is a valid means to compel a servicemember to submit to a test of a body substance. *Murray v. Haldeman, supra*. Evidence of a refusal to obey such an order may be relevant as evidence of consciousness of guilt. *People v. Ellis*, 65 Cal.2d 529, 421 P.2d 393 (1966). *See also State v. Anderson*, Or.App., 631 P.2d 822 (1981); *Newhouse v. Misterly*, 415 F.2d 514 (9th Cir. 1969), *cert. denied* 397 U.S. 966 (1970).

This Rule creates no right to refuse a lawful order. A servicemember may still be compelled to submit to the test. *See, e.g.,* Mil. R. Evid. 312. Any such refusal may be prosecuted separately for violation of an order.

2013 Amendment. Former subsection (c), which contains definitions of words used throughout the rule, was moved so that it immediately follows subsection (a) and is highly visible to the practitioner. Former subsection (h)(3), which discusses denials, was moved to subsection (a)(2) so that it is included near the beginning of the rule to highlight the importance of an accused's right to remain silent. The committee moved and renumbered the remaining subsections so the rule generally follows the chronology of how the issues might arise at trial. In doing so, the committee did not intend to change any result in any ruling on evidence admissibility.

In subsection (b), the committee added the term "allegedly" in reference to derivative evidence to clarify that evidence is not derivative unless a military judge finds, by a preponderance of the evidence, that it is derivative.

In subsections (c)(5), (d), (f)(3)(A), and (f)(7), the committee replaced the word "shall" with "will" or "must" because the committee agreed with the approach of the Advisory Committee on Evidence Rules to minimize the use of words such as "shall" because of the potential disparity in application and interpretation of whether the word is precatory or proscriptive.

The committee also revised this rule for stylistic reasons and to ensure that it addressed admissibility rather than conduct. *See supra*, General Provisions Analysis. In doing so, the committee did not intend to change any result in any ruling on evidence admissibility.

Rule 305 Warnings About Rights

(a) *General Rule.* Rule 305(a) makes statements obtained in violation of Rule 305, *e.g.,* statements obtained in violation of Article 31(b) and the right to counsel, involuntary within the meaning of Rule 304. This approach eliminates any distinction between statements obtained in violation of the common law voluntariness doctrine (which is, in any event, included within Article 31(d) and those statements obtained in violation, for example, of *Miranda* (*Miranda v. Arizona*, 384 U.S. 436 (1966) warning requirements). This is consistent with the approach taken in the 1969 Manual, *e.g.,* Para. 140 *a*(2).

(b) *Definitions.*

(1) *Persons subject to the Uniform Code of Military Justice.* Rule 305(b)(1) makes it clear that under certain conditions a civilian may be a "person subject to the Uniform Code of Military Justice" for purposes of warning requirements, and would be required to give Article 31(b) (Rule 305(c)) warnings. *See, generally, United States v. Penn*, 18 U.S.C.M.A. 194, 39 C.M.R. 194 (1969). Consequently civilian members of the law enforcement agencies of the Armed Forces, *e.g.,* the Naval Investigative Service and the Air Force Office of Special Investigations, will have to give Article 31 (Rule 305(c)) warnings. This provision is taken in substance from Para. 140 *a*(2) of the 1969 Manual.

(2) *Interrogation.* Rule 305(b)(2) defines interrogation to include the situation in which an incriminating response is either sought or is a reasonable consequence of such questioning. The definition is expressly not a limited one and interrogation thus includes more than the putting of questions to an individual. *See e.g., Brewer v. Williams*, 430 U.S. 387 (1977).

The Rule does not specifically deal with the situation in which an "innocent" question is addressed to a suspect and results unexpectedly in an incriminating response which could not have been foreseen. This legislative history and the cases are unclear as to whether Article 31 allows nonincriminating questioning.*See* Frederic Lederer, *Rights, Warnings in the Armed Services,* 72 Mil. L. Rev. 1, 32-33 (1976), and the issue is left open for further development.

(c) *Warnings concerning the accusation, right to remain silent, and use of statement.* Rule 305(c) basically requires that those persons who are required by statute to give Article 31(b) warnings give such warnings. The Rule refrains from specifying who must give such warnings in view of the unsettled nature of the case law in the area.

It was not the intent of the Committee to adopt any particular interpretation of Article 31(b) insofar as who must give warnings except as provided in Rule 305(b)(1) and the Rule explicitly defers to Article 31 for the purpose of determining who must give warnings. The Committee recognized that numerous decisions of the Court of Military Appeals and its subordinate courts have dealt with this issue. These courts have rejected literal application of Article 31(b), but have not arrived at a conclusive rule. *See e.g., United States v. Dohle*, 1 M.J. 223 (C.M.A. 1975). The Committee was of the opinion, however, that both Rule 305(c) and Article 31(b) should be construed at a minimum, and in compliance with numerous cases, as requiring warnings by those personnel acting in an official disciplinary or law enforcement capacity. Decisions such as *United States v. French*, 25 C.M.R. 851 (A.F.B.R. 1958), *aff'd in relevant part,* 10 U.S.C.M.A. 171, 27 C.M.R. 245 (1959) (undercover agent) are not affected by the Rule.

Spontaneous or volunteered statements do not require warnings under Rule 305. The fact that a person may have known of his or her rights under the Rule is of no importance if warnings were required but not given.

Normally, neither a witness nor an accused need to be warned under any part of this Rule when taking the stand to testify at a trial by court-martial. *See,* however, Rule 801(b)(2).

The Rule requires in Rule 305(c)(2) that the accused or suspect be advised that he or she has the "right to remain silent" rather than the statutory Article 31(b) warning which is limited to silence on matters relevant to the underlying offense. The new language was inserted upon the suggestion of the Department of Justice in order to provide clear advice to the accused as to the absolute right to remain silent. *See Miranda v. Arizona,* 384 U.S. 436 (1966).

(d) *Counsel rights and warnings.* Rule 305(d) provides the basic right to counsel at interrogations and requires that an accused or suspect entitled to counsel at an interrogation be warned of that fact. The Rule restates the basic counsel entitlement for custodial interrogations found in both Para. 140 *c*(2), MCM, 1969 (Rev.), and *United States v. Tempia,* 16 U.S.C.M.A. 629, 37 C.M.R. 249 (1967), and recognizes that the right to counsel attaches after certain procedural steps have taken place.

(1) *General rule.* Rule 305(d)(1) makes it clear that the right to counsel only attaches to an interrogation in which an individual's Fifth Amendment privilege against self-incrimination is involved. This is a direct result of the different coverages of the statutory and constitutional privileges. The Fifth Amendment to the Constitution of the United States is the underpinning of the Supreme Court's decision in *Miranda v. Arizona,* 384 U.S. 436 (1966) which is in turn the origin of the military right to counsel at an interrogation. *United States v. Tempia,* 16 U.S.C.M.A. 629, 37 C.M.R. 249 (1967). Article 31, on the other hand, does not provide any right to counsel at an interrogation; *but see United States v. McOmber,* 1 M.J. 380 (C.M.A. 1976). Consequently, interrogations which involve only the Article 31 privilege against self-incrimination do not include a right to counsel. Under present law such interrogations include requests for voice and handwriting samples and perhaps request for bodily fluids. *Compare United States v. Dionivio,* 410 U.S. 1 (1973); *United States v. Mara,* 410 U.S. 19 (1973); and *Schmerber v. California,* 384 U.S. 757 (1967) with *United States v. White,* 17 U.S.C.M.A. 211, 38 C.M.R. 9 (1967); *United States v. Greer,* 3 U.S.C.M.A. 576, 13 C.M.R. 132 (1953); and *United States v. Ruiz,* 23 U.S.C.M.A. 181, 48 C.M.R. 797 (1974). Rule 305(d)(1) requires that an individual who is entitled to counsel under the Rule be advised of the nature of that right before an interrogation involving evidence of a testimonial or communicative nature within the meaning of the Fifth Amendment (an interrogation as defined in Rule 305(d)(2) and modified in this case by Rule 305(d)(1)) may lawfully proceed. Although the Rule does not specifically require any particular wording or format for the right to counsel warning, reasonable specificity is required. At a minimum, the right to counsel warning must include the following substantive matter:

(1) That the accused or suspect has the right to be represented by a lawyer at the interrogation if he or she so desires;

(2) That the right to have counsel at the interrogation includes the right to consult with counsel and to have counsel at the interrogation;

(3) That if the accused or suspect so desires, he or she will have a military lawyer appointed to represent the accused or suspect at the interrogation at no expense to the individual, and the accused or suspect may obtain civilian counsel at no expense to the Government in addition to or instead of free military counsel.

It is important to note that those warnings are in addition to such other warnings and waiver questions as may be required by Rule 305.

Rule 305(d)(1)(A) follows the plurality of civilian jurisdiction

by utilizing an objective test in defining "custodial" interrogation. *See also United States v. Temperley,* 22 U.S.C.M.A. 383, 47 C.M.R. 235 (1978). Unfortunately, there is no national consensus as to the exact nature of the test that should be used. The language used in the Rule results from an analysis of *Miranda v. Arizona,* 384 U.S. 436 (1966) which leads to the conclusion that *Miranda* is predominately a voluntariness decision concerned with the effects of the psychological coercion inherent in official questioning. *See e.g.,* Frederic Lederer, *Miranda v. Arizona—The Law Today,* 78 Mil. L. Rev. 107, 130 (1977).

The variant chosen adopts an objective test that complies with *Miranda's* intent by using the viewpoint of the suspect. The objective nature of the test, however, makes it improbable that a suspect would be able to claim a custodial status not recognized by the interrogator. The test makes the actual belief of the suspect irrelevant because of the belief that it adds nothing in practice and would unnecessarily lengthen trial.

Rule 305(d)(1)(B) codifies the Supreme Court's decisions in *Brewer v. Williams,* 480 U.S. 387 (1977) and *Massiah v. United States,* 377 U.S. 201 (1964). As modified by *Brewer, Massiah* requires that an accused or suspect be advised of his or her right to counsel prior to interrogation, whether open or surreptitious, if that interrogation takes place after either arraignment or indictment. As the Armed Forces lack any equivalent to those civilian procedural points, the initiation of the formal military criminal process has been utilized as the functional equivalent. Accordingly, the right to counsel attaches if an individual is interrogated after preferral of charges or imposition of pretrial arrest, restriction, or confinement. The right is not triggered by apprehension or temporary detention. Undercover investigation prior to the formal beginning of the criminal process will not be affected by this, but jailhouse interrogations will generally be prohibited. *Compare* Rule 305(d)(1)(B) with *United States v. Hinkson,* 17 U.S.C.M.A. 126, 37 C.M.R. 390 (1967) and *United States v. Gibson,* 3 U.S.C.M.A. 746, 14 C.M.R. 164 (1954).

1994 Amendment: Subdivision (d) was amended to conform military practice with the Supreme Court's decision in *McNeil v. Wisconsin,* 501 U.S. 171 (1991). In *McNeil,* the Court clarified the distinction between the Sixth Amendment right to counsel and the Fifth Amendment right to counsel. The court reiterated that the Sixth Amendment right to counsel does not attach until the initiation of adversary proceedings. In the military, the initiation of adversary proceedings normally occurs at preferral of charges. *See United States v. Jordan,* 29 M.J. 177, 187 (C.M.A. 1989); *United States v. Wattenbarger,* 21 M.J. 41, 43 (C.M.A. 1985), *cert. denied,* 477 U.S. 904 (1986). However, it is possible that, under unusual circumstances, the courts may find that the Sixth Amendment right attaches prior to preferral. *See Wattenbarger,* 21 M.J. at 43-44. Since the imposition of conditions on liberty, restriction, arrest, or confinement does not trigger the Sixth Amendment right to counsel, references to these events were eliminated from the rule. These events may, however, be offered as evidence that the government has initiated adversary proceedings in a particular case.

(2) *Counsel.* Rule 305(d)(2) sets forth the basic right to counsel at interrogations required under 1969 Manual Para. 140 *a*(2). The Rule rejects the interpretation of Para. 140 *a*(2) set forth in *United States v. Hofbauer,* 5 M.J. 409 (C.M.A. 1978) and *United States v. Clark,* 22 U.S.C.M.A. 570, 48 C.M.R. 77 (1974) which

held that the Manual only provided a right to military counsel at an interrogation in the event of financial indigency.

Rule 305(d)(2) clarifies prior practice insofar as it explicitly indicates that no right to individual military counsel of the suspect's or accused's choice exists. *See e.g., United States v. Wilcox*, 3 M.J. 803 (A.C.M.R. 1977).

(e) *Notice to Counsel.* Rule 305(e) is taken from *United States v. McOmber*, 1 M.J. 380 (C.M.A. 1976). The holding of that case has been expanded slightly to clarify the situation in which an interrogator does not have actual knowledge that an attorney has been appointed for or retained by the accused or suspect with respect to the offenses, but reasonably should be so aware. In the absence of the expansion, present law places a premium on law enforcement ignorance and has the potential for encouraging perjury. The change rejects the view expressed in *United States v. Roy*, 4 M.J. 840 (A.C.M.R. 1978) which held that in the absence of bad faith a criminal investigator who interviewed the accused one day before the scheduled Article 32 investigation was not in violation of *McOmber* because he was unaware of the appointment of counsel.

Factors which may be considered in determining whether an interrogator should have reasonably known that an individual had counsel for purposes of this Rule include:

Whether the interrogator knew that the person to be questioned had requested counsel;

Whether the interrogator knew that the person to be questioned had already been involved in a pretrial proceeding at which he would ordinarily be represented by counsel;

Any regulations governing the appointment of counsel;

Local standard operating procedures;

The interrogator's military assignment and training; and

The interrogator's experience in the area of military criminal procedure.

The standard involved is purely an objective one.

1994 Amendment: Subdivision (e) was amended to conform military practice with the Supreme Court's decisions in *Minnick v. Mississippi*, 498 U.S. 146 (1990), and *McNeil v. Wisconsin*, 501 U.S. 171 (1991). Subdivision (e) was divided into two subparagraphs to distinguish between the right to counsel rules under the Fifth and Sixth Amendments and to make reference to the new waiver provisions of subdivision (g)(2). Subdivision (e)(1) applies an accused's Fifth Amendment right to counsel to the military and conforms military practice with the Supreme Court's decision in *Minnick*. In that case, the Court determined that the Fifth Amendment right to counsel protected by *Miranda v. Arizona*, 384 U.S. 436 (1966), and *Edwards v. Arizona*, 451 U.S. 477 (1981), as interpreted in *Arizona v. Roberson*, 486 U.S. 675 (1988), requires that when a suspect in custody requests counsel, interrogation shall not proceed unless counsel is *present*. Government officials may not reinitiate custodial *interrogation* in the absence of counsel whether or not the accused has consulted with his attorney. *Minnick*, 498 U.S. at 150-152. This rule does not apply, however, when the accused or suspect initiates reinterrogation regardless of whether the accused is in custody. *Minnick*, 498 U.S. at 154-55; *Roberson*, 486 U.S. at 677. The impact of a waiver of counsel rights upon the *Minnick* rule is discussed in the analysis to subdivision (g)(2) of this rule. Subdivision (e)(2) follows *McNeil* and applies the Sixth Amendment right to counsel to military practice. Under the Sixth Amendment, an accused is

entitled to representation at critical confrontations with the government after the initiation of adversary proceedings. In accordance with *McNeil*, the amendment recognizes that this right is offense-specific and, in the context of military law, that it normally attaches when charges are preferred. *See United States v. Jordan*, 29 M.J. 177, 187 (C.M.A. 1989); *United States v. Wattenbarger*, 21 M.J. 41 (C.M.A. 1985), *cert. denied*, 477 U.S. 904 (1986). Subdivision (e)(2) supersedes the prior notice to counsel rule. The prior rule, based on *United States v. McOmber*, 1 M.J. 380 (C.M.A. 1976), is not consistent with *Minnick* and *McNeil*. Despite the fact that *McOmber* was decided on the basis of Article 27, U.C.M.J., the case involved a Sixth Amendment claim by the defense, an analysis of the Fifth Amendment decisions of *Miranda v. Arizona*, 384 U.S. 436 (1966), and *United States v. Tempia*, 16 U.S.C.M.A. 629, 37 C.M.R. 249 (1967), and the Sixth Amendment decision of *Massiah v. United States*, 377 U.S. 201 (1964). Moreover, the *McOmber* rule has been applied to claims based on violations of both the Fifth and Sixth Amendments. *See, e.g. United States v. Fassler*, 29 M.J. 193 (C.M.A. 1989). *Minnick* and *McNeil* reexamine the Fifth and Sixth Amendment decisions central to the *McOmber* decision; the amendments to subdivision (e) are the result of that reexamination.

(f) *Exercise of rights.* Rule 305(f) restates prior law in that it requires all questioning to cease immediately upon the exercise of either the privilege against self-incrimination or the right to counsel. *See Michigan v. Mosely*, 423 U.S. 96 (1975). The Rule expressly does not deal with the question of whether or when questioning may be resumed following an exercise of a suspect's rights and does not necessarily prohibit it. The Committee notes that both the Supreme Court, *see e.g., Brewer v. Williams*, 480 U.S. 387 (1977); *Michigan v. Mosely*, 423 U.S. 96 (1975), and the Court of Military Appeals, *see, e.g., United States v. Hill*, 5 M.J. 114 (C.M.A. 1978); *United States v. Collier*, 1 M.J. 358 (C.M.A. 1976) have yet to fully resolve this matter.

1994 Amendment: The amendment to subdivision (f) clarifies the distinction between the rules applicable to the exercise of the privilege against self-incrimination and the right to counsel. *Michigan v. Mosley*, 423 U.S. 96 (1975). *See also United States v. Hsu*, 852 F.2d 407, 411 n.3 (9th Cir. 1988). The added language, contained in (f)(2), is based on *Minnick v. Mississippi*, 498 U.S. 146 (1990), and *McNeil v. Wisconsin*, 501 U.S. 171 (1991). Consequently, when a suspect or an accused undergoing interrogation exercises the right to counsel under circumstances provided for under subdivision (d)(l) of this rule, (f)(2) applies the rationale of *Minnick* and *McNeil* requiring that questioning must cease until counsel is present.

(g) *Waiver.* The waiver provision of Rule 305(g) restates current military practice and is taken in part from Para. 140 *a*(2) of the 1969 Manual.

Rule 305(g)(1) sets forth the general rule for waiver and follows *Miranda v. Arizona*, 384 U.S. 436, 475 (1966). The Rule requires that an affirmative acknowledgment of the right be made before an adequate waiver may be found. Thus, three waiver questions are required under Rule 305(g):

Do you understand your rights?
Do you want a lawyer?
Are you willing to make a statement?

The specific wording of the questions is not detailed by the Rule and any format may be used so long as the substantive content is present.

Notwithstanding the above, Rule 305(g)(2), following *North Carolina v. Butler*, 441 U.S. 369 (1979), recognizes that the right to counsel, and only the right to counsel, may be waived even absent an affirmative declination. The burden of proof is on the prosecution in such a case to prove by a preponderance of the evidence that the accused waived the right to counsel.

The second portion of Rule 305(g)(2) dealing with notice to counsel is new. The intent behind the basic notice provision, Rule 305(e), is to give meaning to the right to counsel by preventing interrogators who know or reasonably should know an individual has counsel from circumventing the right to counsel by obtaining a waiver from that person without counsel present. Permitting a Miranda type waiver in such a situation clearly would defeat the purpose of the Rule. Rule 305(g)(2) thus permits a waiver of the right to counsel when notice to counsel is required only if it can be demonstrated either that the counsel, after reasonable efforts, could not be notified, or that the counsel did not attend the interrogation which was scheduled within a reasonable period of time after notice was given.

A statement given by an accused or suspect who can be shown to have his rights as set forth in this Rule and who intentionally frustrated the diligent attempt of the interrogator to comply with this Rule shall not be involuntary solely for failure to comply with the rights warning requirements of this Rule or of the waiver requirements. *United States v. Sikorski*, 21 U.S.C.M.A. 345, 45 C.M.R. 119 (1972).

1994 Amendment: The amendment divided subdivision (2) into three sections. Subsection (2)(A) remains unchanged from the first sentence of the previous rule. Subsection (2)(B) is new and conforms military practice with the Supreme Court's decision in *Minnick v. Mississippi*, 498 U.S. 146 (1990). In that case, the Court provided that an accused or suspect can validly waive his Fifth Amendment right to counsel, after having previously exercised that right at an earlier custodial interrogation, by initiating the subsequent interrogation leading to the waiver. *Id.* at 156. This is reflected in subsection (2)(B)(i). Subsection (2)(B)(ii) establishes a presumption that a coercive atmosphere exists that invalidates a subsequent waiver of counsel rights when the request for counsel and subsequent waiver occur while the accused or suspect is in continuous custody. *See McNeil v. Wisconsin*, 501 U.S. 171 (1991); *Arizona v. Roberson*, 486 U.S. 675 (1991). The presumption can be overcome when it is shown that there occurred a break in custody which sufficiently dissipated the coercive environment. *See United States v. Schake*, 30 M.J. 314 (C.M.A. 1990).

Subsection (2)(C) is also new and conforms military practice with the Supreme Court's decision in *Michigan v. Jackson*, 475 U.S. 625, 636 (1986). In *Jackson*, the Court provided that the accused or suspect can validly waive his or her Sixth Amendment right to counsel, after having previously asserted that right, by initiating the subsequent interrogation leading to the waiver. The Court differentiated between assertions of the Fifth and Sixth Amendment right to counsel by holding that, while exercise of the former barred further interrogation concerning the same or other offenses in the absence of counsel, the Sixth Amendment protection only attaches to those offenses as to which the right

was originally asserted. In addition, while continuous custody would serve to invalidate a subsequent waiver of a Fifth Amendment right to counsel, the existence or lack of continuous custody is irrelevant to Sixth Amendment rights. The latter vest once formal proceedings are instituted by the State and the accused asserts his right to counsel, and they serve to insure that the accused is afforded the right to counsel to serve as a buffer between the accused and the State.

(h) *Non-military interrogations.* Para. 140 *a*(2) of the 1969 Manual, which governed civilian interrogations of military personnel basically restated the holding of *Miranda v. Arizona*, 384 U.S. 436 (1966). Recognizing that the Supreme Court may modify the Miranda rule, the Committee has used the language in Rule 305(h)(1) to make practice in this area dependent upon the way the Federal district courts would handle such interrogations. *See* Article 36.

Rule 305(h)(2) clarifies the law of interrogations as it relates to interrogations conducted abroad by officials of a foreign government or their agents when the interrogation is not conducted, instigated, or participated in by military personnel or their agents. Such an interrogation does not require rights warnings under subdivisions (c) or (d) or notice to counsel under subdivision (e). The only test to be applied in such a case is that of common law voluntariness: whether a statement obtained during such an interrogation was obtained through the use of "coercion, unlawful influence, or unlawful inducement." Article 31(d).

Whether an interrogation has been "conducted, instigated, or participated in by military personnel or their agents" is a question of fact depending on the circumstances of the case. The Rule makes it clear that a United States personnel do not participate in an interrogation merely by being present at the scene of the interrogation, *see United States v. Jones*, 6 M.J. 226 (C.M.A. 1979) and the Analysis to Rule 311(c), or by taking steps which are in the best interests of the accused. Also, an interrogation is not "participated in" by military personnel or their agents who act as interpreters during the interrogation if there is no other participation. *See* Rule 311(c). The omission of express reference to interpreters in Rule 305(h)(2) was inadvertent.

2013 Amendment. The definition of "person subject to the code" was revised to clarify that it includes a person acting as a knowing agent only in subsection (c). Subsection (c) covers the situation where a person subject to the code is interrogating an accused, and therefore an interrogator would include a knowing agent of a person subject to the code, such as local law enforcement acting at the behest of a military investigator. The term "person subject to the code" is also used in subsection (f), which discusses a situation in which a person subject to the code is being interrogated. If an agent of a person subject to the code is being interrogated, subsection (f) is inapplicable, unless that agent himself is subject to the code and is suspected of an offense.

The definition of "custodial interrogation" was moved to subsection (b) from subsection (d) in order to co-locate the definitions. The definition is derived from *Miranda v. Arizona*, 384 U.S. 436, 444-45 (1966), and *Berkemer v. McCarty*, 468 U.S. 420, 442 (1984).

"Accused" is defined as "a person against whom legal proceedings have been initiated." Black's Law Dictionary 23 (8th ed. 2004). "Suspect" is defined as "a person believed to have committed a crime or offense." *Id.* at 1287. In subsection (c)(1), the word "accused" is used in the first sentence because the rule generally addresses the admissibility of a statement at a court-martial, at which legal proceedings have been initiated against the individual. Throughout the remainder of the rule, "accused" and "suspect" are used together to elucidate that an interrogation that triggers the need for Article 31 warnings will often take place before the individual has become an accused and is still considered only a suspect.

Although not specifically outlined in subsection (c), the committee intends that interrogators and investigators fully comply with the requirements of *Miranda v. Arizona*, 384 U.S. 436 (1966). When a suspect is subjected to custodial interrogation, the prosecution may not use statements stemming from that custodial interrogation unless it demonstrates that the suspect was warned of his rights. *Id.* at 444. At a minimum, *Miranda* requires that "the person must be warned that he has a right to remain silent, that any statement he does make may be used as evidence against him, and that he has a right to the presence of an attorney, either retained or appointed. The defendant may waive effectuation of these rights, provided the waiver is made voluntarily, knowingly and intelligently." *Id.* A person subject to the code who is being interrogated may be entitled to both *Miranda* warnings and Article 31(b) warnings, depending on the circumstances.

The committee changed the titles of subsections (c)(2) and (c)(3) to "Fifth Amendment Right to Counsel" and "Sixth Amendment Right to Counsel" respectively because practitioners are more familiar with those terms. In previous editions, the subsections did not expressly state which right was implicated. Although the rights were clear from the text of the former rules, the new titles will allow practitioners to quickly find the desired rule.

Subsection (c)(3) is entitled "Sixth Amendment Right to Counsel" even though the protections of subsection (c)(3) exceed the constitutional minimal standard established by the Sixth Amendment as interpreted by the Supreme Court in *Montejo v. Louisiana*, 556 U.S. 778 (2009). In *Montejo*, the Court overruled its holding in *Michigan v. Jackson*, 475 U.S. 625 (1986), and found that a defendant's request for counsel at an arraignment or similar proceeding or an appointment of counsel by the court does not give rise to the presumption that a subsequent waiver by the defendant during a police-initiated interrogation is invalid. 556 U.S. at 798. In the military system, defense counsel is detailed to a court-martial. R.C.M. 501(b). The accused need not affirmatively request counsel. Under the Supreme Court's holding in *Montejo*, the detailing of defense counsel would not bar law enforcement from initiating an interrogation with the accused and seeking a waiver of the right to have counsel present. However, subsection (c)(3) provides more protection than the Supreme Court requires. Under this subsection, if an accused is represented by counsel, either detailed or retained, he or she may not be interrogated without the presence of counsel. This is true even if, during the interrogation, the accused waives his right to have counsel present. If charges have been preferred but counsel has not yet been detailed or retained, the accused may be interrogated if he voluntarily waives his right to have counsel present.

The words "after such request" were added to subsection (c)(2) to elucidate that any statements made prior to a request for counsel are admissible, assuming, of course, that Article 31(b) rights were given. Without that phrase, the rule could be read to indicate

that all statements made during the interview, even those made prior to the request, were inadmissible. This was not the intent of the committee and therefore the change was necessary.

The word "shall" was changed to "will" in subsections (a), (d), and (f) because the committee agreed with the approach of the Advisory Committee on Evidence Rules to minimize the use of "shall" because of the potential disparity in application and interpretation of whether the word is precatory or proscriptive.

In subsection (e)(1), the committee retained the requirement that the accused's waiver of the privilege against self-incrimination and the waiver of the right to counsel must be affirmative. This rule exceeds the minimal constitutional requirement. In *Berghuis v. Thompkins*, 130 S. Ct. 2250 (2010), the defendant remained mostly silent during a three-hour interrogation and never verbally stated that he wanted to invoke his rights to counsel and to remain silent. The Supreme Court held that the prosecution did not need to show that the defendant expressly waived his rights, and that an implicit waiver is sufficient. *Berghuis*, 130 S. Ct. at 2261. Despite the Supreme Court's holding, under this rule, in order for a waiver to be valid, the accused or suspect must actually take affirmative action to waive his rights. The committee recognizes that this rule places a greater burden on the government to show that the waiver is valid, and it was the intent of the committee to provide more protection to the accused or suspect than is required under the *Berghuis* holding.

In subsection (f)(2), the committee replaced the word "abroad" with "outside of a state, district, commonwealth, territory, or possession of the United States" in order to clearly define where the rule regarding foreign interrogations applies.

The committee also revised this rule for stylistic reasons and to ensure that it addressed admissibility rather than conduct. *See supra*, General Provisions Analysis. In doing so, the committee did not intend to change any result in any ruling on evidence admissibility.

Rule 306 Statements by one of several accused

Rule 306 is taken from the Para. 140 *b* of the 1969 Manual and states the holding of *Bruton v. United States*, 391 U.S. 123 (1968). The remainder of the associated material in the Manual is primarily concerned with the co-conspirator's exception to the hearsay rule and has been superseded by adoption of the Federal Rules of Evidence. *See* Rule 801.

When it is impossible to effectively delete all references to a co-accused, alternative steps must be taken to protect the co-accused. This may include the granting of a severance.

The Committee was aware of the Supreme Court's decision in *Parker v. Randolph*, 442 U.S. 62 (1979) dealing with interlocking confessions. In view of the lack of a consensus in *Parker*, however, the Committee determined that the case did not provide a sufficiently precise basis for drafting a rule, and decided instead to apply *Bruton* to interlocking confessions.

Rule 311 Evidence obtained from unlawful searches and seizures

Rules 311–317 express the manner in which the Fourth Amendment to the Constitution of the United States applies to trials by court-martial, *Cf. Parker v. Levy*, 417 U.S. 733 (1974).

(a) *General rule.* Rule 311(a) restates the basic exclusionary rule for evidence obtained from an unlawful search or seizure and is taken generally from Para. 152 of the 1969 Manual although much of the language of Para. 152 has been deleted for purposes of both clarity and brevity. The Rule requires suppression of derivative as well as primary evidence and follows the 1969 Manual rule by expressly limiting exclusion of evidence to that resulting from unlawful searches and seizures involving governmental activity. Those persons whose actions may thus give rise to exclusion are listed in Rule 311(c) and are taken generally from Para. 152 with some expansion for purposes of clarity. Rule 311 recognizes that discovery of evidence may be so unrelated to an unlawful search or seizure as to escape exclusion because it was not "obtained as a result" of that search or seizure.

The Rule recognizes that searches and seizures are distinct acts the legality of which must be determined independently. Although a seizure will usually be unlawful if it follows an unlawful search, a seizure may be unlawful even if preceded by a lawful search. Thus, adequate cause to seize may be distinct from legality of the search or observations which preceded it. Note in this respect Rule 316(d)(4)(C), Plain View.

(1) *Objection.* Rule 311(a)(1) requires that a motion to suppress or, as appropriate, an objection be made before evidence can be suppressed. Absent such motion or objection, the issue is waived. Rule 311(i).

(2) *Adequate interest.* Rule 311(a)(2) represents a complete redrafting of the standing requirements found in Para. 152 of the 1969 Manual. The Committee viewed the Supreme Court decision in *Rakas v. Illinois*, 439 U.S. 128 (1978), as substantially modifying the Manual language. Indeed, the very use of the term "standing" was considered obsolete by a majority of the Committee. The Rule distinguishes between searches and seizure. To have sufficient interest to challenge a search, a person must have "a reasonable expectation of privacy in the person, place, or property searched." "Reasonable expectation of privacy" was used in lieu of "legitimate expectation of privacy," often used in *Rakas, supra*, as the Committee believed the two expressions to be identical. The Committee also considered that the expression "reasonable expectation" has a more settled meaning. Unlike the case of a search, an individual must have an interest distinct from an expectation of privacy to challenge a seizure. When a seizure is involved rather than a search the only invasion of one's rights is the removal of the property in question. Thus, there must be some recognizable right to the property seized. Consequently, the Rule requires a "legitimate interest in the property or evidence seized." This will normally mean some form of possessory interest. Adequate interest to challenge a seizure does not *per se* give adequate interest to challenge a prior search that may have resulted in the seizure.

The Rule also recognizes an accused's rights to challenge a search or seizure when the right to do so would exist under the Constitution. Among other reasons, this provision was included because of the Supreme Court's decision in *Jones v. United States*, 302 U.S. 257 (1960), which created what has been termed the "automatic standing rule." The viability of *Jones* after *Rakas* and other cases is unclear, and the Rule will apply *Jones* only to the extent that *Jones* is constitutionally mandated.

1986 Amendment: The words "including seizures of the person" were added to expressly apply the exclusionary rule to unlawful apprehensions and arrests, that is, seizures of the person.

Procedures governing apprehensions and arrests are contained in R.C.M. 302. *See also* Mil. R. Evid. 316(c).

(b) *Exceptions:* Rule 311(b) states the holding of *Walder v. United States*, 347 U.S. 62 (1954), and restates with minor change the rule as found in Para. 152 of the 1969 Manual.

1986 Amendment: Rule 311(b)(2) was added to incorporate the "inevitable discovery" exception to the exclusionary rule of *Nix v. Williams*, 467 U.S. 431 (1984). There is authority for the proposition that this exception applies to the primary evidence tainted by an illegal search or seizure, as well as to evidence derived secondarily from a prior illegal search or seizure. *United States v. Romero*, 692 F.2d 699 (10th Cir. 1982), *cited with approval in Nix v. Williams, supra*, 467 U.S. 431, n.2. *See also United States v. Kozak*, 12 M.J. 389 (C.M.A. 1982); *United States v. Yandell*, 13 M.J. 616 (A.F.C.M.R. 1982). *Contra, United States v. Ward*, 19 M.J. 505 (A.F.C.M.R. 1984). There is also authority for the proposition that the prosecution must demonstrate that the lawful means which made discovery inevitable were possessed by the investigative authority and were being actively pursued prior to the occurrence of the illegal conduct which results in discovery of the evidence (*United States v. Satterfield*, 743 F.2d 827, 846 (11th Cir. 1984)).

As a logical extension of the holdings in *Nix* and *United States v. Kozak, supra*, the leading military case, the inevitable discovery exception should also apply to evidence derived from apprehensions and arrests determined to be illegal under R.C.M. 302 (*State v. Nagel*, 308 N.W.2d 539 (N.D. 1981) (alternative holding)). The prosecution may prove that, notwithstanding the illegality of the apprehension or arrest, evidence derived therefrom is admissible under the inevitable discovery exception.

Rule 311(b)(3) was added in 1986 to incorporate the "good faith" exception to the exclusionary rule based on *United States v. Leon*, 468 U.S. 897 (1984) and *Massachusetts v. Sheppard*, 468 U.S. 981 (1984). The exception applies to search warrants and authorizations to search or seize issued by competent civilian authority, military judges, military magistrates, and commanders. The test for determining whether the applicant acted in good faith is whether a reasonably well-trained law enforcement officer would have known the search or seizure was illegal despite the authorization. In *Leon* and *Sheppard*, the applicant's good faith was enhanced by their prior consultation with attorneys.

The rationale articulated in *Leon* and *Sheppard* that the deterrence basis of the exclusionary rule does not apply to magistrates extends with equal force to search or seizure authorizations issued by commanders who are neutral and detached, as defined in *United States v. Ezell*, 6 M.J. 307 (C.M.A. 1979). The United States Court of Military Appeals demonstrated in *United States v. Stuckey*, 10 M.J. 347 (C.M.A. 1981), that commanders cannot be equated constitutionally to magistrates. As a result, commanders' authorizations may be closely scrutinized for evidence of neutrality in deciding whether this exception will apply. In a particular case, evidence that the commander received the advice of a judge advocate prior to authorizing the search or seizure may be an important consideration. Other considerations may include those enumerated in *Ezell* and: the level of command of the authorizing commander; whether the commander had training in the rules relating to search and seizure; whether the rule governing the search or seizure being litigated was clear; whether the evidence supporting the authorization was given under oath; whether the authorization was reduced to writing; and whether the defect in the authorization was one of form or substance.

As a logical extension of the holdings in *Leon* and *Sheppard*, the good faith exception also applies to evidence derived from apprehensions and arrests which are effected pursuant to an authorization or warrant, but which are subsequently determined to have been defective under R.C.M. 302 (*United States v. Mahoney*, 712 F.2d 956 (5th Cir. 1983); *United States v. Beck*, 729 F.2d 1329 (11th Cir. 1984)). The authorization or warrant must, however, meet the conditions set forth in Rule 311(b)(3).

It is intended that the good faith exception will apply to both primary and derivative evidence.

(c) *Nature of search or seizure.* Rule 311(c) defines "unlawful" searches and seizures and makes it clear that the treatment of a search or seizure varies depending on the status of the individual or group conducting the search or seizure.

(1) *Military personnel.* Rule 311(c)(1) generally restates prior law. A violation of a military regulation alone will not require exclusion of any resulting evidence. However, a violation of such a regulation that gives rise to a reasonable expectation of privacy may require exclusion. *Compare United States v. Dillard*, 8 M.J. 213 (C.M.A. 1980), with *United States v. Caceres*, 440 U.S. 741 (1979).

(2) *Other officials.* Rule 311(c)(2) requires that the legality of a search or seizure performed by officials of the United States, of the District of Columbia, or of a state, commonwealth, or possession or political subdivision thereof, be determined by the principles of law applied by the United States district courts when resolving the legality of such a search or seizure.

(3) *Officials of a foreign government or their agents.* This provision is taken in part from *United States v. Jordan*, 1 M.J. 334 (C.M.A. 1976). After careful analysis, a majority of the Committee concluded that portion of the *Jordan* opinion which purported to require that such foreign searches be shown to have complied with foreign law is dicta and lacks any specific legal authority to support it. Further the Committee noted the fact that most foreign nations lack any law of search and seizure and that in some cases, *e.g.*, Germany, such law as may exist is purely theoretical and not subject to determination. The *Jordan* requirement thus unduly complicates trial without supplying any protection to the accused. Consequently, the Rule omits the requirement in favor of a basic due process test. In determining which version of the various due process phrasings to utilize, a majority of the Committee chose to use the language found in Para. 150 *b* of the 1969 Manual rather than the language found in *Jordan* (which requires that the evidence not shock the conscience of the court) believing the Manual language is more appropriate to the circumstances involved.

Rule 311(c) also indicates that persons who are present at a foreign search or seizure conducted in a foreign nation have "not participated in" that search or seizure due either to their mere presence or because of any actions taken to mitigate possible damage to property or person. The Rule thus clarifies *United States v. Jordan*, 1 M.J. 334 (C.M.A. 1976) which stated that the Fourth Amendment would be applicable to searches and seizures conducted abroad by foreign police when United States personnel participate in them. The Court's intent in *Jordan* was to prevent American authorities from sidestepping Constitutional protections by using foreign personnel to conduct a search or seizure that

would have been unlawful if conducted by Americans. This intention is safeguarded by the Rule, which applies the Rules and the Fourth Amendment when military personnel or their agents conduct, instigate, or participate in a search or seizure. The Rule only clarifies the circumstances in which a United States official will be deemed to have participated in a foreign search or seizure. This follows dicta in *United States v. Jones*, 6 M.J. 226, 230 (C.M.A. 1979), which would require an "element of causation," rather than mere presence. It seems apparent that an American servicemember is far more likely to be well served by United States presence— which might mitigate foreign conduct— than by its absence. Further, international treaties frequently require United States cooperation with foreign law enforcement. Thus, the Rule serves all purposes by prohibiting conduct by United States officials which might improperly support a search or seizure which would be unlawful if conducted in the United States while protecting both the accused and international relations.

The Rule also permits use of United States personnel as interpreters viewing such action as a neutral activity normally of potential advantage to the accused. Similarly the Rule permits personnel to take steps to protect the person or property of the accused because such actions are clearly in the best interests of the accused.

(d) *Motion to suppress and objections.* Rule 311(d) provides for challenging evidence obtained as a result of an allegedly unlawful search or seizure. The procedure, normally that of a motion to suppress, is intended with a small difference in the disclosure requirements to duplicate that required by Rule 304(d) for confessions and admissions, the Analysis of which is equally applicable here.

Rule 311(d)(1) differs from Rule 304(c)(1) in that it is applicable only to evidence that the prosecution intends to offer against the accused. The broader disclosure provision for statements by the accused was considered unnecessary. Like Rule 304(d)(2)(C), Rule 311(d)(2)(C) provides expressly for derivative evidence disclosure of which is not mandatory as it may be unclear to the prosecution exactly what is derivative of a search or seizure. The Rule thus clarifies the situation.

(e) *Burden of proof.* Rule 311(e) requires that a preponderance of the evidence standard be used in determining search and seizure questions. *Lego v. Twomey*, 404 U.S. 477 (1972). Where the validity of a consent to search or seize is involved, a higher standard of "clear and convincing," is applied by Rule 314(e). This restates prior law.

February 1986 Amendment: Subparagraphs (e)(1) and (2) were amended to state the burden of proof for the inevitable discovery and good faith exceptions to the exclusionary rule, as prescribed in *Nix v. Williams*, 467 U.S. 431 (1984) and *United States v. Leon*, 468 U.S. 897 (1984), respectively.

1993 Amendment: The amendment to Mil. R. Evid. 311(e)(2) was made to conform Rule 311 to the rule of *New York v. Harris*, 495 U.S. 14 (1990). The purpose behind the exclusion of derivative evidence found during the course of an unlawful apprehension in a dwelling is to protect the physical integrity of the dwelling not to protect suspects from subsequent lawful police interrogation. *See id.* A suspect's subsequent statement made at another location that is the product of lawful police interrogation is not the fruit of the unlawful apprehension. The amendment also contains language added to reflect the "good faith" exception to the exclusionary role set forth in *United States v. Leon,* 468 U.S. 897 (1984), and the "inevitable discovery" exception set forth in *Nix v. Williams,* 467 U.S. 431 (1984).

(f) *Defense evidence.* Rule 311(f) restates prior law and makes it clear that although an accused is sheltered from any use at trial of a statement made while challenging a search or seizure, such statement may be used in a subsequent "prosecution for perjury, false swearing or the making of a false official statement."

(g) *Scope of motions and objections challenging probable cause.* Rule 311(g)(2) follows the Supreme Court decision in *Franks v. Delaware,* 422 U.S. 928 (1978), *see also United States v. Turck,* 49 C.M.R. 49, 53 (A.F.C.M.R. 1974), with minor modifications made to adopt the decision to military procedures. Although Franks involved perjured affidavits by police, Rule 311(a) is made applicable to information given by government agents because of the governmental status of members of the armed services. The Rule is not intended to reach misrepresentations made by informants without any official connection.

1995 Amendment: Subsection (g)(2) was amended to clarify that in order for the defense to prevail on an objection or motion under this rule, it must establish, *inter alia,* that the falsity of the evidence was "knowing and intentional" or in reckless disregard for the truth. *Accord Franks v. Delaware,* 438 U.S. 154 (1978).

(h) *Objections to evidence seized unlawfully.* Rule 311(h) is new and is included for reasons of clarity.

(i) *Effect of guilty plea.* Rule 311(i) restates prior law. *See, e.g., United States v. Hamil,* 15 U.S.C.M.A. 110, 35 C.M.R. 82 (1964).

2013 Amendment. The definition of "unlawful" was moved from subsection (c) to subsection (b) so that it immediately precedes the subsection in which the term is first used in the rule. Other subsections were moved so that they generally follow the order in which the issues described in the subsections arise at trial. The committee renumbered the subsections accordingly and titled each subsection to make it easier for the practitioner to find the relevant part of the rule. The committee also subsumed former subsection (d)(2)(c), addressing a motion to suppress derivative evidence, into subsection (d)(1) because a motion to suppress seized evidence must follow the same procedural requirements as a motion to suppress derivative evidence.

The committee also revised this rule for stylistic reasons and to ensure that it addressed admissibility rather than conduct. *See supra,* General Provisions Analysis. In doing so, the committee did not intend to change any result in any ruling on evidence admissibility.

Rule 312 Body views and intrusions

1984 Amendment: "Body" was substituted for "bodily" in the title and where appropriate in text. *See United States v. Armstrong,* 9 M.J. 374, 378 n.5 (C.M.A. 1980).

(a) *General rule.* Rule 312(a) limits all nonconsensual inspections, searches, or seizures by providing standards for examinations of the naked body and bodily intrusions. An inspection, search, or seizure that would be lawful but for noncompliance with this Rule is unlawful within the meaning of Rule 311.

(b) *Visual examination of the body.* Rule 312(b) governs searches and examinations of the naked body and thus controls what has often been loosely termed "strip searches." Rule 312(b) permits

visual examination of the naked body in a wide but finite range of circumstances. In doing so, the Rule strictly distinguishes between visual examination of body cavities and actual intrusion into them. Intrusion is governed by Rule 312(c) and (e). Visual examination of the male genitals is permitted when a visual examination is permissible under this subdivision. Examination of cavities may include, when otherwise proper under the Rule, requiring the individual being viewed to assist in the examination.

Examination of body cavities within the prison setting has been vexatious. *See, e.g., Hanley v. Ward,* 584 F.2d 609 (2d Cir. 1978); *Wolfish v. Levi,* 573 F.2d 118, 131 (2d Cir. 1978), *reversed sub nom Bell v. Wolfish,* 441 U.S. 520 (1979); *Daughtry v. Harris,* 476 F.2d 292 (10th Cir. 1973), *cert. denied,* 414 U.S. 872 (1973); *Frazier v. Ward,* 426 F.Supp. 1354, 1362–67 (N.D.N.Y. 1977); *Hodges v. Klein,* 412 F.Supp. 896 (D.N.J. 1976). Institutional security must be protected while at the same time only privacy intrusions necessary should be imposed on the individual. The problem is particularly acute in this area of inspection of body cavities as such strong social taboos are involved. Rule 312(b)(2) allows examination of body cavities when reasonably necessary to maintain the security of the institution or its personnel. *See Bell v. Wolfish,* 441 U.S. 520 (1979). Examinations likely to be reasonably necessary include examination upon entry or exit from the institution, examination subsequent to a personal visit, or examination pursuant to a reasonably clear indication that the individual is concealing property within a body cavity. *Frazier v. Ward,* 426 F.Supp. 1354 (N.D.N.Y. 1977); *Hodges v. Klein,* 412 F.Supp. 896 (D.N.J. 1976). Great deference should be given to the decisions of the commanders and staff of military confinement facilities. The concerns voiced by the Court of Appeals for the Tenth Circuit in *Daughtry v. Harris,* 476 F.2d 292 (10th Cir. 1973) about escape and related risks are likely to be particularly applicable to military prisoners because of their training in weapons and escape and evasion tactics.

As required throughout Rule 312, examination of body cavities must be accomplished in a reasonable fashion. This incorporates *Rochin v. California,* 342 U.S. 165 (1952), and recognizes society's particularly sensitive attitude in this area. Where possible, examination should be made in private and by members of the same sex as the person being examined.

1984 Amendment: In subsection (b)(2) and (c), "reasonable" replaced "real" before "suspicion." A majority of Circuit Courts of Appeal have adopted a "reasonable suspicion" test over a "real suspicion" test. *See United States v. Klein,* 592 F.2d 909 (5th Cir. 1979); *United States v. Asbury,* 586 F.2d 973 (2d Cir. 1978); *United States v. Wardlaw,* 576 F.2d 932 (1st Cir. 1978); *United States v. Himmelwright,* 551 F.2d 991 (5th Cir.), *cert. denied,* 434 U.S. 902 (1977). *But see United States v. Aman,* 624 F.2d 911 (9th Cir. 1980). In practice, the distinction may be minimal. *But see Perel v. Vanderford,* 547 F.2d 278, 280 n.1 (5th Cir. 1977). However, the real suspicion formulation has been criticized as potentially confusing. *United States v. Asbury, supra* at 976.

(c) *Intrusion into body cavities.* Actual intrusion into body cavities, *e.g.,* the anus and vagina, may represent both a significant invasion of the individual's privacy and a possible risk to the health of the individual. Rule 312(c) allows seizure of property discovered in accordance with Rules 312(b), 312(c)(2), or 316(d)(4)(C) but requires that intrusion into such cavities be accomplished by personnel with appropriate medical qualifications.

The Rule thus does not specifically require that the intrusion be made by a doctor, nurse, or other similar medical personnel although Rule 312(g) allows the Secretary concerned to prescribe who may perform such procedures. It is presumed that an object easily located by sight can normally be easily extracted. The requirements for appropriate medical qualifications, however, recognize that circumstances may require more qualified personnel. This may be particularly true, for example, for extraction of foreign matter from a pregnant woman's vagina. Intrusion should normally be made either by medical personnel or by persons with appropriate medical qualifications who are members of the same sex as the person involved.

The Rule distinguishes between seizure of property previously located and intrusive searches of body cavities by requiring in Rule 312(c)(2) that such searches be made only pursuant to a search warrant or authorization, based upon probable cause, and conducted by persons with appropriate medical qualifications. Exigencies do not permit such searches without warrant or authorization unless Rule 312(f) is applicable. In the absence of express regulations issued by the Secretary concerned pursuant to Rule 312(g), the determination as to which personnel are qualified to conduct an intrusion should be made in accordance with normal procedures of the applicable medical facility.

Recognizing the peculiar needs of confinement facilities and related institutions, *see, e.g., Bell v. Wolfish*, 441 U.S. 520 (1979), Rule 312(c) authorizes body cavity searches without prior search warrant or authorization when there is a "real suspicion that the individual is concealing weapons, contraband, or evidence of crime."

(d) *Extraction of body fluids.* Seizure of fluids from the body may involve self-incrimination questions pursuant to Article 31 of the Uniform Code of Military Justice, and appropriate case law should be consulted prior to involuntary seizure. *See generally* Rule 301(a) and its Analysis. The Committee does not intend an individual's expelled breath to be within the definition of "body fluids."

The 1969 Manual Para. 152 authorization for seizure of bodily fluids when there has been inadequate time to obtain a warrant or authorization has been slightly modified. The prior language that there be "clear indication that evidence of crime will be found and that there is reason to believe that delay will threaten the destruction of evidence" has been modified to authorize such a seizure if there is reason to believe that the delay "could result in the destruction of the evidence." Personnel involuntarily extracting bodily fluids must have appropriate medical qualifications.

Rule 312 does not prohibit compulsory urinalysis, whether random or not, made for appropriate medical purposes, *see* Rule 312(f), and the product of such a procedure if otherwise admissible may be used in evidence at a court-martial.

1984 Amendment: The first word in the caption of subsection (d) was changed from "*Seizure*" to "*Extraction.*" This is consistent with the text of subsection (d) and should avoid possible confusion about the scope of the subsection. Subsection (d) does not apply to compulsory production of body fluids (*e.g.,* being ordered to void urine), but rather to physical extraction of body fluids (e.g., catheterization or withdrawal of blood). *See Murray v. Haldeman*, 16 M.J. 74 (C.M.A. 1983). *See also* Analysis, Mil. R. Evid. 313(b).

(e) *Other intrusive searches.* The intrusive searches governed by

Rule 312(e) will normally involve significant medical procedures including surgery and include any intrusion into the body including x-rays. Applicable civilian cases lack a unified approach to surgical intrusions, *see, e.g., United States v. Crowder*, 513 F.2d 395 (D.C. Cir. 1976); *Adams v. State*, 299 N.E.2d 834 (Ind. 1973); *Creamer v. State*, 299 Ga. 511, 192 S.E.2d 350 (1972), Note, *Search and Seizure: Compelled Surgical Intrusion*, 27 Baylor L. Rev. 305 (1975), and cases cited therein, other than to rule out those intrusions which are clearly health threatening. Rule 312(e) balances the Government's need for evidence with the individual's privacy interest by allowing intrusion into the body of an accused or suspect upon search authorization or warrant when conducted by person with "appropriate medical qualification," and by prohibiting intrusion when it will endanger the health of the individual. This allows, however, considerable flexibility and leaves the ultimate issue to be determined under a due process standard of reasonableness. As the public's interest in obtaining evidence from an individual other than an accused or suspect is substantially less than the person's right to privacy in his or her body, the Rule prohibits the involuntary intrusion altogether if its purpose is to obtain evidence of crime.

(f) *Intrusions for valid medical purposes.* Rule 312(f) makes it clear that the Armed Forces retain their power to ensure the health of their members. A procedure conducted for valid medical purposes may yield admissible evidence. Similarly, Rule 312 does not affect in any way any procedure necessary for diagnostic or treatment purposes.

(g) *Medical qualifications.* Rule 312(g) permits but does not require the Secretaries concerned to prescribe the medical qualifications necessary for persons to conduct the procedures and examinations specified in the Rule.

2013 Amendment. Former subsection (b)(2) was moved to a discussion paragraph because it addresses the conduct of the examiner rather than the admissibility of evidence. *See supra*, General Provisions Analysis. Failure to comply with the requirement that a person of the same sex conduct the examination does not make the examination unlawful or the evidence inadmissible.

In subsection (c)(2)(a), the words "clear indication" were replaced with "probable cause" because the committee determined that "clear indication" was not well-understood by practitioners nor properly defined in case law, whereas "probable cause" is a recognized Fourth Amendment term. The use of the phrase "clear indication" likely came from the Supreme Court's holding in *Schmerber v. California*, 384 U.S. 757 (1966). In that case, the Court stated: "In the absence of a clear indication that in fact such evidence will be found, these fundamental human interests require law officers to suffer the risk that such evidence may disappear unless there is an immediate search." *Schmerber*, 384 U.S. at 770. However, in *United States v. Montoya de Hernandez*, 473 U.S. 531 (1985), the Supreme Court clarified that it did not intend to create a separate Fourth Amendment standard when it used the words "clear indication." *Montoya de Hernandez*, 473 U.S. at 540 ("[W]e think that the words in *Schmerber* were used to indicate the necessity for particularized suspicion that the evidence sought might be found within the body of the individual, rather than as enunciating still a third Fourth Amendment threshold between "reasonable suspicion" and "probable cause"). The committee decided that the appropriate standard for a search under subsection (c)(2)(a) is probable cause. The committee made this decision with the understanding that doing so raises the level of suspicion required to perform a search under this subsection beyond that which was required in previous versions of this rule. The same reasoning applies to the change in subsection (d), where the committee also replaced the words "clear indication" with "probable cause." This decision is consistent with the Court of Military Appeals' opinion in *United States v. Bickel*, 30 M.J. 277, 279 (C.M.A. 1990) ("We have no doubt as to the constitutionality of such searches and seizures based on probable cause").

In subsection (d), the committee replaced the term "involuntary" with "nonconsensual" for the sake of consistency and uniformity throughout the subsection. The committee did not intend to change the rule in any practical way by using "nonconsensual" in the place of "involuntary."

A discussion paragraph was added following subsection (e) to address a situation in which a person is compelled to ingest a substance in order to locate property within that person's body. This paragraph was previously found in subsection (e), and the committee removed it from the rule itself because it addresses conduct rather than the admissibility of evidence. *See supra*, General Provisions Analysis.

The committee added the last line of subsection (f) to conform the rule to CAAF's holding in *United States v. Stevenson*, 66 M.J. 15 (C.A.A.F. 2008). In *Stevenson*, the court held that any additional intrusion, beyond what is necessary for medical treatment, is a search within the meaning of the Fourth Amendment. *Id.* at 18 ("the Supreme Court has not adopted a *de minimis* exception to the Fourth Amendment's warrant requirement"). The committee moved the first line of former subsection (f) to a discussion paragraph because it addresses conduct rather than the admissibility of evidence, and is therefore more appropriately addressed in a discussion paragraph. *See supra*, General Provisions Analysis.

The committee also revised this rule for stylistic reasons and to ensure that it addressed admissibility rather than conduct. *See supra*, General Provisions Analysis. In doing so, the committee did not intend to change any result in any ruling on evidence admissibility.

Rule 313 Inspections and inventories in the armed forces

Although inspections have long been recognized as being necessary and legitimate exercises of a commander's powers and responsibilities, *see, e.g., United States v. Gebhart*, 10 U.S.C.M.A. 606, 610 n.2, 28 C.M.R. 172, 176 n.2 (1959), the 1969 Manual for Courts-Martial omitted discussion of inspections except to note that the Para. 152 restrictions on seizures were not applicable to "administrative inspections." The reason for the omission is likely that military inspections *per se* have traditionally been considered administrative in nature and free of probable cause requirements. *Cf. Frank v. Maryland*, 359 U.S. 360 (1959). Inspections that have been utilized as subterfuge searches have been condemned. *See, e.g., United States v. Lange*, 15 U.S.C.M.A. 486, 35 C.M.R. 458 (1965). Recent decisions of the United States Court of Military Appeals have attempted, generally without success, to define "inspection" for Fourth Amendment evidentiary purposes, *see, e.g., United States v. Thomas*, 1 M.J. 397 (C.M.A. 1976) (three separate opinions), and have been concerned with the intent, scope, and method of conducting inspections. *See e.g., United States v. Harris*, 5 M.J. 44 (C.M.A. 1978).

(a) *General rule.*

Rule 313 codifies the law of military inspections and inventories. Traditional terms used to describe various inspections, *e.g.* "shakedown inspection" or "gate search," have been abandoned as being conducive to confusion.

Rule 313 does not govern inspections or inventories not conducted within the armed forces. These civilian procedures must be evaluated under Rule 311(c)(2). In general, this means that such inspections and inventories need only be permissible under the Fourth Amendment in order to yield evidence admissible at a court-martial.

Seizure of property located pursuant to a proper inspection or inventory must meet the requirements of Rule 316.

(b) *Inspections.* Rule 313(b) defines "inspection" as an "examination. . . conducted as an incident of command the primary purpose of which is to determine and to ensure the security, military fitness, or good order and discipline of the unit, organization, installation, vessel, aircraft, or vehicle." Thus, an inspection is conducted for the primary function of ensuring mission readiness, and is a function of the inherent duties and responsibilities of those in the military chain of command. Because inspections are intended to discover, correct, and deter conditions detrimental to military efficiency and safety, they must be considered as a condition precedent to the existence of any effective armed force and inherent in the very concept of a military unit. Inspections as a general legal concept have their constitutional origins in the very provisions of the Constitution which authorize the armed forces of the United States. Explicit authorization for inspections has thus been viewed in the past as unnecessary, but in light of the present ambiguous state of the law (*see, e.g. United States v. Thomas, supra; United States v. Roberts*, 2 M.J. 31 (C.M.A. 1976)), such authorization appears desirable. Rule 313 is thus, in addition to its status as a rule of evidence authorized by Congress under Article 36, an express Presidential authorization for inspections with such authorization being grounded in the President's powers as Commander-in-Chief.

The interrelationship of inspections and the Fourth Amendment is complex. The constitutionality of inspections is apparent and has been well recognized; *see e.g., United States v. Gebhart*, 10 C.M.A. 606, 610 n.2, 28 C.M.R. 172, 176 n.2. (1959). There are three distinct rationales which support the constitutionality of inspections.

The first such rationale is that inspections are not technically "searches"within the meaning of the Fourth Amendment. *Cf. Air Pollution Variance Board v. Western Alfalfa Corps*, 416 U.S. 861 (1974); *Hester v. United States*, 265 U.S. 57 (1924). The intent of the framers, the language of the amendment itself, and the nature of military life render the application of the Fourth Amendment to a normal inspection questionable. As the Supreme Court has often recognized, the "Military is, [by necessity, a specialized society separate from civilian society.]" *Brown v. Glines*, 444 U.S. 348, 354 (1980) *citing Parker v. Levy*, 417 U.S. 733, 734 (1974). As the Supreme Court noted in *Glines, supra*, military personnel must be ready to perform their duty whenever the occasion arises. To ensure that they always are capable of performing their mission promptly and reliably, the military services "must insist upon a respect for duty and a discipline without counterpart in civilian life." 444 U.S. at 354 (citations omitted). An effective armed force without inspections is impossible— a fact amply illustrated by the unfettered right to inspect vested in commanders throughout the armed forces of the world. As recognized in *Glines, supra*, and *Greer v. Spock*, 424 U.S. 828 (1976), the *way* that the Bill of Rights applies to military personnel may be different from the way it applies to civilians. Consequently, although the Fourth Amendment is applicable to members of the armed forces, inspections may well not be "searches" within the meaning of the Fourth Amendment by reason of history, necessity, and constitutional interpretation. If they are "searches," they are surely reasonable ones, and are constitutional on either or both of two rationales.

As recognized by the Supreme Court, highly regulated industries are subject to inspection without warrant, *United States v. Biswell*, 406 U.S. 311 (1972); *Colonnade Catering Corp. v. United States*, 397 U.S. 72 (1970), both because of the necessity for such inspections and because of the "limited threats to. . . justifiable expectation of privacy." *United States v. Biswell, supra*, at 316. The court in *Biswell, supra*, found that regulations of firearms traffic involved "large interests," that "inspection is a crucial part of the regulatory scheme," and that when a firearms dealer enters the business "he does so with the knowledge that his business records, firearms, and ammunition will be subject to effective inspection," 406 U.S. 315, 316. It is clear that inspections within the armed forces are at least as important as regulation of firearms; that without such inspections effective regulation of the armed forces is impossible; and that all personnel entering the armed forces can be presumed to know that the reasonable expectation of privacy within the armed forces is exceedingly limited by comparison with civilian expectations. *See e.g., Committee for G.I. Rights v. Callaway*, 518 F.2d 466 (D.C.C. 1975). Under *Colonnade Catering, supra*, and *Bisell, supra*, inspections are thus reasonable searches and may be made without warrant.

An additional rationale for military inspection is found within the Supreme Court's other administrative inspection cases. *See Marshall v. Barlow's, Inc.*, 436 U.S. 397 (1978); *Camara v. Municipal Court*, 387 U.S. 523 (1967); *See v. City of Seattle*, 387 U.S. 541 (1967). Under these precedents an administrative inspection is constitutionally acceptable for health and safety purposes so long as such an inspection is first authorized by warrant. The warrant involved, however, need not be upon probable cause in the traditional sense, rather the warrant may be issued "if reasonable legislative or administrative standards for conducting an area inspection are satisfied. . ." *Camara, supra*, 387 U.S. at 538. Military inspections are intended for health and safety reasons in a twofold sense: they protect the health and safety of the personnel in peacetime in a fashion somewhat analogous to that which protects the health of those in a civilian environment, and, by ensuring the presence and proper condition of armed forces personnel, equipment, and environment, they protect those personnel from becoming unnecessary casualties in the event of combat. Although *Marshall v. Barlow's Inc., Camara*, and *See, supra*, require warrants, the intent behind the warrant requirement is to ensure that the person whose property is inspected is adequately notified that local law requires inspection, that the person is notified of the limits of the inspection, and that the person is adequately notified that the inspector is acting with proper authority. *Camara v. Municipal Court*, 387 U.S. 523, 532 (1967). Within the armed forces, the warrant requirement is met automatically if an inspection is ordered by a commander, as commanders are empowered to grant warrants. *United States v. Ezell*, 6 M.J. 307 (C.M.A. 1979). More importantly, the concerns voiced by the court are met automatically within the military environment in any event as the rank and assignment of those inspecting and their right to do so are known to all. To the extent that the search warrant requirements are intended to prohibit inspectors from utilizing inspections as subterfuge searches, a normal inspection fully meets the concern, and Rule 313(b) expressly prevents such subterfuges. The fact that an inspection that is primarily administrative in nature may result in a criminal prosecution is unimportant. *Camara v. Municipal Court*, 387 U.S. 523, 530–31 (1967). Indeed, administrative inspections may inherently result in prosecutions because such inspections are often intended to discover health and safety defects the presence of which are criminal offenses. *Id.* at 531. What is important, to the extent that the Fourth Amendment is applicable, is protection from unreasonable violations of privacy. Consequently, Rule 313(b) makes it clear that an otherwise valid inspection is not rendered invalid solely because the inspector has as his or her purpose a *secondary* "purpose of obtaining evidence for use in a trial by court-martial or in other disciplinary proceedings. . ." An examination made, however, with a *primary* purpose of prosecution is no longer an administrative inspection. Inspections are, as has been previously discussed, lawful acceptable measures to ensure the survival of the American armed forces and the accomplishment of their mission. They do not infringe upon the limited reasonable expectation of privacy held by service personnel. It should be noted, however, that it is possible for military personnel to be granted a reasonable expectation of privacy greater than the minimum inherently recognized by the Constitution. An installation commander might, for example, declare a BOQ sacrosanct and off limits to inspections. In such a rare case the reasonable expectation of privacy held by the relevant personnel could prevent or substantially limit the power to inspect under the Rule. *See* Rule 311(c). Such extended expectations of privacy may, however, be negated with adequate notice.

An inspection "may be made 'of the whole or part' of a unit, organization, installation, vessel, aircraft, or vehicle. . . (and is) conducted as an incident of command." Inspections are usually quantitative examinations insofar as they do not normally single out specific individuals or small groups of individuals. There is, however, no requirement that the entirety of a unit or organization be inspected. Unless authority to do so has been withheld by competent superior authority, any individual placed in a command or appropriate supervisory position may inspect the personnel and property within his or her control.

Inspections for contraband such as drugs have posed a major problem. Initially, such inspections were viewed simply as a form of health and welfare inspection, *see, e.g., United States v. Unrue*, 22 C.M.A. 466, 47 C.M.R. 556 (1973). More recently, however, the Court of Military Appeals has tended to view them solely as searches for evidence of crime. *See e.g. United States v. Roberts*, 2 M.J. 31 (C.M.A. 1976); *but see United States v. Harris*, 5 M.J. 44, 58 (C.M.A. 1978). Illicit drugs, like unlawful weapons, represent, however, a potential threat to military efficiency of disastrous proportions. Consequently, it is entirely appropriate to treat inspections intended to rid units of contraband that would adversely affect military fitness as being health and welfare inspections, *see, e.g., Committee for G.I. Rights v. Callaway*, 518 F.2d 466 (D.C.C. 1975), and the Rule does so.

A careful analysis of the applicable case law, military and civilian, easily supports this conclusion. Military cases have long recognized the legitimacy of "health and welfare" inspections and have defined those inspections as examinations intended to ascertain and ensure the readiness of personnel and equipment. *See, e.g., United States v. Gebhart*, 10 C.M.A. 606, 610 n.2, 28 C.M.R. 172, 176 n.2 (1959); "(these) types of searches are not to be confused with inspections of military personnel. . . conducted by a commander in furtherance of the security of his command"; *United States v. Brashears*, 45 C.M.R. 438 (A.C.M.R. 1972), *rev'd on other grounds*, 21 C.M.A. 522, 45 C.M.R. 326 (1972). Among the legitimate intents of a proper inspection is the location and confiscation of unauthorized weapons. *See, e.g., United States v. Grace*, 19 C.M.A. 409, 410, 42 C.M.R. 11, 12 (1970). The justification for this conclusion is clear: unauthorized weapons are a serious danger to the health of military personnel and therefore to mission readiness. Contraband that "would affect adversely the security, military fitness, or good order and discipline" is thus identical with unauthorized weapons insofar as their effects can be predicted. Rule 313(b) authorizes inspections for contraband, and is expressly intended to authorize inspections for unlawful drugs. As recognized by the Court of Military Appeals in *United States v. Unrue*, 22 C.M.A. 466, 469–70, 47 C.M.R. 556, 559–60 (1973), unlawful drugs pose unique problems. If uncontrolled, they may create an "epidemic," 47 C.M.R. at 559. Their use is not only contagious as peer pressure in barracks, aboard ship, and in units, tends to impel the spread of improper drug use, but the effects are known to render units unfit to accomplish their missions. Viewed in this light, it is apparent that inspection for those drugs which would "affect adversely the security, military fitness, or good order and discipline of the command" is a proper administrative intent well within the decisions of the United States Supreme Court. *See, e.g., Camara v. Municipal Court*, 387 U.S. 523 (1967); *United States v. Unrue*, 22 C.M.A. 446, 471, 47 C.M.R. 556, 561 (1973) (Judge Duncan dissenting). This conclusion is buttressed by the fact that members of the military have a diminished expectation of privacy, and that inspections for such contraband are "reasonable" within the meaning of the Fourth Amendment. *See, e.g., Committee for G.I. Rights v. Callaway*, 518 F.2d 466 (D.C.C. 1975). Although there are a number of decisions of the Court of Military Appeals that have called the legality of inspections for unlawful drugs into question, *see United States v. Thomas, supra; United States v. Roberts*, 2 M.J. 31 (C.M.A. 1977), those decisions with their multiple opinions are not dispositive. Particularly important to this conclusion is the opinion of Judge Perry in *United States v. Roberts, supra*. Three significant themes are present in the opinion: lack of express authority for such inspections, the perception that unlawful drugs are merely evidence of crime, and the high risk that inspections may be used for subterfuge searches. The new Rule is intended to resolve these matters fully. The Rule, as part of an express Executive Order, supplies the explicit authorization for inspections then lacking. Secondly, the Rule is intended to make plain the fact that an inspection that has as its object the prevention and correction of conditions harmful to readiness is far more than a hunt for evidence. Indeed, it is the express judgment of the Committee that the uncontrolled use of unlawful drugs within the

armed forces creates a readiness crisis and that continued use of such drugs is totally incompatible with the possibility of effectively fielding military forces capable of accomplishing their assigned mission. Thirdly, Rule 313(b) specifically deals with the subterfuge question in order to prevent improper use of inspections.

Rule 313(b) requires that before an inspection intended "to locate and confiscate unlawful weapons or other contraband, that would affect adversely the. . . command" may take place, there must be either "a reasonable suspicion that such property is present in the command" or the inspection must be "a previously scheduled examination of the command." The former requirement requires that an inspection not previously scheduled be justified by "reasonable suspicion that such property is present in the command." This standard is intentionally minimal and requires only that the person ordering the inspection have a suspicion that is, under the circumstances, reasonable in nature. Probable cause is not required. Under the latter requirement, an inspection shall be scheduled sufficiently far enough in advance as to eliminate any reasonable probability that the inspection is being used as a subterfuge, *i.e.*, that it is being used to search a given individual for evidence of crime when probable cause is lacking. Such scheduling may be made as a matter of date or event. In other words, inspections may be scheduled to take place on any specific date, *e.g.*, a commander may decide on the first of a month to inspect on the 7th, 9th, and 21st, or on the occurrence of a specific event beyond the usual control of the commander, *e.g.*, whenever an alert is ordered, forces are deployed, a ship sails, the stock market reaches a certain level of activity, etc. It should be noted that "previously scheduled" inspections that vest discretion in the inspector are permissible when otherwise lawful. So long as the examination, *e.g.*, an entrance gate inspection, has been previously scheduled, the fact that reasonable exercise of discretion is involved in singling out individuals to be inspected is not improper; such inspection must not be in violation of the Equal Protection clause of the 5th Amendment or be used as a subterfuge intended to allow search of certain specific individuals.

The Rule applies special restrictions to contraband inspections because of the inherent possibility that such inspection may be used as subterfuge searches. Although a lawful inspection may be conducted with a secondary motive to prosecute those found in possession of contraband, the primary motive must be administrative in nature. The Rule recognizes the fact that commanders are ordinarily more concerned with removal of contraband from units—thereby eliminating its negative effects on unit readiness—than with prosecution of those found in possession of it. The fact that possession of contraband is itself unlawful renders the probability that an inspection may be a subterfuge somewhat higher than that for an inspection not intended to locate such material.

An inspection which has as its intent, or one of its intents, in whole or in part, the discovery of contraband, however slight, must comply with the specific requirements set out in the Rule for inspections for contraband. An inspection which does not have such an intent need not so comply and will yield admissible evidence if contraband is found incidentally by the inspection. Contraband is defined as material the possession of which is by its very nature unlawful. Material may be declared to be unlawful by appropriate statute, regulation, or order. For example, if liquor is prohibited aboard ship, a shipboard inspection for liquor must comply with the rules for inspections for contraband.

Before unlawful weapons or other contraband may be the subject of an inspection under Rule 313(b), there must be a determination that "such property would affect adversely the security, military fitness, or good order and discipline of the command." In the event of an adequate defense challenge under Rule 311 to an inspection for contraband, the prosecution must establish by a preponderance that such property would in fact so adversely affect the command. Although the question is an objective one, its resolution depends heavily on factors unique to the personnel or location inspected. If such contraband would adversely affect the ability of the command to complete its assigned mission in any significant way, the burden is met. The nature of the assigned mission is unimportant, for that is a matter within the prerogative of the chain of command only. The expert testimony of those within the chain of command of a given unit is worthy of great weight as the only purpose for permitting such an inspection is to ensure military readiness. The physiological or psychological effects of a given drug on an individual are normally irrelevant except insofar as such evidence is relevant to the question of the user's ability to perform duties without impaired efficiency. As inspections are generally quantitative examinations, the nature and amount of contraband sought is relevant to the question of the government's burden. The existence of five unlawful drug users in an Army division, for example, is unlikely to meet the Rule's test involving adverse effect, but five users in an Army platoon may well do so.

The Rule does not require that personnel to be inspected be given preliminary notice of the inspection although such advance notice may well be desirable as a matter of policy or in the interests, as perhaps in gate inspections, of establishing an alternative basis, such as consent, for the examination.

Rule 313(b) requires that inspections be conducted in a "reasonable fashion." The timing of an inspection and its nature may be of importance. Inspections conducted at a highly unusual time are not inherently unreasonable—especially when a legitimate reason of such timing is present. However, a 0200 inspection, for example, may be unreasonable depending upon the surrounding circumstances.

The Rule expressly permits the use of "any reasonable or natural technological aid." Thus, dogs may be used to detect contraband in an otherwise valid inspection for contraband. This conclusion follows directly from the fact that inspections for contraband conducted in compliance with Rule 313 are lawful. Consequently, the technique of inspection is generally unimportant under the new rules. The Committee did, however, as a matter of policy require that the natural or technological aid be "reasonable."

Rule 313(b) recognizes and affirms the commander's power to conduct administrative examinations which are primarily nonprosecutorial in purpose. Personnel directing inspections for contraband must take special care to ensure that such inspections comply with Rule 313(b) and thus do not constitute improper general searches or subterfuges.

1984 Amendment: Much of the foregoing Analysis was rendered obsolete by amendments made in 1984. The third sentence

of Rule 313(b) was modified and the fourth and sixth sentences are new.

The fourth sentence is new. The Military Rule of Evidence did not previously expressly address *production* of body fluids, perhaps because of *United States v. Ruiz*, 23 U.S.C.M.A. 181, 48 C.M.R. 797 (1974). *Ruiz* was implicitly overruled in *United States v. Armstrong*, 9 M.J. 374 (C.M.A. 1980). Uncertainty concerning the course of the law of inspections may also have contributed to the drafter's silence on the matter. *See United States v. Roberts*, 2 M.J. 31 (C.M.A. 1976); *United States v. Thomas*, 1 M.J. 397 (C.M.A. 1976). Much of the uncertainty in this area was dispelled in *United States v. Middleton*, 10 M.J. 123 (C.M.A. 1981). *See also Murray v. Haldeman*, 16 M.J. 74 (C.M.A. 1983).

Despite the absence in the rules of express authority for compulsory production of body fluids, it apparently was the intent of the drafters to permit such production as part of inspections, relying at least in part on the medical purpose exception in Mil. R. Evid. 312(f). Mil. R. Evid. 312(d) applies only to nonconsensual extraction (*e.g.,* catheterization, drawing blood) of body fluids. This was noted in the Analysis, Mil. R. Evid. 312(d), which went on to state that "compulsory urinalysis, whether random or not, made for appropriate medical purposes, *see* Rule 312(f), and the product of such a procedure if otherwise admissible may be used at a court-martial."

There is considerable overlap between production of body fluid for a medical purpose under Mil. R. Evid. 312(f) and for determining and ensuring military fitness in a unit, organization, installation, vessel, aircraft, or vehicle. Frequently the two purposes are coterminous. Ultimately, the overall health of members of the organization is indivisible from the ability of the organization to perform the mission. To the extent that a "medical purpose" embraces anything relating to the physical or mental state of a person and that person's ability to perform assigned duties, then the two purposes may be identical. Such a construction of "medical purpose" would seem to swallow up the specific rules and limitations in Mil. R. Evid. 312(f), however. Therefore, a distinction may be drawn between a medical purpose—at least to the extent that term is construed to concern primarily the health of the individual—and the goal of ensuring the overall fitness of the organization. For example, it may be appropriate to test—by compulsory production of urine—persons whose duties entail highly dangerous or sensitive duties. The primary purpose of such tests is to ensure that the mission will be performed safely and properly. Preserving the health of the individual is an incident—albeit a very important one—of that purpose. A person whose urine is found to contain dangerous drugs is relieved from duty during gunnery practice, for example, not so much to preserve that person's health as to protect the safety of others. On the other hand, a soldier who is extremely ill may be compelled to produce urine (or even have it extracted) not so much so that soldier can return to duty—although the military has an interest in this—as for that soldier's immediate health needs.

Therefore, Mil. R. Evid. 313(b) provides an independent, although often closely related basis for compulsory production of body fluids, with Mil. R. Evid. 312(f). By expressly providing for both, possible confusion or an unnecessarily narrow construction under Mil. R. Evid. 312(f) will be avoided. Note that all of the requirements of Mil. R. Evid. 313(b) apply to an order to produce body fluids under that rule. This includes the requirement that the inspection be done in a reasonable fashion. This rule does not prohibit, as part of an otherwise lawful inspection, compelling a person to drink a reasonable amount of water in order to facilitate production of a urine sample. *See United States v. Mitchell*, 16 M.J. 654 (N.M.C.M.R. 1983).

The sixth sentence is based on *United States v. Middleton, supra. Middleton* was not decided on the basis of Mil. R. Evid. 313, as the inspection in *Middleton* occurred before the effective date of the Military Rules of Evidence. The Court discussed Mil. R. Evid. 313(b), but "did not now decide on the legality of this Rule (or) bless its application." *United States v. Middleton, supra* at 131. However, the reasoning and the holding in *Middleton* suggest that the former language in Mil. R. Evid. 313(b) may have established unnecessary burdens for the prosecution, yet still have been inadequate to protect against subterfuge inspections, under some circumstances.

The former language allowed an inspection for "unlawful weapons and other contraband when such property would affect adversely the security, military fitness, or good order and discipline of the command and when (1) there is a reasonable suspicion that such property is present in the command or (2) the examination is a previously scheduled examination of the command." This required a case-by-case showing of the adverse effects of the weapons or contraband (including controlled substances) in the particular unit, organization, installation, aircraft, or vehicle examined. *See* Analysis, Mil. R. Evid. 313(b). In addition, the examination had to be based on a reasonable suspicion such items were present, or be previously scheduled.

Middleton upheld an inspection which had as one of its purposes the discovery of contraband—i.e., drugs. Significantly, there is no indication in *Middleton* that a specific showing of the adverse effects of such contraband in the unit or organization is necessary. The court expressly recognized (*see United States v. Middleton, supra* at 129; *cf. United States v. Trottier* , 9 M.J. 337 (C.M.A. 1980)) the adverse effect of drugs on the ability of the armed services to perform the mission without requiring evidence on the point. Indeed, it may generally be assumed that if it is illegal to possess an item under a statute or lawful regulation, the adverse effect of such item on security, military fitness, or good order and discipline is established by such illegality, without requiring the commander to personally analyze its effects on a case-by-case basis and the submission of evidence at trial. The defense may challenge the constitutionality of the statute or the legality of the regulation (*cf. United States v. Wilson*, 12 U.S.C.M.A. 165, 30 C.M.R. 165 (1961); *United States v. Nation*, 9 U.S.C.M.A. 724, 26 C.M.R. 504 (1958)) but this burden falls on the defense. Thus, this part of the former test is deleted as unnecessary. Note, however, that it may be necessary to demonstrate a valid military purpose to inspect for some noncontraband items. *See United States v. Brown*, 12 M.J. 420 (C.M.A. 1982).

Middleton upheld broad authority in the commander to inspect for contraband, as well as other things, "when adequate safeguards are present which assure that the 'inspection' was really intended to determine and assure the readiness of the unit inspected, rather than merely to provide a subterfuge for avoiding limitations that apply to a search and seizure in a criminal investigation." As noted above, the Court in *Middleton* expressly re-

served judgment whether Mil. R. Evid. 313(b) as then written satisfied this test.

The two prongs of the second part of the former test were intended to prevent subterfuge. However, they did not necessarily do so. Indeed, the "reasonable suspicion" test could be read to expressly authorize a subterfuge search. *See, e.g., United States v. Lange*, 15 U.S.C.M.A. 486, 35 C.M.R. 458 (1965). The "previously scheduled" test is an excellent way to prove that an inspection was not directed as the result of a reported offense, and the new formulation so retains it. However, it alone does not ensure absence of prosecutorial motive when specific individuals are singled out, albeit well in advance, for special treatment.

At the same time, the former test could invalidate a genuine inspection which had no prosecutorial purpose. For example, a commander whose unit was suddenly alerted for a special mission might find it necessary, even though the commander had no actual suspicion contraband is present, to promptly inspect for contraband, just to be certain none was present. A commander in such a position should not be prohibited from inspecting.

The new language removes these problems and is more compatible with *Middleton*. It does not establish unnecessary hurdles for the prosecution. A commander may inspect for contraband just as for any other deficiencies, problems, or conditions, without having to show any particular justification for doing so. As the fifth sentence in the rule indicates, any examination made primarily for the purpose of prosecution is not a valid inspection under the rule. The sixth sentence identifies those situations which, objectively, raise a strong likelihood of subterfuge. These situations are based on *United States v. Lange, supra* and *United States v. Hay*, 3 M.J. 654, 655–56 (A.C.M.R. 1977) (*quoted in United States v. Middleton, supra* at 127–28 n.7; *see also United States v. Brown, supra*). "Specific individuals" means persons named or identified on the basis of individual characteristics, rather than by duty assignment or membership in a subdivision of the unit, organization, installation, vessel, aircraft, or vehicle, such as a platoon or squad, or on a random basis. *See United States v. Harris*, 5 M.J. 44 (C.M.A. 1978). The first sentence of subsection (b) makes clear that a part of one of the listed categories may be inspected. *Cf. United States v. King*, 2 M.J. 4 (C.M.A. 1976).

The existence of one or more of the three circumstances identified in the fifth sentence does not mean that the examination is, *per se,* not an inspection. The prosecution may still prove, by clear and convincing evidence, that the purpose of the examination was to determine and ensure security, military fitness, and good order and discipline, and not for the primary purpose of prosecution. For example, when an examination is ordered immediately following a report of a specific offense in the unit, the prosecution might prove the absence of subterfuge by showing that the evidence of the particular offense had already been recovered when the inspection was ordered and that general concern about the welfare of the unit was the motivation for the inspection. Also, if a commander received a report that a highly dangerous item (*e.g.*, an explosive) was present in the command, it might be proved that the commander's concern about safety was the primary purpose for the examination, not prosecution. In the case in which specific individuals are examined, or subjected to more intrusive examinations than others, these indicia of subterfuge might be overcome by proof that these persons were not chosen with a view of prosecution, but on neutral ground or for an independent purpose—*e.g.,* individuals were selected because they were new to the unit and had not been thoroughly examined previously. These examples are not exclusive.

The absence of any of the three circumstances in the fifth sentence, while indicative of a proper inspection, does not necessarily preclude a finding of subterfuge. However, the prosecution need not meet the higher burden of persuasion when the issue is whether the commander's purpose was prosecutorial, in the absence of these circumstances.

The new language provides objective criteria by which to measure a subjective standard, *i.e.,* the commander's purpose. Because the standard is ultimately subjective, however, the objective criteria are not conclusive. Rather they provide concrete and realistic guidance for commanders to use in the exercise of their inspection power, and for judicial authorities to apply in reviewing the exercise of that power.

(c) *Inventories.* Rule 313(c) codifies prior law by recognizing the admissibility of evidence seized via bona fide inventory. The rationale behind this exception to the usual probable cause requirement is that such an inventory is not prosecutorial in nature and is a reasonable intrusion. *See, e.g., South Dakota v. Opperman,* 428 U.S. 364 (1976).

An inventory may not be used as subterfuge search, *United States v. Mossbauer,* 20 C.M.A. 584, 44 C.M.R. 14 (1971), and the basis for an inventory and the procedure utilized may be subject to challenge in any specific case. Inventories of the property of detained individuals have usually been sustained. *See, e.g., United States v. Brashears,* 21 C.M.A. 552, 45 C.M.R. 326 (1972).

The committee does not, however, express an opinion as to the lawful scope of an inventory. *See, e.g., South Dakota v. Opperman,* 428 U.S. 364 (1976), in which the court did not determine the propriety of opening the locked trunk or glove box during the inventory of a properly impounded automobile. Inventories will often be governed by regulation.

2013 Amendment. The definition of "inventory" was added to subsection (c) to further distinguish inventories from inspections. The committee also revised this rule for stylistic reasons and to ensure that it addressed admissibility rather than conduct. *See supra,* General Provisions Analysis. In doing so, the committee did not intend to change any result in any ruling on evidence admissibility.

Rule 314 Searches not requiring probable cause

The list of non-probable cause searches contained within Rule 314 is intended to encompass most of the non-probable cause searches common in the military environment. The term "search" is used in Rule 314 in its broadest non-technical sense. Consequently, a "search" for purposes of Rule 314 may include examinations that are not "searches" within the narrow technical sense of the Fourth Amendment. *See, e.g.,* Rule 314(j).

Insofar as Rule 314 expressly deals with a given type of search, the Rule preempts the area in that the Rule must be followed even should the Supreme Court issue a decision more favorable to the Government. If such a decision involves a non-probable cause search of a *type* not addressed in Rule 314, it will be fully applicable to the Armed Forces under Rule 314(k) unless other authority prohibits such application.

(a) *General Rule.* Rule 314(a) provides that evidence obtained

from a search conducted pursuant to Rule 314 and not in violation of another Rule, *e.g.,* Rule 312, Bodily Views and Intrusions, is admissible when relevant and not otherwise inadmissible.

(b) *Border Searches.* Rule 314(b) recognizes that military personnel may perform border searches when authorized to do so by Congress.

(c) *Searches upon entry to United States installations, aircraft, and vessels abroad.* Rule 314(c) follows the opinion of Chief Judge Fletcher in *United States v. Rivera,* 4 M.J. 215, 216 n.2 (C.M.A. 1978), in which he applied the border search doctrine to entry searches of United States installations or enclaves on foreign soil. The search must be reasonable and its intent, in line with all border searches, must be primarily prophylactic. This authority is additional to any other powers to search or inspect that a commander may hold.

Although Rule 314(c) is similar to Rule 313(b), it is distinct in terms of its legal basis. Consequently, a search performed pursuant to Rule 314(c) need not comply with the burden of proof requirement found in Rule 313(b) for contraband inspections even though the purpose of the 314(c) examination is to prevent introduction of contraband into the installation, aircraft or vessel.

A Rule 314(c) examination must, however, be for a purpose denominated in the rule and must be rationally related to such purpose. A search pursuant to Rule 314(c) is possible only upon entry to the installation, aircraft, or vessel, and an individual who chooses not to enter removes any basis for search pursuant to Rule 314(c). The Rule does not indicate whether discretion may be vested in the person conducting a properly authorized Rule 314(c) search. It was the opinion of members of the Committee, however, that such discretion is proper considering the Rule's underlying basis.

1984 Amendment: Subsection (c) was amended by adding "or exit from" based on *United States v. Alleyne,* 13 M.J. 331 (C.M.A. 1982).

(d) *Searches of government property.* Rule 314(d) restates prior law, *see, e.g., United States v. Weshenfelder,* 20 C.M.A. 416, 43 C.M.R. 256 (1971), and recognizes that personnel normally do not have sufficient interest in government property to have a reasonable expectation of privacy in it. Although the rule could be equally well denominated as a lack of adequate interest, *see,* Rule 311(a)(2), it is more usually expressed as a non-probable cause search. The Rule recognizes that certain government property may take on aspects of private property allowing an individual to develop a reasonable expectation of privacy surrounding it. Wall or floor lockers in living quarters issued for the purpose of storing personal property will normally, although not necessarily, involve a reasonable expectation of privacy. It was the intent of the Committee that such lockers give rise to a rebuttable presumption that they do have an expectation of privacy, and that insofar as other government property is concerned such property gives rise to a rebuttable presumption that such an expectation is absent.

Public property, such as streets, parade grounds, parks, and office buildings rarely if ever involves any limitations upon the ability to search.

(e) *Consent Searches.*

(1) *General rule.* The rule in force before 1980 was found in

Para. 152, MCM, 1969 (Rev.), the relevant sections of which state:

A search of one's person with his freely given consent, or of property with the freely given consent of a person entitled in the situation involved to waive the right to immunity from an unreasonable search, such as an owner, bailee, tenant, or occupant as the case may be under the circumstances [is lawful].

If the justification for using evidence obtained as a result of a search is that there was a freely given consent to the search, that consent must be shown by clear and positive evidence.

Although Rule 314(e) generally restates prior law without substantive change, the language has been recast. The basic rule for consent searches is taken from *Schneckloth v. Bustamonte*, 412 U.S. 218 (1973).

(2) *Who may consent.* The Manual language illustrating when third parties may consent to searches has been omitted as being insufficient and potentially misleading and has been replaced by Rule 314(e)(2). The Rule emphasizes the degree of control that an individual has over property and is intended to deal with circumstances in which third parties may be asked to grant consent. *See, e.g., Frazier v. Cupp*, 394 U.S. 731 (1969); *Stoner v. California*, 376 U.S. 483 (1964); *United States v. Mathis*, 16 C.M.A. 511, 37 C.M.R. 142 (1967). It was the Committee's intent to restate prior law in this provision and not to modify it in any degree. Consequently, whether an individual may grant consent to a search of property not his own is a matter to be determined on a case by case basis.

(3) *Scope of consent.* Rule 314(e)(3) restates prior law. *See, e.g., United States v. Castro*, 23 C.M.A. 166, 48 C.M.R. 782 (1974); *United States v. Cady*, 22 C.M.A. 408, 47 C.M.R. 345 (1973).

(4) *Voluntariness.* Rule 314(e)(3) requires that consent be voluntary to be valid. The second sentence is taken in substance from *Schneckloth v. Bustamonte*, 412 U.S. 218, 248–49 (1973).

The specific inapplicability of Article 31(b) warnings follows *Schneckloth* and complies with *United States v. Morris*, 1 M.J. 352 (C.M.A. 1976) (opinion by Chief Judge Fletcher with Judge Cook concurring in the result). Although not required, such warnings are, however, a valuable indication of a voluntary consent. The Committee does not express an opinion as to whether rights warnings are required prior to obtaining an admissible statement as to ownership or possession of property from a suspect when that admission is obtained via a request for consent to search.

(5) *Burden of proof.* Although not constitutionally required, the burden of proof in Para. 152 of the 1969 Manual for consent searches has been retained in a slightly different form—"clear and convincing" in place of "clear and positive"—on the presumption that the basic nature of the military structure renders consent more suspect than in the civilian community. "Clear and convincing evidence" is intended to create a burden of proof between the preponderance and beyond a reasonable doubt standards. The Rule expressly rejects a different burden for custodial consents. The law is this area evidences substantial confusion stemming initially from language used in *United States v. Justice*, 13 C.M.A. 31, 34, 32 C.M.R. 31, 34 (1962): "It [the burden of proof] is an especially heavy obligation if the accused was in custody. . .," which was taken in turn from a number of civilian federal court decisions. While custody should be a factor resulting in an especially careful scrutiny of the circumstances surrounding

a possible consent, there appears to be no legal or policy reason to require a higher burden of proof.

(f) *Frisks incident to a lawful stop.* Rule 314(f) recognizes a frisk as a lawful search when performed pursuant to a lawful stop. The primary authority for the stop and frisk doctrine is *Terry v. Ohio*, 392 U.S. 1 (1968), and the present Manual lacks any reference to either stops or frisks. Hearsay may be used in deciding to stop and frisk. *See, e.g., Adams v. Williams*, 407 U.S. 143 (1972).

The Rule recognizes the necessity for assisting police or law enforcement personnel in their investigations but specifically does not address the issue of the lawful duration of a stop nor of the nature of the questioning, if any, that may be involuntarily addressed to the individual stopped. *See Brown v. Texas*, 440 U.S. 903 (1979), generally prohibiting such questioning in civilian life. Generally, it would appear that any individual who can be lawfully stopped is likely to be a suspect for the purposes of Article 31(b). Whether identification can be demanded of a military suspect without Article 31(b) warnings is an open question and may be dependent upon whether the identification of the suspect is relevant to the offense possibly involved. *See* Frederic Lederer, *Rights Warnings in the Armed Services*, 72 Mil. L. Rev. 1, 40–41 (1976).

1984 Amendment: Subsection (f)(3) was added based on *Michigan v. Long*, 463 U.S. 1032 (1983).

(g) *Searches incident to a lawful apprehension.* The 1969 Manual rule was found in Para. 152 and stated:

A search conducted as an incident of lawfully apprehending a person, which may include a search of his person, of the clothing he is wearing, and of property which, at time of apprehension, is in his immediate possession or control, or of an area from within which he might gain possession of weapons or destructible evidence; and a search of the place where the apprehension is made [is lawful].

Rule 314(g) restates the principle found within the Manual text but utilizes new and clarifying language. The Rule expressly requires that an apprehension be lawful.

(1) *General Rule.* Rule 314(g)(1) expressly authorizes the search of a person of a lawfully apprehended individual without further justification.

(2) *Search for weapons and destructible evidence.* Rule 314(g)(2) delimits the area that can be searched pursuant to an apprehension and specifies that the purpose of the search is only to locate weapons and destructible evidence. This is a variation of the authority presently in the Manual and is based upon the Supreme Court's decision in *Chimel v. California*, 395 U.S. 752 (1969). It is clear from the Court's decision in *United States v. Chadwick*, 438 U.S. 1 (1977), that the scope of a search pursuant to a lawful apprehension must be limited to those areas which an individual could reasonably reach and utilize. The search of the area within the immediate control of the person apprehended is thus properly viewed as a search based upon necessity—whether one based upon the safety of those persons apprehending or upon the necessity to safeguard evidence. *Chadwick*, holding that police could not search a sealed footlocker pursuant to an arrest, stands for the proposition that the *Chimel* search must be limited by its rationale.

That portion of the 1969 Manual dealing with intrusive body searches has been incorporated into Rule 312. Similarly that portion of the Manual dealing with search incident to hot pursuit of a person has been incorporated into that portion of Rule 315 dealing with exceptions to the need for search warrants or authorizations.

1984 Amendment: Subsection (g)(2) was amended by adding language to clarify the permissible scope of a search incident to apprehension of the occupant of an automobile based on *New York v. Belton*, 453 U.S. 454 (1981). The holding of the Court used the term "automobile" so that word is used in the rule. It is intended that the term "automobile" have the broadest possible meaning.

(3) *Examination for other persons.* Rule 314(g)(3) is intended to protect personnel performing apprehensions. Consequently, it is extremely limited in scope and requires a good faith and reasonable belief that persons may be present who might interfere with the apprehension of individuals. Any search must be directed towards the finding of such persons and not evidence.

An unlawful apprehension of the accused may make any subsequent statement by the accused inadmissible.*Dunaway v. New York*, 442 U.S. 200 (1979).

1994 Amendment. The amendment to Mil. R. Evid. 314(g)(3), based on *Maryland v. Buie*, 494 U.S. 325 (1990), specifies the circumstances permitting the search for other persons and distinguishes between protective sweeps and searches of the attack area.

Subsection (A) permits protective sweeps in the military. The last sentence of this subsection clarifies that an examination under the rule need not be based on probable cause. Rather, this subsection adopts the standard articulated in *Terry v. Ohio*, 392 U.S. 1 (1968) and *Michigan v. Long*, 463 U.S. 1032 (1983). As such, there must be articulable facts that, taken together with the rational inferences from those facts, would warrant a reasonably prudent officer in believing the area harbors individuals posing a danger to those at the site of apprehension. The previous language referring to those "who might interfere" was deleted to conform to the standards set forth in *Buie*. An examination under this rule is limited to a cursory visual inspection of those places in which a person might be hiding.

A new subsection (B) was also added as a result of *Buie, supra*. The amendment clarifies that apprehending officials may examine the "attack area" for persons who might pose a danger to apprehending officials. *See Buie*, 494 U.S. at 334. The attack area is that area immediately adjoining the place of apprehension from which an attack could be immediately launched. This amendment makes it clear that apprehending officials do not need any suspicion to examine the attack area.

(h) *Searches within jails, confinement facilities, or similar facilities.* Personnel confined in a military confinement facility or housed in a facility serving a generally similar purpose will normally yield any normal Fourth Amendment protections to the reasonable needs of the facility. *See United States v. Maglito*, 20 C.M.A. 456, 43 C.M.R. 296 (1971). *See also* Rule 312.

(i) *Emergency searches to save life or for related purpose.* This type of search is not found within the 1969 Manual provision but is in accord with prevailing civilian and military case law. *See United States v. Yarborough*, 50 C.M.R. 149, 155 (A.F.C.M.R. 1975). Such a search must be conducted in good faith and may not be a subterfuge in order to circumvent an individual's Fourth Amendment protections.

(j) *Searches of open fields or woodlands.* This type of search is

taken from 1969 Manual paragraph 152. Originally recognized in *Hester v. United States*, 265 U.S. 57 (1924), this doctrine was revived by the Supreme Court in *Air Pollution Variance Board v. Western Alfalfa Corp.*, 416 U.S. 861 (1974). Arguably, such a search is not a search within the meaning of the Fourth Amendment. In *Hester*, Mr. Justice Holmes simply concluded that "the special protection accorded by the 4th Amendment to the people in their [persons, houses, papers, and effects] is not extended to the open fields." 265 U.S. at 59. In relying on *Hester*, the Court in *Air Pollution Variance Board* noted that it was "not advised that he [the air pollution investigator] was on premises from which the public was excluded." 416 U.S. at 865. This suggests that the doctrine of open fields is subject to the caveat that a reasonable expectation of privacy may result in application of the Fourth Amendment to open fields.

(k) *Other searches.* Rule 314(k) recognizes that searches of a *type* not specified within the Rule but proper under the Constitution are also lawful.

2013 Amendment. Language was added to subsection (a) to elucidate that the rules as written afford at least the minimal amount of protection required under the Constitution as applied to servicemembers. If new case law is developed after the publication of these rules which raises the minimal constitutional standards for the admissibility of evidence, that standard will apply to evidence admissibility, rather than the standard established under these rules.

In subsection (c), the committee intentionally limited the ability of a commander to search persons or property upon entry or exit from the installation alone, rather than anywhere on the installation, despite the indication of some courts in dicta that security personnel can search a personally owned vehicle anywhere on a military installation based on no suspicion at all. *See, e.g., United States v. Rogers*, 549 F.2d 490, 493 (8th Cir. 1973). Allowing suspicionless searches anywhere on a military installation too drastically narrows an individual's privacy interest. Although individuals certainly have a diminished expectation of privacy when they are on a military installation, they do not forgo their privacy interest completely.

The committee added a discussion section below subsection (c) to address searches conducted contrary to a treaty or agreement. That material was previously located in subsection (c) and was moved to the discussion because it addresses conduct rather than the admissibility of evidence. *See supra,* General Provisions Analysis.

Although not explicitly stated in subsection (e)(2), the committee intends that the Supreme Court's holding in *Georgia v. Randolph* apply to this subsection. 547 U.S. 103 (2006) (holding that a warrantless search was unreasonable if a physically present co-tenant expressly refused to give consent to search, even if another co-tenant had given consent).

In subsection (f)(2), the phrase "reasonably believed" was changed to "reasonably suspected" to align with recent case law and to alleviate any confusion that "reasonably believed" established a higher level of suspicion required to conduct a stop-and-frisk than required by the Supreme Court in *Terry v. Ohio*, 392 U.S. 1 (1968). The "reasonably suspected" standard conforms to the language of the Supreme Court in *Arizona v. Johnson*, 555 U.S. 323, 328 (2009), in which the Court stated: "To justify a patdown of the driver or a passenger during a traffic stop, however, just as in the case of a pedestrian reasonably suspected of criminal activity, the police must harbor reasonable suspicion that the person subjected to the frisk is Armed and dangerous." The committee intends that this standard, and no higher, be required before an individual can be stopped and frisked under this subsection. Additionally, the committee added a discussion paragraph following this subsection to further expound on the nature and scope of the search, based on case law. *See, e.g., Terry*, 392 U.S. at 30-31; *Pennsylvania v. Mimms*, 434 U.S. 106 (1977).

In subsection (f)(3), the committee changed the phrase "reasonable belief" to "reasonable suspicion" for the same reasons discussed above. The committee added the discussion section to provide more guidance on the nature and scope of the search, based on case law. *See, e.g., Michigan v. Long*, 463 U.S. 1032, 1049 (1983) ("the search of the passenger compartment of an automobile, limited to those areas in which a weapon may be placed or hidden, is permissible if the police officer possesses a reasonable belief based on 'specific and articulable facts which, taken together with the rational inferences from those facts, reasonably warrant' the officers in believing that the suspect is dangerous and the suspect may gain immediate control of weapons"); *Pennsylvania v. Mimms*, 434 U.S. 106 (1977) (there was no Fourth Amendment violation when the driver was ordered out of the car after a valid traffic stop but without any suspicion that he was Armed and dangerous because "what is at most a mere inconvenience cannot prevail when balanced against legitimate concerns for the officer's safety"); *Maryland v. Wilson*, 519 U.S. 408 (1997) (extending the holding in *Mimms* to passengers as well as drivers).

The committee moved the language from former subsection (g)(2), describing the search of an automobile incident to a lawful arrest of an occupant, to the discussion paragraph immediately following the subsection because it addresses conduct rather than the admissibility of evidence. *See supra*, General Provisions Analysis. The discussion section is based on the Supreme Court's holding in *Arizona v. Gant*, 556 U.S. 332 (2009) ("Police may search a vehicle incident to a recent occupant's arrest only if the arrestee is within reaching distance of the passenger compartment at the time of the search or it is reasonable to believe the vehicle contains evidence of the offense of arrest").

The committee also revised this rule for stylistic reasons and to ensure that it addressed admissibility rather than conduct. *See supra*, General Provisions Analysis. In doing so, the committee did not intend to change any result in any ruling on evidence admissibility.

Rule 315 Probable cause searches

(a) *General Rule—* Rule 315 states that evidence obtained pursuant to the Rule is admissible when relevant and not otherwise admissible under the Rules.

(b) *Definitions.*

(1) *Authorization to search.* Rule 315(b)(1) defines an "authorization to search" as an express permission to search issued by proper military authority whether commander or judge. As such, it replaces the term "search warrant" which is used in the Rules only when referring to a permission to search given by proper civilian authority. The change in terminology reflects the unique nature of the armed forces and of the role played by commanders.

(2) *Search warrant.* The expression "search warrant" refers only to the authority to search issued by proper civilian authority.

(c) *Scope of authorization.* Rule 315(c) is taken generally from Para. 152(1)–(3) of the 1969 Manual except that military jurisdiction to search upon military installations or in military aircraft, vessels, or vehicles has been clarified. Although civilians and civilian institutions on military installations are subject to search pursuant to a proper search authorization, the effect of any applicable federal statute or regulation must be considered. *E.g.*, The Right to Financial Privacy Act of 1978, 12 U.S.C. §§ 3401–3422, and DOD Directive 5400.12 (Obtaining Information From Financial Institutions).

Rule 315(c)(4) is a modification of prior law. Subdivision (c)(4)(A) is intended to ensure cooperation between Department of Defense agencies and other government agencies by requiring prior consent to DOD searches involving such other agencies. Although Rule 315(c)(4)(B) follows the 1969 Manual in permitting searches of "other property in a foreign country" to be authorized pursuant to subdivision (d), subdivision (c) requires that all applicable treaties be complied with or that prior concurrence with an appropriate representative of the foreign nation be obtained if no treaty or agreement exists. The Rule is intended to foster cooperation with host nations and compliance with all existing international agreements. The rule does not require specific approval by foreign authority of each search (unless, of course, applicable treaty requires such approval); rather the Rule permits prior blanket or categorical approvals. Because Rule 315(c)(4) is designed to govern intragovernmental and international relationships rather than relationships between the United States and its citizens, a violation of these provisions does not render a search unlawful.

(d) *Power to authorize.* Rule 315(d) grants power to authorize searches to impartial individuals of the included classifications. The closing portion of the subdivision clarifies the decision of the Court of Military Appeals in *United States v. Ezell*, 6 M.J. 307 (C.M.A. 1979), by stating that the mere presence of an authorizing officer at a search does not deprive the individual of an otherwise neutral character. This is in conformity with the decision of the United States Supreme Court in *Lo-Ji Sales v. New York*, 442 U.S. 319 (1979), from which the first portion of the language has been taken. The subdivision also recognizes the propriety of a commander granting a search authorization after taking a pretrial action equivalent to that which may be taken by a federal district judge. For example, a commander might authorize use of a drug detector dog, an action arguably similar to the granting of wiretap order by a federal judge, without necessarily depriving himself or herself of the ability to later issue a search authorization. The question would be whether the commander has acted in the first instance in an impartial judicial capacity.

(1) *Commander.* Rule 315(d)(1) restates the prior rule by recognizing the power of commanders to issue search authorizations upon probable cause. The Rule explicitly allows non-officers serving in a position designated by the Secretary concerned as a position of command to issue search authorizations. If a non-officer assumes command of a unit, vessel, or aircraft, and the command position is one recognized by regulations issued by the Secretary concerned, *e.g.*, command of a company, squadron,

vessel, or aircraft, the non-officer commander is empowered to grant search authorizations under this subdivision whether the assumption of command is pursuant to express appointment or devolution of command. The power to do so is thus a function of position rather than rank.

The Rule also allows a person serving as officer-in-charge or in a position designated by the Secretary as a position analogous to an officer-in-charge to grant search authorizations. The term "officer-in-charge" is statutorily defined, Article 1(4), as pertaining only to the Navy, Coast Guard, and Marine Corps, and the change will allow the Army and Air Force to establish an analogous position should they desire to do so in which case the power to authorize searches would exist although such individuals would not be "officers-in-charge" as that term is used in the U.C.M.J.

(2) *Delegee.* Former subsection (2), which purported to allow delegation of the authority to authorize searches, was deleted in 1984, based on *United States v. Kalscheuer*, 11 M.J. 373 (C.M.A. 1981). Subsection (3) was renumbered as subsection (2).

(3) *Military judge.* Rule 315(d)(2) permits military judges to issue search authorizations when authorized to do so by the Secretary concerned. MILITARY MAGISTRATES MAY ALSO BE EMPOWERED TO GRANT SEARCH AUTHORIZATIONS. This recognizes the practice now in use in the Army but makes such practice discretionary with the specific Service involved.

(e) *Power to search.* Rule 315(e) specifically denominates those persons who may conduct or authorize a search upon probable cause either pursuant to a search authorization or when such an authorization is not required for reasons of exigencies. The Rule recognizes, for example, that all officers and non-commissioned officers have inherent power to perform a probable cause search without obtaining of a search authorization under the circumstances set forth in Rule 315(g). The expression "criminal investigator" within Rule 315(e) includes members of the Army Criminal Investigation Command, the Marine Corps Criminal Investigation Division, the Naval Criminal Investigative Service, the Air Force Office of Special Investigations, and Coast Guard Investigative Service.

(f) *Basis for search authorizations.* Rule 315(f) requires that probable cause be present before a search can be conducted under the Rule and utilizes the basic definition of probable cause found in 1969 Manual Para. 152.

For reasons of clarity the Rule sets forth a simple and general test to be used in all probable cause determinations: probable cause can exist only if the authorizing individual has a "reasonable belief that the information giving rise to the intent to search is believable and has a factual basis." This test is taken from the "two prong test" of *Aguilar v. Texas*, 378 U.S. 108 (1964), which was incorporated in Para. 152 of the 1969 Manual. The Rule expands the test beyond the hearsay and informant area. The "factual basis" requirement is satisfied when an individual reasonably concludes that the information, if reliable, adequately apprises the individual that the property in question is what it is alleged to be and is where it is alleged to be. Information is "believable" when an individual reasonably concludes that it is sufficiently reliable to be believed.

The twin test of "believability" and "basis in fact" must be met in all probable cause situations. The method of application of the test will differ, however, depending upon circumstances. The following examples are illustrative:

(1) An individual making a probable cause determination who observes an incident first hand is only required to determine if the observation is reliable and that the property is likely to be what it appears to be.

For example, an officer who believes that she sees an individual in possession of heroin must first conclude that the observation was reliable (*i.e.*, if her eyesight was adequate—should glasses have been worn—and if there was sufficient time for adequate observation) and that she has sufficient knowledge and experience to be able to reasonably believe that the substance in question was in fact heroin.

(2) An individual making a probable cause determination who relies upon the in person report of an informant must determine both that the informant is believable and that the property observed is likely to be what the observer believes it to be. The determining individual may rely upon the demeanor of the informant in order to determine whether the observer is believable. An individual known to have a "clean record" and no bias against the individual to be affected by the search is likely to be credible.

(3) An individual making a probable cause determination who relies upon the report of an informant not present before the authorizing individual must determine both that the informant is credible and that the property observed is likely to be what the informant believed it to be. The determining individual may utilize one or more of the following factors, among others, in order to determine whether the informant is believable:

(A) *Prior record as a reliable informant.* Has the informant given information in the past which proved to be accurate?

(B) *Corroborating detail.* Has enough detail of the informant's information been verified to imply that the remainder can reasonably be presumed to be accurate?

(C) *Statement against interest.* Is the information given by the informant sufficiently adverse to the fiscal or penal interest of the informant to imply that the information may reasonably be presumed to be accurate?

(D) *Good citizen.* Is the character of the informant, as known by the individual making the probable cause determination, such as to make it reasonable to presume that the information is accurate?

Mere allegations may not be relied upon. For example, an individual may not reasonably conclude that an informant is reliable simply because the informant is so named by a law enforcement agent. The individual making the probable cause determination must be supplied with specific details of the informant's past actions to allow that individual to personally and reasonably conclude that the informant is reliable.

Information transmitted through law enforcement or command channels is presumed to have been reliably transmitted. This presumption may be rebutted by an affirmative showing that the information was transmitted with intentional error.

The Rule permits a search authorization to be issued based upon information transmitted by telephone or other means of communication.

The Rule also permits the Secretaries concerned to impose

additional procedural requirements for the issuance of search authorizations.

1984 Amendment: The second sentence of subsection (f)(1) was deleted based on *Illinois v. Gates,* 462 U.S.213 (1983), which overturned the mandatory two-prong test of *Aguilar v. Texas, supra.* Although the second sentence may be technically compatible with *Gates,* it could be construed as requiring strict application of the standards of *Aguilar.* The former language remains good advice for those deciding the existence of probable cause, especially for uncorroborated tips, but is not an exclusive test. *See also Massachusetts v. Upton,* 466 U.S. 767 (1984).

(g) *Exigencies.* Rule 315(g) restates prior law and delimits those circumstances in which a search warrant or authorization is unnecessary despite the ordinary requirement for one. In all such cases probable cause is required.

Rule 315(g)(1) deals with the case in which the time necessary to obtain a proper authorization would threaten the destruction or concealment of the property or evidence sought.

Rule 315(g)(2) recognizes that military necessity may make it tactically impossible to attempt to communicate with a person who could grant a search authorization. Should a nuclear submarine on radio silence, for example, lack a proper authorizing individual (perhaps for reasons of disqualification), no search could be conducted if the Rule were otherwise unless the ship broke radio silence and imperiled the vessel or its mission. Under the Rule this would constitute an "exigency." "Military operational necessity" includes similar necessity incident to the Coast Guard's performance of its maritime police mission.

The Rule also recognizes in subdivision (g)(3) the "automobile exception" created by the Supreme Court. *See, e.g., United States v. Chadwick,* 433 U.S. 1 (1977); *South Dakota v. Opperman,* 428 U.S. 364 (1976); *Texas v. White,* 423 U.S. 67 (1975), and, subject to the constraints of the Constitution, the Manual, or the Rules, applies it to all vehicles. While the exception will thus apply to vessels and aircraft as well as to automobiles, trucks, *et al,* it must be applied with great care. In view of the Supreme Court's reasoning that vehicles are both mobile and involve a diminished expectation of privacy, the larger a vehicle is, the more unlikely it is that the exception will apply. The exception has no application to government vehicles as they may be searched without formal warrant or authorization under Rule 314(d).

1984 Amendment: The last sentence of subsection (g) was amended by deleting "presumed to be." The former language could be construed to permit the accused to prove that the vehicle was in fact inoperable (that is, to rebut the presumption of operability) thereby negating the exception, even though a reasonable person would have believed the vehicle inoperable. The fact of inoperability is irrelevant; the test is whether the official(s) searching knew or should have known that the vehicle was inoperable.

(h) *Execution.* Rule 314(h)(1) provides for service of a search warrant or search authorization upon a person whose property is to be searched when possible. Noncompliance with the Rule does not, however, result in exclusion of the evidence. Similarly, Rule 314(h)(2) provides for the inventory of seized property and provisions of a copy of the inventory to the person from whom the property was seized. Noncompliance with the subdivision does not, however, make the search or seizure unlawful. Under Rule 315(h)(3) compliance with foreign law is required when execut-

ing a search authorization outside the United States, but noncompliance does not trigger the exclusionary rule.

2013 Amendment. Former subsection (h) was moved so that it immediately follows subsection (a). It was changed to a discussion paragraph because it generally applies to the entire rule, rather than any particular subsection and also because it addresses conduct rather than the admissibility of evidence. *See supra,* General Provisions Analysis.

In subsection (b), the committee changed the term "authorization to search" to "search authorization" to align it with the term more commonly used by practitioners and law enforcement. The committee moved former subsection (c)(4) to a discussion paragraph because it addresses conduct rather than the admissibility of evidence. *See supra,* General Provisions Analysis.

The committee moved the second sentence in former subsection (d)(2) to subsection (d) to elucidate that its content applies to both commanders under subsection (d)(1) and military judges or magistrates under subsection (d)(2). The committee did so in reliance on CAAF's decision in *United States v. Huntzinger,* 69 M.J. 1 (C.A.A.F. 2010), which held that a commander is not *per se* disqualified from authorizing a search under this rule even if he has participated in investigative activities in furtherance of his command responsibilities.

The committee moved former subsection (h)(4), addressing the execution of search warrants, to subsection (e), now entitled "Who May Search," so that it was co-located with the subsection discussing the execution of search authorizations.

In subsection (f)(2), the word "shall" was changed to "will" because the committee agreed with the approach of the Advisory Committee on Evidence Rules to minimize the use of words such as "shall" and "should" because of the potential disparity in application and interpretation of whether the word is precatory or proscriptive. In doing so, the committee did not intend to change any result in any ruling on evidence admissibility.

Subsection (g) was revised to include a definition of exigency rather than to provide examples that may not encompass the wide range of situations where exigency might apply. The definition is derived from Supreme Court jurisprudence. *See Kentucky v. King,* 131 S. Ct. 1849 (2011). The committee retained the language concerning military operational necessity as an exigent circumstance because this rule may be applied to a unique military context where it might be difficult to communicate with a person authorized to issue a search authorization. *See, e.g., United States v. Rivera,* 10 M.J. 55 (C.M.A. 1980) (noting that exigency might exist because of difficulties in communicating with an authorizing official, although the facts of that case did not support such a conclusion). The committee intends that nothing in this rule would prohibit a law enforcement officer from entering a private residence without a warrant to protect the individuals inside from harm, as that is not a search under the Fourth Amendment. *See, e.g., Brigham City v. Stuart,* 547 U.S. 398 (2006) (holding that, regardless of their subjective motives, police officers were justified in entering a home without a warrant, under exigent circumstances exception to warrant requirement, as they had an objectively reasonable basis for believing that an occupant was seriously injured or imminently threatened with injury).

The committee also revised this rule for stylistic reasons and to ensure that it addressed admissibility rather than conduct. *See supra,* General Provisions Analysis. In doing so, the committee did not intend to change any result in any ruling on evidence admissibility.

Rule 316 Seizures

(a) *General Rule.* Rule 316(a) provides that evidence obtained pursuant to the Rule is admissible when relevant and not otherwise inadmissible under the Rules. Rule 316 recognizes that searches are distinct from seizures. Although rare, a seizure need not be proceeded by a search. Property may, for example, be seized after being located pursuant to plain view, *see* subdivision (d)(4)(C). Consequently, the propriety of a seizure must be considered independently of any preceding search.

(b) *Seizures of property.* Rule 316(b) defines probable cause in the same fashion as defined by Rule 315 for probable cause searches. *See* the Analysis of Rule 315(f)(2). The justifications for seizing property are taken from 1969 Manual Para. 152. Their number has, however, been reduced for reasons of brevity. No distinction is made between "evidence of crime" and "instrumentalities or fruits of crime." Similarly, the proceeds of crime are also "evidence of crime."

1984 Amendment: The second sentence of subsection (b) was deleted based on *Illinois v. Gates*, 462 U.S. 213 (1983). *See* Analysis, Mil. R. Evid. 315(f)(1), *supra.*

(c) *Apprehension.* Apprehensions are, of course, seizures of the person and unlawful apprehensions may be challenged as an unlawful seizure. *See, e.g., Dunaway v. New York*, 442 U.S. 200 (1979); *United States v. Texidor-Perez*, 7 M.J. 356 (C.M.A. 1979).

(d) *Seizure of property or evidence.*

(1) *Abandoned property.* Rule 316(d) restates prior law, not addressed specifically by the 1969 Manual chapter, by providing that abandoned property may be seized by anyone at any time.

(2) *Consent.* Rule 316(d)(2) permits seizure of property with appropriate consent pursuant to Rule 314(e). The prosecution must demonstrate a voluntary consent by clear and convincing evidence.

(3) *Government property.* Rule 316(d)(3) permits seizure of government property without probable cause unless the person to whom the property is issued or assigned has a reasonable expectation of privacy therein at the time of seizure. In this regard, note Rule 314(d) and its analysis.

(4) *Other property.* Rule 316(d)(4) provides for seizure of property or evidence not otherwise addressed by the Rule. There must be justification to exercise control over the property. Although property may have been lawfully located, it may not be seized for use at trial unless there is a reasonable belief that the property is of a type discussed in Rule 316(b). Because the Rule is inapplicable to seizures unconnected with law enforcement, it does not limit the seizure of property for a valid administrative purpose such as safety.

Property or evidence may be seized upon probable cause when seizure is authorized or directed by a search warrant or authorization, Rule 316(d)(4)(A); when exigent circumstances pursuant to Rule 315(g) permit proceeding without such a warrant or authorization; or when the property or evidence is in plain view or smell, Rule 316(d)(4)(C).

Although most plain view seizures are inadvertent, there is no necessity that a plain view discovery be inadvertent—notwith-

standing dicta, in some court cases; *see Coolidge v. New Hampshire*, 403 U.S. 443 (1971). The Rule allows a seizure pursuant to probable cause when made as a result of plain view. The language used in Rule 316(d)(4)(C) is taken from the ALI MODEL CODE OF PREARRAIGNMENT PROCEDURES § 260.6 (1975). The Rule requires that the observation making up the alleged plain view be "reasonable." Whether intentional observation from outside a window, via flashlight or binocular, for example, is observation in a "reasonable fashion" is a question to be considered on a case by case basis. Whether a person may properly enter upon private property in order to effect a seizure of matter located via plain view is not resolved by the Rule and is left to future case development.

1984 Amendment: Subsection (d)(5) was added based on *United States v. Place*, 462 U.S. 696 (1983).

(e) *Power to seize.* Rule 316(e) conforms with Rule 315(e) and has its origin in Para. 19, MCM, 1969 (Rev.).

2013 Amendment. In subsection (a), the committee added the word "reasonable" to align the rule with the language found in the Fourth Amendment of the U.S. Constitution and Mil. R. Evid. 314 and 315.

In subsection (c)(5)(C), the committee intends that the term "reasonable fashion" include all action by law enforcement that the Supreme Court has established as lawful in its plain view doctrine. *See, e.g., Arizona v. Hicks*, 480 U.S. 321, 324-25 (1987) (holding that there was no search when an officer merely recorded serial numbers that he saw on a piece of stereo equipment, but that the officer did conduct a search when he moved the equipment to access serial numbers on the bottom of the turntable); *United States v. Lee*, 274 U.S. 559, 563 (1927) (use of a searchlight does not constitute a Fourth Amendment violation). It is not the committee's intent to establish a stricter definition of plain view than that required by the Constitution, as interpreted by the Supreme Court. An officer may seize the item only if his conduct satisfies the three-part test prescribed by the Supreme Court: (1) he does not violate the Fourth Amendment by arriving at the place where the evidence could be plainly viewed; (2) its incriminating character is "readily apparent"; and (3) he has a lawful right of access to the object itself. *Horton v. California*, 496 U.S. 128, 136-37 (1990).

The committee also revised this rule for stylistic reasons and to ensure that it addressed admissibility rather than conduct. *See supra*, General Provisions Analysis. In doing so, the committee did not intend to change any result in any ruling on evidence admissibility.

Rule 317 Interception of wire and oral communication

(a) *General Rule.* The area of interception of wire and oral communications is unusually complex and fluid. At present, the area is governed by the Fourth Amendment, applicable federal statute, DOD directive, and regulations prescribed by the Service Secretaries. In view of this situation, it is preferable to refrain from codification and to vest authority for the area primarily in the Department of Defense or Secretary concerned. Rule 317(c) thus prohibits interception of wire and oral communications for law enforcement purposes by members of the armed forces except as authorized by 18 U.S.C. § 2516, Rule 317(b), and when applicable, by regulations issued by the Secretary of Defense or the

Secretary concerned. Rule 317(a), however, specifically requires exclusion of evidence resulting form noncompliance with Rule 317(c) only when exclusion is required by the Constitution or by an applicable statute. Insofar as a violation of a regulation is concerned, *compare United States v. Dillard,* 8 M.J. 213 (C.M.A. 1980) with *United States v. Caceres,* 440 U.S. 741 (1979).

(b) *Authorization for Judicial Applications in the United States.* Rule 317(b) is intended to clarify the scope of 18 U.S.C. § 2516 by expressly recognizing the Attorney General's authority to authorize applications to a federal court by the Department of Defense, Department of Homeland Security, or the military departments for authority to intercept wire or oral communications.

(c) *Regulations.* Rule 317(c) requires interception of wire or oral communications in the United States be first authorized by statute, *see* Rule 317(b), and interceptions abroad by appropriate regulations. *See* the Analysis to Rule 317(a), *supra.* The Committee intends 317(c) to limit only in interceptions that are non consensual under Chapter 119 of Title 18 of the United States Code.

2013 Amendment. The committee moved former subsections (b) and (c)(3) to a discussion paragraph because they address conduct rather than the admissibility of evidence. *See supra,* General Provisions Analysis.

The committee also revised this rule for stylistic reasons but in doing so did not intend to change any result in any ruling on evidence admissibility.

Rule 321 Eyewitness identification

(a) *General Rule*

(1) *Admissibility.* The first sentence of Rule 321(a)(1) is the basic rule of admissibility of eyewitness identification and provides that evidence of a relevant out-of-court identification is admissible when otherwise admissible under the Rules. The intent of the provision is to allow any relevant out-of-court identification without any need to comply with the condition precedent such as in-court identification, significant change from the prior rule as found in Para. 153 *a,* MCM, 1969 (Rev.).

The language "if such testimony is otherwise admissible under these rules" is primarily intended to ensure compliance with the hearsay rule. *See* Rule 802. It should be noted that Rule 801(d)(1)(C) states that a statement of "identification of a person made after perceiving the person" is not hearsay when "the declarant testifies at the trial or hearing and is subject to cross-examination concerning the statement." An eyewitness identification normally will be admissible if the declarant testifies. The Rule's statement, "the witness making the identification and any person who has observed the previous identification may testify concerning it," is not an express exception authorizing the witness to testify to an out-of-court identification notwithstanding the hearsay rule, rather it is simply an indication that in appropriate circumstances, *see* Rules 803 and 804, a witness to an out-of-court identification may testify concerning it.

The last sentence of subdivision (a)(1) is intended to clarify procedure by emphasizing that an in-court identification may be bolstered by an out-of-court identification notwithstanding the fact that the in-court identification has not been attacked.

(2) *Exclusionary rule.* Rule 321(a)(2) provides the basic exclu-

sionary rule for eyewitness identification testimony. The substance of the Rule is taken from prior Manual paragraph 153 *a* as modified by the new procedure for suppression motions. *See* Rules 304 and 311. Subdivision (a)(2)(A) provides that evidence of an identification will be excluded if it was obtained as a result of an "unlawful identification process conducted by the United States or other domestic authorities" while subdivision (a)(2)(B) excludes evidence of an identification if exclusion would be required by the due process clause of the Fifth Amendment to the Constitution. Under the burden of proof, subdivision (d)(2), an identification is not inadmissible if the prosecution proves by a preponderance of the evidence that the identification process was not so unnecessarily suggestive, in light of the totality of the circumstances, as to create a very substantial likelihood of irreparable mistaken identity. It is the unreliability of the evidence which is determinative. *Manson v. Brathwaite,* 432 U.S. 98 (1977). "United States or other domestic authorities" includes military personnel.

Although it is clear that an unlawful identification may taint a later identification, it is unclear at present whether an unlawful identification requires suppression of evidence other than identification of the accused. Consequently, the Rule requires exclusion of nonidentification derivative evidence only when the Constitution would so require.

(b) *Definition of "unlawful."*

(1) *Lineups and other identification processes.* Rule 321(b) defines "unlawful lineup or other identification processes." When such a procedure is conducted by persons subject to the Uniform Code of Military Justice or their agents, it will be unlawful if it is "unnecessarily suggestive or otherwise in violation of the due process clause of the Fifth Amendment of the Constitution of the United States as applied to members of the armed forces." The expression "unnecessarily suggestive" itself is a technical one and refers to an identification that is in violation of the due process clause because it is unreliable. *See Manson v. Brathwaite, supra; Stovall v. Denno,* 338 U.S. 292 (1967); *Neil v. Biggers,* 409 U.S. 188 (1972). *See also Foster v. California,* 394 U.S. 440 (1969). An identification is not unnecessarily suggestive in violation of the due process clause if the identification process was not so unnecessarily suggestive, in light of the totality of the circumstances, as to create a very substantial likelihood of irreparable mistaken identity. *See Manson v. Brathwaite, supra,* and subdivision (d)(2).

Subdivision (1)(A) differs from subdivision (1)(B) only in that it recognizes that the Constitution may apply differently to members of the armed forces than it does to civilians.

Rule 321(b)(1) is applicable to all forms of identification processes including showups and lineups.

1984 Amendment: Subsections (b)(1) and (d)(2) were modified to make clear that the test for admissibility of an out-of-court identification is reliability. *See Manson v. Brathwaite, supra.* This was apparently the intent of the drafters of the former rule. *See* Analysis, Mil. R. Evid. 321. The language actually used in subsection (b)(1) and (d)(2) was subject to a different interpretation, however. *See* S. Salzburg, L. Schinasi, and D. Schlueter, MILITARY RULES OF EVIDENCE MANUAL at 165–167 (1981); Richard Gasperini, *Eyewitness Identification Under the Military Rules of Evidence,* 1980 Army Law. 42, at 42.

In determining whether an identification is reliable, the military judge should weigh all the circumstances, including: the opportunity of the witness to view the accused at the time of the offense; the degree of attention paid by the witness; the accuracy of any prior descriptions of the accused by the witness; the level of certainty shown by the witness in the identification; and the time between the crime and the confrontation. Against these factors should be weighed the corrupting effect of a suggestive and unnecessary identification. *See Manson v. Brathwaite, supra; Neil v. Biggers, supra.*

Note that the modification of subsection (b)(1) eliminates the distinction between identification processes conducted by persons subject to the code and other officials. Because the test is the reliability of the identification, and not a prophylactic standard, there is no basis to distinguish between identification processes conducted by each group. *See Manson v. Brathwaite, supra.*

(2) *Lineups: right to counsel.* Rule 321(b)(2) deals only with lineups. The Rule does declare that a lineup is "unlawful" if it is conducted in violation of the right to counsel. Like Rule 305 and 311, Rule 321(b)(2) distinguishes between lineups conducted by persons subject to the Uniform Code of Military Justice or their agents and those conducted by others.

Subdivision (b)(2)(A) is the basic right to counsel for personnel participating in military lineups. A lineup participant is entitled to counsel only if that participant is in pretrial restraint (pretrial arrest, restriction, or confinement) under paragraph 20 of the Manual or has had charges preferred against him or her. Mere apprehension or temporary detention does not trigger the right to counsel under the Rule. This portion of the Rule substantially changes military law and adapts the Supreme Court's decision in *Kirby v. Illinois*, 406 U.S. 682, 689 (1972) (holding that the right to counsel attached only when "adversary judicial criminal proceedings" have been initiated or "the government has committed itself to prosecute") to unique military criminal procedure. *See also* Rule 305(d)(1)(B).

Note that *interrogation* of a suspect will require rights warnings, perhaps including a warning of a right to counsel, even if counsel is unnecessary under Rule 321. *See* Rule 305.

As previously noted, the Rule does not define "lineup" and recourse to case law is necessary. Intentional exposure of the suspect to one or more individuals for purpose of identification is likely to be a lineup, *Stovall v. Denno*, 388 U.S. 293, 297 (1967), although in rare cases of emergency (*e.g.,* a dying victim) such an identification may be considered a permissible "showup" rather than a "lineup." Truly accidental confrontations between victims and suspects leading to an identification by the victim are not generally considered "lineups"; *cf. United State ex rel Ragazzin v. Brierley*, 321 F.Supp. 440 (W.D. Pa. 1970). Photolineart identifications are not "lineups" for purposes of the right to counsel. *United States v. Ash*, 413 U.S. 300, 301 n.2 (1973). If a photolineart identification is used, however, the photographs employed should be preserved for use at trial in the event that the defense should claim that the identification was "unnecessarily suggestive." *See subdivision* (b)(1) *supra.*

A lineup participant who is entitled to counsel is entitled to only one lawyer under the Rule and is specifically entitled to free military counsel without regard to the indigency or lack thereof of the participant. No right to civilian counsel or military counsel of the participant's own selection exists under the Rule. *United States v. Wade*, 388 U.S. 218, n.27 (1967). A lineup participant

may waive any applicable right to counsel so long as the participant is aware of the right to counsel and the waiver is made "freely, knowingly, and intelligently." Normally a warning of the right to counsel will be necessary for the prosecution to prove an adequate waiver should the defense adequately challenge the waiver. *See, e.g., United States v. Avers*, 426 F.2d 524 (2d Cir. 1970). *See also* Model Rules for Law Enforcement, Eye Witness Identification, Rule 404 (1974) cited in E. IMWINKELRIED, P. GIANNELLI, F. GILLIGAN, & F. LEDERER, CRIMINAL EVIDENCE 366 (1979).

1984 Amendment: In subsection (b)(2)(A), the words "or law specialist within the meaning of Article 1" were deleted as unnecessary. *See* R.C.M. 103(26).

Subdivision (b)(2)(B) grants a right to counsel at non-military lineups within the United States only when such a right to counsel is recognized by "the principles of law generally recognized in the trial of criminal cases in the United States district courts involving similar lineups." The Rule presumes that an individual participating in a foreign lineup conducted by officials of a foreign nation without American participation has no right to counsel at such a lineup.

(c) *Motions to suppress and objections.* Rule 321(c) is identical in application to Rule 311(d). *See* the Analysis to Rules 304 and 311.

(d) *Burden of proof.* Rule 321(d) makes it clear that when an eyewitness identification is challenged by the defense, the prosecution need reply only to the specific cognizable defense complaint. *See also* Rules 304 and 311. The subdivision distinguishes between defense challenges involving alleged violation of the right to counsel and those involving the alleged unnecessarily suggestive identifications.

(1) *Right to counsel.* Subdivision (d)(1) requires that when an alleged violation of the right to counsel has been raised the prosecution must either demonstrate by preponderance of the evidence that counsel was present or that the right to counsel was waived voluntarily and intelligently. The Rule also declares that if the right to counsel is violated at a lineup that results in an identification of the accused any later identification is considered a result of the prior lineup as a matter of law unless the military judge determines by clear and convincing evidence that the latter identification is not the result of the first lineup. Subdivision (d)(1) is taken in substance from 1969 Manual Para. 153 *a.*

(2) *Unnecessarily suggestive identification.* Rule 321(d)(2) deals with an alleged unnecessarily suggestive identification or with any other alleged violation of due process. The subdivision makes it clear that the prosecution must show, when the defense has raised the issue, that the identification in question was not based upon a preponderance of the evidence, "so unnecessarily suggestive in light of the totality of the circumstances, as to create a very substantial likelihood of irreparable mistaken identity." This rule is taken from the Supreme Court's decisions of *Neil v. Biggers*, 409 U.S. 188 (1972) and *Stovall v. Denno*, 388 U.S. 293 (1967), and unlike subdivision (d)(1), applies to all identification processes whether lineups or not. The Rule recognizes that the nature of the identification process itself may well be critical to the reliability of the identification and provides for exclusion of unreliable evidence regardless of its source. If the prosecution meets its burden, the mere fact that the identification process was

unnecessary or suggestive does not require exclusion of the evidence, *Manson v. Brathwaite, supra.*

If the identification in question is subsequent to an earlier, unnecessarily suggestive identification, the later identification is admissible if the prosecution can show by clear and convincing evidence that the later identification is not the result of the earlier improper examination. This portion of the Rule is consistent both with 1969 Manual Para. 153 *a* and *Kirby v. Illinois*, 406 U.S. 682 (1972).

(e) *Defense evidence.* Rule 321(e) is identical with the analogous provisions in Rules 304 and 311 and generally restates prior law.

(f) *Rulings.* Rule 321(f) is identical with the analogous provisions in Rules 304 and 321 and substantially changes prior law. *See* the Analysis to Rule 304(d)(4).

(g) *Effect of guilty plea.* Rule 321(g) is identical with the analogous provisions in Rules 304 and 311 and restates prior law.

2013 Amendment. The committee revised this rule for stylistic reasons but in doing so did not intend to change any result in any ruling on evidence admissibility.

SECTION IV
RELEVANCY AND ITS LIMITS

Rule 401 Test for Relevant Evidence

The definition of "relevant evidence" found within Rule 401 is taken without change from the Federal Rule and is substantially similar in effect to that used by Para. 137, MCM, 1969 (Rev.). The Rule's definition may be somewhat broader than the 1969 Manual's, as the Rule defines as relevant any evidence that has "any tendency to make the existence of any fact. . . more probable or less probable than it would be without the evidence" while the 1969 Manual defines as "not relevant" evidence "too remote to have any appreciable probative value. . ." To the extent that the 1969 Manual's definition includes considerations of "legal relevance," those considerations are adequately addressed by such other Rules as Rules 403 and 609. *See*, E. IMWINKELRIED, P. GIANNELLI, F. GILLIGAN & F. LEDERER, CRIMINAL EVIDENCE 62–65 (1979) (which, after defining "logical relevance" as involving only probative value, states at 63 that "under the rubric of [legal relevance,] the courts have imposed an additional requirement that the item's probative value outweighs any attendant probative dangers.") The Rule is similar to the 1969 Manual in that it abandons any reference to "materiality" in favor of a single standard of "relevance." Notwithstanding the specific terminology used, however, the concept of materiality survives in the Rule's condition that to be relevant evidence must involve a fact "which is of consequence to the determination of the action."

2013 Amendment. The committee revised this rule for stylistic reasons and to align it with the Federal Rules of Evidence but in doing so did not intend to change any result in any ruling on evidence admissibility.

Rule 402 General Admissibility of Relevant Evidence

Rule 402 is taken without significant change from the Federal Rule. The Federal Rule's language relating to limitations imposed by "the Constitution of the United States, by Act of Congress, by these rules, or by other rules prescribed by the Supreme Court pursuant to statutory authority" has been replaced by material tailored to the unique nature of the Military Rules of Evidence. Rule 402 recognizes that the Constitution may apply somewhat differently to members of the armed forces than to civilians, and the Rule deletes the Federal Rule's reference to "other rules prescribed by the Supreme Court" because such Rules do not apply directly in courts-martial. *See* Rule 101(b)(2).

Rule 402 provides a general standard by which irrelevant evidence is always inadmissible and by which relevant evidence is generally admissible. Qualified admissibility of relevant evidence is required by the limitations in Sections III and V and by such other Rules as 403 and 609 which intentionally utilize matters such as degree of probative value and judicial efficiency in determining whether relevant evidence should be admitted.

Rule 402 is not significantly different in its effect from Para. 137 of the 1969 Manual which it replaces, and procedures used under the 1969 Manual in determining relevance generally remain valid. Offers of proof are encouraged when items of doubtful relevance are proffered, and it remains possible, subject to the discretion of the military judge, to offer evidence "subject to later connection." Use of the latter technique, however, must be made with great care to avoid the possibility of bringing inadmissible evidence before the members of the court.

It should be noted that Rule 402 is potentially the most important of the new rules. Neither the Federal Rules of Evidence nor the Military Rules of Evidence resolve all evidentiary matters; *see* Rule 101(b). When specific authority to resolve an evidentiary issue is absent, Rule 402's clear result is to make relevant evidence admissible.

2013 Amendment. The committee revised this rule for stylistic reasons and to align it with the Federal Rules of Evidence but in doing so did not intend to change any result in any ruling on evidence admissibility.

Rule 403 Exclusion of relevant evidence on grounds of prejudice, confusion or waste of time

Rule 403 is taken without change from the Federal Rule of Evidence. The Rule incorporates the concept often known as "legal relevance," *see* the Analysis to Rule 401, and provides that evidence may be excluded for the reasons stated notwithstanding its character as relevant evidence. The Rule vests the military judge with wide discretion in determining the admissibility of evidence that comes within the Rule.

If a party views specific evidence as being highly prejudicial, it may be possible to stipulate to the evidence and thus avoid its presentation to the court members. *United States v. Grassi*, 602 F.2d 1192 (5th Cir. 1979), a prosecution for interstate transportation of obscene materials, illustrates this point. The defense offered to stipulate that certain films were obscene in order to prevent the jury from viewing the films, but the prosecution declined to join in the stipulation. The trial judge sustained the prosecution's rejection of the stipulation and the Fifth Circuit upheld the judge's decision. In its opinion, however, the Court of Appeals adopted a case by case balancing approach recognizing both the importance of allowing probative evidence to be presented and the use of stipulations as a tool to implement the policies inherent in Rule 403. Insofar as the latter is concerned, the court expressly recognized the power of a Federal district judge to compel the prosecution to accept a defense tendered stipulation.

2013 Amendment. The committee revised this rule for stylistic reasons and to align it with the Federal Rules of Evidence but in doing so did not intend to change any result in any ruling on evidence admissibility.

Rule 404 Character Evidence; Crime or Other Acts

(a) *Character evidence generally.* Rule 404(a) replaces 1969 Manual Para. 138 *f* and is taken without substantial change from the Federal Rule. Rule 404(a) provides, subject to three exceptions, that character evidence is not admissible to show that a person acted in conformity therewith.

Rule 404(a)(1) allows only evidence of a pertinent trait of character of the accused to be offered in evidence by the defense. This is a significant change from Para. 138 *f* of the 1969 Manual which also allows evidence of "general good character" of the accused to be received in order to demonstrate that the accused is less likely to have committed a criminal act. Under the new rule, evidence of general good character is inadmissible because only evidence of a specific trait is acceptable. It is the intention of the Committee, however, to allow the defense to introduce evidence of good military character when that specific trait is pertinent. Evidence of good military character would be admissible, for example, in a prosecution for disobedience of orders. The prosecution may present evidence of a character trait only in rebuttal to receipt in evidence of defense character evidence. This is consistent with prior military law.

Rule 404(a)(2) is taken from the Federal Rule with minor changes. The Federal Rule allows the prosecution to present evidence of the character trait of peacefulness of the victim "in a homicide case to rebut evidence that the victim was the first aggressor." Thus, the Federal Rule allows prosecutorial use of character evidence in a homicide case in which self-defense has been raised. The limitation to homicide cases appeared to be inappropriate and impracticable in the military environment. All too often, assaults involving claims of self-defense take place in the densely populated living quarters common to military life. Whether aboard ship or within barracks, it is considered essential to allow evidence of the character trait of peacefulness of the victim. Otherwise, a substantial risk would exist of allowing unlawful assaults to go undeterred. The Federal Rule's use of the expression "first aggressor" was modified to read "an aggressor," as substantive military law recognizes that even an individual who is properly exercising the right of self-defense may overstep and become an aggressor. The remainder of Rule 404(a)(2) allows the defense to offer evidence of a pertinent trait of character of the victim of a crime and restricts the prosecution to rebuttal of that trait.

Rule 404(a)(3) allows character evidence to be used to impeach or support the credibility of a witness pursuant to Rules 607–609.

2004 Amendment: Subdivision (a) was modified based on the amendment to Fed. R. Evid. 404(a), effective 1 December 2000, and is virtually identical to its Federal Rule counterpart. It is intended to provide a more balanced presentation of character evidence when an accused attacks the victim's character. The accused opens the door to an attack on the same trait of his own character when he attacks an alleged victim's character, giving

the members an opportunity to consider relevant evidence about the accused's propensity to act in a certain manner. The words "if relevant" are added to subdivision (a)(1) to clarify that evidence of an accused's character under this rule must meet the requirements of Mil. R. Evid. 401 and Mil. R. Evid. 403. The drafters believe this addition addresses the unique use of character evidence in courts-martial. The amendment does not permit proof of the accused's character when the accused attacks the alleged victim's character as a witness under Rule 608 or 609, nor does it affect the standards for proof of character by evidence of other sexual behavior or sexual offenses under Rules 412-415.

(b) *Other crimes, wrongs, or acts.* Rule 404(b) is taken without change from the Federal Rule, and is substantially similar to the 1969 Manual rule found in Para. 138 *g*. While providing that evidence of other crimes, wrongs, or acts is not admissible to prove a predisposition to commit a crime, the Rule expressly permits use of such evidence on the merits when relevant to another specific purpose. Rule 404(b) provides examples rather than a list of justifications for admission of evidence of other misconduct. Other justifications, such as the tendency of such evidence to show the accused's consciousness of guilt of the offense charged, expressly permitted in Manual Para. 138 *g*(4), remain effective. Such a purpose would, for example, be an acceptable one. Rule 404(b), like Manual Para. 138 *g*, expressly allows use of evidence of misconduct not amounting to conviction. Like Para. 138 *g*, the Rule does not, however, deal with use of evidence of other misconduct for purposes of impeachment. *See* Rules 608-609. Evidence offered under Rule 404(b) is subject to Rule 403.

1994 Amendment. The amendment to Mil. R. Evid. 404(b) was based on the 1991 amendment to Fed. R. Evid. 404(b). The previous version of Mil. R. Evid. 404(b) was based on the now superseded version of the Federal Rule. This amendment adds the requirement that the prosecution, upon request by the accused, provide reasonable notice in advance of trial, or during trial if the military judge excuses pretrial notice on good cause shown, of the general nature of any such evidence it intends to introduce at trial. Minor technical changes were made to the language of the Federal Rule so that it conforms to military practice.

2013 Amendment. The word "alleged" was added to references to the victim throughout this rule. Stylistic changes were also made to align it with the Federal Rules of Evidence but in doing so did not intend to change any result in any ruling on evidence admissibility.

Rule 405 Methods of proving character

(a) *Reputation or opinion.* Rule 405(a) is taken without change from the Federal Rule. The first portion of the Rule is identical in effect with the prior military rule found in Para. 138 *f*(1) of the 1969 Manual. An individual testifying under the Rule must have an adequate relationship with the community (*see* Rule 405(c)), in the case of reputation, or with the given individual in the case of opinion, in order to testify. The remainder of Rule 405(a) expressly permits inquiry or cross-examination "into relevant specific instances of conduct." This is at variance with prior military practice under which such an inquiry was prohibited. *See* Para. 138 *f*(2), MCM, 1969 (Rev.) (character of the accused). Reputation evidence is exempted from the hearsay rule, Rule 803(21).

(b) *Specific instances of conduct.* Rule 405(b) is taken without significant change from the Federal Rule. Reference to "charge, claim, or defense" has been replaced with "offense or defense" in order to adapt the rule to military procedure and terminology.

(c) *Affidavits.* Rule 405(c) is not found within the Federal Rules and is taken verbatim from material found in Para. 146*b* of the 1969 Manual. Use of affidavits or other written statements is required due to the world wide disposition of the armed forces which makes it difficult if not impossible to obtain witnesses— particularly when the sole testimony of a witness is to be a brief statement relating to the character of the accused. This is particularly important for offenses committed abroad or in a combat zone, in which case the only witnesses likely to be necessary from the United States are those likely to be character witnesses. The Rule exempts statements used under it from the hearsay rule insofar as the mere use of an affidavit or other written statement is subject to that rule.

(d) *Definitions.* Rule 405(d) is not found within the Federal Rules of Evidence and has been included because of the unique nature of the armed forces. The definition of "reputation" is taken generally from 1969 Manual Para. 138 *f*(1) and the definition of "community" is an expansion of that now found in the same paragraph. The definition of "community" has been broadened to add "regardless of size" to indicate that a party may proffer evidence of reputation within any specific military organization, whether a squad, company, division, ship, fleet, group, or wing, branch, or staff corps, for example. Rule 405(d) makes it clear that evidence may be offered of an individual's reputation in either the civilian or military community or both.

2013 Amendment. The committee revised this rule for stylistic reasons and to align it with the Federal Rules of Evidence but in doing so did not intend to change any result in any ruling on evidence admissibility.

Rule 406 Habit; routine practice

Rule 406 is taken without change from the Federal Rule. It is similar in effect to Para. 138*h* of the 1969 Manual. It is the intent of the Committee to include within Rule 406's use of the word, "organization," military organizations regardless of size. *See* Rule 405 and the Analysis to that Rule.

2013 Amendment. The committee revised this rule for stylistic reasons and to align it with the Federal Rules of Evidence but in doing so did not intend to change any result in any ruling on evidence admissibility.

Rule 407 Subsequent remedial measures

Rule 407 is taken from the Federal Rules without change, and has no express equivalent in the 1969 Manual.

2013 Amendment. The committee revised this rule for stylistic reasons and to align it with the Federal Rules of Evidence but in doing so did not intend to change any result in any ruling on evidence admissibility.

Rule 408 Compromise Offers and Negotiations

Rule 408 is taken from the Federal Rules without change, and has no express equivalent in the 1969 Manual.

2013 Amendment. The committee revised this rule for stylistic reasons and to align it with the Federal Rules of Evidence but in

doing so did not intend to change any result in any ruling on evidence admissibility.

Rule 409 Offers to Pay Medical and Similar Expenses

Rule 409 is taken from the Federal Rules without change. It has no present military equivalent and is intended to be applicable to courts-martial to the same extent that is applicable to civilian criminal cases. Unlike Rules 407 and 408 which although primarily applicable to civil cases are clearly applicable to criminal cases, it is arguable that Rule 409 may not apply to criminal cases as it deals only with questions of "liability"—normally only a civil matter. The Rule has been included in the Military Rules to ensure its availability should it, in fact, apply to criminal cases.

2013 Amendment. The committee revised this rule for stylistic reasons and to align it with the Federal Rules of Evidence but in doing so did not intend to change any result in any ruling on evidence admissibility.

Rule 410 Pleas, Plea Discussions, and Related Statements

Rule 410 as modified effective 1 August 1981 is generally taken from the Federal Rule as modified on 1 December 1980. It extends to plea bargaining as well as to statements made during a providency inquiry, civilian or military. *E.g., United States v. Care,* 18 C.M.A. 535 (1969). Subsection (b) was added to the Rule in recognition of the unique possibility of administrative disposition, usually separation, in lieu of court-martial. Denominated differently within the various armed forces, this administrative procedure often requires a confession as a prerequisite. As modified, Rule 410 protects an individual against later use of a statement submitted in furtherance of such a request for administrative disposition. The definition of "on the record" was required because no "record" in the judicial sense exists insofar as request for administrative disposition is concerned. It is the belief of the Committee that a copy of the written statement of the accused in such a case is, however, the functional equivalent of such a record.

Although the expression "false statement" was retained in the Rule, it is the Committee's intent that it be construed to include all related or similar military offenses.

2013 Amendment. The committee revised this rule for stylistic reasons and to align it with the Federal Rules of Evidence but in doing so did not intend to change any result in any ruling on evidence admissibility.

Rule 411 Liability Insurance

Rule 411 is taken from the Federal Rule without change. Although it would appear to have potential impact upon some criminal cases, *e.g.,* some negligent homicide cases, its actual application to criminal cases is uncertain. It is the Committee's intent that Rule 411 be applicable to courts-martial only to the extent that it is applicable to criminal cases.

2013 Amendment. The committee revised this rule for stylistic reasons and to align it with the Federal Rules of Evidence but in doing so did not intend to change any result in any ruling on evidence admissibility.

Rule 412 Nonconsensual sexual offenses; relevance of victim's past behavior

Rule 412 is taken from the Federal Rules. Although substantially similar in substantive scope to Federal Rule of Evidence 412, the application of the Rule has been somewhat broadened and the procedural aspects of the Federal Rule have been modified to adapt them to military practice.

Rule 412 is intended to shield victims of sexual assaults from the often embarrassing and degrading cross-examination and evidence presentations common to prosecutions of such offenses. In so doing, it recognizes that the prior rule, which it replaces, often yields evidence of at best minimal probative value with great potential for distraction and incidentally discourages both the reporting and prosecution of many sexual assaults. In replacing the unusually extensive rule found in Para. 153 *b* (2)(b), MCM, 1969 (Rev.), which permits evidence of the victim's "unchaste" character regardless of whether he or she has testified, the Rule will significantly change prior military practice and will restrict defense evidence. The Rule recognizes, however, in Rule 412(b)(1), the fundamental right of the defense under the Fifth Amendment of the Constitution of the United States to present relevant defense evidence by admitting evidence that is "constitutionally required to be admitted." Further, it is the Committee's intent that the Rule not be interpreted as a rule of absolute privilege. Evidence that is constitutionally required to be admitted on behalf of the defense remains admissible notwithstanding the absence of express authorization in Rule 412(a). It is unclear whether reputation or opinion evidence in this area will rise to a level of constitutional magnitude, and great care should be taken with respect to such evidence.

Rule 412 applies to a "nonconsensual sexual offense" rather than only to "rape or assault with intent to commit rape" as prescribed by the Federal Rule. The definition of "nonconsensual sexual offense" is set forth in Rule 412(e) and "includes rape, forcible sodomy, assault with intent to commit rape or forcible sodomy, indecent assault, and attempts to commit such offenses." This modification to the Federal Rule resulted from a desire to apply the social policies behind the Federal Rule to the unique military environment. Military life requires that large numbers of young men and women live and work together in close quarters which are often highly isolated. The deterrence of sexual offenses in such circumstances is critical to military efficiency. There is thus no justification for limiting the scope of the Rule, intended to protect human dignity and to ultimately encourage the reporting and prosecution of sexual offenses, only to rape and/or assault with intent to commit rape.

Rule 412(a) generally prohibits reputation or opinion evidence of an alleged victim of a nonconsensual sexual offense.

Rule 412(b)(1) recognizes that evidence of a victim's past sexual behavior may be constitutionally required to be admitted. Although there are a number of circumstances in which this language may be applicable, *see,* S. Saltzburg & K. Redden, FEDERAL RULES OF EVIDENCE MANUAL 92–93 (2d ed. Supp. 1979) (giving example of potential constitutional problems offered by the American Civil Liberties Union during the House hearings on Rule 412), one may be of particular interest. If an individual has contracted for the sexual services of a prostitute and subsequent to the performance of the act the prostitute demands increased payment on pain of claiming rape, for exam-

ple, the past history of that person will likely be constitutionally required to be admitted in a subsequent prosecution in which the defense claims consent to the extent that such history is relevant and otherwise admissible to corroborate the defense position. Absent such peculiar circumstances, however, the past sexual behavior of the alleged victim, not within the scope of Rule 412(b)(2), is unlikely to be admissible regardless of the past sexual history. The mere fact that an individual is a prostitute is not normally admissible under Rule 412.

Evidence of past false complaints of sexual offenses by an alleged victim of a sexual offense is not within the scope of this rule and is not objectionable when otherwise admissible.

Rule 412(c) provides the procedural mechanism by which evidence of past sexual behavior of a victim may be offered. The Rule has been substantially modified from the Federal Rule in order to adapt it to military practice. The requirement that notice be given not later than fifteen days before trial has been deleted as being impracticable in view of the necessity for speedy disposition of military cases. For similar reasons, the requirement for a written motion has been omitted in favor of an offer of proof, which could, of course, be made in writing, at the discretion of the military judge. Reference to hearings in chambers has been deleted as inapplicable; a hearing under Article 39(a), which may be without spectators, has been substituted. The propriety of holding a hearing without spectators is dependent upon its constitutionality which is in turn dependent upon the facts of any specific case.

Although Rule 412 is not *per se* applicable to such pretrial procedures as Article 32 and Court of Inquiry hearings, it may be applicable via Rule 303 and Article 31(c). *See* the Analysis to Rule 303.

It should be noted as a matter related to Rule 412 that the 1969 Manual's prohibition in Para. 153 *a* of convictions for sexual offenses that rest on the uncorroborated testimony of the alleged victim has been deleted. Similarly, an express hearsay exception for fresh complaint has been deleted as being unnecessary. Consequently, evidence of fresh complaint will be admissible under the Military Rule only to the extent that it is either nonhearsay, *see* Rule 801(d)(1)(B), or fits within an exception to the hearsay rule. *See* subdivisions (1), (2), (3), (4), and (24) of Rule 803.

1993 Amendment. R.C.M. 405(i) and Mil. R. Evid. 1101(d) were amended to make the provisions of Rule 412 applicable at pretrial investigations. Congress intended to protect the victims of nonconsensual sex crimes at preliminary hearings as well as at trial when it passed Fed. R. Evid. 412. *See* Criminal Justice Subcommittee of the House Judiciary Committee Report, 94th Cong., 2d Session, July 1976.

1998 Amendment. The revisions to Rule 412 reflect changes made to Federal Rule of Evidence 412 by section 40141 of the Violent Crime Control and Law Enforcement Act of 1994, Pub L. No. 103-322, 108 Stat. 1796, 1918-19 (1994). The purpose of the amendments is to safeguard the alleged victim against the invasion of privacy and potential embarrassment that is associated with public disclosure of intimate sexual details and the infusion of sexual innuendo into the factfinding process.

The terminology "alleged victim" is used because there will frequently be a factual dispute as to whether the sexual misconduct occurred. Rule 412 does not, however, apply unless the person against whom the evidence is offered can reasonably be characterized as a "victim of alleged sexual misconduct."

The term "sexual predisposition" is added to Rule 412 to conform military practice to changes made to the Federal Rule. The purpose of this change is to exclude all other evidence relating to an alleged victim of sexual misconduct that is offered to prove a sexual predisposition. It is designed to exclude evidence that does not directly refer to sexual activities or thoughts but that the accused believes may have a sexual connotation for the factfinder. Admission of such evidence would contravene Rule 412's objectives of shielding the alleged victim from potential embarrassment and safeguarding the victim against stereotypical thinking. Consequently, unless an exception under (b)(1) is satisfied, evidence such as that relating to the alleged victim's mode of dress, speech, or lifestyle is inadmissible.

In drafting Rule 412, references to civil proceedings were deleted, as these are irrelevant to courts-martial practice. Otherwise, changes in procedure made to the Federal Rule were incorporated, but tailored to military practice. The Military Rule adopts a 5-day notice period, instead of the 14-day period specified in the Federal Rule. Additionally, the military judge, for good cause shown, may require a different time for such notice or permit notice during trial. The 5-day period preserves the intent of the Federal Rule that an alleged victim receive timely notice of any attempt to offer evidence protected by Rule 412, however, given the relatively short time period between referral and trial, the 5-day period is deemed more compatible with courts-martial practice.

Similarly, a closed hearing was substituted for the in camera hearing required by the Federal Rule. Given the nature of the in camera procedure used in Military Rule of Evidence 505(i)(4), and that an *in camera* hearing in the district courts more closely resembles a closed hearing conducted pursuant to Article 39(a), the latter was adopted as better suited to trial by courts-martial. Any alleged victim is afforded a reasonable opportunity to attend and be heard at the closed Article 39(a) hearing. The closed hearing, combined with the new requirement to seal the motion, related papers, and the record of the hearing, fully protects an alleged victim against invasion of privacy and potential embarrassment.

2007 Amendment: This amendment is intended to aid practitioners in applying the balancing test of Mil. R. Evid. 412. Specifically, the amendment clarifies: (1) that under Mil. R. Evid. 412, the evidence must be relevant for one of the purposes highlighted in subdivision (b); (2) that in conducting the balancing test, the inquiry is whether the probative value of the evidence outweighs the danger of unfair prejudice to the victim's privacy; and (3) that even if the evidence is admissible under Mil. R. Evid. 412, it may still be excluded under Mil. R. Evid. 403. The proposed changes highlight current practice. *See U.S. v. Banker*, 60 M.J. 216, 223 (2004) ("It would be illogical if the judge were to evaluate evidence 'offered by the accused' for unfair prejudice to the accused. Rather, in the context of this rape shield statute, the prejudice in question is, in part, that to the privacy interests of the alleged victim). *See also Sanchez*, 44 M.J. at 178 ("[I]n determining admissibility there must be a weighing of the probative value of the evidence against the interest of shielding the victim's privacy").

Moreover, the amendment clarifies that Mil. R. Evid. 412 applies in all cases involving a sexual offense wherein the person

against whom the evidence is offered can reasonably be characterized as a "victim of the alleged sexual offense." Thus, the rule applies to: "consensual sexual offense," "nonconsensual sexual offenses;" sexual offenses specifically proscribed under the U.C.M.J., e.g., rape, aggravated sexual assault, etc.; those federal sexual offenses DoD is able to prosecute under clause 3 of Article 134, U.C.M.J., e.g., 18 U.S.C. § 2252A (possession of child pornography); and state sexual offenses DoD is able to assimilate under the Federal Assimilative Crimes Act (18 U.S.C. § 13).

In 2011, the Court of Appeals for the Armed Forces expressed concern with the constitutionality of the balancing test from Rule 412(c)(3) as amended in 2007. *See United States v. Gaddis*, 70 M.J. 248 (C.A.A.F. 2011), *United States v. Ellerbrock*, 70 M.J. 314 (C.A.A.F. 2011).

2013 Amendment. In 2011, the Court of Appeals for the Armed Forces expressed concern with the constitutionality of the balancing test from Rule 412(c)(3) as amended in 2007. *See United States v. Gaddis*, 70 M.J. 248 (C.A.A.F. 2011), *United States v. Ellerbrock*, 70 M.J. 314 (C.A.A.F. 2011).

Rule 413 Similar Crimes in Sexual Offense Cases

1998 Amendment. This amendment is intended to provide for more liberal admissibility of character evidence in criminal cases of sexual assault where the accused has committed a prior act of sexual assault.

Rule 413 is nearly identical to its Federal Rule counterpart. A number of changes were made, however, to tailor the Rule to military practice. First, all references to Federal Rule 415 were deleted, as it applies only to civil proceedings. Second, military justice terminology was substituted where appropriate (e.g. accused for defendant, court-martial for case). Third, the 5-day notice requirement in Rule 413(b) replaced a 15-day notice requirement in the Federal Rule. A 5-day requirement is better suited to military discovery practice. This 5-day notice requirement, however, is not intended to restrict a military judge's authority to grant a continuance under R.C.M. 906(b)(1). Fourth, Rule 413(d) has been modified to include violations of the Uniform Code of Military Justice. Also, the phrase "without consent" was added to Rule 413(d)(1) to specifically exclude the introduction of evidence concerning adultery or consensual sodomy. Last, all incorporation by way of reference was removed by adding subsections (e), (f), and (g). The definitions in those subsections were taken from title 18, United States Code §§ 2246(2)–2246(3), and 513(c)(5), respectively.

Although the Rule states that the evidence "is admissible," the drafters intend that the courts apply Rule 403 balancing to such evidence. Apparently, this also was the intent of Congress. The legislative history reveals that "the general standards of the rules of evidence will continue to apply, including the restrictions on hearsay evidence and the court's authority under evidence rule 403 to exclude evidence whose probative value is substantially outweighed by its prejudicial effect." 140 Cong. Rec. S. 12,990 (daily ed. Sept. 20, 1994) (Floor Statement of the Principal Senate Sponsor, Senator Bob Dole, Concerning the Prior Crimes Evidence Rules for Sexual Assault and Child Molestation Cases).

When "weighing the probative value of such evidence, the court may, as part of its rule 403 determination, consider proximity in time to the charged or predicate misconduct; similarity to the charged or predicate misconduct; frequency of the other acts; surrounding circumstances; relevant intervening events; and other relevant similarities or differences." Report of the Judicial Conference of the United States on the Admission of Character Evidence in Certain Sexual Misconduct Cases.

2002 Amendment: Federal Rule of Evidence 415, which created a similar character evidence rule for civil cases, became applicable to the Military Rules of Evidence on January 6, 1996, pursuant to Rule 1102. Federal Rule 415, however, is no longer applicable to the Military Rules of Evidence, as stated in Section 1 of Executive Order, 2002 Amendments to the Manual for Court-Martial, United States, (2000). Rule 415 was deleted because it applies only to federal civil proceedings.

2013 Amendment. The committee changed the time requirement in subsection (b) to align with the time requirements in Mil. R. Evid. 412 and the Federal Rules of Evidence. This change is also in conformity with military practice in which the military judge may accept pleas shortly after referral and sufficiently in advance of trial. Additionally, the committee revised subsection (d) to align with the Federal Rules of Evidence.

The committee also revised this rule for stylistic reasons but in doing so did not intend to change any result in any ruling on evidence admissibility.

Rule 414 Similar Crimes in Child-Molestation Cases

1998 Amendment. This amendment is intended to provide for more liberal admissibility of character evidence in criminal cases of child molestation where the accused has committed a prior act of sexual assault or child molestation.

Rule 414 is nearly identical to its Federal Rule counterpart. A number of changes were made, however, to tailor the Rule to military practice. First, all references to Federal Rule 415 were deleted, as it applies only to civil proceedings. Second, military justice terminology was substituted where appropriate (e.g. accused for defendant, court-martial for case). Third, the 5-day notice requirement in Rule 414(b) replaced a 15-day notice requirement in the Federal Rule. A 5-day requirement is better suited to military discovery practice. This 5-day notice requirement, however, is not intended to restrict a military judge's authority to grant a continuance under R.C.M. 906(b)(1). Fourth, Rule 414(d) has been modified to include violations of the Uniform Code of Military Justice. Last, all incorporation by way of reference was removed by adding subsections (e), (f), (g), and (h). The definitions in those subsections were taken from title 18, United States Code §§ 2246(2), 2246(3), 2256(2), and 513(c)(5), respectively.

Although the Rule states that the evidence "is admissible," the drafters intend that the courts apply Rule 403 balancing to such evidence. Apparently, this was also the intent of Congress. The legislative history reveals that "the general standards of the rules of evidence will continue to apply, including the restrictions on hearsay evidence and the court's authority under evidence rule 403 to exclude evidence whose probative value is substantially outweighed by its prejudicial effect." 140 Cong. Rec. S. 12,990 (daily ed. Sept. 20, 1994) (Floor Statement of the Principal Senate Sponsor, Senator Bob Dole, Concerning the Prior Crimes Evidence Rules for Sexual Assault and Child Molestation Cases).

When "weighing the probative value of such evidence, the court may, as part of its rule 403 determination, consider proximity in time to the charged or predicate misconduct; similarity to the charged or predicate misconduct; frequency of the other acts; surrounding circumstances; relevant intervening events; and other relevant similarities or differences." Report of the Judicial Conference of the United States on the Admission of Character Evidence in Certain Sexual Misconduct Cases.

2002 Amendment: Federal Rule of Evidence 415, which created a similar character evidence rule for civil cases, became applicable to the Military Rules of Evidence on January 6, 1996, pursuant to Rule 1102. Federal Rule 415, however, is no longer applicable to the Military Rules of Evidence, as stated in Section 1 of Executive Order, 2002 Amendments to the Manual for Court-Martial, United States, (2000). Rule 415 was deleted because it applies only to federal civil proceedings.

2013 Amendment. The committee changed the time requirement in subsection (b) to align with the time requirements in Mil. R. Evid. 412 and the Federal Rules of Evidence. This change is also in conformity with military practice in which the military judge may accept pleas shortly after referral and sufficiently in advance of trial. Additionally, the committee revised subsection (d) to align with the Federal Rules of Evidence.

The committee also revised this rule for stylistic reasons but in doing so did not intend to change any result in any ruling on evidence admissibility.

SECTION V

PRIVILEGES

Rule 501 Privilege in General

Section V contains all of the privileges applicable to military criminal law except for those privileges which are found within Rules 301, Privilege Concerning Compulsory Self-Incrimination; Rule 302, Privilege Concerning Mental Examination of an Accused; and Rule 303, Degrading Questions. Privilege rules, unlike other Military Rules of Evidence, apply in "investigative hearings pursuant to Article 32; proceedings for vacation of suspension of sentence under Article 72; proceedings for search authorization; proceedings involving pretrial restraint; and in other proceedings authorized under the Uniform Code of Military Justice of this Manual and not listed in rule 1101(a)." *See* Rule 1101(c); *see also* Rule 1101(b).

In contrast to the general acceptance of the proposed Federal Rules of Evidence by Congress, Congress did not accept the proposed privilege rules because a consensus as to the desirability of a number of specific privileges could not be achieved. *See* generally, S. Saltzburg & K. Redden, FEDERAL RULES OF EVIDENCE MANUAL 200–201 (2d ed. 1977). In an effort to expedite the Federal Rules generally, Congress adopted a general rule, Rule 501, which basically provides for the continuation of common law in the privilege area. The Committee deemed the approach taken by Congress in the Federal Rules impracticable within the armed forces. Unlike the Article III court system, which is conducted almost entirely by attorneys functioning in conjunction with permanent courts in fixed locations, the military criminal legal system is characterized by its dependence upon large numbers of laymen, temporary courts, and inherent geolineartal and personnel instability due to the worldwide deployment of military personnel. Consequently, military law requires far more stability than civilian law. This is particularly true because of the significant number of non-lawyers involved in the military criminal legal system. Commanders, convening authorities, non-lawyer investigating officers, summary court-martial officers, or law enforcement personnel need specific guidance as to what material is privileged and what is not.

Section V combines the flexible approach taken by Congress with respect to privileges with that provided in the 1969 Manual. Rules 502–509 set forth specific rules of privilege to provide the certainty and stability necessary for military justice. Rule 501, on the other hand, adopts those privileges recognized in common law pursuant to Federal Rules of Evidence 501 with some limitations. Specific privileges are generally taken from those proposed Federal Rules of Evidence which although not adopted by Congress were non-controversial, or from the 1969 Manual.

Rule 501 is the basic rule of privilege. In addition to recognizing privileges required by or provided for in the Constitution, an applicable Act of Congress, the Military Rules of Evidence, and the Manual for Courts-Martial, Rule 501(a) also recognizes privileges "generally recognized in the trial of criminal cases in the United States district courts pursuant to Rule 501 of the Federal Rules of Evidence insofar as the application of such principles in trials by court-martial is practicable and not contrary to or inconsistent with the Uniform Code of Military Justice, these rules, or this Manual." The latter language is taken from 1969 Manual Para. 137. As a result of Rule 501(a)(4), the common law of privileges as recognized in the Article III courts will be applicable to the armed forces except as otherwise provided by the limitation indicated above. Rule 501(d) prevents the application of a doctor-patient privilege. Such a privilege was considered to be totally incompatible with the clear interest of the armed forces in ensuring the health and fitness for duty of personnel. *See* 1969 Manual Para. 151 *c*

It should be noted that the law of the forum determines the application of privilege. Consequently, even if a servicemember should consult with a doctor in a jurisdiction with a doctor-patient privilege for example, such a privilege is inapplicable should the doctor be called as a witness before the court-martial.

Subdivision (b) is a non-exhaustive list of actions which constitute an invocation of a privilege. The subdivision is derived from Federal Rule of Evidence 501 as originally proposed by the Supreme Court, and the four specific actions listed are also found in the Uniform Rules of Evidence. The list is intentionally non-exclusive as a privilege might be claimed in a fashion distinct from those listed.

Subdivision (c) is derived from Federal Rule of Evidence 501 and makes it clear that an appropriate representative of a political jurisdiction or other organizational entity may claim an applicable privilege. The definition is intentionally non-exhaustive.

1999 Amendment: The privileges expressed in Rule 513 and Rule 302 and the conforming Manual change in R.C.M. 706, are not physician-patient privileges and are not affected by Rule 501(d).

2013 Amendment. The committee revised this rule for stylistic reasons but in doing so did not intend to change any result in any ruling on evidence admissibility.

Rule 502 Lawyer-client privilege

(a) *General rule of privilege.* Rule 502(a) continues the substance of the attorney-client privilege found in Para. 151 *b*(2) of the

1969 Manual. The Rule does, however, provide additional detail. Subdivision (a) is taken verbatim from subdivision (a) of Federal Rule of Evidence 503 as proposed by the Supreme Court. The privilege is only applicable when there are "confidential communications made for the purpose of facilitating the rendition of professional legal services to the client." A mere discussion with an attorney does not invoke the privilege when the discussion is not made for the purpose of obtaining professional legal services.

(b) *Definitions—*

(1) *Client.* Rule 502(b)(1) defines a "client" as an individual or entity who receives professional legal services from a lawyer or consults a lawyer with a view to obtaining such services. The definition is taken from proposed Federal Rule 503(a)(1) as Para. 151*b*(2) of the 1969 Manual lacked any general definition of a client.

(2) *Lawyer.* Rule 502(b)(2) defines a "lawyer." The first portion of the paragraph is taken from proposed Federal Rule of Evidence 503(a)(2) and explicitly includes any person "reasonably believed by the client to be authorized" to practice law. The second clause is taken from 1969 Manual Para. 151 *b*(2) and recognizes that a "lawyer" includes "a member of the armed forces detailed, assigned, or otherwise provided to represent a person in a court-martial case or in any military investigation or proceeding" regardless of whether that person is in fact a lawyer. *See* Article 27. Thus an accused is fully protected by the privilege even if defense counsel is not an attorney.

The second sentence of the subdivision recognizes the fact, particularly true during times of mobilization, that attorneys may serve in the armed forces in a nonlegal capacity. In such a case, the individual is not treated as an attorney under the Rule unless the individual fits within one of the three specific categories recognized by the subdivision. Subdivision (b)(2)(B) recognizes that a servicemember who knows that an individual is a lawyer in civilian life may not know that the lawyer is not functioning as such in the armed forces and may seek professional legal assistance. In such a case the privilege will be applicable so long as the individual was "reasonably believed by the client to be authorized to render professional legal services to members of the armed forces."

(3) *Representative of a lawyer.* Rule 502(b)(3) is taken from proposed Federal Rule of Evidence 503(a)(3) but has been modified to recognize that personnel are "assigned" within the armed forces as well as employed. Depending upon the particular situation, a paraprofessional or secretary may be a "representative of a lawyer." *See* Para. 151 *b*(2) of the 1969 Manual.

(4) *Confidential communication.* Rule 502(b)(4) defines a "confidential" communication in terms of the intention of the party making the communication. The Rule is similar to the substance of 1969 Manual Para. 151 *b*(2) which omitted certain communications from privileged status. The new Rule is somewhat broader than the 1969 Manual's provision in that it protects information which is obtained by a third party through accident or design when the person claiming the privilege was not aware that a third party had access to the communication. Compare Rule Para. 151 *a* of the 1969 Manual. The broader rule has been adopted for the reasons set forth in the Advisory Committee's notes on proposed Federal Rule 504(a)(4). The provision permitting disclosure to persons in furtherance of legal services or reasonably necessary for the transmission of the communication

is similar to the provision in the 1969 Manual for communications through agents.

Although Para. 151 *c* of the 1969 Manual precluded a claim of the privilege when there is transmission through wire or radio communications, the new Rules protect statements made via telephone, or, "if use of such means of communication is necessary and in furtherance of the communication," by other "electronic means of communication." Rule 511(b).

(c) *Who may claim the privilege.* Rule 502(c) is taken from proposed Federal Rule 503(b) and expresses who may claim the lawyer-client privilege. The Rule is similar to but slightly broader than Para. 151 *b*(2) of the 1969 Manual. The last sentence of the subdivision states that "the authority of the lawyer to claim the privilege is presumed in the absence of evidence to the contrary."

The lawyer may claim the privilege on behalf of the client unless authority to do so has been withheld from the lawyer or evidence otherwise exists to show that the lawyer lacks the authority to claim the privilege.

(d) *Exceptions.* Rule 502(d) sets forth the circumstances in which the lawyer-client privilege will not apply notwithstanding the general application of the privilege.

Subdivision (d)(1) excludes statements contemplating the future commission of crime or fraud and combines the substance of 1969 Manual Para. 151 *b*(2) with proposed Federal Rule of Evidence 503(d). Under the exception a lawyer may disclose information given by a client when it was part of a "communication (which) clearly contemplated the future commission of a crime of fraud," and a lawyer may also disclose information when it can be objectively said that the lawyer's services "were sought or obtained to commit or plan to commit what the client knew or reasonably should have known to be a crime or fraud." The latter portion of the exception is likely to be applicable only after the commission of the offense while the former is applicable when the communication is made.

Subdivisions (d)(2) through (d)(5) provide exceptions with respect to claims through the same deceased client, breach of duty by lawyer of client, documents attested by lawyers, and communications to an attorney in a matter of common interest among joint clients. There were no parallel provisions in the 1969 Manual for these rules which are taken from proposed Federal Rule 503(d). The provisions are included in the event that the circumstances described therein arise in the military practice.

2013 Amendment. The committee revised this rule for stylistic reasons but in doing so did not intend to change any result in any ruling on evidence admissibility.

Rule 503 Communications to clergy

(a) *General rule of privilege.* Rule 503(a) states the basic rule of privilege for communications to clergy and is taken from proposed Federal Rule of Evidence 506(b) and 1969 Manual Para. 151*b*(2). Like the 1969 Manual, the Rule protects communications to a clergyman's assistant in specific recognition of the nature of the military chaplaincy, and deals only with communications "made either as a formal act of religion or as a matter of conscience."

(b) *Definitions.*

(1) *Clergyman.* Rule 503(b)(1) is taken from proposed Federal Rule of Evidence 506(a)(1) but has been modified to include

specific reference to a chaplain. The Rule does not define "a religious organization" and leaves resolution of that question to precedent and the circumstances of the case. "Clergyman" includes individuals of either sex.

(2) *Confidential.* Rule 503(b)(2) is taken generally from proposed Federal Rule of Evidence 506(a)(2) but has been expanded to include communications to a clergyman's assistant and to explicitly protect disclosure of a privileged communication when "disclosure is in furtherance of the purpose of the communication or to those reasonably necessary for the transmission of the communication." The Rule is thus consistent with the definition of "confidential" used in the lawyer-client privilege, Rule 502(b)(4), and recognizes that military life often requires transmission of communications through third parties. The proposed Federal Rule's limitation of the privilege to communications made "privately" was deleted in favor of the language used in the actual Military Rule for the reasons indicated. The Rule is somewhat more protective than the 1969 Manual because of its application to statements which although intended to be confidential are overheard by others. *See* Rule 502(b)(4) and 510(a) and the Analysis thereto.

2007 Amendment: The previous subsection (2) of Mil. R. Evid. 503(b) was renumbered subsection (3) and the new subsection (2) was inserted to define the term "clergyman's assistant."

(c) *Who may claim the privilege.* Rule 503(c) is derived from proposed Federal Rule of Evidence 506(c) and includes the substance of 1969 Manual Para. 151 *b*(2) which provided that the privilege may be claimed by the "penitent." The Rule supplies additional guidance as to who may actually claim the privilege and is consistent with the other Military Rules of Evidence relating to privileges. *See* Rule 502(c); 504(b)(3); 505(c); 506(c).

2013 Amendment. The committee revised this rule for stylistic reasons but in doing so did not intend to change any result in any ruling on evidence admissibility.

Rule 504 Husband-wife privilege

(a) *Spousal incapacity.* Rule 504(a) is taken generally from *Trammel v. United States*, 445 U.S. 40 (1980) and significantly changes military law in this area. Under prior law, *see* 1969 Manual Para. 148 *e*, each spouse had a privilege to prevent the use of the other spouse as an adverse witness. Under the new rule, the *witness'* spouse is the holder of the privilege and may choose to testify or not to testify as the witness' spouse sees fit. *But see* Rule 504(c) (exceptions to the privilege). Implicit in the rule is the presumption that when a spouse chooses to testify against the other spouse the marriage no longer needs the protection of the privilege. Rule 504(a) must be distinguished from Rule 504(b), *Confidential communication made during marriage,* which deals with communications rather than the ability to testify generally at trial.

Although the witness' spouse ordinarily has a privilege to refuse to testify against the accused spouse, under certain circumstances no privilege may exists, and the spouse may be compelled to testify. *See* Rule 504(c).

(b) *Confidential communication made during marriage.* Rule 504(b) deals with communications made during a marriage and is distinct from a spouse's privilege to refuse to testify pursuant to Rule 504(a). *See* 1969 Manual Para. 151 *b*(2).

(1) *General rule of privilege.* Rule 504(b)(1) sets forth the

general rule of privilege for confidential spousal communications and provides that a spouse may prevent disclosure of any confidential spousal communication made during marriage even though the parties are no longer married at the time that disclosure is desired. The accused may always require that the confidential spousal communication be disclosed. Rule 504(b)(3).

No privilege exists under subdivision (b) if the communication was made when the spouses were legally separated.

(2) *Definition.* Rule 504(b)(2) defines "confidential" in a fashion similar to the definition utilized in Rules 502(b)(4) and 503(b)(2). The word "privately" has been added to emphasize that the presence of third parties is not consistent with the spousal privilege, and the reference to third parties found in Rules 502 and 503 has been omitted for the same reason. Rule 504(b)(2) extends the definition of "confidential" to statements disclosed to third parties who are "reasonably necessary for transmission of the communication." This recognizes that circumstances may arise, especially in military life, where spouses may be separated by great distances or by operational activities, in which transmission of a communication via third parties may be reasonably necessary.

(3) *Who may claim the privilege.* Rule 504(b)(3) is consistent with 1969 Manual Para. 151 *b*(2) and gives the privilege to the spouse who made the communication. The accused may, however, disclose the communication even though the communication was made to the accused.

(c) *Exceptions.*

(1) *Spouse incapacity only.* Rule 504(c)(1) provides exceptions to the spousal incapacity rule of Rule 504(a). The rule is taken from 1969 Manual Para. 148 *e* and declares that a spouse may not refuse to testify against the other spouse when the marriage has been terminated by divorce or annulment. Annulment has been added to the present military rule as being consistent with its purpose. Separation of spouses via legal separation or otherwise does not affect the privilege of a spouse to refuse to testify against the other spouse. For other circumstances in which a spouse may be compelled to testify against the other spouse, *see* Rule 504(c)(2).

Confidential communications are not affected by the termination of a marriage.

(2) *Spousal incapacity and confidential communications.* Rule 504(c)(2) prohibits application of the spousal privilege, whether in the form of spousal incapacity or in the form of a confidential communication, when the circumstances specified in paragraph (2) are applicable. Subparagraphs (A) and (C) deal with anti-marital acts, *e.g.,* acts which are against the spouse and thus the marriage. The Rule expressly provides that when such an act is involved a spouse may not refuse to testify. This provision is taken from proposed Federal Rule 505(c)(1) and reflects in part the Supreme Court's decision in *Wyatt v. United States*, 362 U.S. 525 (1960). *See also Trammel v. United States*, 445 U.S. 40, 46 n.7 (1980). The Rule thus recognizes society's overriding interest in prosecution of anti-marital offenses and the probability that a spouse may exercise sufficient control, psychological or otherwise, to be able to prevent the other spouse from testifying voluntarily. The Rule is similar to 1969 Manual Para. 148 *e* but has deleted the Manual's limitation of the exceptions to the privilege

to matters occurring after marriage or otherwise unknown to the spouse as being inconsistent with the intent of the exceptions.

Rule 504(c)(2)(B) is derived from Para. 148 *e* and 151 *b*(2) of the 1969 Manual. The provision prevents application of the privileges as to privileged communications if the marriage was a sham at the time of the communication, and prohibits application of the spousal incapacity privilege if the marriage was begun as a sham and is a sham at the time the testimony of the witness is to be offered. Consequently, the Rule recognizes for purposes of subdivision (a) that a marriage that began as a sham may have ripened into a valid marriage at a later time. The intent of the provision is to prevent individuals from marrying witnesses in order to effectively silence them.

2012 Amendment: Subdivision (c)(2)(D) was added by Executive Order 13593 to create an exception to the privilege when both parties have been substantial participants in illegal activity.

2007 Amendment: (d) *Definition.* Rule 504(d) modifies the rule and is intended to afford additional protection to children. Previously, the term "a child of either," referenced in Rule 504(c)(2)(A), did not include a "de facto" child or a child who is under the physical custody of one of the spouses but lacks a formal legal parent-child relationship with at least one of the spouses. *See U.S. v. McCollum*, 58 M.J. 323 (C.A.A.F. 2003). Prior to this amendment, an accused could not invoke the spousal privilege to prevent disclosure of communications regarding crimes committed against a child with whom he or his spouse had a formal, legal parent-child relationship; however, the accused could invoke the privilege to prevent disclosure of communications where there was not a formal, legal parent-child relationship. This distinction between legal and "de facto" children resulted in unwarranted discrimination among child victims and ran counter to the public policy of protecting children. Rule 504(d) recognizes the public policy of protecting children by addressing disparate treatment among child victims entrusted to another. The "marital communications privilege should not prevent 'a properly outraged spouse with knowledge from testifying against a perpetrator' of child abuse within the home regardless of whether the child is part of that family." *U.S. v. McCollum*, 58 M.J. 323, 342 n.6 (C.A.A.F. 2003) (citing *U.S. v. Bahe*, 128 F.3d 1440, 1446 (10th Cir. 1997)).

2013 Amendment. Subsection (c)(2)(D) was added pursuant to Exec. Order No. 13643. The committee also revised this rule for stylistic reasons but in doing so did not intend to change any result in any ruling on evidence admissibility.

Rule 505 Classified information

Rule 505 is based upon H.R. 4745, 96th Cong., 1st Sess. (1979), which was proposed by the Executive Branch as a response to what is known as the "graymail" problem in which the defendant in a criminal case seeks disclosure of sensitive national security information, the release of which may force the government to discontinue the prosecution. The Rule is also based upon the Supreme Court's discussion of executive privilege in *United States v. Reynolds*, 345 U.S. 1 (1953), and *United States v. Nixon*, 418 U.S. 683 (1974). The rule attempts to balance the interests of an accused who desires classified information for his or her defense and the interests of the government in protecting that information.

(a) *General rule of privilege.* Rule 505(a) is derived from *United*

States v. Reynolds, supra and 1969 Manual Para. 151. Classified information is only privileged when its "disclosure would be detrimental to the national security."

1993 Amendment: The second sentence was added to clarify that this rule, like other rules of privilege, applies at all stages of all actions and is not relaxed during the sentencing hearing under Mil. R. Evid. 1101(c).

(b) *Definitions.*

(1) *Classified information.* Rule 505(b)(1) is derived from section 2 of H.R. 4745. The definition of "classified information" is a limited one and includes only that information protected "pursuant to an executive order, statute, or regulation," and that material which constitutes restricted data pursuant to 42 U.S.C. § 2014(y) (1976).

(2) *National security.* Rule 505(b)(2) is derived from section 2 of H.R. 4745.

(c) *Who may claim the privilege.* Rule 505(c) is derived from Para. 151 of the 1969 Manual and is consistent with similar provisions in the other privilege rules. *See* Rule 501(c). The privilege may be claimed only "by the head of the executive or military department or government agency concerned" and then only upon "a finding that the information is properly classified and that disclosure would be detrimental to the national security." Although the authority of a witness or trial counsel to claim the privilege is presumed in the absence of evidence to the contrary, neither a witness nor a trial counsel may claim the privilege without prior direction to do so by the appropriate department or agency head. Consequently, expedited coordination with senior headquarters is advised in any situation in which Rule 505 appears to be applicable.

(d) *Action prior to referral of charges.* Rule 505(d) is taken from section 4(b)(1) of H.R. 4745. The provision has been modified to reflect the fact that pretrial discovery in the armed forces, prior to referral, is officially conducted through the convening authority. The convening authority should disclose the maximum amount of requested information as appears reasonable under the circumstances.

(e) *Pretrial session.* Rule 505(e) is derived from section 3 of H.R. 4745.

(f) *Action after referral of charges.* Rule 505(f) provides the basic procedure under which the government should respond to a determination by the military judge that classified information "apparently contains evidence that is relevant and material to an element of the offense or a legally cognizable defense and is otherwise admissible in evidence." *See generally* the Analysis to Rule 507(d).

It should be noted that the government may submit information to the military judge for *in camera* inspection pursuant to subdivision (i). If the defense requests classified information that it alleges is "relevant and material" and the government refuses to disclose the information to the military judge for inspection, the military judge may presume that the information is in fact "relevant and material."

(g) *Disclosure of classified information to the accused.* Paragraphs (1) and (2) of Rule 505(g) are derived from section 4 of H.R. 4745. Paragraph (3) is taken from section 10 of H.R. 4745 but has been modified in view of the different application of the Jencks Act, 18 U.S.C. § 3500 (1976) in the armed forces. Para-

graph (4) is taken from sections 4(b)(2) and 10 of H.R. 4745. The reference in H.R. 4745 to a recess has been deleted as being unnecessary in view of the military judge's inherent authority to call a recess.

1993 Amendment: Subsection (g)(1)(D) was amended to make clear that the military judge's authority to require security clearances extends to persons involved in the conduct of the trial as well as pretrial preparation for it. The amendment requires persons needing security clearances to submit to investigations necessary to obtain the clearance.

(h) *Notice of the accused's intention to disclose classified information.* Rule 505(h) is derived from section 5 of H.R. 4745. The intent of the provision is to prevent disclosure of classified information by the defense until the government has had an opportunity to determine what position to take concerning the possible disclosure of that information. Pursuant to Rule 505(h)(5), failure to comply with subdivision (h) may result in a prohibition on the use of the information involved.

1993 Amendment: Subsection (h)(3) was amended to require specificity in detailing the items of classified information expected to be introduced. The amendment is based on *United States v. Collins*, 720 F.2d. 1195 (11th Cir. 1983).

(i) *In camera proceedings for cases involving classified information.* Rule 505(i) is derived generally from section 5 of H.R. 4745. The "*in camera*" procedure utilized in subdivision (i) is generally new to military law. Neither the accused nor defense counsel may be excluded from the *in camera* proceeding. However, nothing within the Rule requires that the defense be provided with a copy of the classified material in question when the government submits such information to the military judge pursuant to Rule 505(i)(3) in an effort to obtain an *in camera* proceeding under this Rule. If such information has not been disclosed previously, the government may describe the information by generic category, rather than by identifying the information. Such description is subject to approval by the military judge, and if not sufficiently specific to enable the defense to proceed during the *in camera* session, the military judge may order the government to release the information for use during the proceeding or face the sanctions under subdivision (i)(4)(E).

1993 Amendment: Subsection (i)(3) was amended to clarify that the classified material and the government's affidavit are submitted only to the military judge. The word "only" was placed at the end of the sentence to make it clear that it refers to "military judge" rather than to "examination." The military judge is to examine the affidavit and the classified information without disclosing it before determining to hold an *in camera* proceeding as defined in subsection (i)(1).

The second sentence of subsection (i)(4)(B) was added to provide a standard for admission of classified information in sentencing proceedings.

(j) *Introduction of classified information.* Rule 505(j) is derived from section 8 of H.R. 4745 and *United States v. Grunden*, 2 M.J. 116 (C.M.A. 1977).

1993 Amendment: Subsection (j)(5) was amended to provide that the military judge's authority to exclude the public extends to the presentation of any evidence that discloses classified information, and not merely to the testimony of witnesses. *See generally, United States v. Hershey*, 20 M.J. 433 (C.M.A. 1985), *cert. de-*

nied, 474 U.S. 1062 (1986) (specifies factors to be considered in the trial judge's determination to close the proceedings).

(k) *Security procedures to safeguard against compromise of classified information disclosed to courts-martial.* Rule 505(k) is derived from section 9 of H.R. 4745.

2013 Amendment. The committee significantly restructured this rule to bring greater clarity and regularity to military practice. The changes focus primarily on expanding the military judge's explicit authority to conduct *ex parte* pretrial conferences in connection with classified information and detailing when the military judge is required to do so, limiting the disclosure of classified information per order of the military judge, specifically outlining the process by which the accused gains access to and may request disclosure of classified information, and the procedures for using classified material at trial. The changes were intended to ensure that classified information is not needlessly disclosed while at the same time ensuring that the accused's right to a fair trial is maintained. Some of the language was adopted from the Military Commissions Rules of Evidence and the Classified Information Procedures Act.

Rule 506 Government information other than classified information

(a) *General rule of privilege.* Rule 506(a) states the general rule of privilege for nonclassified government information. The Rule recognizes that in certain extraordinary cases the government should be able to prohibit release of government information which is detrimental to the public interest. The Rule is modeled on Rule 505 but is more limited in its scope in view of the greater limitations applicable to nonclassified information. *Compare United States v. Nixon,* 418 U.S. 683 (1974) with *United States v. Reynolds,* 345 U.S. 1 (1953). Rule 506 addresses those similar matters found in 1969 Manual Para. 151 *b*(1) and 151 *b*(3). Under Rule 506(a) information is privileged only if its disclosure would be "detrimental to the public interest." It is important to note that pursuant to Rule 506(c) the privilege may be claimed only "by the head of the executive or military department or government agency concerned" unless investigations of the Inspectors General are concerned.

Under Rule 506(a) there is no privilege if disclosure of the information concerned is required by an Act of Congress such as the Freedom of Information Act, 5 U.S.C. § 552 (1976). Disclosure of information will thus be broader under the Rule than under the 1969 Manual. *See United States v. Nixon, supra.*

(b) *Scope.* Rule 506(b) defines "Government information" in a nonexclusive fashion, and expressly states that classified information and information relating to the identity of informants are solely within the scope of other Rules.

(c) *Who may claim the privilege.* Rule 506(c) distinguishes between government information in general and investigations of the Inspectors General. While the privilege for the latter may be claimed "by the authority ordering the investigation or any superior authority," the privilege for other government information may be claimed *only* "by the head of the executive or military department or government agency concerned." *See generally* the Analysis to Rule 505(c).

1990 Amendment: Subsection (c) was amended by substituting the words "records and information" for "investigations", which

is a term of art vis-a-vis Inspector General functions. Inspectors General also conduct "inspections" and "inquiries," and use of the word "records and information" is intended to cover all documents and information generated by or related to the activities of Inspectors General. "Records" includes reports of inspection, inquiry, and investigation conducted by an Inspector General and extracts, summaries, exhibits, memoranda, notes, internal correspondence, handwritten working materials, untranscribed shorthand or stenotype notes of unrecorded testimony, tape recordings and other supportive records such as automated data extracts. In conjunction with this change, the language identifying the official entitled to claim the privilege for Inspector General records was changed to maintain the previous provision which allowed the superiors of Inspector General officers, rather than the officers themselves, to claim the privilege.

(d) *Action prior to referral of charges.* Rule 506(d) specifies action to be taken prior to referral of charges in the event of a claim of privilege under the Rule. *See generally* Rule 505(d) and its Analysis. Note that disclosures can be withheld only if action under paragraph (1)–(4) of subdivision (d) cannot be made "without causing identifiable damage to the public interest" (emphasis added).

(e) *Action after referral of charges. See generally* Rule 505(f) and its Analysis. Note that unlike Rule 505(f), however, Rule 506(e) does not require a finding that failure to disclose the information in question "would materially prejudice a substantial right of the accused." Dismissal is required when the relevant information is not disclosed in a "reasonable period of time."

1995 Amendment: It is the intent of the Committee that if classified information arises during a proceeding under Rule 506, the procedures of Rule 505 will be used.

The new subsection (e) was formerly subsection (f). The matters in the former subsection (f) were adopted without change. The former subsection (e) was amended and redesignated as subsection (f) (see below).

(f) *Pretrial session.* Rule 506(f) is taken from Rule 505(e). It is the intent of the Committee that if classified information arises during a proceeding under Rule 506, the procedures of Rule 505 will be used.

1995 Amendment: See generally Rule 505(f) and its accompanying Analysis. Note that unlike Rule 505(f), however, Rule 506(f) does not require a finding that failure to disclose the information in question "would materially prejudice a substantial right of the accused." Dismissal is not required when the relevant information is not disclosed in a "reasonable period of time."

Subsection (f) was formerly subsection (e). The subsection was amended to cover action after a defense motion for discovery, rather than action after referral of charges. The qualification that the government claim of privilege pertains to information "that apparently contains evidence that is relevant and necessary to an element of the offense or a legally cognizable defense and is otherwise admissible in evidence in a court-martial proceeding" was deleted as unnecessary. Action by the convening authority is required if, after referral, the defense moves for disclosure and the Government claims the information is privileged from disclosure.

(g) *Disclosure of government information to the accused.* Rule 506(g) is taken from Rule 505(g) but deletes references to classified information and clearances due to their inapplicability.

(h) *Prohibition against disclosure.* Rule 506(h) is derived from

Rule 505(h)(4). The remainder of Rule 505(h)(4) and Rule 505(h) generally has been omitted as being unnecessary. No sanction for violation of the requirement has been included.

1995 Amendment: Subsection (h) was amended to provide that government information may not be disclosed by the accused unless authorized by the military judge.

(i) *In camera proceedings.* Rule 506(i) is taken generally from Rule 505(i), but the standard involved reflects 1969 Manual Para. 151 and the Supreme Court's decision in *United States v. Nixon, supra.* In line with *Nixon,* the burden is on the party claiming the privilege to demonstrate why the information involved should not be disclosed. References to classified material have been deleted as being inapplicable.

1995 Amendment: Subsection (i) was amended to clarify the procedure for in camera proceedings. The definition in subsection (i)(1) was amended to conform to the definition of in camera proceedings in Mil. R. Evid. 505(i)(1). Subsections (i)(2) and (i)(3) were unchanged. Subsection (i)(4)(B), redesignated as (i)(4)(C), was amended to include admissible evidence relevant to punishment of the accused, consistent with *Brady v. Maryland,* 373 U.S. 83, 87 (1963). Subsection (i)(4)(C) was redesignated as (i)(4)(D), but was otherwise unchanged. The amended procedures provide for full disclosure of the government information in question to the accused for purposes of litigating the admissibility of the information in the protected environment of the in camera proceeding; *i.e.,* the Article 39(a) session is closed to the public and neither side may disclose the information outside the in camera proceeding until the military judge admits the information as evidence in the trial. Under subsection (i)(4)(E), the military judge may authorize alternatives to disclosure, consistent with a military judge's authority concerning classified information under Mil. R. Evid. 505. Subsection (i)(4)(F) allows the Government to determine whether the information ultimately will be disclosed to the accused. However, the Government's continued objection to disclosure may be at the price of letting the accused go free, in that subsection (i)(4)(F) adopts the sanctions available to the military judge under Mil. R. Evid. 505(i)(4)(E). *See United States v. Reynolds,* 345 U.S. 1, 12 (1953).

(k) *Introduction of government information subject to a claim of privilege.* Rule 506(k) is derived from Rule 505(j) with appropriate modifications being made to reflect the nonclassified nature of the information involved.

1995 Amendment: Subsection (j) was added to recognize the Government's right to appeal certain rulings and orders. *See* R.C.M. 908. The former subsection (j) was redesignated as subsection (k). The subsection speaks only to government appeals; the defense still may seek extraordinary relief through interlocutory appeal of the military judge's orders and rulings. *See generally,* 28 U.S.C. § 1651(a); *Waller v. Swift,* 30 M.J. 139 (C.M.A. 1990); *Dettinger v. United States,* 7 M.J. 216 (C.M.A. 1979).

(l) *Procedures to safeguard against compromise of government information disclosed to courts-martial.* Rule 506(k) is derived from Rule 505(k). Such procedures should reflect the fact that material privileged under Rule 506 is not classified.

2013 Amendment. The committee significantly revised this rule to both bring greater clarity to it and also to align it with changes made to Mil. R. Evid. 505.

Rule 507 Identity of informant

(a) *Rule of privilege.* Rule 507(a) sets forth the basic rule of privilege for informants and contains the substance of 1969 Manual Para. 151 *b*(1). The new Rule, however, provides greater detail as to the application of the privilege than did the 1969 manual.

The privilege is that of the United States or political subdivision thereof and applies only to information relevant to the identity of an informant. An "informant" is simply an individual who has supplied "information resulting in an investigation of a possible violation of law" to a proper person and thus includes good citizen reports to command or police as well as the traditional "confidential informants" who may be consistent sources of information.

(b) *Who may claim the privilege.* Rule 507(b) provides for claiming the privilege and distinguishes between representatives of the United States and representatives of a state or subdivision thereof. Although an appropriate representative of the United States may always claim the privilege when applicable, a representative of a state or subdivision may do so only if the information in question was supplied to an officer of the state or subdivision. The Rule is taken from proposed Federal Rule of Evidence 510(b), with appropriate modifications, and is similar in substances to Para. 151 *b*(1) of the 1969 Manual which permitted "appropriate governmental authorities" to claim the privilege.

The Rule does not specify who an "appropriate representative" is. Normally, the trial counsel is an appropriate representative of the United States. The Rule leaves the question open, however, for case by case resolution. Regulations could be promulgated which could specify who could be an appropriate representative.

(c) *Exceptions.* Rule 507(c) sets forth the circumstances in which the privilege is inapplicable.

(1) *Voluntary disclosures; informant as witness.* Rule 507(c)(1) makes it clear that the privilege is inapplicable if circumstances have nullified its justification for existence. Thus, there is no reason for the privilege, and the privilege is consequently inapplicable, if the individual who would have cause to resent the informant has been made aware of the informant's identity by a holder of the privilege or by the informant's own action or when the witness testifies for the prosecution thus allowing that person to ascertain the informant's identity. This is in accord with the intent of the privilege which is to protect informants from reprisals. The Rule is taken from Para. 151 *b*(1) of the 1969 Manual.

(2) *Testimony on the issue of guilt or innocence.* Rule 507(c)(2) is taken from 1969 Manual Para. 151 *b* (1) and recognizes that in certain circumstances the accused may have a due process right under the Fifth Amendment, as well as a similar right under the Uniform Code of Military Justice, to call the informant as a witness. The subdivision intentionally does not specify what circumstances would require calling the informant and leaves resolution of the issue to each individual case.

(3) *Legality of obtaining evidence.* Rule 507(c)(3) is new. The Rule recognizes that circumstances may exist in which the Constitution may require disclosure of the identity of an informant in the context of determining the legality of obtaining evidence under Rule 311; *see, e.g., Franks v. Delaware,* 438 U.S. 154, 170 (1978); *McCray v. Illinois,* 386 U.S. 300 (1976) (both cases indicate that disclosure may be required in certain unspecified circumstances but do not in fact require such disclosure). In view

of the highly unsettled nature of the issue, the Rule does not specify whether or when such disclosure is mandated and leaves the determination to the military judge in light of prevailing case law utilized in the trial of criminal cases in the Federal district courts.

(d) *Procedures*. Rule 507(d) sets forth the procedures to be followed in the event of a claim of privilege under Rule 507. If the prosecution elects not to disclose the identity of an informant when the judge has determined that disclosure is required, that matter shall be reported to the convening authority. Such a report is required so that the convening authority may determine what action, if any, should be taken. Such actions could include disclosure of the informant's identity, withdrawal of charges, or some appropriate appellate action.

2013 Amendment. The committee added subsection (b) to define terms that are used throughout the rule and added subsection (e)(1) to permit the military judge to hold an in camera review upon request by the prosecution. The committee also revised this rule for stylistic reasons but in doing so did not intend to change any result in any ruling on evidence admissibility.

Rule 508 Political vote

Rule 508 is taken from proposed Federal Rule of Evidence 507 and expresses the substance of 18 U.S.C. § 596, which is applicable to the armed forces. The privilege is considered essential for the armed forces because of the unique nature of military life.

Rule 509 Deliberation of courts and juries

Rule 509 is taken from 1969 Manual Para. 151 but has been modified to ensure conformity with Rule 606(b) which deals specifically with disclosure of deliberations in certain cases.

2013 Amendment. The committee added the language "courts-martial, military judges" to this rule in light of CAAF's holding in *United States v. Matthews*, 68 M.J. 29 (C.A.A.F. 2009). In that case, CAAF held that this rule as it was previously written created an implied privilege that protected the deliberative process of a military judge from disclosure and that testimony that revealed the deliberative thought process of the military judge is inadmissible. *Matthews*, 68 M.J. at 38-43. The changes simply express what the court found had previously been implied.

Rule 510 Waiver of privilege by voluntary disclosure

Rule 510 is derived from proposed Federal Rule of Evidence 511 and is similar in substance to 1969 Manual Para. 151 *a* which notes that privileges may be waived. Rule 510(a) simply provides that "disclosure of any significant part of the matter or communication under such circumstances that it would be inappropriate to claim the privilege" will defeat and waive the privilege. Disclosure of privileged matter may be, however, itself privileged; *see* Rules 502(b)(4); 503(b)(2); 504(b)(2). Information disclosed in the form of an otherwise privileged telephone call (*e.g.,* information overheard by an operator) is privileged, Rule 511(b), and information disclosed via transmission using other forms of communication may be privileged; Rule 511(b). Disclosure under certain circumstances may not be "inappropriate" and the information will retain its privileged character. Thus, disclosure of an

informant's identity by one law enforcement agency to another may well be appropriate and not render Rule 507 inapplicable.

Rule 510(b) is taken from Para. 151 *b*(1) of the 1969 Manual and makes it clear that testimony pursuant to a grant of immunity does not waive the privilege. Similarly, an accused who testifies in his or her own behalf does not waive the privilege unless the accused testifies voluntarily to the privileged matter of communication.

Rule 511 Privileged matter disclosed under compulsion or without opportunity to claim privilege

Rule 511(a) is similar to proposed Federal Rule of Evidence 512. Placed in the context of the definition of "confidential" utilized in the privilege rules, *see,* Rule 502(b)(4), the Rule is substantially different from prior military law inasmuch as prior law permitted utilization of privileged information which had been gained by a third party through accident or design. *See* Para. 151 *b* (1), MCM, 1969 (Rev.). Such disclosures are generally safeguarded against via the definition "confidential" used in the new Rules. Generally, the Rules are more protective of privileged information than was the 1969 Manual.

Rule 511(b) is new and deals with electronic transmission of information. It recognizes that the nature of the armed forces today often requires such information transmission. Like 1969 Manual Para. 151 *b*(1), the new Rule does not make a non-privileged communication privileged; rather, it simply safeguards already privileged information under certain circumstances.

The first portion of subdivision (b) expressly provides that otherwise privileged information transmitted by telephone remains privileged. This is in recognition of the role played by the telephone in modern life and particularly in the armed forces where geolineartal separations are common. The Committee was of the opinion that legal business cannot be transacted in the 20th century without customary use of the telephone. Consequently, privileged communications transmitted by telephone are protected even though those telephone conversations are known to be monitored for whatever purpose.

Unlike telephonic communications, Rule 511(b) protects other forms of electronic communication only when such means "is necessary and in furtherance of the communication." It is irrelevant under the Rule as to whether the communication in question was in fact necessary. The only relevant question is whether, once the individual decided to communicate, the *means* of communication was necessary and in furtherance of the communication. Transmission of information by radio is a means of communication that must be tested under this standard.

2013 Amendment. Titles were added to the subsections of this rule for clarity and ease of use.

Rule 512 Comment upon or inference from claim of privilege; instruction

(a) *Comment or inference not permitted.* Rule 512(a) is derived from proposed Federal Rule 513. The Rule is new to military law but is generally in accord with the Analysis of Contents of the 1969 Manual; United States Department of the Army, Pamphlet No. 27-2, Analysis of Contents, Manual for Courts-Martial 1969, *Revised Edition,* 27-33, 27-38 (1970).

Rule 512(a)(1) prohibits any inference or comment upon the

exercise of a privilege by the accused and is taken generally from proposed Federal Rule of Evidence 513(a).

Rule 512(a)(2) creates a qualified prohibition with respect to any inference or comment upon the exercise of a privilege by a person not the accused. The Rule recognizes that in certain circumstances the interests of justice may require such an inference and comment. Such a situation could result, for example, when the government's exercise of a privilege has been sustained, and an inference adverse to the government is necessary to preserve the fairness of the proceeding.

(b) *Claiming privilege without knowledge of members.* Rule 512(b) is intended to implement subdivision (a). Where possible, claims of privilege should be raised at an Article 39(a) session or, if practicable, at sidebar.

(c) *Instruction.* Rule 512(c) requires that relevant instructions be given "upon request." *Cf.* Rule 105. The military judge does not have a duty to instruct *sua sponte.*

Rule 513 Psychotherapist-patient privilege

1999 Amendment: Military Rule of Evidence 513 establishes a psychotherapist-patient privilege for investigations or proceedings authorized under the Uniform Code of Military Justice. Rule 513 clarifies military law in light of the Supreme Court decision in *Jaffee v. Redmond*, 518 U.S. 1, 116 S. Ct. 1923, 135 L.Ed.2d 337 (1996). *Jaffee* interpreted Federal Rule of Evidence 501 to create a federal psychotherapist-patient privilege in civil proceedings and refers federal courts to state laws to determine the extent of privileges. In deciding to adopt this privilege for courts-martial, the committee balanced the policy of following federal law and rules, when practicable and not inconsistent with the UCMJ or MCM, with the needs of commanders for knowledge of certain types of information affecting the military. The exceptions to the rule have been developed to address the specialized society of the military and separate concerns that must be met to ensure military readiness and national security. *See Parker v. Levy*, 417 U.S. 733, 743 (1974); *U.S. ex rel. Toth v. Quarles*, 350 U.S. 11, 17 (1955); *Dept. of the Navy v. Egan*, 484 U.S. 518, 530 (1988). There is no intent to apply Rule 513 in any proceeding other than those authorized under the UCMJ. Rule 513 was based in part on proposed Fed. R. Evid. 504 (not adopted) and state rules of evidence. Rule 513 is not a physician-patient privilege. It is a separate rule based on the social benefit of confidential counseling recognized by *Jaffee*, and similar to the clergy-penitent privilege. In keeping with American military law since its inception, there is still no physician-patient privilege for members of the Armed Forces. *See* the analyses for Rule 302 and Rule 501.

(a) *General rule of privilege.* The words "under the UCMJ" in this rule mean Rule 513 applies only to UCMJ proceedings, and do not limit the availability of such information internally to the services, for appropriate purposes.

(d) *Exceptions* These exceptions are intended to emphasize that military commanders are to have access to all information that is necessary for the safety and security of military personnel, operations, installations, and equipment. Therefore, psychotherapists are to provide such information despite a claim of privilege.

2012 Amendment: Executive Order 13593 removed communications about spouse abuse as an exception to the privilege by deleting the words "spouse abuse" and "the person of the other

spouse or" from Rule 513(d)(2), thus expanding the overall scope of the privilege. In removing the spouse abuse exception to Rule 513, the privilege is now consistent with Rule 514 in that spouse victim communications to a provider who qualifies as both a psychotherapist for purposes of Rule 513 and victim advocate for purposes of Mil. R. Evid. 514 are covered by the privilege.

2013 Amendment. In Exec. Order No. 13643, the President removed communications about spouse abuse as an exception to the spousal privilege by deleting the words "spouse abuse" and "the person of the other spouse or" from Mil. R. Evid. 513(d)(2), thus expanding the overall scope of the privilege. The privilege is now consistent with Mil. R. Evid. 514 in that spouse victim communications to a provider who qualifies as both a psychotherapist for purposes of Mil. R. Evid. 513 and as a victim advocate for purposes of Mil. R. Evid. 514 are covered.

In subsection (e)(3), the committee changed the language to further expand the military judge's authority and discretion to conduct in camera reviews. The committee also revised this rule for stylistic reasons but in doing so did not intend to change any result in any ruling on evidence admissibility.

Rule 514 Victim advocate-victim privilege

2012 Amendment: Like the psychotherapist-patient privilege created by Rule 513, Rule 514 establishes a victim advocate-victim privilege for investigations or proceedings authorized under the Uniform Code of Military Justice. Implemented as another approach to improving the military's overall effectiveness in addressing the crime of sexual assault, facilitating candor between victims and victim advocates, and mitigating the impact of the court-martial process on victims, the rule specifically emerged in response to concerns raised by members of Congress, community groups, and *The Defense Task Force on Sexual Assault in the Military Services* (DTFSAMS). In its 2009 report, DTFSAMS noted the following: 35 states had a privilege for communications between victim advocates and victims of sexual assault; victims did not believe they could communicate confidentially with medical and psychological support services provided by DoD; victims perceived interference with the victim-victim advocate relationship and continuing victim advocate services when the victim advocate was identified as a potential witness in a court-martial; and service members reported being "re-victimized" when their prior statements to victim advocates were used to cross-examine them in court-martial proceedings. DTFSAMS recommended that Congress "enact a comprehensive military justice privilege for communications between a Victim Advocate and a victim of sexual assault." Both the DoD Joint Service Committee on Military Justice and Congress began considering a privilege. The Committee modeled proposed Rule 514 after Rule 513, including its various exceptions, in an effort to balance the privacy of the victim's communications with a victim advocate against the accused's legitimate needs. Differing proposals for a victim advocate privilege were suggested as part of the National Defense Authorization Act for 2011 (NDAA), but were not enacted. A victim advocate privilege passed the House of Representatives as part of the NDAA for 2012, while the Senate version required the President to issue a Military Rule of Evidence providing a privilege. Congress removed both provisions because Rule 514 was pending the President's signature and Congress was satisfied that once implemented, this Rule accomplished the objective of ensuring privileged communications for sexual assault victims.

(a) *General rule of privilege.* The words "under the UCMJ" in Rule 514 mean that the privilege only applies to UCMJ proceedings. It does not apply in situations in which the offender cannot be prosecuted under the UCMJ. Furthermore, this Rule only applies to communications between a victim advocate and the victim of a sexual or violent offense.

(b) *Definitions.* The Committee intended the definition of "victim advocate" from Rule 514 to include, but not be limited to, personnel performing victim advocate duties within the DoD Sexual Assault Prevention and Response Office (such as a Sexual Assault Response Coordinator), and the DoD Family Advocacy Program (such as a domestic abuse victim advocate). A victim liaison appointed pursuant to the Victim and Witness Assistance Program is not a "victim advocate" for purposes of this Rule, nor are personnel working within an Equal Opportunity or Inspector General office. For purposes of this Rule, the Committee intended "violent offense" to mean an actual or attempted murder, manslaughter, rape, sexual assault, aggravated assault, robbery, assault consummated by a battery and similar offenses. A simple assault may be a violent offense where the violence has been physically attempted or menaced. A mere threatening in words is not a violent offense. The Committee recognizes that this Rule will be applicable in situations where there is a factual dispute as to whether a sexual or violent offense occurred and whether a person actually suffered direct physical or emotional harm of such an offense. The fact that such findings have not been judicially established shall not prevent application of this Rule to alleged victims reasonably intended to be covered by this Rule.

(d) *Exceptions.* The exceptions to Rule 514 are similar to the exceptions found in Rule 513, and are intended to be applied in the same manner. Rule 514 does not include comparable exceptions found within Rule 513(d)(2) and 513(d)(7). In drafting the "constitutionally required" exception, the Committee intended that communication covered by the privilege would be released only in the narrow circumstances where the accused could show harm of constitutional magnitude if such communication was not disclosed. In practice, this relatively high standard of release is not intended to invite a fishing expedition for possible statements made by the victim, nor is it intended to be an exception that effectively renders the privilege meaningless. If a military judge finds that an exception to this privilege applies, special care should be taken to narrowly tailor the release of privileged communications to only those statements which are relevant and whose probative value outweighs unfair prejudice. The fact that otherwise privileged communications are admissible pursuant to an exception of Rule 514 does not prohibit a military judge from imposing reasonable limitations on cross-examination. *See Delaware v. Van Arsdall*, 475 U.S. 673, 679 (1986); *United States v. Gaddis*, 70 M.J. 248, 256 (C.A.A.F. 2011); *United States v. Ellerbrock*, 70 M.J. 314 (C.A.A.F. 2011). *See also* Rule 611.

2013 Amendment. Like the psychotherapist-patient privilege created by Mil. R. Evid. 513, Mil. R. Evid. 514 establishes a victim advocate-victim privilege for investigations or proceedings authorized under the Uniform Code of Military Justice. Implemented as another approach to improving the military's overall effectiveness in addressing the crime of sexual assault, facilitating candor between victims and victim advocates, and mitigating the

impact of the court-martial process on victims, the rule specifically emerged in response to concerns raised by members of Congress, community groups and *The Defense Task Force on Sexual Assault in the Military Services* (DTFSAMS). In its 2009 report, DTFSAMS noted: 35 states had a privilege for communications between victim advocates and victims of sexual assault; victims did not believe they could communicate confidentially with medical and psychological support services provided by DoD; there was interference with the victim-victim advocate relationship and continuing victim advocate services when the victim advocate was identified as a potential witness in a court-martial; and servicemembers reported being "re-victimized" when their prior statements to victim advocates were used to cross-examine them in court-martial proceedings. DTFSAMS recommended that Congress "enact a comprehensive military justice privilege for communications between a Victim Advocate and a victim of sexual assault." Both the DoD Joint Service Committee on Military Justice and Congress began considering a privilege. The committee chose to model a proposed Mil. R. Evid. 514 on Mil. R. Evid. 513, including its various exceptions, in an effort to balance the privacy of the victim's communications with a victim advocate against the accused's legitimate needs. Differing proposals for a victim advocate privilege were suggested as part of the FY2011 National Defense Authorization Act (NDAA), but were not enacted. A victim advocate privilege passed the House as part of the FY2012 NDAA, while the Senate version would have required the President to issue a Military Rule of Evidence providing a privilege. Congress removed both provisions because Mil. R. Evid. 514 was pending the President's signature and this rule accomplished the objective of ensuring privileged communications for sexual assault victims.

Under subsection (a), *General Rule*, the words "under the Uniform Code of Military Justice" in Mil. R. Evid. 514 mean that the privilege only applies to misconduct situations constituting a case that could result in UCMJ proceedings. It does not apply in situations in which the offender is not subject to UCMJ jurisdiction. There is no intent to apply Mil. R. Evid. 514 in any proceeding other than those authorized under the UCMJ. However, service regulations dictate how the privilege is applied to non-UCMJ proceedings. Furthermore, this rule only applies to communications between a victim advocate and the victim of a sexual or violent offense.

Under subsection (b), *Definitions*, the committee intended the definition of "victim advocate" to include, but not be limited to, personnel performing victim advocate duties within the DoD Sexual Assault Prevention and Response Office (such as a Sexual Assault Response Coordinator), and the DoD Family Advocacy Program (such as a domestic abuse victim advocate). To determine whether an official's duties encompass victim advocate responsibilities, DoD and military service regulations should be consulted. A victim liaison appointed pursuant to the Victim and Witness Assistance Program is not a "victim advocate" for purposes of this rule, nor are personnel working within an Equal Opportunity or Inspector General office. For purposes of this rule, the committee intended "violent offense" to mean an actual or attempted murder, manslaughter, rape, sexual assault, aggravated assault, robbery, assault consummated by a battery, or similar offense. A simple assault may be a violent offense where the violence has been physically attempted or menaced. A mere threatening in words is not a violent offense. The committee recognizes that this rule will be applicable in situations where there is a factual dispute as to whether a sexual or violent offense occurred and whether a person actually suffered direct physical or emotional harm from such an offense. The fact that such findings have not been judicially established shall not prevent application of this rule to alleged victims reasonably intended to be covered by this rule.

Under subsection (d), *Exceptions*, the exceptions to Mil. R. Evid. 514 are similar to the exceptions found in Mil. R. Evid. 513, and are intended to be applied in the same manner. Mil. R. Evid. 514 does not include comparable exceptions found within Mil. R. Evid. 513(d)(2) and 513(d)(7). In drafting the "constitutionally required" exception, the committee intended that communication covered by the privilege would be released only in the narrow circumstances where the accused could show harm of constitutional magnitude if such communication was not disclosed. In practice, this relatively high standard of release is not intended to invite a fishing expedition for possible statements made by the victim, nor is it intended to be an exception that effectively renders the privilege meaningless. If a military judge finds that an exception to this privilege applies, special care should be taken to narrowly tailor the release of privileged communications to only those statements which are relevant and whose probative value outweighs unfair prejudice. The fact that otherwise privileged communications are admissible pursuant to an exception of Mil. R. Evid. 514 does not prohibit a military judge from imposing reasonable limitations on cross-examination. *See Delaware v. Van Arsdall*, 475 U.S. 673, 679 (1986); *United States v. Gaddis*, 70 M.J. 248, 256 (C.A.A.F. 2011); *United States v. Ellerbrock*, 70 M.J. 314 (C.A.A.F. 2011).

SECTION VI

WITNESSES

Rule 601 Competency to Testify in General

Rule 601 is taken without change from the first portion of Federal Rule of Evidence 601. The remainder of the Federal Rule was deleted due to its sole application to civil cases.

In declaring that subject to any other Rule, all persons are competent to be witnesses, Rule 601 supersedes Para. 148 of the 1969 Manual which required, among other factors, that an individual know the difference between truth and falsehood and understand the moral importance of telling the truth in order to testify. Under Rule 601 such matters will go only to the weight of the testimony and not to its competency. The Rule's reference to other rules includes Rules 603 (Oath or Affirmation), 605 (Competency of Military Judge as Witness), 606 (Competency of Court Member as Witness), and the rules of privilege.

The plain meaning of the Rule appears to deprive the trial judge of any discretion whatsoever to exclude testimony on grounds of competency unless the testimony is incompetent under those specific rules already cited *supra; see, United States v. Fowler*, 605 F.2d 181 (5th Cir. 1979), a conclusion bolstered by the Federal Rules of Evidence Advisory Committee's Note, S. Saltzburg & K. Redden, FEDERAL RULES OF EVIDENCE MANUAL 270 (2d ed. 1977). Whether this conclusion is accurate, especially in the light of Rule 403, is unclear. *Id.* at 269; *see*

also United States v. Calahan, 442 F.Supp. 1213 (D. Minn. 1978).

2013 Amendment. The committee revised this rule for stylistic reasons and to align it with the Federal Rules of Evidence but in doing so did not intend to change any result in any ruling on evidence admissibility.

Rule 602 Need for Personal Knowledge

Rule 602 is taken without significant change from the Federal Rule and is similar in content to Para. 138 *d*, MCM, 1969 (Rev.). Although the 1969 Manual expressly allowed an individual to testify to his or her own age or date of birth, the Rule is silent of the issue.

Notwithstanding that silence, however, it appears that it is within the meaning of the Rule to allow such testimony. Rule 804(b)(4) (Hearsay Exceptions; Declarant Unavailable—Statement of Personal or Family History) expressly permits a hearsay statement "concerning the declarant's own birth . . . or other similar fact of personal or family history, even though declarant had no means of acquiring personal knowledge of the matter stated." It seems evident that if such a hearsay statement is admissible, in-court testimony by the declarant should be no less admissible. It is probable that the expression "personal knowledge" in Rule 804(b)(4) is being used in the sense of "first hand knowledge" while the expression is being used in Rule 602 in a somewhat broader sense to include those matters which an individual could be considered to reliably know about his or her personal history.

2013 Amendment. The committee revised this rule for stylistic reasons and to align it with the Federal Rules of Evidence but in doing so did not intend to change any result in any ruling on evidence admissibility.

Rule 603 Oath or Affirmation to Testify Truthfully

Rule 603 is taken from the Federal Rule without change. The oaths found within Chapter XXII of the Manual satisfy the requirements of Rule 603. Pursuant to Rule 1101(c), this Rule is inapplicable to the accused when he or she makes an unsworn statement.

2013 Amendment. The committee revised this rule for stylistic reasons and to align it with the Federal Rules of Evidence but in doing so did not intend to change any result in any ruling on evidence admissibility.

Rule 604 Interpreters

Rule 604 is taken from the Federal Rule without change and is consistent with Para. 141, MCM, 1969 (Rev.). The oath found in Paras. 114 *e*, MCM, 1969 (Rev.) (now R.C.M. 807(b)(2) (Discussion), MCM, 1984), satisfies the oath requirements of Rule 604.

2013 Amendment. The committee amended this rule to match the Federal Rules of Evidence. However, the word "qualified" is undefined both in these rules and in the Federal Rules. R.C.M. 502(e)(1) states that the Secretary concerned may prescribe qualifications for interpreters. Practitioners should therefore refer to the Secretary's guidance to determine if a translator is qualified under this rule. The committee also revised this rule for stylistic reasons and to align it with the Federal Rules of Evidence but in doing so did not intend to change any result in any ruling on evidence admissibility.

Rule 605 Military Judge's Competency as a Witness

Rule 605(a) restates the Federal Rule without significant change. Although Article 26(d) of the Uniform Code of Military Justice states in relevant part that "no person is eligible to act as a military judge if he is a witness for the prosecution ..." and is silent on whether a witness for the defense is eligible to sit, the Committee believes that the specific reference in the code was not intended to create a right and was the result only of an attempt to highlight the more grievous case. In any event, Rule 605, unlike Article 26(d), does not deal with the question of eligibility to sit as a military judge, but deals solely with the military judge's competency as a witness. The rule does not affect *voir dire.*

Rule 605(b) is new and is not found within the Federal Rules of Evidence. It was added because of the unique nature of the military judiciary in which military judges often control their own dockets without clerical assistance. In view of the military's stringent speedy trial roles, *see, United States v. Burton,* 21 U.S.C.M.A 112, 44 C.M.R. 166 (1971), it was necessary to preclude expressly any interpretation of Rule 605 that would prohibit the military judge from placing on the record details relating to docketing in order to avoid prejudice to a party. Rule 605(b) is consistent with present military law.

2013 Amendment. The committee revised subsection (a) for stylistic reasons and to align it with the Federal Rules of Evidence but in doing so did not intend to change any result in any ruling on evidence admissibility.

Rule 606 Member's Competency as a Witness

(a) *At the court-martial.* Rule 606(a) is taken from the Federal Rule without substantive change. The Rule alters prior military law only to the extent that a member of the court could testify as a defense witness under prior precedent. Rule 606(a) deals only with the competency of court members as witnesses and does not affect other Manual provisions governing the eligibility of the individuals to sit as members due to their potential status as witnesses.*See, e.g.,* Paras. 62 *f* and 63, MCM, 1969 (Rev.). The Rule does not affect *voir dire.*

(b) *Inquiry into validity of findings or sentence.* Rule 606(b) is taken from the Federal Rule with only one significant change. The rule, retitled to reflect the sentencing function of members, recognizes unlawful command influence as a legitimate subject of inquiry and permits testimony by a member on that subject. The addition is required by the need to keep proceedings free from any taint of unlawful command influence and further implements Article 37(a) of the Uniform Code of Military Justice. Use of superior rank or grade by one member of a court to sway other members would constitute unlawful command influence for purposes of this Rule under Para. 74 *d*(1), MCM, 1969 (Rev.). Rule 606 does not itself prevent otherwise lawful polling of members of the court, *see generally, United States v. Hendon,* 6 M.J. 171, 174 (C.M.A. 1979), and does not prohibit attempted lawful clarification of an ambiguous or inconsistent verdict. Rule 606(b) is in general accord with prior military law.

2013 Amendment. The committee added subsection (c) to this rule to align it with the Federal Rules of Evidence. The committee also revised this rule for stylistic reasons but in doing so did not intend to change any result in any ruling on evidence admissibility.

Rule 607 Who May Impeach a Witness

Rule 607 is taken without significant change from the Federal Rule. It supersedes Para. 153 *b*(1), MCM, 1969 (Rev.), which restricted impeachment of one's own witness to those situations in which the witness is indispensable or the testimony of the witness proves to be unexpectedly adverse.

Rule 607 thus allows a party to impeach its own witness. Indeed, when relevant, it permits a party to call a witness for the sole purpose of impeachment. It should be noted, however, that an apparent inconsistency exists when Rule 607 is compared with Rules 608(b) and 609(a). Although Rule 607 allows impeachment on direct examination, Rules 608(b) and 609(a) would by their explicit language restrict the methods of impeachment to cross-examination. The use of the expression "cross-examination" in these rules appears to be accidental and to have been intended to be synonymous with impeachment while on direct examination. *See generally* S. Saltzburg & K. Redden, FEDERAL RULES OF EVIDENCE MANUAL 298–99 (2d ed. 1977). It is the intent of the Committee that the Rules be so interpreted unless the Article III courts should interpret the Rules in a different fashion.

2013 Amendment. The committee revised this rule for stylistic reasons and to align it with the Federal Rules of Evidence but in doing so did not intend to change any result in any ruling on evidence admissibility.

Rule 608 A Witness's Character for Truthfulness or Untruthfulness

(a) *Opinion and reputation evidence of character.* Rule 608(a) is taken verbatim from the Federal Rule. The Rule, which is consistent with the philosophy behind Rule 404(a), limits use of character evidence in the form of opinion or reputation evidence on the issue of credibility by restricting such evidence to matters relating to the character for truthfulness or untruthfulness of the witness. General good character is not admissible under the Rule. Rule 608(a) prohibits presenting evidence of good character until the character of the witness for truthfulness has been attacked. The Rule is similar to Para. 153 *b* of the 1969 Manual except that the Rule, unlike Para. 153 *b*, applies to all witnesses and does not distinguish between the accused and other witnesses.

(b) *Specific instances of conduct.* Rule 608(b) is taken from the Federal Rule without significant change. The Rule is somewhat similar in effect to the military practice found in Para. 153 *b*(2) of the 1969 Manual in that it allows use of specific instances of conduct of a witness to be brought out on cross-examination but prohibits use of extrinsic evidence. Unlike Para. 153 *b*(2), Rule 608(b) does not distinguish between an accused and other witnesses.

The fact that the accused is subject to impeachment by prior acts of misconduct is a significant factor to be considered by the military judge when he or she is determining whether to exercise the discretion granted by the Rule. Although the Rule expressly limits this form of impeachment to inquiry on cross-examination, it is likely that the intent of the Federal Rule was to permit inquiry on direct as well, *see* Rule 607, and the use of the term "cross-examination" was an accidental substitute for "impeachment." *See* S. Saltzburg & K. Redden, FEDERAL RULES OF EVIDENCE MANUAL 312–13 (2d ed. 1977). It is the intent of the Committee to allow use of this form of evidence on direct examination to the same extent, if any, it is so permitted in the Article III courts.

The Rule does not prohibit receipt of extrinsic evidence in the form of prior convictions, Rule 609, or to show bias. Rule 608(c). *See also* Rule 613 (Prior statements of witnesses). When the witness has testified as to the character of another witness, the witness may be cross-examined as to the character of that witness. The remainder of Rule 608(b) indicates that testimony relating only to credibility does not waive the privilege against self-incrimination. *See generally* Rule 301.

Although 608(b) allows examination into specific acts, counsel should not, as a matter of ethics, attempt to elicit evidence of misconduct unless there is a reasonable basis for the question. *See generally* ABA PROJECT ON STANDARDS FOR CRIMINAL JUSTICE, STANDARDS RELATING TO THE PROSECUTION FUNCTION AND THE DEFENSE FUNCTION, Prosecution Function 5.7(d); Defense Functions 7.6(d) (Approved draft 1971).

(c) *Evidence of bias.* Rule 608(c) is taken from 1969 Manual Para. 153*d* and is not found within the Federal Rule. Impeachment by bias was apparently accidentally omitted from the Federal Rule, *see* S. Saltzburg & K. Redden, FEDERAL RULES OF EVIDENCE MANUAL 313–14 (2d ed. 1977), but is acceptable under the Federal Rules; *see, e.g., United States v. Leja*, 568 F.2d 493 (6th Cir. 1977); *United States v. Alvarez-Lopez*, 559 F.2d 1155 (9th Cir. 1977). Because of the critical nature of this form of impeachment and the fact that extrinsic evidence may be used to show it, the Committee believed that its omission would be impracticable.

It should be noted that the Federal Rules are not exhaustive, and that a number of different types of techniques of impeachment are not explicitly codified.

The failure to so codify them does not mean that they are no longer permissible. *See, e.g., United states v. Alvarez-Lopez , supra* 155; Rule 412. Thus, impeachment by contradiction, *see also* Rule 304(a)(2); 311(j), and impeachment via prior inconsistent statements, Rule 613, remain appropriate. To the extent that the Military Rules do not acknowledge a particular form of impeachment, it is the intent of the Committee to allow that method to the same extent it is permissible in the Article III courts. *See, e.g.,* Rules 402; 403.

Impeachment of an alleged victim of a sexual offense through evidence of the victim's past sexual history and character is dealt with in Rule 412, and evidence of fresh complaint is admissible to the extent permitted by Rules 801 and 803.

2013 Amendment. The committee revised this rule for stylistic reasons and to align it with the Federal Rules of Evidence but in doing so did not intend to change any result in any ruling on evidence admissibility.

Rule 609 Impeachment by Evidence of a Criminal Conviction

(a) *General Rules.* Rule 609(a) is taken from the Federal Rule but has been slightly modified to adopt it to military law. For example, an offense for which a dishonorable discharge may be adjudged may be used for impeachment. This continues the rule as found in Para. 153 *b*(2)(b)(1) of the 1969 Manual. In determining whether a military offense may be used for purposes of impeachment under Rule 609(a)(1), recourse must be made to the maximum punishment imposable if the offense had been tried by general court-martial.

Rule 609(a) differs slightly from the prior military rule. Under Rule 609(a)(1), a civilian conviction's availability for impeachment is solely a function of its maximum punishment under "the law in which the witness was convicted." This is different from Para. 153 *b*(2)(b)(3) of the 1969 Manual which allowed use of a non-federal conviction analogous to a federal felony or characterized by the jurisdiction as a felony or "as an offense of comparable gravity." Under the new rule, comparisons and determinations of relative gravity will be unnecessary and improper.

Convictions that "involve moral turpitude or otherwise affect . . . credibility" were admissible for impeachment under Para. 153 *b*(2)(b) of the 1969 Manual. The list of potential convictions expressed in Para. 153 *b*(2)(b) was illustrative only and non-exhaustive. Unlike the 1969 Manual rule, Rule 609(a) is exhaustive.

Although a conviction technically fits within Rule 609(a)(1), its admissibility remains subject to finding by the military judge that its probative value outweighs its prejudicial effect to the accused.

Rule 609(a)(2) makes admissible convictions involving "dishonesty or false statement, regardless of punishment." This is similar to intent in Para. 153*b*(2)(b)(4) of the 1969 Manual which makes admissible "a conviction of any offense involving fraud, deceit, larceny, wrongful appropriation, or the making of false statement." The exact meaning of "dishonesty" within the meaning of Rule 609 is unclear and has already been the subject of substantial litigation. The Congressional intent appears, however, to have been extremely restrictive with "dishonesty" being used in the sense of untruthfulness. *See generally* S. Saltzburg & K. Redden, FEDERAL RULES OF EVIDENCE MANUAL 336–45 (2d ed. 1977). Thus, a conviction for fraud, perjury, or embezzlement would come within the definition, but a conviction for simple larceny would not. Pending further case development in the Article III courts, caution would suggest close adherence to this highly limited definition.

It should be noted that admissibility of evidence within the scope of Rule 609(a)(2) is not explicitly subject to the discretion of the military judge. The application of Rule 403 is unclear.

While the language of Rule 609(a) refers only to cross-examination, it would appear that the Rule does refer to direct examination as well. *See* the Analysis to Rules 607 and 608(b).

As defined in Rule 609(f), a court-martial conviction occurs when a sentence has been adjudged.

1993 Amendment. The amendment to Mil. R. Evid. 609(a) is based on the 1990 amendment to Fed. R. Evid. 609(a). The previous version of Mil. R. Evid. 609(a) was based on the now superseded version of the Federal Rule. This amendment removes from the rule the limitation that the conviction may only be elicited during cross-examination. Additionally, the amendment clarifies the relationship between Rules 403 and 609. The amendment clarifies that the special balancing test found in Mil. R. Evid. 609(a)(1) applies to the accused's convictions. The convictions of all other witnesses are only subject to the Mil. R. Evid. 403 balancing test. *See Green v. Bock Laundry Machine Co.,* 490 U.S. 504 (1989).

2012 Amendment: Rule 609(a) was amended to conform to the

Federal Rule by replacing the word "credibility" with the words "character for truthfulness." Rule 609(a)(2) was amended to conform to the Federal Rule.

(b) *Time limit.* Rule 609(b) is taken verbatim from the Federal Rule. As it has already been made applicable to the armed forces, *United States v. Weaver*, 1 M.J. 111 (C.M.A. 1975), it is consistent with the present military practice.

(c) *Effect of pardon, annulment, or certificate of rehabilitation.* Rule 609(c) is taken verbatim from the Federal Rule except that convictions punishable by dishonorable discharge have been added. Rule 609(c) has no equivalent in present military practice and represents a substantial change as it will prohibit use of convictions due to evidence of rehabilitation. In the absence of a certificate of rehabilitation, the extent to which the various Armed Forces post-conviction programs, such as the Air Force's 3320th Correction and Rehabilitation Squadron and the Army's Retraining Brigade, come within Rule 609(c) is unclear, although it is probable that successful completion of such a program is "an equivalent procedure based on the finding of the rehabilitation of the persons convicted" within the meaning of the Rule.

2012 Amendment: Rule 609(c) was amended to conform to the Federal Rule.

(d) *Juvenile adjudications.* Rule 609(d) is taken from the Federal Rule without significant change. The general prohibition in the Rule is substantially different from Para. 153*b*(2)(b) of the 1969 Manual which allowed use of juvenile adjudications other than those involving an accused. The discretionary authority vested in the military judge to admit such evidence comports with the accused's constitutional right to a fair trial. *Davis v. Alaska,* 415 U.S. 308 (1974).

(e) *Pendency of appeal.* The first portion of Rule 609(e) is taken from the Federal Rule and is substantially different from Para. 153 *b*(2)(b) of the 1969 Manual which prohibited use of convictions for impeachment purposes while they were undergoing appellate review. Under the Rule, the fact of review may be shown but does not affect admissibility. A different rule applies, however, for convictions by summary court-martial or by special court-martial without a military judge. The Committee believed that because a legally trained presiding officer is not required in these proceedings, a conviction should not be used for impeachment until review has been completed.

February 1986 Amendment: The reference in subsection (e) to "Article 65(c)" was changed to "Article 64" to correct an error in MCM, 1984.

(f) *Definition.* This definition of conviction has been added because of the unique nature of the court-martial. Because of its recognition that a conviction cannot result until at least sentencing, *cf. Frederic Lederer, Reappraising the Legality of Post-trial Interviews,* 1977 Army Law. 1, 12, the Rule may modify *United States v. Mathews,* 6 M.J. 357 (C.M.A. 1979).

2013 Amendment. Pursuant to Exec. Order No. 13643, the committee amended subsections (a), (b)(2), and (c)(1) to conform the rule with the Federal Rules of Evidence. The committee also revised this rule for stylistic reasons but in doing so did not intend to change any result in any ruling on evidence admissibility.

Rule 610 Religious beliefs or opinions

Rule 610 is taken without significant change from the Federal Rules and had no equivalent in the 1969 Manual for Courts-Martial. The Rule makes religious beliefs or opinions inadmissible for the purpose of impeaching or bolstering credibility. To the extent that such opinions may be critical to the defense of a case, however, there may be constitutional justification for overcoming the Rule's exclusion. *Cf.Davis v. Alaska*, 415 U.S. 308 (1974).

2013 Amendment. The committee revised this rule for stylistic reasons and to align it with the Federal Rules of Evidence but in doing so did not intend to change any result in any ruling on evidence admissibility.

Rule 611 Mode and Order of Examining Witnesses and Presenting Evidence

(a) *Control by the military judge.* Rule 611(a) is taken from the Federal Rule without change. It is a basic source of the military judge's power to control proceedings and replaces 1969 Manual Para. 149 *a* and that part of Para. 137 dealing with cumulative evidence. It is within the military judge's discretion to control methods of interrogation of witnesses. The Rule does not change prior law. Although a witness may be required to limit an answer to the question asked, it will normally be improper to require that a "yes" or "no" answer be given unless it is clear that such an answer will be a complete response to the question. A witness will ordinarily be entitled to explain his or her testimony at some time before completing this testimony. The Manual requirement that questions be asked through the military judge is now found in Rule 614.

Although the military judge has the discretion to alter the sequence of proof to the extent that the burden of proof is not affected, the usual sequence for examination of witnesses is: prosecution witnesses, defense witnesses, prosecution rebuttal witnesses, defense rebuttal witnesses, and witnesses for the court. The usual order of examination of a witness is: direct examination, cross-examination, redirect examination, recross-examination, and examination by the court. Para. 54 *a*, MCM, 1969 (Rev.).

1995 Amendment: When a child witness is unable to testify due to intimidation by the proceedings, fear of the accused, emotional trauma, or mental or other infirmity, alternative to live in-court testimony may be appropriate.*See Maryland v. Craig,* 497 U.S. 836 (1990); *United States v. Romey,* 32 M.J. 180 (C.M.A.), *cert. denied,* 502 U.S. 924 (1991); *United States v. Batten,* 31 M.J. 205 (C.M.A. 1990); *United States v. Thompson,* 31 M.J. 168 (C.M.A. 1990), *cert. denied,* 111 S. Ct. 956 (1991). This is an evolving area of law with guidance available in case law. The drafters, after specifically considering adoption of 18 U.S.C. § 3509, determined it more appropriate to allow the case law evolutionary process to continue.

(b) *Scope of cross-examination.* Rule 611(b) is taken from the Federal Rule without change and replaces Para. 149 *b*(1) of the 1969 Manual which was similar in scope. Under the Rule the military judge may allow a party to adopt a witness and proceed as if on direct examination. *See* Rule 301(b)(2) (judicial advice as to the privilege against self-incrimination for an apparently uninformed witness); Rule 301(f)(2) (effect of claiming the privilege against self-incrimination on cross-examination); Rule 303 (Degrading Questions); and Rule 608(b) (Evidence of Character, Conduct, and Bias of Witness).

(c) *Leading questions.* Rule 611(c) is taken from the Federal Rule without significant change and is similar to Para. 149 *c* of the 1969 Manual. The reference in the third sentence of the Federal Rule to an "adverse party" has been deleted as being applicable to civil cases only.

A leading question is one which suggests the answer it is desired that the witness give. Generally, a question that is susceptible to being answered by "yes" or "no" is a leading question.

The use of leading questions is discretionary with the military judge. Use of leading questions may be appropriate with respect to the following witnesses, among others: children, persons with mental or physical disabilities, the extremely elderly, hostile witnesses, and witnesses identified with the adverse party.

It is also appropriate with the military judge's consent to utilize leading questions to direct a witness's attention to a relevant area of inquiry.

1999 Amendment: Rule 611(d) is new. This amendment to Rule 611 gives substantive guidance to military judges regarding the use of alternative examination methods for child victims and witnesses in light of the U.S. Supreme Court's decision in *Maryland v. Craig*, 497 U.S. 836 (1990) and the change in Federal law in 18 U.S.C. § 3509. Although *Maryland v. Craig* dealt with child witnesses who were themselves the victims of abuse, it should be noted that 18 U.S.C. § 3509, as construed by Federal courts, has been applied to allow non-victim child witnesses to testify remotely. *See, e.g., United States v. Moses*, 137 F.3d 894 (6th Cir. 1998) (applying § 3509 to a non-victim child witness, but reversing a child sexual assault conviction on other grounds) and *United States v. Quintero*, 21 F.3d 885 (9th Cir. 1994) (affirming conviction based on remote testimony of non-victim child witness, but remanding for resentencing). This amendment recognizes that child witnesses may be particularly traumatized, even if they are not themselves the direct victims, in cases involving the abuse of other children or domestic violence. This amendment also gives the accused an election to absent himself from the courtroom to prevent remote testimony. Such a provision gives the accused a greater role in determining how this issue will be resolved.

2013 Amendment. The committee amended subsection (d)(3) to conform with the United States Supreme Court's holding in *Maryland v. Craig*, 497 U.S. 836 (1990), and CAAF's holding in *United States v. Pack*, 65 M.J. 381 (C.A.A.F. 2007). In *Craig*, the Supreme Court held that, in order for a child witness to be permitted to testify via closed-circuit one-way video, three factors must be met: (1) the trial court must determine that it is necessary "to protect the welfare of the particular child witness"; (2) the trial court must find "that the child witness would be traumatized, not by the courtroom generally, but by the presence of the defendant"; and (3) the trial court must find "that the emotional distress suffered by the child witness in the presence of the defendant is more than *de minimis.*" *Craig,* 497 at 855-56. In *Pack*, CAAF held that, despite the Supreme Court's decision in *Crawford v. Washington*, the Supreme Court did not implicitly overrule *Craig* and that all three factors must be present in order to permit a child witness to testify remotely. *Pack*, 65 M.J. at 384-85. This rule as previously written contradicted these cases because it stated that any one of four factors, rather than all three of those identified in *Craig*, would be sufficient to allow a child

to testify remotely. The committee made the changes to ensure that this subsection aligned with the relevant case law.

The language for subsection (5) was taken from 18 U.S.C. § 3509, which covers child victims' and child witnesses' rights. There is no comparable Federal Rule of Evidence but the committee believes that a military judge may find that an Article 39(a) session outside the presence of the accused is necessary to make a decision regarding remote testimony. The committee intended to limit the number of people present at the Article 39(a) session in order to make the child feel more at ease, which is why the committee included the language limiting those present to "a representative" of the defense and prosecution, rather than multiple representatives.

The committee also revised this rule for stylistic reasons but in doing so did not intend to change any result in any ruling on evidence admissibility.

Rule 612 Writing Used to Refresh a Witness's Memory

Rule 612 is taken generally from the Federal Rule but a number of modifications have been made to adapt the Rule to military practice. Language in the Federal Rule relating to the Jencks Act, 18 U.S.C. § 3500, which would have shielded material from disclosure to the defense under Rule 612 was discarded. Such shielding was considered to be inappropriate in view of the general military practice and policy which utilizes and encourages broad discovery on behalf of the defense.

The decision of the president of a special court-martial without a military judge under this rule is an interlocutory ruling not subject to objection by the members, Para. 57 *a*, MCM, 1969 (Rev.).

Rule 612 codifies the doctrine of past recollection refreshed and replaces that portion of Para. 146*a* of the 1969 Manual which dealt with the issue. Although the 1969 Manual rule was similar, in that it authorized inspection by the opposing party of a memorandum used to refresh recollection and permitted it to be offered into evidence by that party to show the improbability of it refreshing recollection, the Rule is somewhat more extensive as it also deals with writings used before testifying.

Rule 612 does not affect in any way information required to be disclosed under any other rule or portion of the Manual. *See*, Rule 304(c)(1).

2013 Amendment. The committee revised subsection (b) of this rule to align with the Federal Rules of Evidence. The committee also revised this rule for stylistic reasons but in doing so did not intend to change any result in any ruling on evidence admissibility.

Rule 613 Witness's Prior Statement

(a) *Examining witness concerning prior statement.* Rule 613(a) is taken from the Federal Rule without change. It alters military practice inasmuch as it eliminates the foundation requirements found in Para. 153*b*(2)(c) of the 1969 Manual. While it will no longer be a condition precedent to admissibility to acquaint a witness with the prior statement and to give the witness an opportunity to either change his or her testimony or to reaffirm it, such a procedure may be appropriate as a matter of trial tactics.

It appears that the drafters of Federal Rule 613 may have inadvertently omitted the word "inconsistent" from both its caption and the text of Rule 613(a). The effect of that omission, if any, is unclear.

(b) *Extrinsic evidence of prior inconsistent statement of witness.* Rule 613(b) is taken from the Federal Rule without change. It requires that the witness be given an opportunity to explain or deny a prior inconsistent statement when the party proffers extrinsic evidence of the statement. Although this foundation is not required under Rule 613(a), it is required under Rule 613(b) if a party wishes to utilize more than the witness' own testimony as brought out on cross-examination. The Rule does not specify any particular timing for the opportunity for the witness to explain or deny the statement nor does it specify any particular method. The Rule is inapplicable to introduction of prior inconsistent statements on the merits under Rule 801.

2013 Amendment. The committee revised this rule for stylistic reasons and to align it with the Federal Rules of Evidence but in doing so did not intend to change any result in any ruling on evidence admissibility.

Rule 614 Court-Martial's Calling or Examining a Witness

(a) *Calling by the court-martial.* The first sentence of Rule 614(a) is taken from the Federal Rule but has been modified to recognize the power of the court members to call and examine witnesses. The second sentence of the subdivision is new and reflects the members' power to call or recall witnesses. Although recognizing that power, the Rule makes it clear that the calling of such witnesses is contingent upon compliance with these Rules and this Manual. Consequently, the testimony of such witnesses must be relevant and not barred by any Rule or Manual provision.

(b) *Interrogation by the court-martial.* The first sentence of Rule 614(b) is taken from the Federal Rule but modified to reflect the power under these Rules and Manual of the court-members to interrogate witnesses. The second sentence of the subdivision is new and modifies Para. 54*a* and Para. 149*a* of the present manual by requiring that questions of members be submitted to the military judge in writing. This change in current practice was made in order to improve efficiency and to prevent prejudice to either party. Although the Rule states that its intent is to ensure that the questions will "be in a form acceptable to the military judge," it is not the intent of the Committee to grant *carte blanche* to the military judge in this matter. It is the Committee's intent that the president will utilize the same procedure.

(c) *Objections.* Rule 614(c) is taken from the Federal Rule but modified to reflect the powers of the members to call and interrogate witnesses. This provision generally restates prior law but recognizes counsel's right to request an Article 39(a) session to enter an objection.

2013 Amendment. In subsection (a), the committee substituted the word "relevant" for "appropriate" because relevance is the most accurate threshold for admissibility throughout these rules. Additionally, the committee added the phrase "Following the opportunity for review by both parties" to subsection (b) to align it with the standard military practice to allow the counsel for both sides to review a question posed by the members, and to voice objections before the military judge rules on the propriety of the question. The committee also revised this rule for stylistic reasons and to align it with the Federal Rules of Evidence but in doing so

did not intend to change any result in any ruling on evidence admissibility.

Rule 615 Excluding Witnesses

Rule 615 is taken from the Federal Rule with only minor changes of terminology. The first portion of the Rule is in conformity with prior practice, *e.g.,* Para. 53*f*, MCM, 1969 (Rev.). The second portion, consisting of subdivisions (2) and (3), represents a substantial departure from prior practice and will authorize the prosecution to designate another individual to sit with the trial counsel. Rule 615 thus modifies Para. 53 *f*. Under the Rule, the military judge lacks any discretion to exclude potential witnesses who come within the scope of Rule 615(2) and (3) unless the accused's constitutional right to a fair trial would be violated. Developing Article III practice recognizes the defense right, upon request, to have a prosecution witness, not excluded because of Rule 615, testify before other prosecution witnesses.

Rule 615 does not prohibit exclusion of either accused or counsel due to misbehavior when such exclusion is not prohibited by the Constitution of the United States, the Uniform Code of Military Justice, this Manual, or these Rules.

2002 Amendment: These changes are intended to extend to victims at courts-martial the same rights granted to victims by the Victims' Rights and Restitution Act of 1990, 42 U.S.C. § 10606(b)(4), giving crime victims "[t]he right to be present at all public court proceedings related to the offense, unless the court determines that testimony by the victim would be materially affected if the victim heard other testimony at trial," and the Victim Rights Clarification Act of 1997, 18 U.S.C. § 3510, which is restated in subsection (5). For the purposes of this rule, the term "victim" includes all persons defined as victims in 42 U.S.C. § 10607(e)(2), which means "a person that has suffered direct physical, emotional, or pecuniary harm as a result of the commission of a crime, including"—(A) in the case of a victim that is an institutional entity, an authorized representative of the entity; and (B) in the case of a victim who is under 18 years of age, incompetent, incapacitated, or deceased, one of the following (in order of preference): (i) a spouse; (ii) a legal guardian; (iii) a parent; (iv) a child; (v) a sibling; (vi) another family member; or (vii) another person designated by the court. The victim's right to remain in the courtroom remains subject to other rules, such as those regarding classified information, witness deportment, and conduct in the courtroom. Subsection (4) is intended to capture only those statutes applicable to courts-martial.

2013 Amendment. The committee revised this rule for stylistic reasons but in doing so did not intend to change any result in any ruling on evidence admissibility.

SECTION VII
OPINIONS AND EXPERT TESTIMONY

Rule 701 Opinion testimony by lay witnesses

Rule 701 is taken from the Federal Rule without change and supersedes that portion of Para. 138 *e*, MCM, 1969 (Rev.), which dealt with opinion evidence by lay witnesses. Unlike the prior Manual rule which prohibited lay opinion testimony except when the opinion was of a "kind which is commonly drawn and which cannot, or ordinarily cannot, be conveyed to the court by a mere recitation of the observed facts," the Rule permits opinions or inferences whenever rationally based on the perception of the witness and helpful to either a clear understanding of the testimony or the determination of a fact in issue. Consequently, the Rule is broader in scope than the Manual provision it replaces. The specific examples listed in the Manual, "the speed of an automobile, whether a voice heard was that of a man, woman or child, and whether or not a person was drunk" are all within the potential scope of Rule 701.

2004 Amendment: Rule 701 was modified based on the amendment to Fed. R. Evid. 701, effective 1 December 2000, and is taken from the Federal Rule without change. It prevents parties from proffering an expert as a lay witness in an attempt to evade the gatekeeper and reliability requirements of Rule 702 by providing that testimony cannot qualify under Rule 701 if it is based on "scientific, technical, or other special knowledge within the scope of Rule 702."

2013 Amendment. The committee revised this rule for stylistic reasons and to align it with the Federal Rules of Evidence but in doing so did not intend to change any result in any ruling on evidence admissibility.

Rule 702 Testimony by Expert Witnesses

Rule 702 is taken from the Federal Rule verbatim, and replaces that portion of Para. 138 *e*, MCM, 1969 (Rev.), dealing with expert testimony. Although the Rule is similar to the prior Manual rule, it may be broader and *may* supersede *Frye v. United States*, 293 F.1013 (C.D. Cir. 1923), an issue now being extensively litigated in the Article III courts. The Rule's sole explicit test is whether the evidence in question "will assist the trier of fact to understand the evidence or to determine a fact in issue." Whether any particular piece of evidence comes within the test is normally a matter within the military judge's discretion.

Under Rule 103(a) any objection to an expert on the basis that the individual is not in fact adequately qualified under the Rule will be waived by a failure to so object.

Para. 142 *e* of the 1969 Manual, "Polygraph tests and drug-induced or hypnosis-induced interviews," has been deleted as a result of the adoption of Rule 702. Para. 142 *e* states, "The conclusions based upon or lineartally represented by a polygraph test and conclusions based upon, and the statements of the person interviewed made during a drug-induced or hypnosis-induced interview are inadmissible in evidence." The deletion of the explicit prohibition on such evidence is not intended to make such evidence *per se* admissible, and is not an express authorization for such procedures. Clearly, such evidence must be approached with great care. Considerations surrounding the nature of such evidence, any possible prejudicial effect on a fact finder, and the degree of acceptance of such evidence in the Article III courts are factors to consider in determining whether it can in fact "assist the trier of fact." As of late 1979, the Committee was unaware of any significant decision by a United States Court of Appeals sustaining the admissibility of polygraph evidence in a criminal case, *see e.g., United States v. Masri*, 547 F.2d 932 (5th Cir. 1977); *United States v. Cardarella*, 570 F.2d 264 (8th Cir. 1978), although the Seventh Circuit, *see e.g., United States v. Bursten*, 560 F.2d 779 (7th Cir. 1977) (holding that polygraph admissibility is within the sound discretion of the trial judge) and perhaps the Ninth Circuit, *United States v. Benveniste*, 564 F.2d 335, 339

n.3 (9th Cir. 1977), at least recognize the possible admissibility of such evidence. There is reason to believe that evidence obtained via hypnosis may be treated somewhat more liberally than is polygraph evidence. *See, e.g., Kline v. Ford Motor Co.*, 523 F.2d 1067 (9th Cir. 1975).

2004 Amendment: Rule 702 was modified based on the amendment to Fed. R. Evid. 702, effective 1 December 2000, and is taken from the Federal Rule without change. It provides guidance for courts and parties as to the factors to consider in determining whether an expert's testimony is reliable in light of *Daubert v. Merrell Dow Pharmaceuticals, Inc.*, 509 U.S. 579 (1993), and *Kumho Tire Co. v. Carmichael*, 526 U.S. 137 (1999) (holding that gatekeeper function applies to all expert testimony, not just testimony based on science).

2013 Amendment. The committee revised this rule for stylistic reasons and to align it with the Federal Rules of Evidence but in doing so did not intend to change any result in any ruling on evidence admissibility.

Rule 703 Bases of an Expert's Opinion of Testimony

Rule 703 is taken from the Federal Rule without change. The Rule is similar in scope to Para. 138 *e* of the 1969 Manual, but is potentially broader as it allows reliance upon "facts or data" whereas the 1969 Manual's limitation was phrased in terms of the personal observation, personal examination or study, or examination or study "of reports of others of a kind customarily considered in the practice of the expert's specialty." Hypothetical questions of the expert are not required by the Rule.

A limiting instruction may be appropriate if the expert while expressing the basis for an opinion states facts or data that are not themselves admissible. *See* Rule 105.

Whether Rule 703 has modified or superseded the *Frye* test for scientific evidence, *Frye v. United States*, 293 F.1013 (D.C. Cir. 1923), is unclear and is now being litigated within the Article III courts.

2004 Amendment: Rule 703 was modified based on the amendment to Fed. R. Evid. 703, effective 1 December 2000, and is virtually identical to its Federal Rule counterpart. It limits the disclosure to the members of inadmissible information that is used as the basis of an expert's opinion. *Compare* Mil. R. Evid. 705.

2013 Amendment. The committee revised this rule to align with the Federal Rules of Evidence but in doing so the committee did not intend to change any result in any ruling on evidence admissibility.

Rule 704 Opinion on ultimate issue

Rule 704 is taken from the Federal Rule verbatim. The 1969 Manual for Courts-Martial was silent on the issue. The Rule does not permit the witness to testify as to his or her opinion as to the guilt or innocence of the accused or to state legal opinions. Rather it simply allows testimony involving an issue which must be decided by the trier of fact. Although the two may be closely related, they are distinct as a matter of law.

February 1986 Amendment: Fed. R. Evid. 704(b), by operation of Mil. R. Evid. 1102, became effective in the military as Mil. R. Evid. 704(b) on 10 April 1985. The Joint-Service Committee on Military Justice considers Fed. R. Evid. 704(b) an integral part of the Insanity Defense Reform Act, ch. IV, Pub.L. No. 98–473, 98 Stat. 2067–68 (1984), (hereafter the Act). Because proposed legislation to implement these provisions of the Act relating to insanity as an affirmative defense had not yet been enacted in the UCMJ by the date of this Executive Order, the Committee recommended that the President rescind the application of Fed. R. Evid. 704(b) to the military. Even though in effect since 10 April 1985, this change was never published in the Manual.

1986 Amendment: While writing the Manual provisions to implement the enactment of Article 50a, UCMJ ("Military Justice Amendments of 1986," National Defense Authorization Act for fiscal year 1987, Pub.L. No. 99–661, 100 Stat. 3905 (1986)), the drafters rejected adoption of Fed. R. Evid. 704(b). The statutory qualifications for military court members reduce the risk that military court members will be unduly influenced by the presentation of ultimate opinion testimony from psychiatric experts.

2013 Amendment. The committee revised this rule for stylistic reasons but in doing so did not intend to change any result in any ruling on evidence admissibility.

Rule 705 Disclosing the Facts or Data Underlying an Expert's Opinion

Rule 705 is taken from the Federal Rule without change and is similar in result to the requirement in Para. 138 *e* of the 1969 Manual that the "expert may be required, on direct or cross-examination, to specify the data upon which his opinion was based and to relate the details of his observation, examination, or study." Unlike the 1969 Manual, Rule 705 requires disclosure on direct examination only when the military judge so requires.

2013 Amendment. The committee revised this rule for stylistic reasons and to align it with the Federal Rules of Evidence but in doing so did not intend to change any result in any ruling on evidence admissibility.

Rule 706 Court-Appointed Expert Witnesses

(a) *Appointment and compensation.* Rule 706(a) is the result of a complete redraft of subdivision (a) of the Federal Rule that was required to be consistent with Article 46 of the Uniform Code of Military Justice which was implemented in Paras. 115 and 116, MCM, 1969 (Rev.). Rule 706(a) states the basic rule that prosecution, defense, military judge, and the court members all have equal opportunity under Article 46 to obtain expert witnesses. The second sentence of the subdivision replaces subdivision (b) of the Federal Rule which is inapplicable to the armed forces in light of Para. 116, MCM, 1969 (Rev.).

(b) *Disclosure of employment.* Rule 706(b) is taken from Fed. R. Evid. 706(c) without change. The 1969 Manual was silent on the issue, but the subdivision should not change military practice.

(c) *Accused's expert of own selection.* Rule 706(c) is similar in intent to subdivision (d) of the Federal Rule and adapts that Rule to military practice. The subdivision makes it clear that the defense may call its own expert witnesses at its own expense without the necessity of recourse to Para. 116.

2013 Amendment. The committee removed subsection (b) because the committee believes that the authority of the military judge to tell members that he or she has called an expert witness is implicit in his or her authority to obtain the expert, and there-

fore the language was unnecessary. Although the language has been removed, the committee intends that the military judge may, in the exercise of discretion, notify the members that he or she called the expert. The committee also revised this rule for stylistic reasons but in doing so did not intend to change any result in any ruling on evidence admissibility.

Rule 707 Polygraph Examinations

Rule 707 is new and is similar to Cal. Evid. Code 351.1 (West 1988 Supp.). The Rule prohibits the use of polygraph evidence in courts-martial and is based on several policy grounds. There is a real danger that court members will be misled by polygraph evidence that "is likely to be shrouded with an aura of near infallibility." *United States v. Alexander*, 526 F.2d 161, 168-69 (8th Cir. 1975). To the extent that the members accept polygraph evidence as unimpeachable or conclusive, despite cautionary instructions from the military judge, the members "traditional responsibility to collectively ascertain the facts and adjudge guilt or innocence is preempted." *Id.* There is also a danger of confusion of the issues, especially when conflicting polygraph evidence diverts the members' attention from a determination of guilt or innocence to a judgment of the validity and limitations of polygraphs. This could result in the court-martial degenerating into a trial of the polygraph machine. *State v. Grier*, 300 S.E.2d 351 (N.C. 1983). Polygraph evidence also can result in a substantial waste of time when the collateral issues regarding the reliability of the particular test and qualifications of the specific polygraph examiner must be litigated in every case. Polygraph evidence places a burden on the administration of justice that outweighs the probative value of the evidence. The reliability of polygraph evidence has not been sufficiently established and its use at trial impinges upon the integrity of the judicial system. *See People v. Kegler*, 242 Cal. Rptr. 897 (Cal. Ct. App. 1987). Thus, this amendment adopts a bright-line rule that polygraph evidence is not admissible by any party to a court-martial even if stipulated to by the parties. This amendment is not intended to accept or reject *United States v. Gipson*, 24 M.J. 343 (C.M.A. 1987), concerning the standard for admissibility of other scientific evidence under Mil. R. Evid. 702 or the continued vitality of *Frye v. United States*, 293 F. 1013 (D.C. Cir. 1923). Finally, subsection (b) of the rule ensures that any statements which are otherwise admissible are not rendered inadmissible solely because the statements were made during a polygraph examination.

2013 Amendment. The committee revised this rule for stylistic reasons but in doing so did not intend to change any result in any ruling on evidence admissibility.

SECTION VIII

HEARSAY

Rule 801 Definitions that Apply to this Section; Exclusions from Hearsay

(a) *Statement.* Rule 801(a) is taken from the Federal Rule without change and is similar to Para. 139 *a* of the 1969 Manual.

(b) *Declarant.* Rule 801(b) is taken from the Federal Rule verbatim and is the same definition used in prior military practice.

(c) *Hearsay.* Rule 801(c) is taken from the Federal Rule verbatim. It is similar to the 1969 Manual definition, found in Para.

139 *a*, which stated: "A statement which is offered in evidence to prove the truth of the matters stated therein, but which was not made by the author when a witness before the court at a hearing in which it is so offered, is hearsay." Although the two definitions are basically identical, they actually differ sharply as a result of the Rule's exceptions which are discussed *infra.*

(d) *Statements which are not hearsay.* Rule 801(d) is taken from the Federal Rule without change and removes certain categories of evidence from the definition of hearsay. In all cases, those categories represent hearsay within the meaning of the 1969 Manual definition.

(1) *Prior statement by witness.* Rule 801(d)(1) is taken from the Federal Rule without change and removes certain prior statements by the witness from the definition of hearsay. Under the 1969 Manual rule, an out-of-court statement not within an exception to the hearsay rule and unadopted by the testifying witness, is inadmissible hearsay notwithstanding the fact that the declarant is now on the stand and able to be cross-examined, Para. 139a; *United States v. Burge,* 1 M.J. 408 (C.M.A. 1976) (Cook, J., concurring). The justification for the 1969 Manual rule is presumably the traditional view that out-of-court statements cannot be adequately tested by cross-examination because of the time differential between the making of the statement and the giving of the in-court testimony. The Federal Rules of Evidence Advisory Committee rejected this view in part believing both that later cross-examination is sufficient to ensure reliability and that earlier statements are usually preferable to later ones because of the possibility of memory loss. *See generally,* 4 J. Weinstein & M. Berger, WEINSTEIN'S EVIDENCE Para. 801(d)(1)(01) (1978). Rule 801(d)(1) thus not only makes an important shift in the military theory of hearsay, but also makes an important change in law by making admissible a number of types of statements that were either inadmissible or likely to be inadmissible under prior military law.

Rule 801(d)(1)(A) makes admissible on the merits a statement inconsistent with the in-court testimony of the witness when the prior statement "was given under oath subject to the penalty of perjury at a trial, hearing, or other proceeding, or in a deposition." The Rule does not require that the witness have been subject to cross-examination at the earlier proceeding, but requires that the witness must have been under oath and subject to penalty of perjury. Although the definition of "trial, hearing, or other proceeding" is uncertain, it is apparent that the Rule was intended to include grand jury testimony and may be extremely broad in scope. *See United States v. Castro-Ayon,* 537 F.2d 1055 (9th Cir.), *cert. denied,* 429 U.S. 983 (1976) (tape recorded statements given under oath at a Border Patrol station found to be within the Rule). It should clearly apply to Article 32 hearings. The Rule does not require as a prerequisite a statement "given under oath subject to the penalty of perjury." The mere fact that a statement was given under oath may not be sufficient. No foundation other than that indicated as a condition precedent in the Rule is apparently necessary to admit the statement under the Rule. *But see* WEINSTEIN'S EVIDENCE 801–74 (1978).

Rule 801(d)(1)(B) makes admissible as substantive evidence on the merits a statement consistent with the in-court testimony of the witness and "offered to rebut an express or implied charge against the declarant of recent fabrication or improper influence or motive." Unlike Rule 801(d)(1)(A), the earlier consistent state-

ment need not have been made under oath or at any type of proceeding. On its face, the Rule does not require that the consistent statement offered have been made prior to the time the improper influence or motive arose or prior to the alleged recent fabrication. Notwithstanding this, the Supreme Court has read such a requirement into the rule. *Tome v. United States,* 513 U.S. 150 (1995); *see also United States v. Allison,* 49 M.J. 54 (C.A.A.F. 1998). The limitation does not, however, prevent admission of a consistent statement made after an inconsistent statement but before the improper influence or motive arose. *United States v. Scholle,* 553 F.2d 1109 (8th Cir. 1977). Rule 801(d)(1)(B) provides a possible means to admit evidence of fresh complaint in prosecution of sexual offenses. Although limited to circumstances in which there is a charge, for example, of recent fabrication, the Rule, when applicable, would permit not only fact of fresh complaint, as is presently possible, but also the entire portion of the consistent statement.

Under Rule 801(d)(1)(C) a statement of identification is not hearsay. The content of the statement as well as the fact of identification is admissible. The Rule must be read in conjunction with Rule 321 which governs the admissibility of statements of pretrial identification.

(2) *Admission by party opponent.* Rule 801(d)(2) eliminates a number of categories of statements from the scope of the hearsay rule. Unlike those statements within the purview of Rule 801(d)(1), statements within the purview of Rule 801(d)(2) would have come within the exceptions to the hearsay rule as recognized in the 1969 Manual. Consequently, their "reclassification" is a matter of academic interest only. No practical differences result. The reclassification results from a belief that the adversary system impels admissibility and that reliability is not a significant factor.

Rule 801(d)(2)(A) makes admissible against a party a statement made in either the party's individual or representative capacity. This was treated as an admission or confession under Para. 140 *a* of the 1969 Manual, and is an exception of the prior hearsay rule.

Rule 801(d)(2)(B) makes admissible "a statement of which the party has manifested the party's adoption or belief in its truth." This is an adoptive admission and was an exception to the prior hearsay rule. *Cf.* Para. 140 *a*(4) of the 1969 Manual. While silence may be treated as an admission on the facts of a given case, *see* Rule 304(h)(3) and the analysis thereto, under Rule 801(d)(2) that silence must have been intended by the declarant to have been an assertion. Otherwise, the statement will not be hearsay within the meaning of Rule 801(d)(2) and will presumably be admissible, if at all, as circumstantial evidence.

Rule 801(d)(2)(C) makes admissible "a statement by a person authorized by the party to make a statement concerning the subject." While this was not expressly dealt with by the 1969 Manual, it would be admissible under prior law as an admission; *Cf.* Para. 140 *b*, utilizing agency theory.

Rule 801(d)(2)(D) makes admissible "a statement by the party's agent or servant concerning a matter within the scope of the agency or employment of the agent or servant, made during the existence of the relationship." These statements would appear to be admissible under prior law. Statements made by interpreters, as by an individual serving as a translator for a service member in a foreign nation who is, for example, attempting to consummate a drug transaction with a non-English speaking person, should be admissible under Rule 801(d)(2)(D) or Rule 801(d)(2)(C).

Rule 801(d)(2)(E) makes admissible "a statement by a co-conspirator of a party during the course and in furtherance of the conspiracy." This is similar to the military hearsay exception found in Para. 140 *b* of the 1969 Manual. Whether a conspiracy existed for purposes of this Rule is solely a matter for the military judge. Although this is the prevailing Article III rule, it is also the consequence of the Military Rules' modification to Federal Rule of Evidence 104(b). Rule 801(d)(2)(E) does not address many critical procedural matters associated with the use of co-conspirator evidence. *See generally* Comment, Restructuring the Independent Evidence Requirement of the Coconspirator Hearsay Exception, 127 U. Pa. L. Rev. 1439 (1979). For example, the burden of proof placed on the proponent is unclear although a preponderance appears to be the developing Article III trend. Similarly, there is substantial confusion surrounding the question of whether statements of an alleged co-conspirator may themselves be considered by the military judge when determining whether the declarant was in fact a co-conspirator. This process, known as bootstrapping, was not permitted under prior military law. *See, e.g., United States v. Duffy,* 49 C.M.R. 208, 210 (A.F.C.M.R. 1974); *United States v. LaBossiere,* 13 C.M.A. 337, 339, 32 C.M.R. 337, 339 (1962). A number of circuits have suggested that Rule 104(a) allows the use of such statements, but at least two circuits have held that other factors prohibit bootstrapping. *United States v. James,* 590 F.2d 575 (5th Cir.) (en banc), *cert. denied,* 442 U.S. 917 (1979); *United States v. Valencia,* 609 F.2d 603 (2d Cir. 1979). Until such time as the Article III practice is settled, discretion would dictate that prior military law be followed and that bootstrapping not be allowed. Other procedural factors may also prove troublesome although not to the same extent as bootstrapping. For example, it appears to be appropriate for the military judge to determine the co-conspirator question in a preliminary Article 39(a) session. Although receipt of evidence "subject to later connection" or proof is legally possible, the probability of serious error, likely requiring a mistrial, is apparent.

Rule 801(d)(2)(E) does not appear to change what may be termed the "substantive law" relating to statements made by co-conspirators. Thus, whether a statement was made by a co-conspirator in furtherance of a conspiracy is a question for the military judge, and a statement made by an individual after he or she was withdrawn from a conspiracy is not made "in furtherance of the conspiracy."

Official statements made by an officer—as by the commanding officer of a battalion, squadron, or ship, or by a staff officer, in an endorsement of other communication—are not excepted from the operation of the hearsay rule merely by reason of the official character of the communication or the rank or position of the officer making it.

The following examples of admissibility under this Rule may be helpful:

(1) *A is being tried for assaulting B.* The defense presents the testimony of C that just before the assault C heard B say to A that B was about to kill A with B's knife. The testimony of C is not hearsay, for it is offered to show that A acted in self-defense because B made the statement and not to prove the truth of B's statement.

(2) *A is being tried for rape of B.* If B testifies at trial, the testimony of B that she had previously identified A as her attacker at an identification lineup would be admissible under Rule 801(d)(1)(C) to prove that it was A who raped B.

(3) *Private A is being tried for disobedience of a certain order given him orally by Lieutenant B.* C is able to testify that he heard Lieutenant B give the order to A. This testimony, including testimony of C as to the terms of the order, would not be hearsay.

(4) *The accused is being tried for the larceny of clothes from a locker.* A is able to testify that B told A that B saw the accused leave the quarters in which the locker was located with a bundle resembling clothes about the same time the clothes were stolen. This testimony from A would not be admissible to prove that facts stated by B.

(5) *The accused is being tried for wrongfully selling government clothing.* A policeman is able to testify that while on duty he saw the accused go into a shop with a bundle under his arm; that he entered the shop and the accused ran away; that he was unable to catch the accused; and that thereafter the policeman asked the proprietor of the shop what the accused was doing there; and that the proprietor replied that the accused sold him some uniforms for which he paid the accused $30. Testimony by the policeman as to the reply of the proprietor would be hearsay if it was offered to prove the facts stated by the proprietor. The fact that the policeman was acting in the line of duty at the time the proprietor made the statement would not render the evidence admissible to prove the truth of the statement.

(6) *A defense witness in an assault case testifies on direct examination that the accused did not strike the alleged victim.* On cross-examination by the prosecution, the witness admits that at a preliminary investigation he stated that the accused had struck the alleged victim. The testimony of the witness as to this statement will be admissible if he was under oath at the time and subject to a prosecution for perjury.

2013 Amendment. The committee changed the title of subsection (2) from "Admission by party-opponent" to "An Opposing Party's Statement" to conform to the Federal Rules of Evidence. The term "admission" is misleading because a statement falling under this exception need not be an admission and also need not be against the party's interest when spoken. In making this change, the committee did not intend to change any result in any ruling on evidence admissibility.

Rule 802 The Rule Against Hearsay

Rule 802 is taken generally from the Federal Rule but has been modified to recognize the application of any applicable Act of Congress.

Although the basic rule of inadmissibility for hearsay is identical with that found in Para. 139*a* of the 1969 Manual, there is a substantial change in military practice as a result of Rule 103(a). Under the 1969 Manual, hearsay was incompetent evidence and did not require an objection to be inadmissible. Under the new Rules, however, admission of hearsay will not be error unless there is an objection to the hearsay. *See* Rule 103(a).

2013 Amendment. The committee revised this rule for stylistic reasons and to align it with the Federal Rules of Evidence but in doing so did not intend to change any result in any ruling on evidence admissibility.

Rule 803 Exceptions to the Rule Against Hearsay – Regardless of Whether the Declarant is Available as a Witness

Rule 803 is taken generally from the Federal Rule with modifications as needed for adaptation to military practice. Overall, the Rule is similar to practice under Manual Paras. 142 and 144 of the 1969 Manual. The Rule is, however, substantially more detailed and broader in scope than the 1969 Manual.

(1) *Present sense impression.* Rule 803(1) is taken from the Federal Rule verbatim. The exception it establishes was not recognized in the 1969 Manual for Courts-Martial. It is somewhat similar to a spontaneous exclamation, but does not require a startling event. A fresh complaint by a victim of a sexual offense may come within this exception depending upon the circumstances.

(2) *Excited utterance.* Rule 803(2) is taken from the Federal Rule verbatim. Although similar to Para. 142 b of the 1969 Manual with respect to spontaneous exclamations, the Rule would appear to be more lenient as it does not seem to require independent evidence that the startling event occurred. An examination of the Federal Rules of Evidence Advisory Committee Note indicates some uncertainty, however. S. Saltzburg & K. Redden, FEDERAL RULES OF EVIDENCE MANUAL 540 (2d ed. 1977). A fresh complaint of a sexual offense may come within this exception depending on the circumstances.

(3) *Then existing mental, emotional, or physical condition.* Rule 803(3) is taken from the Federal Rule verbatim. The Rule is similar to that found in 1969 Manual Para. 142d but may be slightly more limited in that it may not permit statements by an individual to be offered to disclose the intent of another person. Fresh complaint by a victim of a sexual offense may come within this exception.

(4) *Statements for purposes of medical diagnosis or treatment.* Rule 803(4) is taken from the Federal Rule verbatim. It is substantially broader than the state of mind or body exception found in Para. 142 d of the 1969 Manual. It allows, among other matters, statements as to the cause of the medical problem presented for diagnosis or treatment. Potentially, the Rule is extremely broad and will permit statements made even to non-medical personnel (*e.g.,* members of one's family) and on behalf of others so long as the statements are made for the purpose of diagnosis or treatment. The basis for the exception is the presumption that an individual seeking relief from a medical problem has incentive to make accurate statements. *See generally,* 4 J. Weinstein & M. Berger, WEINSTEIN'S EVIDENCE Para. 804(4)(01) (1978). The admissibility under this exception of those portions of a statement not relevant to diagnosis or treatment is uncertain. Although statements made to a physician, for example, merely to enable the physician to testify, do not appear to come within the Rule, statements solicited in good faith by others in order to ensure the health of the declarant would appear to come within the Rule. Rule 803(4) may be used in an appropriate case to present evidence of fresh complaint in a sexual case.

(5) *Recorded recollection.* Rule 803(5) is taken from the Federal Rule without change, and is similar to the present exception for past recollection recorded found in Paras. 146 a and 149 c(1)(b) of the 1969 Manual except that under the Rule the memorandum may be read but not presented to the fact finder unless offered by the adverse party.

(6) *Record of regularly conducted activity.* Rule 803(6) is taken generally from the Federal Rule. Two modifications have been made, however, to adapt the rule to military practice. The definition of "business" has been expanded to explicitly include the armed forces to ensure the continued application of this hearsay exception, and a descriptive list of documents, taken generally from 1969 Manual Para. 144 d, has been included. Although the activities of the armed forces do not constitute a profit making business, they do constitute a business within the meaning of the hearsay exception, *see* Para. 144 c, of the 1969 Manual, as well as a "regularly conducted activity."

The specific types of records included within the Rule are those which are normally records of regularly conducted activity within the armed forces. They are included because of their importance and because their omission from the Rule would be impracticable. The fact that a record is of a type described within subdivision does not eliminate the need for its proponent to show that the *particular* record comes within the Rule when the record is challenged; the Rule does establish that the *types* of records listed are normally business records.

Chain of custody receipts or documents have been included to emphasize their administrative nature. Such documents perform the critical function of accounting for property obtained by the United States Government. Although they may be used as prosecution evidence, their primary purpose is simply one of property accountability. In view of the primary administrative purpose of these matters, it was necessary to provide expressly for their admissibility as an exception to the hearsay rule in order to clearly reject the interpretation of Para. 144 d of the 1969 Manual with respect to chain of custody forms as set forth in *United States v. Porter,* 7 M.J. 32 (C.M.A. 1979) and *United States v. Nault,* 4 M.J. 318 (C.M.A. 1978) insofar as they concerned chain of custody forms.

Laboratory reports have been included in recognition of the function of forensic laboratories as impartial examining centers. The report is simply a record of "regularly conducted" activity of the laboratory. *See, e.g., United States v. Strangstalien,* 7 M.J. 225 (C.M.A. 1979); *United States v. Evans,* 21 U.S.C.M.A. 579, 45 C.M.R. 353 (1972).

Paragraph 144 d prevented a record "made principally with a view to prosecution, or other disciplinary or legal action . . .rdquo; from being admitted as a business record. The limitation has been deleted, *but see* Rule 803(8)(B) and its Analysis. It should be noted that a record of "regularly conducted activity" is unlikely to have a prosecutorial intent in any event.

The fact that a record may fit within another exception, *e.g.,* Rule 803(8), does not generally prevent it from being admissible under this subdivision although it would appear that the exclusion found in Rule 803(8)(B) for "matters observed by police officers and other personnel acting in a law enforcement capacity" prevent any such record from being admissible as a record of regularly conducted activity. Otherwise the limitation in subdivision (8) would serve no useful purpose. *See also* Analysis to Rule 803(8)(B).

Rule 803(6) is generally similar to the 1969 Manual rule but is potentially broader because of its use of the expression "regularly conducted" activity in addition to "business." It also permits records of opinion which were prohibited by Para. 144 d of the

1969 Manual. Offsetting these factors is the fact that the Rule requires that the memorandum was "made at or near the time by, or from information transmitted by a person with knowledge . . ., " but Para. 144 *c* of the 1969 Manual rule expressly did not require such knowledge as a condition of admissibility.

2004 Amendment: Rule 803(6) was modified based on the amendment to Fed. R. Evid. 803(6), effective 1 December 2000. It permits a foundation for business records to be made through certification to save the parties the expense and inconvenience of producing live witnesses for what is often perfunctory testimony. The Rule incorporates federal statutes that allow certification in a criminal proceeding in a court of the United States. *See, e.g.,* 18 U.S.C. § 3505 (Foreign records of regularly conducted activity.) The Rule does not include foreign records of regularly conducted business activity in civil cases as provided in its Federal Rule counterpart. This Rule works together with Mil. R. Evid. 902(11).

(7) *Absence of entry in records kept in accordance with the provisions of paragraph (6).* Rule 803(7) is taken verbatim from the Federal Rule. The Rule is similar to Paras. 143 *a*(2)(h) and 143 *b*(3) of the 1969 Manual.

(8) *Public records and reports.* Rule 803(8) has been taken generally from the Federal Rule but has been slightly modified to adapt it to the military environment. Rule 803(8)(B) has been redrafted to apply to "police officers and other personnel acting in a law enforcement capacity" rather the Federal Rule's "police officers and other law enforcement personnel." The change was necessitated by the fact that all military personnel may act in a disciplinary capacity. Any officer, for example, regardless of assignment, may potentially act as a military policeman. The capacity within which a member of the armed forces acts may be critical.

The Federal Rule was also modified to include a list of records that, when made pursuant to a duty required by law, will be admissible notwithstanding the fact that they may have been made as "matters observed by police officers and other personnel acting in a law enforcement capacity." Their inclusion is a direct result of the fact, discussed above, that military personnel may all function within a law enforcement capacity. The Committee determined it would be impracticable and contrary to the intent of the Rule to allow the admissibility of records which are truly administrative in nature and unrelated to the problems inherent in records prepared only for purposes of prosecution to depend upon whether the maker was at that given instant acting in a law enforcement capacity. The language involved is taken generally from Para. 144 *b* of the 1969 Manual. Admissibility depends upon whether the record is "a record of a fact or event if made by a person within the scope of his official duties and those duties included a duty to know or ascertain through appropriate and trustworthy channels of information the truth of the fact or event . . ." Whether any given record was obtained in such a trustworthy fashion is a question for the military judge. The explicit limitation on admissibility of records made "principally with a view to prosecution" found in Para. 144 *d* has been deleted.

The fact that a document may be admissible under another exception to the hearsay rule, *e.g.,* Rule 803(6), does not make it inadmissible under this subdivision.

Military Rule of Evidence 803(8) raises numerous significant questions. Rule 803(8)(A) extends to "records, reports, statements, or data compilations" of public offices or agencies, setting

forth (A) the activities of the office or agency. The term "public office or agency" within this subdivision is defined to include any government office or agency including those of the armed forces. Within the civilian context, the definition of "public offices or agencies" is fairly clear and the line of demarcation between governmental and private action can be clearly drawn in most cases. The same may not be true within the armed forces. It is unlikely that every action taken by a servicemember is an "activity" of the department of which he or she is a member. Presumably, Rule 803(8) should be restricted to activities of formally sanctioned instrumentalities roughly similar to civilian entities. For example, the activities of a squadron headquarters or a staff section would come within the definition of "office or agency." Pursuant to this rationale, there is no need to have a military regulation or directive to make a statement of a "public office or agency" under Rule 803(8)(A). However, such regulations or directives might well be highly useful in establishing that a given administrative mechanism was indeed an "office or agency" within the meaning of the Rule.

Rule 803(8)(B) encompasses "matters observed pursuant to duty imposed by law as to which matters there was a duty to report. . .." This portion of Rule 803(8) is broader than subdivision (8)(A) as it extends to far more than just the normal procedures of an office or agency. Perhaps because of this extent, it requires that there be a specific duty to observe and report. This duty could take the form of a statement, general order, regulation, or any competent order.

The exclusion in the Federal Rule for "matters observed by police officers" was intended to prevent use of the exception for evaluative reports as the House Committee believed them to be unreliable. Because of the explicit language of the exclusion, normal statutory construction leads to the conclusion that reports which would be within Federal or Military Rule 803(8) but for the exclusion in (8)(B) are not otherwise admissible under Rule 803(6). Otherwise the inclusion of the limitation would serve virtually no purpose whatsoever. There is no contradiction between the exclusion in Rule 803(8)(B) and the specific documents made admissible in Rule 803(8) (and Rule 803(6)) because those documents are not matters "observed by police officers and other personnel acting in a law enforcement capacity." To the extent that they might be so considered, the specific language included by the Committee is expressly intended to reject the subdivision (8)(B) limitation. Note, however, that all forms of evidence not within the specific item listing of the Rule but within the (8)(B) exclusion will be admissible insofar as Rule 803(8) is concerned, whether the evidence is military or civilian in origin.

A question not answered by Rule 803(8) is the extent to which a regulation or directive may circumscribe Rule 803(8). Thus, if a regulation establishes a given format or procedure for a report which is not followed, is an otherwise admissible piece of evidence inadmissible for lack of conformity with the regulation or directive? The Committee did not address this issue in the context of adopting the Rule. However, it would be at least logical to argue that a record not made in substantial conformity with an implementing directive is not sufficiently reliable to be admissible. *See* Rule 403. Certainly, military case law predating the Military Rules may resolve this matter to the extent to which it is not based purely on now obsolete Manual provisions. As the modifications to subdivision (8) dealing with specific records retains the present Manual language, it is particularly likely that present case law will survive in this area.

Rule 803(8)(C) makes admissible, but only against the Government, "factual findings resulting from an investigation made pursuant to authority granted by law, unless the sources of information or other circumstances indicate lack of trustworthiness." This provision will make factual findings made, for example, by an Article 32 Investigating Officer or by a Court of Inquiry admissible on behalf of an accused. Because the provision applies only to "factual findings," great care must be taken to distinguish such factual determinations from opinions, recommendations, and incidental inferences.

(9) *Records of vital statistics.* Rule 803(9) is taken verbatim from the Federal Rule and had no express equivalent in the 1969 Manual.

(10) *Absence of public record or entry.* Rule 803(10) is taken verbatim from the Federal Rules and is similar to 1969 Manual Para. 143 *a*(2)(g).

(11-13) *Records of religious organizations: Marriage, baptismal, and similar certificates: Family records.* Rule 802(11)–(13) are all taken verbatim from the Federal Rules and had no express equivalents in the 1969 Manual.

(14-16) *Records of documents affecting an interest in property: Statements in documents affecting an interest in property; Statements in ancient documents.* Rules 803(14)–(16) are taken verbatim from the Federal Rules and had no express equivalents in the 1969 Manual. Although intended primarily for civil cases, they all have potential importance to courts-martial.

(17) *Market reports, commercial publications.* Rule 803(17) is taken generally from the Federal Rule. Government price lists have been added because of the degree of reliance placed upon them in military life. Although included within the general Rule, the Committee believed it inappropriate and impracticable not to clarify the matter by specific reference. The Rule is similar in scope and effect to the 1969 Manual Para. 144 *f* except that it lacks the Manual's specific reference to an absence of entries. The effect, if any, of the difference is unclear.

(18) *Learned treatise.* Rule 803(18) is taken from the Federal Rule without change. Unlike Para. 138 *e* of the 1969 Manual, which allowed use of such statements only for impeachment, this Rule allows substantive use on the merits of statements within treaties if relied upon in direct testimony or called to the expert's attention on cross-examination. Such statements may not, however, be given to the fact finder as exhibits.

(19-20) *Reputation concerning personal or family history; reputation concerning boundaries or general history.* Rules 803(19)–(20) are taken without change from the Federal Rules and had no express equivalents in the 1969 Manual.

(21) *Reputation as to character.* Rule 803(21) is taken from the Federal Rule without change. It is similar to Para. 138 *f* of the 1969 Manual in that it creates an exception to the hearsay rule for reputation evidence. "Reputation" and "community" are defined in Rule 405(d), and "community" includes a "military organization regardless of size." Affidavits and other written statements are admissible to show character under Rule 405(c), and, when offered pursuant to that Rule, are an exception to the hearsay rule.

(22) *Judgment or previous conviction.* Rule 803(22) is taken from the Federal Rule but has been modified to recognize convic-

tions of a crime punishable by a dishonorable discharge, a unique punishment not present in civilian life. *See also* Rule 609 and its Analysis.

There is no equivalent to this Rule in military law. Although the Federal Rule is clearly applicable to criminal cases, its original intent was to allow use of a prior criminal conviction in a subsequent civil action. To the extent that it is used for criminal cases, significant constitutional issues are raised, especially if the prior conviction is a foreign one, a question almost certainly not anticipated by the Federal Rules Advisory Committee.

(23) *Judgment as to personal, family or general history, or boundaries.* Rule 803(23) is taken verbatim from the Federal Rule, and had no express equivalent in the 1969 Manual. Although intended for civil cases, it clearly has potential use in courts-martial for such matters as proof of jurisdiction.

2013 Amendment. The committee removed subsection (24), which stated: "Other Exceptions: [Transferred to M.R.E. 807]" because practitioners are generally aware that Mil. R. Evid. 807 covers statements not specifically covered in this rule, and therefore the subsection was unnecessary. The committee also revised this rule for stylistic reasons and to align it with the Federal Rules of Evidence but in doing so did not intend to change any result in any ruling on evidence admissibility.

Rule 804 Exceptions to the Rule Against Hearsay – When the Declarant is Unavailable as a Witness

(a) *Definition of unavailability.* Subdivisions (a)(1)–(a)(5) of Rule 804 are taken from the Federal Rule without change and are generally similar to the relevant portions of Paras. 145 *a* and 145 *b* of the 1969 Manual, except that Rule 804(a)(3) provides that a witness who "testifies as to a lack of memory of the subject matter of the declarant's statement" is unavailable. The Rule also does not distinguish between capital and non-capital cases.

February 1986 Amendment: The phrase "claim or lack of memory" was changed to "claim of lack of memory" to correct an error in MCM, 1984.

Rule 804(a)(6) is new and has been added in recognition of certain problems, such as combat operations, that are unique to the armed forces. Thus, Rule 804(a)(6) will make unavailable a witness who is unable to appear and testify in person for reason of military necessity within the meaning of Article 49(d)(2). The meaning of "military necessity" must be determined by reference to the cases construing Article 49. The expression is not intended to be a general escape clause, but must be restricted to the limited circumstances that would permit use of a deposition.

(b) *Hearsay exceptions*

(1) *Former testimony.* The first portion of Rule 804(b)(1) is taken from the Federal Rule with omission of the language relating to civil cases. The second portion is new and has been included to clarify the extent to which those military tribunals in which a verbatim record normally is not kept come within the Rule.

The first portion of Rule 804(b)(1) makes admissible former testimony when "the party against whom the testimony is now offered had an opportunity and similar motive to develop the testimony by direct, cross, or redirect examination." Unlike Para. 145 *b* of the 1969 Manual, the Rule does not explicitly require that the accused, when the evidence is offered against him or her, have been "afforded at the former trial an opportunity, to be adequately represented by counsel." Such a requirement should be read into the Rule's condition that the party have had "opportunity and similar motive." In contrast to the 1969 Manual, the Rule does not distinguish between capital and non-capital cases.

The second portion of Rule 804(b)(1) has been included to ensure that testimony from military tribunals, many of which ordinarily do not have verbatim records, will not be admissible unless such testimony is presented in the form of a verbatim record. The Committee believed substantive use of former testimony to be too important to be presented in the form of an incomplete statement.

Investigations under Article 32 of the Uniform Code of Military Justice present a special problem. Rule 804(b)(1) requires that "the party against whom the testimony is now offered had an opportunity and similar motive to develop the testimony" at the first hearing. The "similar motive" requirement was intended primarily to ensure sufficient identity of issues between the two proceedings and thus to ensure an adequate interest in examination of the witness. *See, e.g.*, J. Weinstein & M. Berger, WEINSTEIN'S EVIDENCE Para. 804(b)(1)((04)) (1978). Because Article 32 hearings represent a unique hybrid of preliminary hearings and grand juries with features dissimilar to both, it was particularly difficult for the Committee to determine exactly how subdivision (b)(1) of the Federal Rule would apply to Article 32 hearings. The specific difficulty stems from the fact that Article 32 hearings were intended by Congress to function as discovery devices for the defense as well as to recommend an appropriate disposition of charges to the convening authority. *Hutson v. United States*, 19 U.S.C.M.A. 437, 42 C.M.R. 39 (1970); *United States v. Samuels*, 10 U.S.C.M.A. 206, 212, 27 C.M.R. 280, 286 (1959). *See generally Hearing on H.R. 2498 Before a Subcomm. of the House Comm. on Armed Services*, 81st Cong., 1st Sess., 997 (1949). It is thus permissible, for example, for a defense counsel to limit cross-examination of an adverse witness at an Article 32 hearing using the opportunity for discovery alone, for example, rather than impeachment. In such a case, the defense would not have the requisite "similar motive" found within Rule 804(b)(1).

Notwithstanding the inherent difficulty of determining the defense counsel's motive at an Article 32 hearing, the Rule is explicitly intended to prohibit use of testimony given at an Article 32 hearing unless the requisite "similar motive" was present during that hearing. It is clear that some Article 32 testimony is admissible under the Rule notwithstanding the Congressionally sanctioned discovery purpose of the Article 32 hearing. Consequently, one is left with the question of the extent to which the Rule actually does apply to Article 32 testimony. The only apparent practical solution to what is otherwise an irresolvable dilemma is to read the Rule as permitting only Article 32 testimony preserved via a verbatim record that is not objected to as having been obtained without the requisite "similar motive." While defense counsel's assertion of his or her intent in not examining one or more witnesses or in not fully examining a specific witness is not binding upon the military judge, clearly the burden of establishing admissibility under the Rule is on the prosecution and the burden so placed may be impossible to meet should the defense counsel adequately raise the issue. As a matter of good trial practice, a defense counsel who is limiting cross-examination

at the Article 32 hearing because of discovery should announce that intent sometime during the Article 32 hearing so that the announcement may provide early notice to all concerned and hopefully avoid the necessity for counsel to testify at the later trial.

The Federal Rule was modified by the Committee to require that testimony offered under Rule 804(b)(1) which was originally "given before courts-martial, courts of inquiry, military commissions, other military tribunals, and before proceedings pursuant to or equivalent to those required by Article 32" and which is otherwise admissible under the Rule be offered in the form of a verbatim record. The modification was intended to ensure accuracy in view of the fact that only summarized or minimal records are required of some types of military proceedings.

An Article 32 hearing is a "military tribunal." The Rule distinguishes between Article 32 hearings and other military tribunals in order to recognize that there are other proceedings which are considered the equivalent of Article 32 hearings for purposes of former testimony under Rule 804(b)(1).

(2) *Statement under belief of impending death.* Rule 804(b)(2) is taken from the Federal Rule except that the language, "for any offense resulting in the death of the alleged victim," has been added and reference to civil proceedings has been omitted. The new language has been added because there is no justification for limiting the exception only to those cases in which a homicide charge has actually been preferred. Due to the violent nature of military operations, it may be appropriate to charge a lesser included offense rather than homicide. The same justifications for the exception are applicable to lesser included offenses which are also, of course, of lesser severity. The additional language, taken from Para. 142 *a*, thus retains the 1969 Manual rule, modification of which was viewed as being impracticable.

Rule 804(b)(2) is similar to the dying declaration exception found in Para. 142 *a* of the 1969 Manual, except that the Military Rule does not require that the declarant be dead. So long as the declarant is unavailable and the offense is one for homicide or other offense resulting in the death of the alleged victim, the hearsay exception may be applicable. This could, for example, result from a situation in which the accused, intending to shoot A, shoots both A and B; uttering the hearsay statement, under a belief of impending death, B dies, and although A recovers, A is unavailable to testify at trial. In a trial of the accused for killing B, A's statement will be admissible.

There is no requirement that death immediately follow the declaration, but the declaration is not admissible under this exception if the declarant had a hope of recovery. The declaration may be made by spoken words or intelligible signs or may be in writing. It may be spontaneous or in response to solicitation, including leading questions. The utmost care should be exercised in weighing statements offered under this exception since they are often made under circumstances of mental and physical debility and are not subject to the usual tests of veracity. The military judge may exclude those declarations which are viewed as being unreliable. *See* Rule 403.

A dying declaration and its maker may be contradicted and impeached in the same manner as other testimony and witnesses. Under the prior law, the fact that the deceased did not believe in a deity or in future rewards or punishments may be offered to affect the weight of a declaration offered under this Rule but does not defeat admissibility. Whether such evidence is now admissible in the light of Rule 610 is unclear.

(3) *Statement against interest.* Rule 804(b) is taken from the Federal Rule without change, and has no express equivalent in the 1969 Manual. It has, however, been made applicable by case law, *United States v. Johnson,* 3 M.J. 143 (C.M.A. 1977). It makes admissible statements against a declarant's interest, whether pecuniary, proprietary, or penal when a reasonable person in the position of the declarant would not have made the statement unless such a person would have believed it to be true.

The Rule expressly recognizes the penal interest exception and permits a statement tending to expose the declarant to criminal liability. The penal interest exception is qualified, however, when the declaration is offered to exculpate the accused by requiring the "corroborating circumstances clearly indicate the trustworthiness of the statement." This requirement is applicable, for example, when a third party confesses to the offense the accused is being tried for and the accused offers the third party's statement in evidence to exculpate the accused. The basic penal interest exception is established as a matter of constitutional law by the Supreme Court's decision in *Chambers v. Mississippi,* 410 U.S. 284 (1973), which may be broader than the Rule as the case may not require either corroborating evidence or an unavailable declarant.

In its present form, the Rule fails to address a particularly vexing problem—that of the declaration against penal interest which implicates the accused as well as the declarant. On the face of the Rule, such a statement should be admissible, subject to the effects, if any, of *Bruton v. United States,* 391 U.S. 123 (1968) and Rule 306. Notwithstanding this, there is considerable doubt as to the applicability of the Rule to such a situation. *See generally* 4 J. Weinstein & M. Berger, WEINSTEIN'S EVIDENCE 804–93, 804–16 (1978). Although the legislative history reflects an early desire on the part of the Federal Rules of Evidence Advisory Committee to prohibit such testimony, a provision doing so was not included in the material reviewed by Congress. Although the House included such a provision, it did so apparently in large part based upon a view that *Bruton, supra,* prohibited such statements—arguably an erroneous view of *Bruton. See Bruton, supra* at 128 n.3. *Dutton v. Evans,* 400 U.S. 74 (1970). The Conference Committee deleted the House provision, following the Senate's desires, because it believed it inappropriate to "codify constitutional evidentiary principles." WEINSTEIN'S EVIDENCE at 804–16 (1978) citing CONG.REC.H 11931–32 (daily ed. Dec. 14, 1974). Thus, applicability of the hearsay exception to individuals implicating the accused may well rest only on the extent to which *Bruton, supra,* governs such statement. The Committee intends that the Rule extend to such statements to the same extent that subdivision 804(b)(4) is held by the Article III courts to apply to such statements.

(4) *Statement of personal or family history.* Rule 804(b)(4) of the Federal Rule is taken verbatim from the Federal Rule, and had no express equivalent in the 1969 Manual. The primary feature of Rule 803(b)(4)(A) is its application even though the "declarant had no means of acquiring personal knowledge of the matter stated."

2013 Amendment. In subsection (b)(3)(B), the committee intentionally left undisturbed the phrase "and is offered to exculpate the accused," despite the fact that it is not included in the current or former versions of the Federal Rules of Evidence. Unlike in Mil. R. Evid. 803, the committee did not remove subsection (5), which directs practitioners to the residual exception in Mil. R. Evid. 807, because doing so would cause the remaining subsections to be renumbered. Although subsection (5) is not necessary, renumbering the subsections within this rule would have a detrimental effect on legal research and also would lead to inconsistencies in numbering between these rules and the Federal Rules. The committee also revised this rule for stylistic reasons and to align it with the Federal Rules of Evidence but in doing so did not intend to change any result in any ruling on evidence admissibility.

Rule 805 Hearsay within hearsay

Rule 805 is taken verbatim from the Federal Rule. Although the 1969 Manual did not exactly address the issue, the military rule is identical with the new rule.

2013 Amendment. The committee revised this rule for stylistic reasons and to align it with the Federal Rules of Evidence but in doing so did not intend to change any result in any ruling on evidence admissibility.

Rule 806 Attacking and Supporting the Declarant's Credibility

Rule 806 is taken from the Federal Rule without change. It restates the prior military rule that a hearsay declarant or statement may always be contradicted or impeached. The Rule eliminates any requirement that the declarant be given "an opportunity to deny or explain" an inconsistent statement or inconsistent conduct when such statement or conduct is offered to attack the hearsay statement. As a result, Rule 806 supersedes Rule 613(b) which would require such an opportunity for a statement inconsistent with in-court testimony.

2013 Amendment. The committee revised this rule for stylistic reasons and to align it with the Federal Rules of Evidence but in doing so did not intend to change any result in any ruling on evidence admissibility.

Rule 807 Residual exception

Rule 807 was adopted on 30 May 1998 without change from the Federal Rule and represents the residual exception to the hearsay rule formerly contained in Mil. R. Evid. 803(24) and Mil. R. Evid. 804(b)(5).

The Rule strikes a balance between the general policy behind the Rules of Evidence of permitting admission of probative and reliable evidence and the congressional intent "that the residual hearsay exceptions will be used very rarely, and only in exceptional circumstances." S. Rep. No. 93-1277, *reprinted in* 1974 U.S.C.C.A.N. 7051, 7066. Mil. R. Evid. 807 represents the acceptance of the so-called "catch-all" or "residual" exception to the hearsay rule. Because of the constitutional concerns associated with hearsay statements, the courts have created specific foundational requirements in order for residual hearsay to be admitted. *See United States v. Haner,* 49 M.J. 72, 77-78 (C.A.A.F. 1998). These requirements are: necessity, materiality, reliability, and notice.

The necessity prong "essentially creates a 'best evidence' requirement." *United States v. Kelley,* 45 M.J. 275, 280 (C.A.A.F.

1996) (quoting *Larez v. City of Los Angeles*, 946 F.2d 630, 644 (9th Cir. 1991)). Coupled with the rule's materiality requirement, necessity represents an important fact that is more than marginal or inconsequential and is in furtherance of the interests of justice and the general purposes of the rules of evidence.

There are two alternative tests in order to fulfill the reliability condition. If the residual hearsay is a "non-testimonial statement," the proponent of the statement must demonstrate that the statement has particularized guarantees of trustworthiness as shown from the totality of the circumstances. *Idaho v. Wright*, 497 U.S. 805 (1990). The factors surrounding the taking of the statement and corroboration by other evidence should be examined to test the statement for trustworthiness. The Court of Appeals for the Armed Forces has held that the Supreme Court's prohibition against bolstering the indicia of reliability under a Sixth Amendment analysis does not apply to a residual hearsay analysis. Therefore, in addition to evidence of the circumstances surrounding the taking of the statement, extrinsic evidence can be considered. *United States v. McGrath*, 39 M.J. 158, 167 (C.M.A. 1994). However, if the residual hearsay is a "testimonial statement," e.g. "affidavits, custodial examinations, prior testimony that the [accused] was unable to cross-examine, or similar pretrial statements that declarants would reasonably expect to be used prosecutorially," the proponent of the statement must demonstrate that the declarant of the statement is unavailable and the accused had a prior opportunity to cross-examine the declarant on the statement. *Crawford v. Washington*, 541 U.S. 36 (2004).

2013 Amendment. The committee revised this rule for stylistic reasons and to align it with the Federal Rules of Evidence but in doing so did not intend to change any result in any ruling on evidence admissibility.

SECTION IX
AUTHENTICATION AND INDENTIFICATION

Rule 901 Authenticating or Identifying Evidence

(a) *General provision.* Rule 901(a) is taken verbatim from the Federal Rule, and is similar to Para. 143 *b* of the 1969 Manual, which stated in pertinent part that: "A writing may be authenticated by any competent proof that it is genuine—is in fact what it purports or is claimed to be." Unlike the 1969 Manual provision, however, Rule 901(a) is not limited to writings and consequently is broader in scope. The Rule supports the requirement for logical relevance. *See* Rule 401.

There is substantial question as to the proper interpretation of the Federal Rule equivalent of Rule 901(a). The Rule requires only "evidence sufficient to support a finding that the matter in question is what its proponent claims." It is possible that this phrasing supersedes any formulaic approach to authentication and that rigid rules such as those that have been devised to authenticate taped recordings, for example, are no longer valid. On the other hand, it appears fully appropriate for a trial judge to require such evidence as is needed "to support a finding that the matter in question is what its proponent claims," which evidence may echo in some cases the common law formulations. There appears to be no reason to believe that the Rule will change the present law as it affects chains of custody for real evidence—especially if fungible. Present case law would appear to be consistent with the

new Rule because the chain of custody requirement has not been applied in a rigid fashion. A chain of custody will still be required when it is necessary to show that the evidence is what it is claimed to be and, when appropriate, that its condition is unchanged. Rule 901(a) may make authentication somewhat easier, but is unlikely to make a substantial change in most areas of military practice.

As is generally the case, failure to object to evidence on the grounds of lack of authentication will waive the objection. *See* Rule 103(a).

(b) *Illustration.* Rule 901(b) is taken verbatim from the Federal Rule with the exception of a modification to Rule 901(b)(10). Rule 901(b)(10) has been modified by the addition of "or by applicable regulations prescribed pursuant to statutory authority." The new language was added because it was viewed as impracticable in military practice to require statutory or Supreme Court action to add authentication methods. The world wide disposition of the armed forces with their frequent redeployments may require rapid adjustments in authentication procedures to preclude substantial interference with personnel practices needed to ensure operational efficiency. The new language does not require new statutory authority. Rather, the present authority that exists for the various Service and Departmental Secretaries to issue those regulations necessary for the day to day operations of their department is sufficient.

Rule 901(b) is a non-exhaustive list of illustrative examples of authentication techniques. None of the examples are inconsistent with prior military law and many are found within the 1969 Manual, *see*, Para. 143 *b*. Self-authentication is governed by Rule 902.

2013 Amendment. The committee revised this rule to align with the Federal Rules of Evidence but in doing so did not intend to change any result in any ruling on evidence admissibility.

Rule 902 Evidence that is Self-Authenticating

Rule 902 has been taken from the Federal Rule without significant change except that a new subdivision, 4a, has been added and subdivisions (4) and (10) have been modified. The Rule prescribes forms of self-authentication.

(1) *Domestic public documents under seal.* Rule 902(1) is taken verbatim from the Federal Rule, and is similar to aspects of Paras. 143 *b*(2)(c) and (d) of the 1969 Manual. The Rule does not distinguish between original document and copies. A seal is self-authenticating and, in the absence of evidence to the contrary, is presumed genuine. Judicial notice is not required.

(2) *Domestic public documents not under seal.* Rule 902(2) is taken from the Federal Rule without change. It is similar in scope to aspects of Paras. 143 *b*(2)(c) and (d) of the 1969 Manual in that it authorizes use of a certification under seal to authenticate a public document not itself under seal. This provision is not the only means of authenticating a domestic public record under this Rule. *Compare* Rule 902(4); 902(4a).

(3) *Foreign public documents.* Rule 902(3) is taken without change from the Federal Rule. Although the Rule is similar to Paras. 143 *b*(2)(e) and (f) of the 1969 Manual, the Rule is potentially narrower than the prior military one as the Rule does not permit "final certification" to be made by military personnel as did the Manual rule nor does it permit authentication made by military personnel as did the Manual rule nor does it permit

authentication made solely pursuant to the laws of the foreign nation. On the other hand, the Rule expressly permits the military judge to order foreign documents to "be treated as presumptively authentic without final certification or permit them to be evidenced by an attested summary with or without final certification."

(4) *Certified copies of public records.* Rule 902(4) is taken verbatim from the Federal Rule except that it has been modified by adding "or applicable regulations prescribed pursuant to statutory authority." The additional language is required by military necessity and includes the now existing statutory powers of the President and various Secretaries to promulgate regulations. *See, generally,* Analysis to Rule 901(b).

Rule 902(4) expands upon prior forms of self-authentication to acknowledge the propriety of certified public records or reports and related materials domestic or foreign, the certification of which complies with subdivisions (1), (2), or (3) of the Rule.

(4a) *Documents or records of the United States accompanied by attesting certificates.* This provision is new and is taken from the third rule.subparagraph of Para. 143 *b*(2)(c) of the 1969 Manual. It has been inserted due to the necessity to facilitate records of the United States in general and military records in particular. Military records do not have seals and it would not be practicable to either issue them or require submission of documents to those officials with them. In many cases, such a requirement would be impossible to comply with due to geolineartal isolation or the unwarranted time such a requirement could demand.

An "attesting certificate" is a certificate or statement, signed by the custodian of the record or the deputy or assistant of the custodian, which in any form indicates that the writing to which the certificate or statement refers is a true copy of the record or an accurate "translation" of a machine, electronic, or coded record, and the signer of the certificate or statement is acting in an official capacity as the person having custody of the record or as the deputy or assistant thereof. *See* Para. 143 *a*(2)(a) of the 1969 Manual. An attesting certificate does not require further authentication and, absent proof to the contrary, the signature of the custodian or deputy or assistant thereof on the certificate is presumed to be genuine.

(5-9) *Official publications; Newspapers and periodicals; Trade inscriptions and the like; Acknowledged documents; Commercial paper and related documents.* Rules 902(5)–(9) are taken verbatim from the Federal Rules and have no equivalents in the 1969 Manual or in military law.

(10) *Presumptions under Acts of Congress and Regulations.* Rule 902(10) was taken from the Federal Rule but was modified by adding "and Regulations" in the caption and "or by applicable regulation prescribed pursuant to statutory authority." *See generally* the Analysis to Rule 901(b)(10) for the reasons for the additional language. The statutory authority referred to includes the presently existing authority for the President and various Secretaries to prescribe regulations.

(11) *2004 Amendment:* Rule 902(11) was modified based on the amendment to Fed. R. Evid. 902(11), effective 1 December 2000, and is taken from the Federal Rule without change. It provides for self-authentication of domestic business records and sets forth procedures for preparing a declaration of a custodian or other qualified witness that will establish a sufficient foundation for the admissibility of domestic business records. This Rule works together with Mil. R. Evid. 803(6).

2013 Amendment. The committee added language to subsection (11) to permit the military judge to admit non-noticed documents even after the trial has commenced if the offering party shows good cause to do so. The committee also revised this rule for stylistic reasons and to align it with the Federal Rules of Evidence but in doing so did not intend to change any result in any ruling on evidence admissibility.

Rule 903 Subscribing Witness's Testimony

Rule 903 is taken verbatim from the Federal Rule and has no express equivalent in the 1969 Manual.

2013 Amendment. The committee revised this rule for stylistic reasons and to align it with the Federal Rules of Evidence but in doing so did not intend to change any result in any ruling on evidence admissibility.

SECTION X
CONTENTS OF WRITINGS, RECORDINGS, AND PHOTOGRAPHS

Rule 1001 Definitions that Apply to this Section

(1) *Writings and recordings.* Rule 1001(1) is taken verbatim from the Federal Rule and is similar in scope to Para. 143 *d* of the 1969 Manual. Although the 1969 Manual was somewhat more detailed, the Manual was clearly intended to be expansive. The Rule adequately accomplishes the identical purpose through a more general reference.

(2) *Photographs.* Rule 1001(2) is taken verbatim from the Federal Rule and had no express equivalent in the 1969 Manual. It does, however, reflect current military law.

(3) *Original.* Rule 1001(3) is taken verbatim from the Federal Rule and is similar to Para. 143 *a*(1) of the 1969 Manual. The 1969 Manual, however, treated "duplicate originals," *i.e.*, carbon and photolineart copies made for use as an original, as an "original" while Rule 1001(4) treats such a document as a "duplicate."

(4) *Duplicate.* Rule 1004(4) is taken from the Federal Rule verbatim and includes those documents Para. 143 *a*(1) of the 1969 Manual defined as "duplicate originals." In view of Rule 1003's rule of admissibility for "duplicate," no appreciable negative result stems from the reclassification.

2013 Amendment. The committee revised this rule to align with the Federal Rules of Evidence but in doing so did not intend to change any result in any ruling on evidence admissibility.

Rule 1002 Requirement of the original

Rule 1002 is taken verbatim from the Federal Rule except that "this Manual" has been added in recognition of the efficacy of other Manual provisions. The Rule is similar in scope to the best evidence rule found in Para. 143 *a*(19) of the 1969 Manual except that specific reference is made in the rule to recordings and photographs. Unlike the 1969 Manual, the Rule does not contain the misleading reference to "best evidence" and is plainly applicable to writings, recordings, or photographs.

It should be noted that the various exceptions to Rule 1002 are similar to but not identical with those found in the 1969 Manual. *Compare* Rules 1005–1007 *with* Para. 143 *a*(2)(f) of the 1969 Manual. For example, Paras. 143 *a* (2)(e) and 144 *c* of the 1969 Manual excepted banking records and business records from the rule as categories while the Rule does not. The actual difference in practice, however, is not likely to be substantial as Rule 1003 allows admission of duplicates unless, for example, "a genuine question is raised as to the authenticity of the original." This is similar in result to the treatment of business records in Para. 144 *a* of the 1969 Manual. Omission of other 1969 Manual exceptions, *e.g.*, certificates of fingerprint comparison and identity, *see* Rule 703, 803, evidence of absence of official or business entries, and copies of telegrams and radiograms, do not appear substantial when viewed against the entirety of the Military Rules which are likely to allow admissibility in a number of ways.

The Rule's reference to "Act of Congress" will now incorporate those statutes that specifically direct that the best evidence rule be inapplicable in one form or another. *See, e.g.*, 1 U.S.C. § 209 (copies of District of Columbia Codes of Laws). As a rule, such statutes permit a form of authentication as an adequate substitute for the original document.

2013 Amendment. The committee revised this rule for stylistic reasons and to align it with the Federal Rules of Evidence but in doing so did not intend to change any result in any ruling on evidence admissibility.

Rule 1003 Admissibility of duplicates

Rule 1003 is taken verbatim from the Federal Rule. It is both similar to and distinct from the 1969 Manual. To the extent that the Rule deals with those copies which were intended at the time of their creation to be used as originals, it is similar to the 1969 Manual's treatment of "duplicate originals," Para. 143 *a*(1), except that under the 1969 Manual there was no distinction to be made between originals and "duplicate originals". Accordingly, in this case the Rule would be narrower than the 1969 Manual. To the extent that the Rule deals with copies not intended at their time of creation to serve as originals, however, *e.g.*, when copies are made of pre-existing documents for the purpose of litigation, the Rule is broader than the 1969 Manual because that Manual prohibited such evidence unless an adequate justification for the non-production of the original existed.

2013 Amendment. The committee revised this rule for stylistic reasons and to align it with the Federal Rules of Evidence but in doing so did not intend to change any result in any ruling on evidence admissibility.

Rule 1004 Admissibility of other evidence of contents

Rule 1004 is taken from the Federal Rule without change, and is similar in scope to the 1969 Manual. Once evidence comes within the scope of Rule 1004, secondary evidence is admissible without regard to whether "better" forms of that evidence can be obtained. Thus, no priority is established once Rule 1002 is escaped. Although the 1969 Manual stated in Para. 143 *a*(2) that "the contents may be proved by an authenticated copy or by the testimony of a witness who has seen and can remember the substance of the writing" when the original need not be produced, that phrasing appears illustrative only and not exclusive. Accord-

ingly, the Rule, the Manual, and common law are in agreement in not requiring categories of secondary evidence.

(1) *Originals lost or destroyed.* Rule 1004(1) is similar to the 1969 Manual except that the Rule explicitly exempts originals destroyed in "bad faith." Such an exemption was implicit in the 1969 Manual.

(2) *Original not obtained.* Rule 1004(2) is similar to the justification for nonproduction in Para. 143 *a*(2) of the 1969 Manual, "an admissible writing. . . cannot feasibly be produced."

(3) *Original in possession of opponent.*

Rule 1004(3) is similar to the 1969 Manual provision in Para. 143 *a*(2) that when a document is in the possession of the accused the original need not be produced except that the 1969 Manual explicitly did not require notice to the accused, and the Rule may require such notice. Under the Rule, the accused must be "put on notice, by the pleadings or otherwise, that the contents would be subject of proof at the hearing." Thus, under certain circumstances, a formal notice to the accused may be required. Under no circumstances should such a request or notice be made in the presence of the court members. The only purpose of such notice is to justify use of secondary evidence and does not serve to compel the surrender of evidence from the accused. It should be noted that Rule 1004(3) acts in favor of the accused as well as the prosecution and allows notice to the prosecution to justify defense use of secondary evidence.

(4) *Collateral matters.* Rule 1004 is not found within the Manual but restates prior military law. The intent behind the Rule is to avoid unnecessary delays and expense. It is important to note that important matters which may appear collateral may not be so in fact due to their weight. *See, e.g., United States v. Parker*, 13 U.S.C.M.A. 579, 33 C.M.R. 111 (1963) (validity of divorce decree of critical prosecution witness not collateral when witness would be prevented from testifying due to spousal privilege if the divorce were not valid). The Rule incorporates this via its use of the expression "related to a controlling issue."

2013 Amendment. The committee revised this rule for stylistic reasons and to align it with the Federal Rules of Evidence but in doing so did not intend to change any result in any ruling on evidence admissibility.

Rule 1005 Copies of Public Records to Prove Content

Rule 1005 is taken verbatim from the Federal Rule except that "or attested to" has been added to conform the Rule to the new Rule 902(4a). The Rule is generally similar to Para. 143 *a*(2)(c) of the 1969 Manual although some differences do exist. The Rule is somewhat broader in that it applies to more than just "official records." Further, although the 1969 Manual permitted "a properly authenticated" copy in lieu of the official record, the Rule allows secondary evidence of contents when a certified or attested copy cannot be obtained by the exercise of reasonable diligence. The Rule does, however, have a preference for a certified or attested copy.

2013 Amendment. The committee revised this rule for stylistic reasons and to align it with the Federal Rules of Evidence but in doing so did not intend to change any result in any ruling on evidence admissibility.

Rule 1006 Summaries to Prove Content

Rule 1006 is taken from the Federal Rule without change, and is similar to the exception to the best evidence rule now found in Para. 143 a(2)(b) of the 1969 Manual. Some difference between the Rule and the 1969 Manual exists, however, because the Rule permits use of "a chart, summary, or calculation" while the Manual permitted only "a summarization." Additionally, the Rule does not include the 1969 Manual requirement that the summarization be made by a "qualified person or group of qualified persons," nor does the Rule require, as the Manual appeared to, that the preparer of the chart, summary, or calculation testify in order to authenticate the document. The nature of the authentication required is not clear although some form of authentication is required under Rule 901(a).

It is possible for a summary that is admissible under Rule 1006 to include information that would not itself be admissible if that information is reasonably relied upon by an expert preparing the summary. *See generally* Rule 703 and S. Saltzburg & K. Redden, FEDERAL RULES OF EVIDENCE MANUAL 694 (2d ed. 1977).

2013 Amendment. The committee revised this rule for stylistic reasons and to align it with the Federal Rules of Evidence but in doing so did not intend to change any result in any ruling on evidence admissibility.

Rule 1007 Testimony or Statement of a Party to Prove Content

Rule 1007 is taken from the Federal Rule without change and had no express equivalent in the 1969 Manual. The Rule establishes an exception to Rule 1002 by allowing the contents of a writing, recording or photograph to be proven by the testimony or deposition of the party against whom offered or by the party's written admission.

2013 Amendment. The committee revised this rule for stylistic reasons and to align it with the Federal Rules of Evidence but in doing so did not intend to change any result in any ruling on evidence admissibility.

Rule 1008 Functions of military judge and members

Rule 1008 is taken from the Federal Rule without change, and had no formal equivalent in prior military practice. The Rule specifies three situations in which members must determine issues which have been conditionally determined by the military judge. The members have been given this responsibility in this narrow range of issues because the issues that are involved go to the very heart of a case and may prove totally dispositive. Perhaps the best example stems from the civil practice. Should the trial judge in a contract action determine that an exhibit is in fact the original of a contested contract, that admissibility decision could determine the ultimate result of trial if the jury were not given the opportunity to be the final arbiter of the issue. A similar situation could result in a criminal case, for example, in which the substance of a contested written confession is determinative (this would be rare because in most cases the fact that a written confession was made is unimportant, and the only relevant matter is the content of the oral statement that was later transcribed) or in a case in which the accused is charged with communication of a written threat. A

decision by the military judge that a given version is authentic could easily determine the trial. Rule 1008 would give the member the final decision as to accuracy. Although Rule 1008 will rarely be relevant to the usual court-martial, it will adequately protect the accused from having the case against him or her depend upon a single best evidence determination by the military judge.

2013 Amendment. The committee revised this rule for stylistic reasons and to align it with the Federal Rules of Evidence but in doing so did not intend to change any result in any ruling on evidence admissibility.

SECTION XI
MISCELLANEOUS RULES

Rule 1101 Applicability of rules

The Federal Rules have been revised extensively to adapt them to the military criminal legal system. Subdivision (a) of the Federal Rule specifies the types of courts to which the Federal Rules are applicable, and Subdivision (b) of the Federal Rule specifies the types of proceedings to be governed by the Federal Rules. These sections are inapplicable to the military criminal legal system and consequently were deleted. Similarly, most of Federal Rule of Evidence 1101(d) is inapplicable to military law due to the vastly different jurisdictions involved.

(a) *Rules applicable.* Rule 1101(a) specifies that the Military Rules are applicable to all courts-martial including summary courts-martial, to Article 39(a) proceedings, limited factfinding proceedings ordered on review, revision proceedings, and contempt proceedings. This limited application is a direct result of the limited jurisdiction available to courts-martial.

(b) *Rules of privilege.* Rule 1101(b) is taken from subdivision (c) of the Federal Rule and is similar to prior military law. Unlike the Federal Rules, the Military Rules contain detailed privileges rather than a general reference to common law. *Compare* Federal Rule of Evidence 501 with Military Rule of Evidence 501–512.

(c) *Rules relaxed.* Rule 1101(c) conforms the rules of evidence to military sentencing procedures as set forth in the 1969 Manual Para. 75 c. Courts-martial are bifurcated proceedings with sentencing being an adversarial proceeding. Partial application of the rules of evidence is thus appropriate. The Rule also recognizes the possibility that other Manual provisions may now or later affect the application of the rules of evidence.

(d) *Rules inapplicable.* Rule 1101(d) is taken in concept from subdivision (d) of the Federal Rule. As the content of the Federal Rule is, however, generally inapplicable to military law, the equivalents of the Article III proceedings listed in the Federal Rule have been listed here. They included Article 32 investigative hearings, the partial analog to grand jury proceedings, proceedings for search authorizations, and proceedings for pretrial release.

1993 Amendment. Mil. R. Evid. 1101(d) was amended to make the provisions of Mil. R. Evid. 412 applicable at pretrial investigations.

1998 Amendment. The Rule is amended to increase to 18 months the time period between changes to the Federal Rules of Evidence and automatic amendment of the Military Rules of

Evidence. This extension allows for timely submission of changes through the annual review process.

2013 Amendment. The committee revised this rule to align with the Federal Rules of Evidence but in doing so did not intend to change any result in any ruling on evidence admissibility.

Rule 1102 Amendments

Rule 1102 has been substantially revised from the original Federal Rule which sets forth a procedure by which the Supreme Court promulgates amendments to the Federal Rules subject to Congressional objection. Although it is the Committee's intent that the Federal Rules of Evidence apply to the armed forces to the extent practicable, *see* Article 36(a), the Federal Rules are often in need of modification to adapt them to military criminal legal system. Further, some rules may be impracticable. As Congress may make changes during the initial period following Supreme Court publication, some period of time after an amendment's effective date was considered essential for the armed forces to review the final form of amendments and to propose any necessary modifications to the President. Six months was considered the minimally appropriate time period.

Amendments to the Federal Rules are not applicable to the armed forces until 180 days after the effective date of such amendment, unless the President directs earlier application. In the absence of any Presidential action, however, an amendment to the Federal Rule of Evidence will be automatically applicable on the 180th day after its effective date. The President may, however, affirmatively direct that any such amendment may not apply, in whole or in part, to the armed forces and that direction shall be binding upon courts-martial.

1998 Amendment: The Rule is amended to increase to 18 months the time period between changes to the Federal Rules of Evidence and automatic amendment of the Military Rules of Evidence. This extension allows for the timely submission of changes through the annual review process.

2004 Amendment: See Executive Order 13365, dated 3 December 2004. The amendment to the Federal Rules of Evidence, effective in United States District Courts, 1 December 2000, creating Rule 902(12) is not adopted. Federal Rules 301, 302, and 415, were not adopted because they were applicable only to civil proceedings.

2013 Amendment. The committee revised this rule for stylistic reasons and to align it with the Federal Rules of Evidence but in doing so did not intend to change any result in any ruling on evidence admissibility.

Rule 1103 Title

In choosing the title, Military Rules of Evidence, the Committee intends that it be clear that military evidentiary law should echo the civilian federal law to the extent practicable, but should also ensure that the unique and critical reasons behind the separate military criminal legal system be adequately served.

2013 Amendment. The committee revised this rule for stylistic reasons and to align it with the Federal Rules of Evidence but in doing so did not intend to change any result in any ruling on evidence admissibility.

PIN 104253–000